God Is Not Fair, Thank God!

God Is Not Fair, **Thank God!**

Biblical Paradox in the Life and Worship of the Parish

George E. Thompson

RESOURCE *Publications* • Eugene, Oregon

GOD IS NOT FAIR, THANK GOD!
Biblical Paradox in the Life and Worship of the Parish

Copyright © 2014 George E. Thompson. All rights reserved. Except for brief quotations in critical publications or reviews, no part of this book may be reproduced in any manner without prior written permission from the publisher. Write: Permissions, Wipf and Stock Publishers, 199 W. 8th Ave., Suite 3, Eugene, OR 97401.

Resource Publications
An Imprint of Wipf and Stock Publishers
199 W. 8th Ave., Suite 3
Eugene, OR 97401

www.wipfandstock.com

ISBN 13: 978-1-62032-844-6

Manufactured in the U.S.A.

Song lyrics to "Try to Remember" from the stage play, *The Fantasticks*, by Thomas Jones are printed by permission of the author.

"For the Healing of the Nations," words by Fred Kaan, copyright 1968, Hope Publishing Company, Carol Stream, Illinois 60188. All rights reserved. Used by permission.

Dedicated to
Pat

"My bounty is as boundless as the sea,
My love as deep; the more I give to thee,
The more I have, for both are infinite."

—WILLIAM SHAKESPEARE'S *ROMEO AND JULIET*, ACT 2, SCENE 2

Contents

Introduction: Pondering a Pastor's Pilgrimage   ix

Part I: Paradox and the Doctrine of God
1. God Is Not Fair, Thank God!   3
2. The Wise Foolishness of God   12
3. Divine Presence During the Eclipse of God   20
4. The Good Thing about Bad News   28
5. Fear of A Loving God   36
6. Healed by God's Wounds   43
7. The Tenderness of God's Tough Judgment   52
8. Comforted by God's Tears   59
9. Chosen by Rejection   67
10. Paradox and the Mathematics of Mystery   73

Part II: Paradox and Christology
11. The Blessing of Misfortune   85
12. The Resilient Power of Failure   95
13. Christ as Servant Leader   104
14. Emptied to Be Filled   112
15. The Sacrament of Jesus' Suffering   120
16. The Sword of Peace   132
17. King Upon a Cross   144
18. Starting to Live by Stopping for Death   155
19. Resisting Resurrection   163
20. In Christ the Future Is Present   173

Part III: **PARADOX AND THE HOLY SPIRIT AS AN EXTENSION OF THE INCARNATION**

    21 Ship of Fools   187

    22 Less Is More   196

    23 Being Alone Together   204

    24 The Paradox of Church History   213

    25 The Urgency of Patience   223

    26 Winning by Losing   231

    27 Good for Nothing   239

    28 A Royal Waste of Time   248

    29 Common Nobility   259

    30 One God in Three Persons, Blessed Trinity   272

Bibliography   281
Subject Index   291
Scripture Index   303

Introduction: Pondering a Pastor's Pilgrimage

LIFE IS FILLED WITH contradictions. This is the anguish and glory of human existence. I am writing these lines in a spring of incomparable beauty amidst the budding of rhododendrons and the lush greening of mountain scenery. But on Monday of last week, as the Midwest also experienced its seasonal renaissance, a cloud funnel formed in the "tornado alley" of Oklahoma. Within sixteen minutes after the National Weather Service's alert, a 210-mph twister had scarred a capricious trail one mile wide and seventeen miles long through the suburban town of Moore, Oklahoma, home to a population of some 56,000. Hardly a home or commercial building was left standing. The lifeless bodies of seven children were pulled from the rubble of Plaza Towers Elementary. Amidst the anguish of this disaster, rescuers discovered teachers who had heroically protected their young students with their own bodies, saving precious lives.

The tragedy in Moore, Oklahoma, is parabolic, for each of us has been scarred by some unanticipated, painful experience: a sudden illness, the untimely loss of a spouse, the elimination of a valued job, the blossom of marital bliss blown apart, a teenager's drug addiction, vocational failure, or other evaporations of one's dreams. We all struggle to make sense of life's many contradictions and polarities. But this is especially the case within Christian faith communities that maintain a steadfast commitment to the authority of Scripture and belief in a God of justice. Those of us who seek to interpret our personal stories in light of biblical narrative are constantly confronted with contradictions, polarities, and unfairness, both within our own personal experience and in episodes of the biblical story.

This volume is not a fool's attempt to resolve the logical tensions within life's inherent ambiguities or to balance the scales of justice upon the authoritative pages of holy writ. It is an attempt, however, to guide readers in the direction of trust and acceptance of these polarities in order that our faith may find peace in a more profound understanding of the Bible's paradoxical messages. This volume has been written by a parish theologian whose context of experience in the worship and life of the church encourages the coherence of contradictions, a holding together in dramatic tension s of either/or with both/and. In this volume, we shall glean from our common heritage

Introduction: Pondering a Pastor's Pilgrimage

in biblical wisdom literature the great paradoxical truths that enable us to cope with life's most perplexing contradictions. Author, educator, and activist Parker J. Palmer turned to Niels Bohr, a Nobel Prize-winning physicist—not a theologian—for his definition of paradox. The scientist, reflecting upon the deep mysteries of his own field of expertise, is purported to have said, "The opposite of a correct statement is a false statement. But the opposite of a profound truth may be another profound truth."[1]

This volume is an exploration into some of the most profound paradoxical disclosures concerning the mysteries of divine being contained within the biblical texts. Although this author is far from being a biblical literalist, I am unabashedly a biblical "literaturist" insofar as I recognize that a vast multiplicity of literary forms are contained within the sacred canon of the Christian tradition. Each is a medium for communicating truth about God's activity of grace and mercy: parables, allegories, myths, apocalyptic writings, epic sagas, hagiographic biographies, subjective history, epistles, theological tracts, poetic drama, and numerous styles of Hebraic poetry. I have discovered intriguing theological themes amidst these various forms of biblical literature, and in this volume I have gathered eternal biblical truths that seem paradoxical in character. In these pages, we shall examine a sweeping variety of sacred passages under the microscope of reason, the wisdom of Christian tradition, and adventurous experiences within the worship and missional activity of the local church. In no way will these pages imply that the paradoxical themes of the Bible are the only, or even the primary, vehicles for cogently exploring the mysteries of life's most perplexing contradictions. But the reader will discover that this theme is abundantly prevalent within the core messages of sacred texts.

The thesis of this book is that the God we discover within the various forms of biblical literature most profoundly reveals divine nature through the mystery and power of paradox. I have developed this thesis in a Trinitarian pattern. Certainly I have made no attempt to be comprehensive in exploring all biblical facets of the paradoxical disclosure of God as Father/Creator, but each of the first ten chapters will examine one facet of this theme. In the first third of this volume we shall, therefore, postulate the existence of a Father/Creator God whose mercy contradicts our desire for fairness, whose wisdom is foolishness to the world, whose presence is most profoundly experienced through divine absence, whose good news is best recognized amidst life's tragedies, whom we grow to love through our fear of the Almighty, whose tenderness is ultimately expressed through tough judgments, who brings strength and healing through the weakness of divine tears and suffering, who chooses us in acts of rejection, and whose clarity of order and design is revealed through the mysteries and paradoxes within the disciplines of science and mathematics.

The second section of this volume deals with Christology through an exploration of the various facets of the nature and reality of the Christ of faith. Here we shall experience the radiance of a historical person who courageously lived a paradoxical

---

1. A paraphrase offered by Palmer, *Promise of Paradox*, xxix.

Introduction: Pondering a Pastor's Pilgrimage

life, becoming like us in order that we may become more like him. We discover that the Man of Nazareth took upon himself all the paradoxical elements of God's being that we explored in the initial ten chapters. Thus, in this second third of the book, we shall immerse ourselves in Jesus' paradoxical beatitudes. We shall discover that his failures are the sources of resilient success. We shall boldly assert that the paradoxical Christ is our model for the sort of humble servant leadership that may subtly transform the world. We shall enter the pilgrimage of Jesus' passion in order to experience the fullness of life through the emptying of self and redemptive suffering. We shall be challenged by the fact that Jesus was an aggressive pacifist in a warring world. His kingdom is not of this world, but because of his death upon the cross, he is truly in charge of the world's destiny. In facing death, he paradoxically teaches us how to live, even though we resist the responsibility that his resurrection demands of his followers. Because of the Christ event, his disciples have a new understanding of time. A Christology that parallels the nature of Christ with the paradoxical nature of the Father/Creator God truly personalizes the Christian faith. A book that gained prominence during my collegiate years, Donald M. Baillie's *God Was in Christ*, asks the question, "How do we have a language of theology if we cannot speak of God in the third person with human words and categories of the finite mind?" This Scottish theologian of a previous generation wisely answers, "We shall have to pay the price—it will always be a theology of paradox. The price is not too great to pay, for we must theologize; and indeed the very act of worship, particularly corporate worship, involves the use of words and thoughts about God, and to think to speak of God at all is to run into antinomy, dialectical contradiction, paradox."[2]

Evidence within the scriptural accounts of the life of Jesus of Nazareth personalizes, concretizes, and makes palpable the discussion of the various facets regarding the paradoxical nature of God's identity outlined in the initial ten chapters. These two sections, therefore, hold together in symmetry because God's mercy (*hesed*) and covenant love (*agape*) are expressed in the activity of Christ-centered worship through the language of *antinomy*, *dialectical contradiction*, and *paradox*. Through the paradoxical disclosure of the Messiah, God the Creator/Father indeed becomes experiential and personal.

Yet, these two diamonds of paradoxical personae (God the Father and God the Son) fail to glow with shimmering beauty until they are joined in triangular completeness with the paradoxical facet of the Holy Spirit. Thus, I shall resolutely assert in the third section of this book that this whole theological construct is a house of cards unless the paradoxical nature of God's being is evidenced within the worship and life of the church through the power of the Holy Spirit. In this third and final section, we shall marvel at the mysterious facets of the Holy Spirit that glow with increasing luminosity and grandeur as an extension of the incarnation. The darkness of this world is indeed hungry for its glow. The Holy Spirit resides within the church and is most prominent and transforming when it evokes a Christ-like, paradoxical identity within

2. Baillie, *God Was in Christ*, 108.

Introduction: Pondering a Pastor's Pilgrimage

the congregation. The church then becomes a joyful community of the redeemed, but not the gathering of the sanctified. The church is always becoming; thus, it appears to be a ship of fools moving toward the destination of its authentic paradoxical identity. It is called toward a communal life of simplicity and costly sharing. Its pilgrimage moves the believer from loneliness through solitude to the miracle of community. The church need not be in charge; but it should announce the present reality of God's rule through King Jesus. In its suffering and losses, it is called to remain urgently patient. Its best use of time is "wasted" absorption into periods of worship. Its reward arrives upon seeking no recompense or prominence. In this final section, I shall, therefore, make a passionate plea for faithful congregations to maintain oral and written narratives of Christ-like individuals and missional activities. Their stories constitute the precious meta-narratives of salvation history.

I am a pastoral theologian. This assertion is a tautology; for the central role of a Christian pastor is to engage the community of faith in an understanding of its biblical and historical traditions, to give leadership to a vibrant worship of the triune God, and to provide administrative channels by which the theology of the church is manifested in sacrificial, Christ-centered ministries. Christian theology is vacuous if it does not emerge from the life and worship of a congregation that believes and practices a life of paradoxical behavior. A carefully articulated Christian theology is irrelevant if it does not aggressively engage in transforming the lives of individuals and groups through immersion into the holy habits of an aberrant faith community.

Consequently, parish ministry is the most challenging and exciting profession available for any professing Christian. Every baptized Christian is called to some expression of ministry and mission. A pastor's role is no more important than the ministry of the laity; in fact, laypeople often hold positions of power and influence through business and public office that are rarely available to a pastor. But the pastor is gifted with a lifetime of absorption into the study of Scripture and theological traditions in order to interpret, defend, and practice the essential tenants of faith.

The parish is, and always has been, a laboratory for doing theology. The rubber hits the road in the daily pilgrimage of pastoral functions: counseling those in crisis, visiting the sick and infirm, teaching in small groups, providing comfort for the bereaved, burying the dead with eulogies that affirm the faithful, and giving order to meaningful activities of mission. The parish theologian, through holy habits of theological reflection, learns from the great works of academic theologians, but the pastor is also blessed with daily opportunities to enter the laboratory of practical theology in the care of the parish and the administration of the church's mission.

As I enter the retirement phase of my ministry, I feel compelled to reflect theologically upon these years of blessing during which I have experienced the opportunity and responsibility of pastoral leadership. During years of pastoral encounters in teaching classes and preparing sermons, I have been inspired and enlightened by a great variety of biblical and theological themes: the many facets of grace, the primacy

Introduction: Pondering a Pastor's Pilgrimage

of eschatology and Christian hope, helpful interpretations of salvation history, the act of justification, and the process of sanctification. My experience in the parish and a lifetime of probing the Scriptures has, therefore, gradually taught me to find comfort in biblical paradox. Theological and personal struggles remain and are at times more pronounced. Biblical paradox does not resolve mystery; to the contrary, it embraces life's ambiguities. My personal faith requires trust amidst the pain of unresolved tension, or else I would not be an authentic believer. My sense of hope emerges out of the tension of unfulfilled expectations and unrealized promises. Any other form of hope is merely wishful thinking, as was testified by the Apostle Paul when he wrote, "For in hope we were saved. Now hope that is seen is not hope. For who hopes for what is seen? But if we hope for what we do not see, we wait for it with patience."[3] I have not passed through a single month in my parish pilgrimage without walking in the shadow of the question of theodicy: If God is truly good, why does God allow for the existence of evil? But I have come to discover the depths of a greater faith by living within the tension of a paradoxical God who conquers evil by dying and addresses the injustices of this world through mercy instead of punitive justice.

This indeed is an exciting time to be a pastor. Rapid change in contemporary culture is a challenge within every parish. But the ways of God are subtle and mysterious. In an era when western secular journalists have persistently announced the funeral of the institutional church, such pundits of doom have missed the really big story. As the church languishes in affluent North America and Europe, the congregational life of Christianity has exploded in the impoverished southern hemisphere. This irony can only be understood within the context of the paradoxical message of the Jesus. Consequently, I was not even mildly stunned by the assertion of the sociologist of religion, Philip Jenkins, who has recently observed,

> Already today, Africans and Asians represent some 30 percent of all Christians, and the proportion will rise steadily. Conceivably, the richest Christian harvest of all might yet be in China, a nation of inestimable importance to the politics of the coming decades. Some projections suggest that by 2050, China might contain the second-largest population of Christians on the planet, exceeded only by the United States. More confidently, we can predict that by that date, there should be around three billion Christians in the world, of whom only around one-fifth or fewer will be non-Hispanic whites.[4]

It is not true that Protestant laity of North America are altogether bewildered, frail of faith, and deplete of confidence in God's future. Local parishes have not been passive observers of these revolutionary social trends, nor are most parishes hopelessly adrift in a turbulent sea of theological chaos. It is my experience that parish life continues to be the primary laboratory for doing Christian theology. I have

---

3. Rom 8:24–25 NRSV.
4. Jenkins, *New Faces of Christianity*, 9.

Introduction: Pondering a Pastor's Pilgrimage

experienced a viable active remnant within nearly each parish to which I have been appointed. This faithful remnant is receptive to costly discipleship, aggressive participation, engaging dialogue, and painful confrontation. What amazes me most is not the theological apathy or confusion of laity, but the resilience of faith within so many parishioners. Most of these are well acquainted with biblical paradoxes and life's most recurring ambiguities. They are not satisfied with swallowing prescribed platitudes when experiencing the raging fever of doubt. Still they continue to believe, trust, and practice the disciplines of a reasonable faith. But when reason runs out of gas at the edge of the soft sod near some cemetery ridge on a wet Wednesday, these people recite the mysterious liturgies of paradox and resurrection praise! They continue to worship and pray with fervor and resilience.

For whom have I written this book? I earnestly pray that this volume will stimulate and encourage a variety of conscientious laity for whom sustaining a vibrant faith and practice has been a struggle. I hope that this Trinitarian structure will concretize the thinking and inspire missional activity among many laity for whom life is not fair, but who will be guided from cynicism's inertia into a hope-filled and joyous participation in ministries of compassion that reflect the paradoxical nature of Christ's dwelling within their lives.

I have very consciously written these reflections for the benefit of seminary students preparing for a life in parish ministry and for the many young pastors who are just beginning their pastoral pilgrimage. But I am primarily writing these chapters with a profound sense of affirmation for my clergy colleagues and many faithful laity that continue to labor so faithfully in obscure places, performing ordinary tasks with an extraordinary grace. During the time of our labors, mainstream churches have lost many members. A spirit of malaise permeates the heart of many pastors and church leaders who have given it their best shot. Many of these have been faithful to the Word that both afflicts the comfortable and comforts the afflicted. Growing churches do not typically preach the gospel of God's pain. They are often uncomfortable with paradox. But the church, which shall be preserved until the end of the ages, does so preach, live, and worship. Such a church has as its central mission a participation in the pain of this world, which is being redeemed through a suffering God. This theological reflection is a word of affirmation and hope for faithful pastors and lay leaders that have labored paradoxically and bravely in the eye of overwhelming storms.

This theology emerges from congregational life. These reflections emanate from the witness of authentic people of faith: parishioners who refuse to believe that life is meaningless, wasted, or useless; conscientious Christians who cannot endure the suggestion that evil will have the last word in history or at life's end. These people have faced personal disaster and catastrophe courageously and gracefully. The paradox they have embraced is the notion that the Almighty God of creation is not above it all, calling the shots. This God is sharing the blows below. We are a people of hope, not because we project our human wishes upon the screen of some fantasized future, as in

American civil religion. Rather, we share the confidence that God-in-Christ is holding open the future so that its potential for our meaningful participation will remain and our lives will be fit for living and dying. This we have learned, in the words of Thomas Merton, by "traveling [together] toward [our] destiny in the belly of a paradox."[5]

---

5. Merton, *Sign of Jonas*, 11.

Part I

PARADOX AND THE DOCTRINE OF GOD

1

God Is Not Fair, Thank God!

LIFE IS NOT FAIR. The sooner we can accept this reality, the better we are able to cope with what life brings to us. The genius of the biblical story is the paradoxical tension between the obvious unfairness that God allows within the human saga and the subtle threads of mercy that hold together the fabric of history's tapestry. When we ignore this paradoxical theme and become obsessed with justifying the many abominations that God allows, we paint ourselves into a theological corner of disturbing contradictions. "Fairness" is a post-Enlightenment expectation that was not a central concern in the biblical narrative. Jeffersonian ideals are noble aspirations indeed, but they are not the core of Mosaic covenant theology. "We hold these truths to be self-evident, that all men are created equal, that they are endowed by their Creator with certain unalienable rights, that among these are life, liberty, and the pursuit of happiness" were not the words spoken from Mount Sinai. Scripture tells the story of a cracked creation in which slavery, oppression, misery, and suffering of the righteous are an abundant reality. A restored Eden, the Kingdom of God, or other biblical metaphors and expressions of hope are the result of divine initiative in which *mercy*, not necessarily *fairness*, is enthroned. In the biblical narrative, happiness is not the achievement of some economic utopia of shared material abundance and wealth for all. Happiness is the serendipitous gift of a merciful God whose presence and love is sufficient reward. The initial biblical account of creation concludes with the grand assertion that "God saw all that he had made, and it was very good."[1] But the two great Hebrew legends of creation also remind us that this pristine order was fractured by human disobedience. Adam and Eve—the mythological archetypes of all humanity—rebelled against the authority of God, causing an inevitable influx of debilitating consequences.

But the biblical narrative does not imply a theological dualism with a Creator God whose absolute power is threatened by the guiles of a competing sinister demigod.

---

1. Gen 1:31a NIV.

Part I: Paradox and the Doctrine of God

The Bible reveals the consistent and abiding presence of an all-powerful God who does not cause evil but clearly allows it to happen. Thus, God's ways are not fair. Moreover, the comprehensive spectrum of the biblical saga is really not about the fairness of God. The central theme is the mercy of God. The most frequent Hebrew word for mercy is *hesed*, which suggests that among the attributes of divine being are *loving kindness*, *loyalty*, and *faithfulness*. *Hesed* is never used in Hebrew Scripture apart from the context of covenant. It is because of God's promise to Abraham and Sarah and their spiritual descendents that God continues to provide mercy, despite the disobedience of God's chosen ones. The word *hesed*—as it is defined progressively through the narrative surrounding patriarchs, matriarchs, and prophets—becomes synonymous with the concept of *grace*. In one biblical account after another, disobedience results in punishment, suffering, and periods of abandonment. But despite the unfairness of children suffering from the sins of their parents or atrocities befalling innocent people, the biblical narrative is written upon the parchment of *hesed*—unmerited love, irrational kindness, and unfair loyalty. Thus, the righteousness and justice of God do not conform to standard measures of human fairness.

The unfairness of life is experienced within the ebb and flow of daily existence of each parish. The suffering of a child afflicted by an incurable disease, the daily ministries of the church among a city's homeless, and the constant awareness of radical economic disparity within every community demonstrate life's unfairness. Those who inhabit the pews of faithful worship on Sunday morning are keenly aware of this reality. When the worshiper lives with a global consciousness, this discrepancy becomes especially acute. Early in my experience as a pastor I was privileged to participate in a study-tour in Mexico. I was submerged in reading that nation's lamentable history after the Spanish conquest. The group of pastors with whom I traveled spent time with Catholic social workers and priests who ministered among refugee residents of squatter villages from agricultural regions near Cuernavaca and Mexico City. On one occasion, we helped relocate a destitute family that had been living on the roof of a modest adobe home in a space previously reserved for chickens. Two of the children were blind from the effects of severe malnutrition. As we traveled together over rough rural highway, we learned that this family's plight was shared by many forced to accept wretched poverty and appalling hunger as a way of life.

Every faithful worshiper—through liturgy, intercessory prayers, and an authentic proclamation of biblical theology—enters into the plight of pain within his or her local neighborhood and amidst the lives of fellow Christians. Christ United Methodist Church (UMC) in Greensboro, North Carolina, challenged my apathy through its spiritual fervor and decades-long relationships with parishes in Cochabamba, Bolivia. In response to the biblical mandate to live with grateful sensitivity to the poor, that affluent congregation sustained a resource center for agricultural development in that destitute region. In a similar spirit, the people of Providence UMC in Charlotte, North Carolina, have maintained two medical clinics near Cap-Haïtien, Haiti, for forty years and have recently initiated macroeconomics programs for unemployed women in several villages. They sent waves of volunteers to minister amidst the rubble and carnage following the earthquake of 2010. These meager efforts hardly restore *economic fairness* within the two poorest countries of the Western Hemisphere—but they provide hope to the hopeless. These congregations have developed loving relationships with "the least of these"[2] living far away as well as within their own cities. By fusing worship with service, church members have developed effective missions of mercy. While singing "The Battle Hymn of the Republic" with a Bolivian congregation that stood on the dirt floor of a makeshift sanctuary, our mission team felt the paradox of divine mercy amidst the misery and desolation of abject poverty. These faithful disciples have consistently challenged earth's abysmal unfairness by embodying the biblical message of *hesed*.

Through the centuries, faithful congregations have proclaimed that the true nature of God was profoundly revealed through the advent of Jesus of Nazareth. His teachings, the conduct of his life in human history, and the redemptive power of his unjust and cruel death disclosed an authentic glimpse at the essence of God. Jesus' historical existence defined *hesed*—the only power of redemption for a fractured creation. When Jesus began teaching his disciples on the tranquil hillsides of Galilee overlooking the village of Capernaum, his audience likely stood in reverent attention. It was the custom in those days for learned rabbis to give instruction while seated. Their pupils, in an act of respect, remained standing throughout the lesson. Jesus' apostles and the throng of enthralled followers, therefore, stood in courteous concentration as this layman from a tiny nearby village began painting a verbal picture: "For the kingdom of heaven is like a landowner who went out early in the morning to hire laborers for his vineyard."[3] By the time Jesus had completed his tale about these laborers, however, we can imagine that many within his audience would have begun to sit down upon the grass, collapsing in passive protest. This prophet of justice, through this disturbing little parable, had apparently endorsed an ethic of inequity in which lazy laborers, arriving for work at sunset, received the same compensation as those who had sweltered in the heat of the day. Jesus' offended listeners must have begun murmuring, "If the kingdom of heaven is like this, I want no part in it. The doctrine of God, proclaimed by this son of Joseph the carpenter, just isn't fair."

When Matthew recorded the parable, he suggested that Jesus added this enigmatic summary, "So the last will be first, and the first will be last."[4] Apparently Matthew editorialized with these words, for they are extraneous to the fabric of Jesus' original story. But Matthew was instructing catechumens within his congregation in the theology of paradox that was at the core of Jesus' life and message. We, like those who first read this disturbing parable from the manuscript of the First Gospel,

---

2. Matt 25:40 NRSV.
3. Matt 20:1 NRSV.
4. Matt 20:16 NRSV.

Part I: Paradox and the Doctrine of God

respond with a sense of consternation. Some of us have known from our youth what it means to make our way into the fields before sunrise with the smell of fertile earth in our nostrils. Others of us, with a similar commitment to an honest day's labor, have consistently cranked up our car's engine at daybreak and joined with other sleepy-faced motorists, punching in our timecard just as the factory whistle begins to blow. We have had our share of melancholy Mondays, grumbling beneath our breath the protest of Ecclesiastics: "Vanity of vanities . . . All is vanity. What do people gain from all the toil at which they toil under the sun? . . . All things are wearisome; more than one can express."[5] This is why, after forty-three years of faithful labor, I recently pulled the lever of our United Methodist Church's pension program, began cashing in upon my obligatory investments in Social Security, and finally (after all those years of arduous work) feel justified in receiving an earned monetary reward for retirement. At least there is a measure of fairness when our sweat equity guarantees a payoff.

But Jesus did not measure justice with any such a mathematical equation for fairness in this paradoxical parable. *Quid* does not equal *quo*. His implicit fair labor code ruffles our neatly feathered formula for fairness. In our point of view, this is no way to run a vineyard, a factory, a ship, and certainly not the church. If the Kingdom of God is like this, perhaps we too will want no part in it. And Jesus, just one chapter in Matthew's text away from the passion narrative and his final week, was giving his disciples ample opportunity to bail out before it was too late. So let's look carefully at this enigmatic story—the parable of the Laborers—to see whether there is a relevant word for us.

Jesus' parable accurately described labor in Palestine during his day. Rabbinical literature tells us that working hours lasted from the dawning of the sun to the rising of the stars. Hebrew literature rarely glorified work. Labor was drudgery. Palestinian heat was intense. Pay was minimal. People of the land received only subsistence wage. So, naturally, none of the early workers in the parable protested the promised recompense: one denarius, perhaps a dollar for one day of strenuous exertion. Unemployment was rampant in Palestine. A contemporary scholar of ancient texts, Thomas Carney, describes Galilean culture during the time of Jesus as "a society based on patronage, not class stratification; so little pyramids of power abounded . . . Thus, society resembled a mass of little pyramids of influence, each headed by a major family—or one giant pyramid headed by an autocrat—not the three-decker sandwich of upper, middle, and lower classes familiar to us from industrial society."[6]

Nonetheless, the landowner desperately needed work done in this vineyard, so he went to the marketplace around noon and hired the idle ones. He repeated this process throughout the afternoon, even until the sun was setting on the early laborers returning in exhaustion from the fields. It is left open to the speculation of the listener whether these who stood idle in the market came to work so late because of lack

---

5. Eccl 1:2, 1:3, 1:8 NRSV.
6. Carney, *Shape of the Past*, 63. See also John Dominic Crossan, *Historical Jesus*, 59.

of opportunity or their own laziness. Either way, they arrived only moments before the time for compensation. The law of Leviticus strictly stated, "The wages of a hired servant shall not remain with you all night until the morning."[7] It was kosher to pay at dusk. This was protective compassion for the poor, all of whom lived from hand to mouth. Thus, in this strange parable, the last hired, who clocked only a few minutes of work, were the first paid. Moreover, they received the same compensation as those who had labored by the sweat of their brow since sunrise! It was in this crucial scene that the first workers suddenly saw how the last had been rewarded. In this moment, their solid satisfaction at mere employment melted in the boiling juices of resentment.

Dripping with the perspiration of an exhausting day's toil, they protested the unfairness of the owner's action. They were incensed because they expected equal pay for equal work. The first laborers of sunrise were enraged, for they had done at least twelve times as much work and had borne the oppressive pain of the midday heat. They were indignant that the landowner had equally rewarded these with fresh faces and garments unsoiled by sweat.

But note this: had these early laborers not witnessed the payoff of the latecomers, they would never have raised a word of protest. From the beginning, they had been content with the promised compensation. They got exactly what they had been promised. They received all they had originally expected. They had been saved from the agony of unemployment. Yet their indignation exploded at the sight of reward for those who had not done equal labor. The landowner's actions now appeared grossly unfair.

We too are shocked by the apparent message of this parable, for it goes against the grain of our natural expectation of fairness. It mocks our sense of justice. Perhaps we are more drawn to the message of Danish writer Jens Peter Jacobsen in his novel *Niels Lyhne*, which tells the story of a man who rejected God. As he grew older, he secretly desired the peace of faith, but he refused to come weak-kneed to God toward life's ending. Fate had been harsh to him, with death visiting those he loved most. Tenaciously, he held on to disbelief, nihilism, and existential despair even though he wanted the peace of God. In the last hour of his life, he refused to see a pastor, though secretly he wanted absolution and faith's consolation. Hjerrild, his loving and affirming physician, was moved by his valor and whispered, "If I were God . . . I would far sooner save the man who does not repent at the last minute."[8]

Deep down inside, our sense of even-scaled justice admires the hardened skeptic, Niels Lyhne. Jesus' parable, however, communicates the opposite message. It shatters all our preconceived assumptions about the justice of God. Here is a story with a coded message that brings us to the core of what Jesus of Nazareth is all about. The key to interpreting the parable is in remembering that the vineyard is always the symbol of God's kingdom, the new community of Christ, the new reality announced by the

7. Lev 19:13 RSV.
8. Jacobsen, *Niels Lyhne*, 186.

advent of our Lord. In point of fact, the vineyard represents the church. Moreover, God owns the vineyard—lock, stock, and barrel. The parable suggests that we are privileged to labor in God's vineyard (the church) and receive the security that there will be adequate compensation for everyone. But our real pay is not the wage offered to us at the end of day, or the conclusion of our life. Our work itself is our gift, our immeasurable privilege! The work—the sacrificial ministry, caring for the downtrodden, acts of piety, and deeds of mercy—carries its own reward. In point of fact, our arduous work in God's vineyard brings us near to our compassionate Lord and the blessed assurance that we are meaningfully employed in the fulfilling activity of his righteous Kingdom.

Jesus' parable tells us that we cannot come to God in resentful obedience, entering God's temple of worship with a dour countenance. We cannot join in the labors of the church reluctantly, toughing it out until the end in order to receive a heavenly reward. No! Our reward is found amidst our labors.

This shocking parable runs counter to all we commonly accept about fairness.[9] It proclaims the extravagant goodness of God. It demonstrates the Lord's spendthrift mercy. God's measure of fairness cannot be weighed on human scales. It is difficult for us to calculate the cost of a pound of grace on the open market.

Matthew, in compiling the teachings of Jesus, was primarily addressing the problems of the early church, perhaps even of his own congregation. This parable, therefore, does not outline any philosophy of economics. Establishing a fair labor code is not the story's primary intent, according to the theology of Matthew. Jesus startled his followers with this story, for many had joined his parade with one primary concern: What's in it for me? This provocative story suggests that God's judgment falls upon those who are jealous of the good fortune of others. Jesus was saying in this parable that God's judgment is not our own. God's measure of fairness is not calibrated to our own, and we can thank God for that fact! This parable, in the estimation of George Buttrick, demonstrates that the "verdicts of heaven cause amazing reversals in the verdicts of earth."[10]

Matthew's Gospel was perhaps the early church's catechism; it was a book of instruction for new converts. Luke's Gospel, however, was the early church's inclusive call to mission for the believer. The Lucan parallel to this parable is the story of the prodigal son, especially the second stanza concerning the elder son. His indignant response to the joy of his father and the reward of his brother is comparable to the response of the laborers in the vineyard. In his impetuous reaction to his father's graciousness, he unwittingly put all his emotional cards on the table. He was steaming with envy, refusing to join the banquet. He argued with his father about the unfairness of his paternal demeanor, saying, "Listen! For all these years I have been working like a slave for you, and I have never disobeyed your command; yet you have never given me

9. Hunter, *Interpreting the Parables*, 52.
10. Buttrick, *Parables of Jesus*, 163.

even a young goat so that I might celebrate with my friends."[11] In other words, "Your forgiveness is unfair; I want no part of these celebrations." Thus, the older brother unraveled his inner self like a pungent onion with these words of protest, "But when this son of yours came back, who has devoured your property with prostitutes, you killed the fatted calf for him!"[12] Ah, now we see the elder son's very soul, down past the superego to his id. Nothing had been said, to this point, about *harlots*. The brother's wish projection fell out of his secret mental compartment. His soul was stripped bare. So the loving father, picking up the pieces of his son's shredded self-esteem, gently said, "Son, you are always with me, and all that is mine is yours."[13] In effect, "You are already in the kingdom. Just to be in the family, just to be able to plow the fields, just to be able to labor at my side, just to know the security of my presence, just to know of my unfaltering love is reward enough!" Thus, the father said, "But we had to celebrate and rejoice, because this brother of yours was dead and has come to life; he was lost and has been found."[14]

Malcolm Muggeridge was an irascible cynic who wrote with a sardonic pen. A literary genius, he offered devastating critiques of literature and culture. He was an agnostic and an arrogant intellectual who pursued every sort of self-centered, hedonistic activity throughout his youth and adulthood. In his final years, Muggeridge, whose voice was well known over the BBC, converted. He became a zealous Christian, admired by millions of the devout across the globe. Now, is that fair? Look at all the fun he had while not being a disciple: not having to attend all those lengthy Anglican Eucharists, not having to squirm through all those boring sermons, not spending his money and time in advocacy for the poor. In his last years, he wrote a two-volume autobiography. The title he gave reveals his assessment of all his years lived outside the faith: *Chronicles of Wasted Time*.

What do we want out of our life's labors? When we have put in our forty-plus years, we perhaps sense that it is time to pull the lever and receive the reward: a life of leisure in retirement. What if it does not come out that way? What if our life at that idyllic lake retirement home is not exactly real estate in paradise? What if our life, when compared with the retirement rewards of others, does not feel fair? What if our body is infested with the pain of a worn-out instrument? What if some of our friends have earned their money the old-fashioned way—by inheritance—and we have just enough left to meet the monthly bills? What if the old reprobate, once a petulant sinner, finally begins to attend church after his second heart attack? Cynically, we wonder if he is cramming for his final exams.

Jesus' parable forthrightly responds to our suspicion by saying that fairness is not the primary concern of God. Life's reward is within life itself. If you want to get to

11. Luke 15:29 NRSV.
12. Luke 15:30 NRSV.
13. Luke 15:31 NRSV.
14. Luke 15:32 NRSV.

heaven, if you want everlasting reward, you must take a slice of heaven in your heart with you. Moreover, this heaven—this love, forgiveness, and communion with God—is offered freely to everyone. All who enter the vineyard will receive the same reward.

There is no place for spiritual envy in the Kingdom of God. The ground is level at the foot of the cross. This is why, when Dante contemplated the fate of the envious in his *Inferno*, he had their eyelids sewn together so that they would not compare their plight with the fate of others. This parable is about the generosity of God. It punctures all our preconceptions about God's justice and points us to the paradoxical relationship between justice and mercy. This parable clearly illustrates that fairness is not God's ultimate concern. In Jesus' surprising story, the last are treated with the same favor as the first. The parable of Jesus, consequently, shocks us with a jolt of divine generosity which can only be called *hesed—mercy*. Suddenly all our conventional concepts of fairness are challenged. Perhaps it is Portia in Shakespeare's *The Merchant of Venice* who best comprehends this paradox of justice when she says to Shylock, who has come to the king's court demanding justice,

> The quality of mercy is not strained.
> It droppeth as the gentle rain from heaven
> Upon the place beneath....
> ....
> But mercy is above this sceptered sway;
> It is enthroned in the hearts of kings;
> It is an attribute of God himself;
> And earthly power doth then show like God's
> When mercy seasons justice.[15]

Our assumed goodness is inadequate when it becomes a strategy—a clever conspiracy—to break into heaven like a thief. Paradise is not our pay for earthwork. It is the fruit of knowing that we labor with and for God in his vineyard, the church. Our labors here are our overpayment. God pays not on the basis of our volume of work but on the spirit of our labors.

On the surface, God's forgiveness and generosity do not seem fair. This parable could be reported to the US Department of Labor. But God offers us mercy and grace, not fairness. We would all be lost if fairness were the standard for God's acceptance. Occasionally I consult a disturbing website, http://www.globalrichlist.com. Even in my state of retirement as a middle-class citizen living on a fixed income, I discover that my anticipated annual financial resources remain among the top one percentile of the world's population! Will the rich be saved? Shall I receive my *deserved wages* at the end of my life's pilgrimage? I must receive seriously the scrutiny of Jesus' rebuke, based upon principles of fairness: "For it is easier for a camel to go through the eye

---

15. Shakespeare, *The Merchant of Venice*, Act 4, Scene 1, lines 173–86.

of a needle than for a rich man to enter the kingdom of God."[16] Thus, I am eternally grateful that Jesus added a codicil to his reprimand of the wealthy aristocrat who inquired, "Who can be saved?" Our merciful master answered him (and me), "What is impossible with men is possible with God."[17]

With theological consistency, Jesus lived his life in accordance with the parable of the Laborers. He embodied the Hebrew concept of *hesed*. In his actions and teachings, we encounter the radical dimension of divine justice. As Harold Bosley warns, "Justice is something less than justice unless it is something more."[18] God's justice, tempered by divine mercy, is that something more. We need not begrudge God's measure of generosity, for without it, we are indeed lost. For, according to time-tested records, there was once a man who labored arduously all his life to do only what was just and righteous. Instead of being rewarded, he was hoisted into the air upon a cruel instrument of torture. Yet, strangely enough, he did not envy his executioners. He died slowly, with plenty of time to contemplate his plight. It was all so unfair. Yet even in agony he whispered a prayer: "Father, forgive them; for they do not know what they do."[19] This is how Jesus interpreted the unfairness of his own fate. This man who died in misery knew well the misery of those who tortured him. He knew the agony of all those who sat in the marketplace, all those whose lives are empty and whose labors have no purpose. He did not envy his executioners; rather, he prayed that they might inherit his joy—the inner peace of laboring in God's Kingdom and the tranquility of knowing that none of our righteous labors are ever in vain.

The God who Jesus revealed is not fair, thank God! Yet because of this crucified God, we can return to the vineyard of our labors, knowing that we are already receiving the generosity of a merciful employer.

---

16. Luke 18:25 RSV.
17. Luke 18:27 RSV.
18. Bosley, *He Spoke to Them*, 170.
19. Luke 23:34 NRSV.

2

The Wise Foolishness of God

ANY STUDENT OF THE Bible quickly discovers that the sacred narrative contains many paradoxical themes; thus, it is appropriate to ask if the core biblical message is an affront to reason, relegating believers to irrationality. Does the Christian belief in a God whose fairness is inconsistent, but whose mercy is everlasting, defy human reason? Are the paradoxical themes of Christian affirmation contrary to common sense or rational consistency? Does our Judeo-Christian heritage resist logic?

After experiencing a profoundly discouraging trip to Moscow in 1968, Elie Wiesel, the renowned Holocaust survivor and internationally acclaimed novelist, was struck by the terror that haunted the lives of devout Russian Jews twelve years after the death of Stalin. He decided to testify to their resilient courage by composing a riveting drama titled *Zalmen, or the Madness of God*. The play had its theatrical debut as a television production in the United States during 1975. It is set in a small town's post-Stalinist Russian synagogue. Zalmen, the old rabbi of the community, has practically given up hope of ever seeing his people practice their ancient faith, live in accordance with Torah, or breathe the untainted air of freedom. His own son and daughter-in-law are ashamed of Zalmen—a fossilized relic of religious tradition. Kremlin spies monitor his sermons, looking for reasons to imprison him or commit him to an asylum. He experiences radical rejection that eventually drives him to verbal explosions of catatonic rage. Everyone considers Zalmen to be hopelessly insane and a danger to the Communist philosophical consensus. Everyone, that is, except his grandson, young Misha. The child is torn between loyalty to his conciliatory father, who refuses to instill in him even the most rudimentary expressions of Judaism, and his eccentric grandfather, a man of uncompromising faith. Misha is inexorably drawn to the defiant personality of his ridiculed and ostracized grandfather. A chemistry of connection between the eyes of Zalmen and Misha carry the hopeful theme of this enthralling drama's final scene. Only the grandson sympathetically hears the voice of the rabbi's pain as the voice of God's agony. He refuses to abandon emotionally his ostracized grandfather in a Communist culture committed to the core values of reason and the rejection of all religious tradition. After all, reason had guided the new Russia to an ascendancy of the proletariat and a culture liberated from the myths and irrationality of faith's dogma. When the Communist Party Inspector asks Misha if he feels sorry for his grandfather, the twelve-year-old responds, "I don't. It's something else I feel. I don't know what I feel right now . . . I only know I . . . love him very much."[1]

Even though belief in YHWH and the observance of such rituals as Yom Kippur (the Jewish ritual of Atonement) were considered to be expressions of fanatical madness in Soviet culture, Misha's eyes remain sympathetically fixed upon his counter-cultural, defiant grandfather. For Wiesel, this was the gaze of hope and the discernment of a coming transformation in the political philosophy and theological tolerance within Russian and Eastern European social order. The drama's author boldly illustrates how the faith and traditions of Judaism will indeed survive both the Nazi Holocaust and post-Stalinist gulags as long as even one believer continues in the land of the living. The hope of humanity is sustained by the madness of God, which is saner than the wisdom of mortals.

This intriguing drama speaks profoundly to both devout Jews and Christians tempted by the despair, the saturation of secularity, and the hostility toward all things sacred and mysterious in the twenty-first century. Before we are seduced by reliance upon the absolute authority and prowess of human reason, we need to hear the subtle wisdom of Wiesel's hauntingly staged reassessment of reality. When we resolve to expunge from our culture all that is enigmatic, transcendent, or unfathomable, we fail to acknowledge that the *madness* of the mysterious is wiser than human rationality.

In the twenty-first century, we have entered an era that requires enormous stockpiles of information. Access to information ensures power and financial reward. Thus, we have come to live with the illusion that the accumulation of information automatically produces wisdom. We have, therefore, arrogantly condoned the worship of all things contemporary. We discard that which is antiquated or mysterious, including the wisdom literature of ancient traditions and its various paradoxical themes.

During the summer of 1999, I attended a symposium at Montreat College in the mountains of North Carolina. Among the theologians and writers that addressed that assemblage was Douglas John Hall, whose works have intrigued me throughout his illustrious career. In one of his lectures he provided this prophetic insight into the context of biblical wisdom in relation to our contemporary passion for information: "Information, though necessary, without knowledge is superficial, chaotic, and potentially dangerous. Knowledge, though indispensable, by itself is insufficient to supply the human need for discernment and purpose. Wisdom, the very goal of our

---

1. Wiesel, *Zalmen*, 140.

creaturehood, is in its fullness always eluding us. Faith is essential to the soul's fulfillment and the species' wellbeing."[2]

Information is low on the ladder that leads to truth and reality. The power of wisdom cannot be grasped apart from the pilgrimage of faith. Information alone cannot produce knowledge, let alone the wisdom to make decisions that enhance quality of life and lead to the realization of admirable goals in the saga of human history. Thus, Alan Greenspan and his team of information-gathering experts were totally surprised by the appalling arrival of economic recession during the early months of 2008. Enron's executive officers were all graduates of Ivy League business schools with truckloads of financial information. The architects of this nation's long war in Afghanistan were trained in the technology of warfare and social science of the Middle East at such prestigious institutions as West Point and Johns Hopkins University. The "masters of the universe"[3] who command six-figure annual incomes through prestigious Wall Street firms have inadvertently led our nation to the precipice of economic disaster and a fourteen trillion dollar national deficit. The wrath of the thousands who have joined citizen protests in major US cities and around the world is evidence of a movement that recognizes the insufficiencies of reason devoid of both ethics and divinely inspired wisdom.

When my fourth grade Sunday school class focused on the lesson of King Solomon, we discussed together how we, like the great and successful king of Israel, could attain wisdom. I shared with these elementary schoolchildren the following diagram, which illustrates in simple visual form the progression articulated by Douglas John Hall:

Ascending Ladder of Wisdom

Wisdom

Faith

Knowledge

Information

---

2. Douglas John Hall, "But Where Shall Wisdom Be Found?" (presentation transcript, Reclaiming the Text Conference, Montreat, North Carolina, June 1, 2000).

3. Wolfe, *Bonfire of the Vanities*, 73.

The Wise Foolishness of God

In the first chapter of this book, we explored the fallacies of "fairness" as a core Christian value. It is generally true that the rules governing fairness are quantitative and calculable. Fairness can easily be measured in the court of public opinion. Fairness is usually the product of common sense. It is reasonable. But history plows through the delicate soil of fairness. If fairness is our prerequisite for a restored Eden, then each advancing era of human history remains equidistant from that restoration. My seven decades of existence have been defined by these atrocious symbols of degradation: Auschwitz's unprecedented cruelty, racial injustice from Selma to Soweto, the Berlin Wall, the My Lai Massacre, a congregational flock of nine hundred poisoned by a religious fanatic's hysteria in Guyana, the killing fields of Cambodia, the carnage of Hutus and Tutsis in Rwanda, the formidable wall that separates the West Bank of Israel and Palestine, and the terrified bodies plunging hopelessly from the World Trade Center's Twin Towers. So it seems that although humanity has grown more intelligent, more technological, and better informed, we have become oblivious to our irrational journey toward chaos and annihilation.

Jesus of Nazareth was born into a similar context of history's horrors. According to Matthew's account, his advent was marked by the death of Herod the Great—a cruel egotistical tyrant who murdered three of his own sons in order to consolidate his puppet power and favor with the Roman Caesar. *Pax Romana* came at a great price to subjugated Judah and Galilee. Jesus lived with his parents in a small, insignificant Galilean village. He was not an urbanite, but some historians speculate that he labored in construction with his father in nearby Sepphoris as a stonemason or carpenter. This Galilean peasant's entire ministry was conducted in the context of a three-fold division of power. Herod Antipas was the tetrarch of Galilee and Peraea; Pontius Pilate was the rigid prefect of Judaea who lived in Caesarea on the Mediterranean coast in a luxurious palace built by Herod the Great, father of Antipas. Only Pilate, the Roman prefect, had the right to sentence anyone to death. He was given the power to execute even a Roman military officer without a full trial, so he could treat citizens of the subjugated Jewish state with impunity, deprived of due process. Joseph Caiaphas was the high priest during Jesus' adult life. He made sure that the Sanhedrin did not offend the Roman authorities, especially Pontius Pilate. Jesus came as a lowly, powerless peasant who taught in the tradition of Hebrew wisdom literature. John Dominic Crossan, in recent scholarly pursuit of the historical Jesus, referred to the Man of Nazareth as "a Mediterranean Jewish peasant."[4] Jesus' "strange teachings" did not resemble the Greek philosophers' systematic formulations of wisdom. Mysteriously, this magnetic teacher combined acts of miraculous healing with parables and bizarre idioms.

Luke the Evangelist sought to write a narrative of Jesus' life and teachings that would address questions raised by many Gentiles—Greek-speaking constituents of his burgeoning congregation in Antioch or Caesarea. Thus, the Third Evangelist presents to us the story of a Jesus who utters startling words and does unanticipated

---

4. Crossan, *Historical Jesus*, 4.

things. This happened, for example, when in the region of Galilee he encountered the faith of those who had lowered their paralyzed friend through a ceiling of a home. These compassionate ones literally raised the roof in order to demonstrate their trust in the remarkable peasant teacher's healing power. Jesus surprisingly commanded the afflicted one to take up his pallet and walk. The Evangelist reported that "amazement seized all of them, and they glorified God and were filled with awe, saying, 'We have seen *strange things* today.'"[5] A similar translation reports that the Galilean people saw "remarkable things," and Eugene Peterson even interprets the phrase to mean, "We've never seen anything like that!"[6] The Greek text here in Luke's Gospel employs the unusual word *paradoxa*, from which we receive our English "paradox." Luke was saying to his congregation and subsequent readers that Jesus lived a paradoxical life and taught paradoxical wisdom. He not only taught "strange things," but his actions were awesome and impossible to explain. Those who encountered him personally were instructed by his wisdom and dazzled by his miraculous healings. They were *awestruck*. Jesus' strange activities and startling Galilean ministries were consistent with the content of his remarkable teachings in the tradition of the wisdom literature of his Hebraic tradition. He was indeed the paradoxical Messiah.

Every parable, utterance of biblical wisdom, and miraculous healing in the life of Jesus points to a mystery that eludes a superficial hearing or shallow interpretations. Each of the biblical stories and paradoxical teachings we examine in these chapters presents a bipolar and seemingly contradictory notion: *para* "alongside of" + *doxa* "belief" or "opinion." Every biblical paradox reflects the vital tension between two opposite ideas or beliefs. Whenever we discover that the opposite of a true statement is another true statement, we have most certainly entered the twilight zone of paradoxical reality. A biblical paradox usually consists of two opposing propositions placed beside each other—both equally true, and when spoken together, representative of an even more profound reality.

Luke's second volume, the book of Acts, makes much of a dream in which the Apostle Paul was called to preach in Macedonia. By responding positively, Paul brought an Eastern gospel into the Western world. Structured Western philosophy was not altogether receptive to Paul's Eastern, Hebraic orientation. For the Greeks, gods must dwell in might upon Mount Olympus. They do not share significantly in the human situation. But, for Paul, the gospel of Christ defies human wisdom. It is the story of a mighty God appearing paradoxically in weakness. It is the account of the powerless form of a dying man on the cross, one whose very weakness transforms all human history. When Paul preached at Mars Hill, the intellectuals said his words were foolish. They could not comprehend the paradox of God's power revealed in the form of a servant. The mere idea of a king on a cross was a contradiction. The apostle, specifically addressing the sophisticated church in Corinth and indirectly the

---

5. Luke 5:26 NRSV, emphasis mine.
6. Peterson, *Message*, 1,862.

brilliant minds of the Western empire, stated forcefully, "For the message of the cross is foolishness to those who are perishing, but to us who are being saved it is the power of God."[7] Then Paul taunted these inflexible men of Greek wisdom by asking, "Where is the wise man? Where is the philosopher of this age?"[8] He answered his rhetorical question with this credo: "For God's foolishness is wiser than human wisdom, and God's weakness is stronger than human strength."[9]

The wisdom of the Western world in the time of Jesus was dominated by the philosophy of Greek culture. Truth was hammered out upon the anvil of intense intellectual debate. Carefully crafted syllogisms became the building blocks of truth. Jesus, however, emerged out of a Hebraic culture that was more oriental than it was Western. His teachings were, therefore, packed with ironic parables and astounding statements of paradox, not Aristotelian logic. He told his followers that if they wanted to gain eternal life, they must lose their lives. The first among the disciples will be last, and the last first. Whoever wishes to become truly great must become the servant of all. Jesus' parables in particular turned around all the furniture and scrambled all the price tags. Heavenly values became the antithesis of earthly ones. The wrong sorts of people get invited to sumptuous banquets in the Kingdom that Jesus envisioned. A rich man dies and goes to a place of anguish; a peasant named Lazarus dies and is transported to the bosom of Abraham. Blessings come unexpectedly. Nothing makes logical sense, except to the mind of the faithful and to the eye of the spiritually perceptive. But biblical paradox is not counter-reason. It is not alien to real life experience. However, it often runs counter to common sense. Paradox follows a different route of reason—the path of faith.

During the Renaissance, when brilliant scientific minds were moving toward the assumption that empirical research would eventually disclose all the mysteries of the universe, a skeptical Erasmus wrote his classic defense of paradoxical truth, *In Praise of Folly*. There are exalted truths embodied within the life of Jesus that point precisely to a wisdom that transcends the limits of our rational thought and can only be embraced by faith. The German mystic Nicholas of Cusa wrote a meditation titled *On Learned Ignorance*, in which he confessed,

> If we can fully attain unto this [knowledge of our ignorance], we will attain unto learned ignorance. For a man—even one very well-versed in learning—will attain unto nothing more perfect than to be found to be most learned in the ignorance which is distinctively his. The more he knows that he is unknowing, the more learned he will be. Unto this end I have undertaken the task of writing a few things about learned ignorance.[10]

---

7. 1 Cor 1:18 NIV.
8. 1 Cor 1:20 NIV.
9. 1 Cor 1:25 RSV.
10. Nicholas of Cusa, *On Learned Ignorance*, 6.

Part I: Paradox and the Doctrine of God

What this renowned mystic taught is that the more we learn, the more we understand the limitations of our knowing. Only through the recognition of our ignorance do we attain the wisdom of humility that brings us eternal and internal peace. The more a person knows that he or she is unknowing, the more learned that person becomes.

In our Western logic, the opposite of a truth is considered a falsehood. Yet in portions of Hebraic wisdom literature and certain Jewish proverbs, the opposite of a truth may well be another truth. This reality is not counter-intelligent, but is rather a higher form of wisdom. Often a greater truth is held between them like the two sides of the same coin. The faith of the Jews, after all, began with the story of Abraham, the most paradoxical figure of all, holding a knife over the quivering body of his beloved Isaac in response to God's command. This scene depicts the tension of faith: God as the fierce judge who tests our faith with potential tragedy, and the merciful God who supplies a proper sacrifice. We enter this paradox, as did Abraham, not by understanding God's reason, but by drawing near with faith.

I saw the faces of paradoxical faith when I visited Chinese Christians at a crowded early morning prayer service in Xi'an. I was traveling with a group of pastors on a study tour sponsored by Duke Divinity School, during which we made contact with faith communities in many of the major cities within the People's Republic of China. An older woman beside me wept during the prayers for the persecuted. A small, but visible, puddle of tears had accumulated in front of her bended knees. All of these humble souls had survived the Cultural Revolution with emotional and physical scars. They did not know what the future held for them, but they trusted in the blessings of God's power to create a new future. Each worshiper in that simple setting firmly believed that the God to whom they prayed would have the last word in their lives and in human history. These simple peasants are among the truly blessed. None dreaded the horizon of the future. They had not borne impossible burdens in order to merit eternal payoffs, yet they were constantly surprised by a joy that transcended their grief. Their beliefs were not an affront to human reason, but a path to a greater truth.

Taylor Branch's *Parting the Waters*, a book that chronicles the first phase of the civil rights movement in this country, may be the most significant single account of this period in American history, if only because Branch deals so singularly with the theological commitments of several key black church leaders. For example, he reminds us of the courage of many black laity during the Montgomery Bus Boycott. Each evening, after walking to work and back again, many attended spiritual life rallies in the church in order to maintain the fervor of their commitment to this righteous cause. One night, when little apparent progress had been made in the movement to desegregate city buses, one of the clergy shared the testimony of a certain elderly lady known affectionately as Mother Pollard. She had refused polite suggestions that she drop out of the boycott due to her age. The crowded congregation was told of Mother

Pollard's response: "My feets is tired, but my soul is rested."[11] Her words became a classic refrain of encouragement for the fainthearted and a cornerstone of the movement that transformed American history.

Over a period of forty-three years of pastoral service I have had the privilege of knowing countless authentic followers of Christ who have led paradoxical lives inspired by the core narratives of the Bible. One of these revered individuals was Calvin Michaels, a man of profound faith and inspiring example from Greensboro, North Carolina. When I became his pastor, Calvin was already an established community leader. He was the personnel manager for a major industry in the city. He conducted his life with such ethical courage, integrity, and consistency that people throughout the community looked to him as a role model for compassion and sensitivity to human need. Calvin led his company and many leaders in the city in a program of education and advocacy for victims of HIV/AIDS. This was a highly controversial act at the time. Upon his recommendation, Christ UMC (Calvin's congregation) invited the Executive Director of AIDS Action to speak from the pulpit. His activism on behalf of victims and their families was an affront to some within the congregation. But everyone respected his passion and integrity in campaigning against this enormously destructive disease.

Our entire congregation was appalled upon learning that Calvin had become the victim of an equally destructive disease—amyotrophic lateral sclerosis (ALS, or Lou Gehrig's disease). He soon began to lose control of his muscles. Day by day, his body became more like melted wax. When he could no longer raise his head due to the weakness of his neck muscles, he reported to his golf buddies that he now had an advantage over them: His eyes would always be on the ball before teeing off. He never complained or rebelled against his plight. He persisted in a life of courageous faith. Eventually, he became paralyzed. But he continued to attend worship services each Sunday with the assistance of his loving family. In early Epiphany on the Baptism of our Lord Sunday, those in attendance were invited to renew their baptism by coming down the carpeted nave, approaching the font, and receiving water from the pastor's hand upon the forehead in the sign of the cross. I said to each participating worshiper, "Remember your baptism and be thankful." Calvin's young grandson pushed his beloved grandfather's wheelchair, despite the fact that this stricken man's head was nearly in his lap. When his emaciated body was directly in front of me, I administrated this renewal of the sacrament. Drops of water gently wound down his face. Then he suddenly raised the thumb of his right hand as if to say, "I indeed remember and affirm my baptism." Two days later I rushed to his home, where he died the death of a beloved saint of that bereaved family, congregation, and city.

Even though I cannot explain the paradoxical reason why the pure in heart see the face of God, I can affirm the reality of that mysterious truth and tell the story of my friend Calvin.

---

11. Quoted in Branch, *Parting the Waters*, 149.

3

Divine Presence During the Eclipse of God

GOD MAKES GOD'S SELF most powerfully present during times of God's absence. There are moments in which many of us experience the eclipse of God. We do not cease believing. We do not even doubt God's existence. But we feel the dreadful absence of a divine presence. We may even harbor hostility toward the Almighty. It is as if we have dialed the 911 emergency number in desperation and received a busy signal. The power of God remains apparent to us even in these times of stark darkness. Our parched lips begrudgingly form the words of faith, "the Lord giveth; the Lord taketh away," but our throat turns to cotton as we force the final tragic line from the mouth of Job, "Blessed be the name of the Lord."[1]

When I was a pastor in Greensboro, an aggressive fire a few miles from our home unmercifully swept through a modest wooden farmhouse. The flames quickly engulfed the seventy-five-year-old structure and its inhabitants. Four lovely, angelic children were killed, including eight-month-old twins, their twenty-two-month-old sister, and a four-year-old brother. The mother was taken by helicopter to the Chapel Hill Burn Center. In a state of pensive reflection, the mother's father told a local reporter, "A man gets up in the morning and loses everything he's got before suppertime."[2]

We all exist in a world of uncertainty and potential tragedy. The rains fall upon the just and the unjust alike. Calamity does not discriminate. Disease and viruses attack at will in wanton fashion. Fires burn palatial mansions of proud starlets on the slopes of Malibu Beach as well as the humble hovels of rural North Carolina. Genetic predispositions for cancer or heart disease are carried by the rich and famous as well as the anonymous poor.

Daniel Hans, a Presbyterian pastor from Gettysburg, Pennsylvania, writing for *Pulpit Digest*, reflected upon the agonizing death of his three-year-old daughter, who

---

1. Job 1:21 KJV.
2. Solomon, "Four Children Killed in Fire West of Troy."

had recently succumbed to cancer. He identified with the role of Mary, mother of Jesus, who watched helplessly at the foot of Golgotha's agony. Daniel did not lose his faith while watching his beloved daughter slip away in that futile fight. He did, however, experience the eclipse of God's presence. The character and content of his personal faith will, therefore, never be the same. He testified: "Whatever may be the cause of loss, whatever the source of suffering, the presence of an absence results when there is absence of a presence. As the church we are called to fill those absences with our presence."[3]

The Hebrew Bible maintained for centuries a rather simplistic explanation for most tragic events. During the era of the monarchy, devout descendants of Abraham began to record the oral traditions of their inherited faith. The so-called Deuteronomic theology was articulated and served the emotional needs of the faith community during eras of stability. It succinctly stated that righteous people are rewarded; sinners are punished. *Quid pro quo.* God will zap those who perform evil deeds. The Decalogue of Moses especially supported and preserved this theory. If we obey the commandments of YHWH, we shall be rewarded. If we honor our parents and our ancestry of faith, we shall live long, prosperous lives. Those who are devout in prayer and the disciplines of the Torah never experience the eclipse of the Almighty.

This judicial formula was rarely challenged, even by the great prophets of Judah. After all, men like Jeremiah easily documented the debauchery of the nation, which had triggered the destruction of Jerusalem and initiated an era of slavery in Babylon. It was assumed that the Hebrews got what they deserved. But, even during the lifetime of Jeremiah, analytical Hebrew writers challenged this concept of retribution as the cause of human suffering. A generation of devout sons and daughters had been born in exile. They were not responsible for the sins of their parents and grandparents. They wept in faithfulness by the waters of Babylon and tasted salty tears of remorse. Prophets of the exile such as Ezekiel began to insist that this new generation must be accountable for its own sins, ceasing to blame their plight upon the debauchery of their ancestors. Moreover, their plight of poverty, suffering, and humiliation was not caused by their own transgressions.

The book of Job was probably penned during this period. It is truly an Everyman story. This saga is contained within the so-called wisdom literature of the Hebrew Bible. It is akin to Ecclesiastes (in Hebrew, *Qoheleth*, a term literally meaning "leader of an assembly" or simply "the preacher"), which gave utterance to skepticism after the restoration of Israel and somber return to a barren Jerusalem with no Temple. *Qoheleth* affirmed the existence and authority of God but viewed the created order as an expression of absurd vanity. Wisdom literature emerged after the scattered Jews began to return to a prosaic, pulverized Palestine. The writers of wisdom poetry remembered a righteous ruler, Josiah, who had instituted many honorable reforms—but this pious leader suffered an early death, and the nation of Israel again became subservient

---

3. Hans, "Absence and Presence," 44.

to a pagan power. Where was God amidst such tragic circumstances? Evil prospered. Bad things happened to good people like King Josiah. Wisdom literature tended to raise these skeptical questions and to confess with candor the feeling that the God of Torah is often silent. The purposes of God are not apparent or easily perceived. "A generation goes, and a generation comes, but the earth remains forever . . . All things are wearisome; more than one can express."[4]

The book of Job was the earliest and most formidable challenge to orthodox Hebraic theology. It initiated the profound tradition of Jewish skepticism reflected in much of the later wisdom writings. Its poetry was probably written by a Jerusalem sage who had been deported into Lower Mesopotamia during the early stages of the Babylonian exile. This poet shows the influence of Jeremiah, Habakkuk, and Ezekiel, but addresses the unique concerns of a post-exilic Judaism.

Its narrative is recapitulated in nearly every parish in some fashion and at persistently regular intervals. Each time a pastor climbs into the pulpit and invokes the text of Job, the preacher takes comfort in the work of the Deuteronomic redactor whose fingerprints are upon the prologue (Job 1:1—2:13) and the epilogue (Job 42:7–17) in which the pitiful man who loses all his children and possessions has his family and fortunes restored at the end of the story. But any contemporary pastor knows that the original text of this revered book was the poetic section and that the prose was the later addition of a redactor who was drastically disturbed by the implication that a righteous person's life can end in the agony of unremitting grief, the intense pain of physical torture, and the eclipse of God.

Every conscientious pastor knows that eventually he or she must deal with the reality of Job's plight disclosed in the poetic portion that is devoid of restitution, earthly reward, and exoneration. Bad things—horrendously unjust things—happen to good people in the community. Some, if not many, of these do not have their broken lives put back together. They feel the absence, silence, and eclipse of the God of their creation. The book of Job has withstood the test of time, not because it capitulates to an easy Deuteronomic formula to explain the nature of things, but because it discloses a God that makes God's self most profoundly present at the times of perceived absence.

The story of this foreigner from the land of Uz began in the form of oral tradition told by respected seers of the community around campfires during the exile and in synagogues throughout Babylon. It may have been a dramatic presentation at the autumn festivals along the rivers of Babel during this era of anguish and slavery. Job represented the plight of many Jews during those discouraging times. The writer poignantly raised the question: Does the faithful believer have the right to judge the wisdom and justice of God? Job was truly a good man. His three friends pestered him to confess his sins, for they assumed that Job had surely disobeyed God and thereby caused his own calamitous circumstance. But Job argued that his suffering was not caused by his evil deeds.

4. Eccl 1:4–8a NRSV.

Divine Presence During the Eclipse of God

The core issue in this dramatic book is the matter of theodicy. Simply stated, theodicy is a theological attempt to justify the ways of God to humanity. Theodicy asks, "If God is good, whence evil?" In Archibald MacLeish's modern Job—a stage play titled *JB*—Nickles, as the Adversary, succinctly states the ambiguity of the theodicy question:

> I heard upon his dry dung heap
> That man cry out who cannot sleep:
> "If God is God He is not good,
> If God is good He is not God;
> Take the even, take the odd,
> I would not sleep here if I could . . ."[5]

Nickles voices our lament. He has, in fact, stolen my line in the play of my life in the parish. For I have answered the phone in the middle of the night and met the patrolman with the family at the hospital's morgue in the terrifying moment of identifying a beloved body, broken and lifeless. Nickles speaks my line in life's most tragic drama when I watched a little leukemia victim in a Greensboro hospital grasp his stuffed monkey, appropriately named Curious George. I stood with his anguished single mother as we watched his little bald head sobbing in pain. Through the night we watched him as he panted for breath until his last gasp brought the dubious tranquility of death. This moment provoked more than my theological curiosity; it produced a vehement rage at the core of my being. In that moment of God's eclipse, I protested with the intensity of Job: "Truly the thing that I fear comes upon me, and what I dread befalls me. I am not at ease, nor am I quiet; I have no rest; but trouble comes."[6]

What, then, is the central message of Job that has such relevance for those Curious George events of anguish experienced in nearly every parish? Certainly the book dispenses with the partially valid Deuteronomic formula, but it also makes a mockery of all our attempts to mold God into some sort of systematic theologian. For good reason this bold, time-tested expression of sacred wisdom literature has been revered for some twenty-six centuries. It was among the great treasures carefully preserved in the caves of Qumran. Perhaps its endurance is due to its grasp of the true human situation and its embrace of the paradoxical nature of God's presence in a broken and unjust world.

The key to understanding Job's haunting message may be encapsulated in the startling language of God in the whirlwind scenario toward the end of the book. Speaking out of the turbulence, God forces Job to examine the whole of God's created order—the stars above, the desert and watered terrain, the wild lion, the stately horse, the huge oxen-like beast called Behemoth. God reminds Job that "there is no

---

5. MacLeish, *JB*, 14.
6. Job 3:25–26 NRSV.

one on land who can dominate him / Made as he is without fear."[7] When the voice of God describes the vastness of the Lord's creation and the place of humanity in the scheme of things, Job suddenly understands that his worldview had been myopic. His assumptions about God's justice had been premature. In the context of this revelation amidst the chaos of a whirlwind, he shouts remorsefully, "Indeed, I spoke without understanding / Of things beyond me, which I did not know."[8]

The wisdom of Job asserts that we, like this universal man of suffering, are not masters of all we survey. Our vision of reality is always limited or skewed. We cannot possibly behold the vast dimensions of God's dealings with fallen creation. Humanity is only one portion of a suffering world that is crying out in pain for its redemption. God is in the process of redeeming us, and with us, the whole cosmos. God is still in charge, even when we experience God's absence, the great theological eclipse. Out of the whirlwind, God spoke to Job. The message of this God-in-a-whirlwind seems insensitive to Job's pain, with its unsympathetic tone and preoccupation with the vastness of God's creation. God babbles on incessantly like a circus owner about his wild animals and sea monsters. But the God we meet in these pages is not oblivious to Job's agony. Such suffering, God is quick to demonstrate, is shared and absorbed into the whole of the created order. It is especially shared by God himself. Job's pain is God's pain. Job does not suffer in isolation. The voice from the whirlwind finally convinces him of this reality. God, in these crucial verses, guides Job into a greater compassion and understanding of the painful plight and suffering that infests the whole of the created order.

The paradoxical message of Job is akin to the profundity of the great body of wisdom literature in the Bible that was at the heart of Jesus' faith. The teacher of Galilee quoted from these sources, including the Psalms, more than any other references among the Scriptures of his tradition. The subtle message of Job reflects the astoundingly realistic assertion of *Qoheleth*: "All streams run to the sea, but the sea is not full; to the place where the streams flow, there they continue to flow."[9]

Elie Wiesel is arguably a contemporary Job. As a child who survived the Holocaust, his eyes have perhaps witnessed a severity of inhumane suffering that far exceeded the Babylonian captivity of the ancient Israelites. Like Job, Wiesel witnessed the cruel annihilation of his family in the death camp of Auschwitz and the destruction of all his worldly possessions. When this man of enduring faith and immeasurable suffering wrote his memoirs, he titled the first volume *All Rivers Run to the Sea* and the second *And the Sea Is Never Full*. The overarching theme of the great wisdom tradition of Israel is that despite evidence that all things appear absurd and all seems vanity, God is working out God's divine purpose. The rivers have a destination. History is not a tale told by an idiot, signifying nothing. In point of fact, those who entered the

---

7. Job 41:25. Translation by Greenburg et al., *The Writings: Kethubim*.
8. Job 42:3b. *The Writings: Kethubim*..
9. Eccl 1:7 NRSV.

Divine Presence During the Eclipse of God

gas chambers of Auschwitz reverently repeating the Shema experienced the depths of God's Being. When we have the faith of Job, we are not passive or particularly patient. But we go on trusting in the ultimate will of a loving, compassionate God whose ways are shrouded in mystery and paradox—a God who makes God's Being most profoundly present during times of God's absence.

Job's response to the voice of God in chapter 42 has inadvertently been misunderstood. Verse six of this crucial chapter has been translated: "therefore I despise myself and *repent* in dust and ashes."[10] The Hebrew verb *naham* is usually translated "to repent." But when it is used with the preposition *al*, it more accurately means "to change one's mind" or "to reverse one's opinion." The decision of Job was, consequently, to change his mind about his wearing the apparel of "dust and ashes"—that is, his spirit of lamentation and dejection. Job decided that he would no longer lick his sores in self-pity or blame God for his unjust plight. Job came to the realization that he had described God as a prisoner of a particular way of thinking about justice. It is this outlook that Job now abandons. He concludes that no one can define God, especially through human categories of justice and fairness. The *repentance* of Job—if we consider this response to be contrition—was his confession of arrogance. After all, he had attempted to define and limit God. Gustavo Gutiérrez, in his insightful *On Job*, summarizes the astounding new realization that came to a transformed Job. The man of pain suddenly realized that "justice alone does not have the final say about how we are to speak of God."[11] God is primarily known through his love, even and especially suffering love. God's love, however, like all true love, does not operate in a world of mere cause and effect. God's love enters human experience with a spirit of freedom and graciousness. It tempers justice with mercy. The ways of God are not boxed in or limited by human categories or conventional logic. God does not make God's self known only in forms of retribution: punishing evil and rewarding good. God is not a slave to some singular formula for justice that says, "If I give to God, I shall get something in return." The God we meet in the book of Job does not abandon justice nor forsake the just. Neither does the Lord force us from the necessity of practicing justice. But Job is guided by the mysterious voice of God to reject the temptation of imprisoning God within a narrow way of thinking about justice or a myopic view of human history.

In the end, Job learns paradoxically to trust the God he cannot define, control, or comprehend. This is the imperishable value and universal significance of this profound Hebrew book. This observation prompts me to contemplate the central agenda that I constantly face as a pastor and theologian. I discover the trusting faith of Job within the people of each new congregation. These heroic, Job-like faithful of the church struggle against great adversity and bravely bear their anguish. They bury their dead with confident trust. They continue to believe, even though they reside within

10. Job 42:6 NRSV.
11. Gutiérrez, *On Job*, 87.

Part I: Paradox and the Doctrine of God

the eye of a hurricane's most ferocious doubts. They remain silent amidst storms. They possess a noble strength described in Gray's *Elegy:* "Along the cool sequestered vale of life / They kept the noiseless tenor of their way."[12] Their names shall be written large in the Book of Life!

One of the most important people in my life was a young adult member of my second parish who lived in a rural region near Winston-Salem, North Carolina. Kathy Sprinkle was born a hydrocephalic. This congenital condition is caused by an abnormal accumulation of cerebrospinal fluid in the ventricles or cavities of the brain. When Kathy was a child, her head circumference enlarged rapidly due to her condition, causing the development of a posterior fontanelle. Fluid tended to build up inside her brain, causing severe headaches that persisted throughout her life. She underwent surgery nearly every year at Baptist Hospital to insert various shunts that helped drain the excess fluid. Often these shunts would malfunction or become infected. On a regular basis, she experienced nausea, vomiting, and seizures.

Despite these obstacles and intimations that God had callously abandoned her, Kathy maintained a positive spirit. She learned to use crutches and, in an era before the enforcement of handicapped accessibility codes for churches, she ascended the steep steps of Shady Grove United Methodist Church and participated in corporate worship. I have rarely encountered such courage or depth of faith. She had all the aspirations and desires of a normal teenager and managed to complete her high school degree with the help of tutors and home study. Although most patients with this condition do not live into adulthood, she survived until the age of forty-two. Her devoted parents, both caring members of the congregation, and her uncommon courage kept her alive amidst unrelenting pain. A wise older man within that congregation insisted upon accompanying me on many of my pastoral visits at the Sprinkle home. At the conclusion of an especially meaningful conversation and moment of prayer with Kathy, he turned to me as we left the Sprinkles and poignantly said, "George, I never feel sorry for Kathy when we make these visits, despite all the suffering we observe during our time with her. I only feel sorry for those in this community who have not taken the time to experience the privilege of knowing her."

The theology of Job reminds me of the central character in Gail Godwin's novel *Father Melancholy's Daughter.* He is an Episcopalian pastor who takes the pain of his struggling little parish upon himself. He is a man who suffers intensely but continues to minister fervently and faithfully. Adrian Bonner, the story's young clergy colleague, gives a stirring tribute to this Job-like pastor when he speaks candidly with the daughter of his clergy mentor:

> He's not trendy; he doesn't pose . . . He's just himself—himself offered daily. He worries about people, he worries about himself . . . He baptizes and marries and buries and listens to people's fears and confessions and isn't above

---

12. Gray, "Elegy Written in a Country Churchyard," 543–44.

sharing some of his own . . . He's a dedicated man, your father. He's lonely and bedeviled like the rest of us, but he has time for it all and tries to do it right. He lives by the grace of daily obligation. He's what the priests in books used to be like, but today he's a rarity.[13]

These words describe the faith of the modern Jobs we often meet in the most pedestrian parishes. Through the empathetic pain of such caring followers of Christ, we begin to hear the voice of God from the other side of silence, from the void of the divine eclipse. Through the cries of a transformed Job, we are drawn in wondrous awe to a mysterious grace that we can neither comprehend nor control.

When I am transported from this reality unto a heavenly one, I shall surely pass through the misty portals of divine mystery with my hand raised in questioning protest. The Almighty has some explaining to do! But, now in this interim before death, I desire the trusting faith of Job and the persevering posture of Kathy Sprinkle or Father Melancholy. I wish to be a person who lives faithfully "by the grace of daily obligation."[14] In so doing, I shall discover the God whose love transcends the neat categories of human justice, whose mystery is disclosed in the form of his innocent son's death upon a cross, whose presence is profoundly revealed during times of his assumed absence, and whose glory fills the earth with a joy which transcends all our earthly sufferings.

---

13. Godwin, *Father Melancholy's Daughter*, 208–209.
14. Ibid., 209.

4

The Good Thing about Bad News

IN THESE INITIAL CHAPTERS we have explored how the doctrine of God confronts us with the paradoxical nature of divine Being: A righteous God whose mercy is often unfair, whose absolute wisdom transcends our deficient human understanding, and whose caring presence is most profoundly revealed during times of perceived callous absence. The most essential components of the biblical narrative, in fact, disclose a God whose activity in human history is paradoxical. The wholeness of the biblical story is gospel, the message of good news. The four narrative accounts of the life of Jesus are the culmination of the biblical gospel, not the exclusive reservoir of biblical good news. The Scriptures of Jesus—the law (*Torah*), the prophets (*Neviim*), and wisdom literature or writings (*Kethubim*)—are an integral and essential component of the fullness of the message of salvation history. When we immerse ourselves in the comprehensive narrative of the Bible that includes the books of Moses, Hebrew wisdom literature, all the prophetic books, the four Evangelists, the Letters of Paul, and the Pastoral Epistles, we are startled by the stark realism of sacred writ. Vestiges of good news are difficult to find through a cursory reading of the biblical narrative from Genesis to Revelation.

The great preponderance of these writings muddle through expansive sagas of human sadness, horrific wars, oppression and exile of the people of Israel, and the desperate plight of the persecuted faithful. Most biblical authors provide a grandparent version of the faith family's story. Parents tend to have an idyllic, selective memory of the past so that they become the heroes of much of the narrative. But grandparents are truth-telling redactors who shake out all the dirty linen on the family clothesline. Thus, most of the biblical story is composed of appalling accounts of atrocious, ghastly events: humanity's departure from Eden, the near-destruction of all living things in the great flood, Abraham's averted sacrifice of Isaac, the theological and ethical struggles of Jacob the trickster, centuries of slavery in Egypt, repeated disobedience of Israel during demonic dynasties, the rejection of righteous prophets, the multiple destructions of Jerusalem, the demolition of the first sacred Temple, the Babylonian captivity, the desecration of the new Temple, the humiliation of the Jews under the Seleucid dynasty, Herod's massacre of innocent children upon the news of a Messiah's birth, the Passion Narrative, and the persecution of the early church. These pages of the biblical story pile high in a heap of human residue. None of the authors of the corpus of biblical canon conclude their narrative with the line, "and they lived happily ever after." Very few sacred texts, if any, are likely to be converted into film fodder for the Hallmark television network. Joshua's idyllic stories of heroic valor and triumphant entry into Canaan's soil is immediately countered by the book of Judges' saga of stained military leaders whose exploits were inevitably negated by the bad behavior of God's chosen people. In the era of the kings of Israel and Judah, there were at least ten conniving Ahabs for every good Josiah. The promissory message of Second Isaiah is balanced by the dreary realities of *Qoheleth*. The soothing word of restorative justice in the appealing poetry of Hosea is countered by the vindictive, appallingly harsh voice of the prophet Nahum, who rejoices in the brutal defeat and tortuous destruction of Judah's enemy.

Thus, at a superficial level, much of the biblical story seems like a good news/bad news joke. Until we recognize the paradoxical nature of God's activity in the vast scope of the biblical narrative, our vision remains myopic, and we rarely perceive authentic good news beneath the rubble of all the excruciatingly bad. The Bible appears to be a collection of ancient mythical tales told by a vast variety of fallible human authors, unless the readers of sacred texts allow the Story to intersect and interpret their personal stories. When the text has become an integral part of one's existence and has taken a central place in one's psyche, Scripture begins to interpret redemptively the intimacies of one's personal narrative. Thus, we begin to see how God speaks to us in the language of events—both the good and the bad. Through a reverent, disciplined, and intimate relationship with the Story, we begin to discover the good thing about bad news within our stories.

During the last months of my older brother Albert's life, we spent some valuable time on the phone reflecting upon memories of our childhood and youth. Our adult lives had been separated by many miles, making it impossible to be together or share our personal memories except on special occasions. But we both vividly recalled a pivotal incident when Albert was six and I was three. Our parents had planned a family road trip to Texas at the invitation of my mother's sister. The first phase of this lengthy post-war journey was a stopover in Milledgeville, Georgia, my mother's ancestral home. The trunk of our family car was packed with boxes for Christmas to be distributed to relatives there. The journey was supposed to encompass the entire week of Christmas with time for further exploration. My father faced the threat of a jobless future, and so one purpose of this family adventure was to investigate employment opportunities in the Lone Star State.

Part I: Paradox and the Doctrine of God

As darkness fell on a narrow road somewhere in central Georgia, we encountered a reckless driver careening off both sides of the highway. We later discovered that the careless driver was inebriated with holiday spirits. In order to avoid a head-on collision, our father instinctively drove the vehicle off the road and down a steep ravine, where our car catapulted until it came to rest on its passenger side. Our father somehow managed to pull each of us out through the mangled car door. Fearing an explosion from a leaking gas tank, he exerted uncommon strength and lifted our mother's bloodied body through that narrow passage. Eventually two soldiers, recently returned from assignments abroad during World War II, spotted our trouble and loaded us into their car to rush us to the nearest hospital. Rural ambulance service was not readily available during that era. After enduring several weeks of incompetent diagnosis and delay in a small-town medical facility, our mother was transferred to Charlotte, North Carolina, where specialists discovered several broken bones at the base of her neck and portions of her spine.

Needless to say, our parents never pursued their dreams of monetary security in the elusive state of Texas. Even though our mother continued to teach elementary children in a western North Carolina public school, she endured pain from the accident for the rest of her life.

As Albert and I shared our memories of this crucial event, I observed that our family story could have been one of greater financial security and fewer physical challenges had this tragic episode never happened. My older brother interrupted our phone conversation by stating the obvious: "You are forgetting that, if this horrendous event had never occurred, you wouldn't have met the love of your life in high school. No forty years of marital bliss. And I would never have found the wife and family of my dreams."

Only a mature and comprehensive perspective of faith enables us to see our stories in the context of a greater Story. Only through the discipline of scriptural holiness and absorption into the biblical text can we experience a sort of spiritual *gestalt* within our personal narratives. Only by focusing eyes of faith upon a memory of sacred narrative are we able to perceive good news despite all that is bad. God's activity in our personal stories, therefore, is paradoxical. God speaks to us in the episodic language of personal events, weaving together a tapestry of good and bad. Just as revered biblical characters (patriarchs, matriarchs, prophets, martyrs, and other saints) could not see the fullness of their stories, so we too must enter the future not knowing specific outcomes, but trusting in the ultimate triumph of God's goodness. Only the perspective of faith embraces the paradoxical nature of human history. Good is hidden within the bad. Only a voice of faith can avow with confidence the affirmation of the Apostle Paul, who wrote, "We know that in everything God works for good with those who love him, who are called according to his purpose."[1] Certainly not all things are good.

---

1. Rom 8:28 RSV. It is evident to the writer that the Apostle Paul did not intend for *pánta* to be translated in the nominative case. All things do not work for good. But if this Greek word, which can

The Good Thing about Bad News

Not even all things work toward goodness. But God works amidst and despite all things—very bad things and evil events—in order to guide the ultimate destination of human history toward God's ultimate goodness. God certainly works against some things with subtle interventions of unanticipated grace and splendor.

Some the most enduring and beloved passages of the Hebrew Bible are contained within the prophetic book commonly called "Second Isaiah"—chapters 40 through 66. This poetry was originally put to parchment just before October 29, 539 B.C. and the conquest of Cyrus, King of Persia, which resulted in the fall of the Babylonian Empire and the end of its cruel enslavement of the Jews. Before his army's assault upon Babylon, this benevolent conqueror announced that he would allow the liberated Jews to return to their homeland in Judah, rebuild their demolished Temple, and reinstitute their historic rituals and festivals of worship. This was exceedingly good news for Isaiah, a poet-prophet of the late exile. More than a full generation of Jews had lived in the Diaspora of the pagan and perverse Babylonian Empire. Restoration had been a quixotic dream of despairing, devout Jews. When the liberating armies of the benevolent King Cyrus, sovereign of the Persian Empire, ended Babylonian domination and blessed the Hebrew minority that had sustained dreams of restoration, the ecstatic prophet penned a series of "servant songs" that articulated the joy of a coming reality. In the fourth of these poetic celebrations, the exilic Isaiah compared the people of Israel to a forsaken wife, married in the passion of youth, divorced, but now restored in everlasting marital covenant. He wrote this riveting line: "*For a brief moment* I abandoned you, but with great compassion I will gather you. In overflowing wrath *for a moment* I hid my face from you, but with everlasting love I will have compassion on you, says the Lord, your redeemer."[2] This "brief moment" had lasted forty-seven years—an entire generation! The prophet compared this expansive era to the trial of Noah, when God nearly destroyed the earth and all its inhabitants but changed his mind and initiated a covenant of peace through the symbol of the rainbow.

Through the years of my pastorates, I have been fortified in faith by the many laity in each parish who have endured "brief moments" of bad news. I have known and revered many older friends from a generation that endured the austere years of the Great Depression, followed by global warfare during which they personally experienced poverty and violence on a massive scale. "For a moment," great throngs

---

be either nominative or accusative, is the object of a preposition, the contextual translation of the Revised Standard Version ("in *everything* God works for good") is preferable to the King Jas or New Revised Standard Version. In the theology of paradox I am articulating, it makes sense to assert that God works for good *through all things*. As a pastor, I found it unfaithful to the intent of the Apostle Paul to assert to a bereaved parishioner that had just experienced some tragic loss that this was in fact a good thing and an expression of God's providential will. Evil events defy the intentional will of God and retard the realization of God's kingdom of righteousness. Many things, indeed, work for evil. But God works *amidst* all things (and even *against* many things) in order to bring about God's ultimate good.

2. Isa 54:7–8 NRSV, emphasis mine.

Part I: Paradox and the Doctrine of God

of faithful people in churches around the world experienced little encouraging news during the prolonged era of 1929 to 1945.

Lillian Jelly was an emigrant from England who came to the mountains of Asheville, North Carolina, in order to pursue a better life with her children after surviving the devastation of her native Nottingham. From her, I learned to view personal adversity from a broader perspective than the immediacy of one's experience. She came to this country in the post-war era lacking financial resources. She soon began teaching music to children of the community with the help of the McMannen Methodist Church, which provided her with a piano and space for instruction. She reciprocated by introducing many young lives in the parish to the joy of classical music and the profundity of her faith. She demonstrated to all within that parish a theology of confidence amidst adversity. When I became a summer youth director in the church and boarded in her modest home, this widow shared with me her memories of Nazi air raids and frightful nights spent in bomb shelters with her two children. Through it all, she discovered a sense of hope within a network of courageous Christians.

She also told me about the inspiration of clergymen like Leslie Weatherhead, who reminded his congregation and a nation of radio listeners of God's greater vision in the midst of those chaotic times. During the spring of 1940, for example, Weatherhead's City Temple parish in London celebrated its tercentennial—three hundred years of ministry. The church had endured many hardships, including the economic and emotional stress of the First World War, but had managed to eliminate a longstanding debt just as the new war with Germany began. But by the fall of that year, bombs had fallen upon London, pulverizing the City Temple. Amidst the carnage, Weatherhead preached a series of sermons on national radio that were published as the Christian classic, *The Will of God*. In these addresses, he distinguished between the intentional, the circumstantial, and the ultimate will of God. Weatherhead's parish newsletter article on the week of the ancient sanctuary's destruction perhaps best illustrates his comprehension of God's activity amidst the absurdity of this frightful time. The pastor whose faith had inspired and fortified Lillian Jelly wrote this to his despondent congregation:

> [The Church of Jesus Christ] is invisible and invincible, indestructible and indissoluble. Smash the form of its expression here and it breaks out there. Burn its local habitation to the ground one day and it has found another the next . . . So, resolute and determined, with quiet hearts and steady nerves, and with no bitterness, remembering the thousands of our fellow Christians who, through all ages, have been driven from pillar to post for Christ's sake, the City Temple goes forward into its fourth century.[3]

This was precisely the quality of faith and the wise insight that I gleaned from my friendship with Lillian Jelly, whose resilient and joyful existence bore witness to

---

3. Weatherhead, *Leslie Weatherhead*, 177–78.

the primacy of the gospel amidst the tragic dimensions of her personal life. In every congregation I have served in these decades of ministry, I have shared a faith pilgrimage with people who have experienced the worst of news with resilience, courage, and hope. What carries these people of uncommon faith?

My first parish appointment was in the campus town of Wingate, North Carolina. My wife and I were quickly drawn to Ben and Eva Bivens, a young couple about our age. They were bright and attractive, with deep roots in the community. Eva's father was the town's respected mayor, and Ben's parents were connected with the citizens of the town through a flourishing business. Everyone in the Wingate United Methodist Church took pride in the marital union of these promising role models, who had also been blessed by the birth of a lovely baby girl named Beth.

One evening this little blonde, blue-eyed angel registered a slight fever. Beth's parents had no reason to be alarmed until the thermometer registered a sudden spike. Without medical consultation, they gave their three-year-old child aspirin—a safe adult remedy, but an inadvertent mistake. I met them at the local county hospital as precious moments passed without a diagnosis. The frustrated emergency doctor recommended a transfer to Presbyterian Hospital in nearby Charlotte. Shortly after the ambulance arrived accompanied by a bewildered Ben and Eva, a competent diagnostic physician told the stunned parents that their child was the victim of Reye's syndrome, a disease marked by liver inflammation and severe swelling in the brain. It was too late to save Beth.

On that dreadful night, I stood for hours in paralyzed disbelief beside these beleaguered parents who had been strangers to tragedy as we watched their fragile child fall into a coma and fade into death. Nothing about this tragic ending was good. Ben and Eva were devastated, and I could only give to them respectful silence and the empathy of my tears as I drove them back to their empty home.

No one can prepare for such a moment. I met with Ben and Eva the next day as they made arrangements for the funeral. The couple was inundated with sorrowful visits by intimate friends and casual acquaintances, but the only condolences that penetrated their parental grief were from Beth's little Sunday school classmates. One neighborhood child picked daises along the sidewalk on the way to that grief-stricken house. He presented these to the emotionally broken mother with the words, "I picked these for Beth."

A few weeks after the funeral, Eva began searching the obituaries published in regional papers, including the *Charlotte Observer*. She began writing messages of condolence to other parents who had lost young children. This activity not only became a therapeutic endeavor for Eva, but it also resulted in a vital ministry of empathy that elicited many phone conversations and written responses of gratitude from bereaved parents near and far.

With the passage of time, Ben was offered a promotion, and the couple made the difficult decision to leave the nurturing parish of Wingate and loving people who had

Part I: Paradox and the Doctrine of God

so consistently reached out to them with kindness and compassion. For over forty years, we have kept in touch with these friends who relocated to Houston, Texas. We always discuss our memories of Beth, the anguish of her death, and the ever-present emptiness in their lives. Although Ben and Eva were later gifted with three healthy sons, they continue to carry the scar of that incomparable grief. But these two faithful servants of resurrection and hope have come to peace with their bad news by continuing to share with empathy in the suffering and sorrow of others. Their three sons, now adults with children of their own, will never fill the emptiness of Beth's death. But they are evidence of a divine grace that has confidently carried them, and countless other faithful ones, through years of grief. This family has become the embodiment of the paradoxical progression of faith suggested by the Apostle Paul when he testified that "suffering produces endurance, and endurance produces character, and character produces hope, and hope does not disappoint us, because God's love has been poured into our hearts through the Holy Spirit that has been given to us."[4]

In the moment of epic crisis (either personal, private tragedy or large-scale catastrophe), it is not the role of the pastor or the laity to explain bad news or justify the ways of God. Systematic theology can offer neither reason nor remedy. On that infamous day of September 11, 2001, Rowan Williams, Archbishop of Canterbury, was leading a spiritual life retreat at Trinity Episcopal Church, just blocks away from the World Trade Center. He was compelled to write his theological reflections without any attempt to explain or defend the Being of God in such a calamitous context. He merely described his emotions upon witnessing the chaos and scope of human anguish suffered by victims of the attack. He wanted his written theological reflections to imitate the bizarre action of Jesus recorded in the eighth chapter of John, when our Lord witnessed a woman about to be stoned for adultery. The scribes and Pharisees wanted Jesus to make an ethical assessment about the justification of this punishment in order to trap him. The Messiah refrained from ethical pontification, but merely wrote a message in the dirt. Arising from bended knee, Jesus said to them, "Let him who is without sin among you be the first to throw a stone at her."[5] In similar manner, Archbishop Williams refrained from offering a theological defense of a deity who would allow such carnage. Like Jesus, Rowan Williams hesitated. He did not articulate a fixed interpretation. He did not dictate the just fate of the perpetrators of this violence. He invited the reader merely to see differently, precisely because the writer and theologian refused to make sense of this bad news. All of southern Manhattan was covered in dust from the collapsing Twin Towers. Thus, Williams titled his reflections *Writing in the Dust: After September 11*. In keeping with his intention to write that which is personal but transitory, Williams candidly noted, "We who call ourselves Christian have every reason to say no to any system at all that uses suffering to prove things: to

---

4. Rom 5:3b–5 NRSV.

5. John 8:7 RSV. This pericope is placed as a footnote in the best translations of John's Gospel. It was a later addition to the original manuscript of the Fourth Gospel.

prove the sufferer's guilt as sinner being punished, or—perhaps more frequently in our world—to prove the sufferer's innocence as a martyr whose heroism must never be forgotten or betrayed."[6] Hours after witnessing desperate strangers hold hands and leap from the seventy-eighth floor of the South Tower, Bishop Williams invited us to hold the memory of this moment in our mind "long enough for some of our demons to walk away."[7]

A theology of paradox resists a neat, systematic explanation of bad news. But it provides a context of resilient trust by which even the anguish of bad news cannot destroy the hope planted in the heart of every pilgrim that abides in scriptural holiness. The context of this trusting faith, grounded in scriptural awareness and reverence for the Story, is the source of redemption for all our stories.

---

6. Williams, *Writing in the Dust*, 71.
7. Ibid., 78.

5

Fear of A Loving God

EARLY IN MY MINISTRY I was drawn to the practical wisdom and theological viability of the writings of Wayne Oates, a remarkable pioneer in the field of pastoral psychology. In a volume titled *When Religion Gets Sick*, Oates reminds readers that bad theology can result in psychological and even physical harm. The symptoms of sick religion are usually elusive until some major crisis arises. The destructive behavioral patterns of someone indoctrinated by sick theology are compared to a condition of severe fear. For example, Oates tells of a man who was laden with years of guilt and trepidation and consequently gouged out his eyes. He had taken literally the injunction of Jesus, "If your right eye causes you to sin, tear it out and throw it away."[1] Oates also related a story concerning a certain hospital chaplain who was assigned by a physician to counsel a young girl whose right hand had been amputated. She disclosed to him that God, whom she had disobeyed, had instructed her to sever her offending hand. In fear, she had obeyed the inner voice of judgment.[2]

These are extreme cases of abnormal behavior prompted by religious terror. But we all can think of psychological damage caused by the fear of God's judgment. An eleven-year-old boy, for example, was confined to a juvenile detention center after his parents had resigned themselves to the fact that he was incorrigible. He had repeatedly run away from home and often left school in the afternoons to assist a neighboring construction contractor at a job. He slipped away from home late at night and joined an auto mechanic at his repair shop. These places were more attractive than home. The detention center's psychologist investigated the child's motivations and discovered that the root of the problem was his fear of God's wrath. The child's parents had told him that God was angry with him. If he did not get right with God, he would have

---

1. Matt 5:29a NRSV.
2. Oates, *When Religion Gets Sick*, 5–10.

Fear of A Loving God

"an encounter with the Holy Spirit."[3] The child did not comprehend what his parents meant by this threat, but he did understand the wrath of his own father. He therefore frequently ran away from God and his father alike.

Religion becomes sick when its overarching impulse is fear. Religious allegiance that is the product of intimidation or threat does not produce a happy, well-adjusted life. Obedience forged by force or fear cannot sustain a joyous, healthy existence.

Nonetheless, a consistent theme of Hebrew wisdom literature is the affirmation that the fear of God is the origin and impetus of human wisdom. Proverbs of sacred writ abound with admonitions like "The fear of the Lord is the beginning of wisdom,"[4] or "The fear of the Lord prolongs life, but the years of the wicked will be short,"[5] and "The fear of the Lord is a fountain of life, so that one may avoid the snares of death."[6] Even the Decalogue cautions, "If only they had such a mind as this, to fear me and to keep all my commandments always, so that it might go well with them and with their children forever!"[7] This was the faith heritage Jesus' parents taught their son. Thus, it should be no surprise that Mary's Magnificat repeats the poetry of her Hebrew heritage, "His mercy is for those who fear him from generation to generation."[8] Altogether, there are well over 150 biblical references that admonish the devout believer to fear God.

Bernhard Anderson, in his helpful study of the Psalter, designates Psalm 111 as a hymn of praise.[9] The focus of this poem is upon the God who created and chose Israel. This is a temple hymn to be sung or recited by the gathered community, beginning with the words, "Praise the Lord. I will give thanks to the Lord with my whole heart, in the company of the upright, in the congregation."[10] We can best visualize the origins of this psalm by imagining a procession of bearded priests entering a newly constructed Temple in Jerusalem after the Babylonian exile. They are wearing long, flowing prayer shawls. Amidst the pungent smoke of sacrifice burning upon the altar, the crash of cymbals, the shaking of tambourines, and the melody of strings and horns, the people chant in loud cadence, "The fear of the Lord is the beginning of wisdom; all those who practice it have a good understanding."[11] This hymn reflected the central teachings of wisdom literature of the period and captured the tone of the times. This popular poetry became an oft-quoted poem, easily memorized. Psalm 111 is in the form of an acrostic, meaning that the first letter of the first word in each line constitutes the

3. Ibid., 5.
4. Prov 9:10 NRSV.
5. Prov 10:27 NRSV.
6. Prov 14:27 NRSV.
7. Deut 5:29 NRSV.
8. Luke 1:50 NRSV.
9. Anderson, *Out of the Depths*, 160.
10. Ps 111: 1 NRSV.
11. Ps 111:10 NRSV.

consecutive letters of the Hebrew alphabet. It was a sort of "Now I Know My ABCs" poem taught to Jewish children. In all likelihood, Jesus had been taught this poem in early childhood through the synagogue of Nazareth and his parents' tutelage. The affirmation, "The fear of the Lord is the beginning of wisdom," is therefore integral to the faith of any disciple of Jesus.

How do we square this teaching with the prayerful and playful lifestyle of a Jesus who prayed to God as *Abba*, "Father"? Our Lord used an affectionate Aramaic reference to God as "Daddy" when he prayed. Is it possible both to love and fear the object of our prayers?

We live in an era of too many abusive fathers who use violence to control their children. We live in the context of rampant fears, locked doors, terrorist attacks on city streets, and intimidation. The biblical admonition to fear God appears to add insult to our injury in this environment of intimidation and violence. Our society verges on the edge of paranoia. Why should we dig up these lines from Hebrew antiquity, dust them off, and display them in calligraphy on worship bulletins and Sunday school walls? After all, phobias can be fatal. Some among us attend therapy in order to overcome our fears. Check any thesaurus to discover legions of names referring to the fears that plague our times. Some fear confined places (claustrophobia); others fear open spaces (agoraphobia). The list in medical journals seems endless. Webster's dictionary has even embraced the word "phobophobia," the fear of developing phobias!

When the father of Michael Jordan, one of the most famous athletes in the world, was murdered near a major highway in North Carolina, many of us reached the conclusion that none of us were really secure from harm. We live in a world permeated by legitimate fear. The last thing we need in theology, it seems, is a reminder that the fear of God is the root of all wisdom. So what might we make of this post-exilic wisdom teaching? If the fear of God is the origin of human wisdom, then is it folly to be wise? Does this passage speak any sense for these terrifying times?

In response to this critical question, let us first examine what the authors of wisdom literature do not mean by this conspicuous reference. The Psalter projects many verbal images of God. The various authors of Hebrew wisdom poetry do not imply that fear is the exclusive, or even dominant, response that God desires from the believer. Psalm 111, for example, is a hymn of praise. Joy and adoration is the main mood of the poem. We all recall dominant symbols of God throughout the rest of the Psalter. God is like a kind, compassionate shepherd. God comes to us as a righteous judge who sets things right. God is the strong deliverer who takes away the oppression of the poor and downtrodden. God rescues those who have sinned and are repentant. God is our refuge in times of trouble. God takes away our fear. Thus, the writer of the Tenth Psalm prays, "O Lord, you will hear the desire of the meek; you will strengthen their heart, you will incline your ear to do justice for the orphan and the oppressed, so that those from earth may strike terror no more."[12] God takes our hand and leads

---

12. Ps 10:17–18 NRSV.

us into the valley of peace. God is the source of light and salvation; therefore, with the confidence of a triumphant spirit, the psalmist asked, "The Lord is the stronghold of my life; of whom shall I be afraid?"[13]

I see no evidence that Psalm 111 posits a contradiction to the theology of Israel's great common book of prayer, the Psalter. This poem, however, speaks the language of a great paradox. The God who loves us and desires nothing but fulfillment from our lives is also the God who expects our obedience. The good shepherd who walks beside us through the valley of the shadow of death is also the mighty Creator who is far removed from our understanding. God's ways are not our ways. The God who stands beside us is also the Lord who hovers high above us. This God is shrouded in mystery.

Stewart McCullough, that remarkable professor of Oriental Languages at the University of Toronto, insisted that the phrase, "the fear of God," actually means "reverence for God."[14] God comes to us in God's *otherness*. It is not a domesticated deity that we worship. When we abandon God's law, when we fail to honor God's justice, when we make a mockery of God's righteousness, we kindle the hot breath of God's wrath. We often suffer from the consequences of these actions and attitudes. When we stand in fear before a God of love, we take the posture of wonderment.

The theology of mainline Protestant liberalism of the last century had the tendency to regard God's love as the dominant motif of Christianity while attempting to comprehend God's righteousness in the light of that love. This understanding failed to be faithful to the paradoxical tension between love and righteousness that presides over biblical narrative, both in Hebrew wisdom literature and in the teachings of Jesus. God's righteousness is indeed connected to the importance of God's wrath. Divine love is an expression of tough love. Professor James Cone of Union Theological Seminary used to say that the elimination of the concept of God's wrath from Christian theology has the effect of making God's love mere sentimentality. In one parish appointment that I served, the congregation had been taught by its previous pastor to substitute the phrase "the love of God" at any place in the Psalter's liturgical reading that included the textual words, "the fear of God." If I had not corrected this liturgical heresy, I would have been guilty of Dietrich Bonhoeffer's description of "cheap grace."[15]

God's love and God's righteousness are not antithetical realities; they are two ways of paradoxically talking about the same reality. Perhaps we of the contemporary church have become so terrorized by our times that we have failed to become lost in wonder, love, and praise. When we do not fear disobedience to the God who loves us, we are vulnerable to the fear of everything. Fear, reverence, awe, and wonder are perhaps clumsy words of our tradition used to describe the depths of our devotion to the God of love that requires our uncompromised obedience. The concept of "the fear

---

13. Ps 27:1b NRSV.
14. McCullough, "Exegesis of Psalms 101–119," 595.
15. Bonoeffer, *Cost of Discipleship*, 45–60.

of God," reminds us of the paradoxical nature of our covenant. Joy and fear are held in paradoxical tension in any authentically reliable pilgrimage of faith.

It has always been the temptation of the church to abolish the theological tension between the wrath of God and the love of God. During the second century, the theologian Marcion confronted the issue head-on with a simple solution. He insisted that the gospel of Christ is a completely new phenomenon, unconnected to the demand for righteousness in the Hebrew canon. This Gnostic philosopher and theologian taught his disciples that there are two cosmic gods: a vain and angry Creator God who ruthlessly demands justice, and a superior God who, out of sheer goodness, sent his son Jesus Christ to save humanity from the material world and bring people to a new home. According to Marcion, the Old Testament presents a Creator God who is transcendent and detached. This god often expresses himself through anger in response to human disobedience to the covenant requirement of righteousness. This god created the material world of which humanity—body and soul—is a part. The New Testament, however, has introduced to the human predicament the Redeemer God. This God has become flesh in the person of Jesus. The Redeemer God is good, benevolent, and self-giving. In the Marcion construct of theology, this God of love is contrasted with the God of wrath revealed in Hebrew heritage. Marcion was rightly declared a heretic in A.D. 144 and his movement was condemned. When the saintly Polycarp met Marcion in Rome, he identified him as "the firstborn of Satan."[16] The movement he initiated forced the early church to fix an approved canon of theologically acceptable texts and an inclusion of the three segments of sacred Hebrew literature—Torah, wisdom literature, and the prophets.

When contemporary Christians reject the paradoxical relationship between the fear of God and the love of God, they revive the spirit and influence of Marcion. From the origins of the formulation of orthodoxy and the designation of the Christian canon, the Church has fought to maintain in paradoxical tension the reality of God's righteousness and God's love.

The focal event in all of Scripture is, of course, the resurrection of Christ. Nothing is more joyous than the celebration of Easter. Every Sunday in the life of the church is, in point of fact, an exultant gathering of God's Easter people. Without this faith event, we would have nothing joyous to proclaim. This is the substance of all our hopes. But it is important to note that the First Gospel Evangelist was Mark, who concluded his narrative in this way: "So they (the disciples) went out and fled from the tomb, for terror and amazement had seized them; and they said nothing to anyone, for they were afraid."[17] Period. This stark line concluded the original manuscript of Mark's Gospel. Terror and amazement, fear and joy: these were held in paradoxical tension within the hearts of the early believers.

---

16. Fox, *Pagans and Christians*, 492.
17. Mark 16:8 NRSV.

Fear of A Loving God

Thomas Jefferson, a skeptic of many aspects of the Christian tradition, was a wise man who did not discard the theology of Hebrew wisdom literature. Having affixed his signature to the Declaration of Independence, he knew he was a hunted man. Had the colonies lost the war with Britain, Jefferson would have been among the first executed. He lived bravely in an atmosphere of terror during the years of colonial rebellion. But his authentic religious convictions were revealed in this confession:

> Indeed I tremble for my country. When I reflect that God is just: that his justice cannot sleep forever: that considering numbers, nature, and natural means only, a revolution of the wheel of fortune, an exchange of situation, is among possible events; that it may become probable by supernatural interference! The Almighty has no attribute which can take sides with us in such a contest.[18]

Jefferson put his life on the line for the cause of God-sanctioned liberty. His wisdom was rooted in the fear of a righteous God. When we lose our sense of fear, reverence, and awe, the very fabric of our society is torn asunder. When we have come to peace with the reality of God's awesome power and God's proclivity toward righteousness, then we shall fear no one and experience the security of God's perfect love.

Shall the faithful, therefore, fear God? The Epistles of John remind us that perfect love casts out all our fears—even the fear of God. The overriding emotion that describes our relationship to God is love, not fear; however, we do fear the consequences of our disobedience. We bow in awe and reverence before the mysterious God of the Bible. We do not fear God's anger, but rather our own weakness. Moreover, when we renew our covenant with the God who loves us, when we continue to grow in God's grace, when we consistently conduct our lives through the discipline of holy habits, we fear no person or power in this world!

Reverend Samuel Om is the Cambodian pastor of a multicultural United Methodist Church in Charlotte, North Carolina, and I was his district superintendent for eight years. Sam lived under stark conditions during the Vietnam War's incursion into his country and risked his life to escape from Communist authorities. He converted to Christianity during his years in a refugee camp. While cynically tearing pages from a Bible donated by missionaries in order to roll cigarettes, Sam was intrigued by chapter three of John's Gospel. He was mesmerized by Jesus' words to Nicodemus about a God that loved the world enough to send God's son to die for the world's redemption. His was a world of violence and retribution. How could he reconcile the reality of a violent and unjust world with the notion of a loving Creator God? Through the witness of caring Christians in the austere camp for refugees and the preaching of evangelical clergy, Sam was converted to the gospel message. At one time a soldier of the Communist government apprehended him. Unmercifully, this combatant held a pistol to Sam's temple and asked if Sam had anything to say before he pulled the trigger. Sam calmly told the soldier, "Go ahead and take my life. You send me to be with the God

---

18. Jefferson, "Notes on the State of Virginia" in Ellis, *American Sphinx*, 102.

who loves me. But allow me time to pray for the soul of the one who will take my life." The man's hand began to tremble until he dropped the revolver and ran away.

When we render absolute reverence to the God who loves us and holds us accountable to standards of righteousness, we shall no longer be enslaved by fear of others. We shall paradoxically love the God we fear in our times of disobedience. If the fear of God is indeed the beginning of wisdom, it is truly wise to love and obey the God who first loved us.

In the African-American church there is a saying one often finds inscribed upon walls in the homes of faithful believers. These lines were a particular favorite of Martin Luther King Jr.:

> Fear knocked at the door.
> Faith answered.
> There was no one there.[19]

---

19. King, *Strength to Love*, 117.

6

Healed by God's Wounds

EACH OF US HURTS somewhere. We are acquainted with the agony of physical pain, the aggravation of unresolved tension, the scar of a broken relationship, the distress of an unresolved addiction, or the misery of an unfulfilled life. We know what it means to be wounded—physically, verbally, or emotionally. Thus, much of our time is dedicated to the elimination of suffering and the reduction of our pain. Art, drama, literature, cinema, spectator sports, travel, sexual fantasy, or pharmaceutical escapism: all these and more are mobilized for the eradication of suffering and healing of our wounds.

Our attempts to sooth our wounds are justifiable. To desire pain is masochistic, an intolerable sickness. But, despite all our marvelous drugs, ingenious psychotherapies, and escapist fantasies, we are still a people riveted by self-induced pain. We hide our hidden hurts, harbor our secret wounds, and preserve both our toughened, exterior scabs and our interior scars. Perhaps this partially explains the current popularity of violence in entertainment. Through violence on the screen, pain occurs to someone else. We can witness a mysterious murder case on television and know it is all fiction while we remain detached, uninvolved observers. Through this pornography of violence, we attempt to achieve a catharsis of our fears or an escape from our personal distress. But this is a delusion. Why? Because we have avoided the discovery of God's redemption amidst our hurts, God's caring touch upon our wounds, and God's healing power within our brokenness. The good news of faith is not that, if we believe in Jesus, our pain and problems will disappear; rather the paradoxical message of our therapeutic faith is that "by his bruises we are healed."[1] Through the compassion of the Wounded One, our severest injuries can become the conduit through which we shall receive greater strength and wholeness. Our therapeutic message of hope in a world of violence and intense suffering is that the source of our healing is a suffering God who is empathetically present amidst our wounds.

1. Isa 53:5b NRSV.

Part I: Paradox and the Doctrine of God

The Japanese theologian Kazōh Kitamori discovered that his personal agony had the potential of bringing him to the very heart of God, for God is that being who vicariously enters into the pain of those whom he loves. Vicarious suffering is the mission of God's love; it is indeed the essence of God's Being, for as Kitamori asserts, "the pain of God is the essence of God; this is the heart of God!"[2] Moreover, the ultimate purpose of God and the destination of God's saving grace are the transformation of personal pathos and the healing of this wounded creation by the therapeutic presence of divine love. The Apostle Paul reflected upon the reality of the cosmic scope of God's desire to heal creation's infirmity when he wrote, "For I reckon that the sufferings we now endure bear no comparison with the splendor, as yet unrevealed, which is in store for us. For the created universe waits with eager expectation for God's sons to be revealed."[3]

There is nothing innately redemptive, however, about human suffering. Yet our experience of suffering may point us toward the anguish of God, which has the power to redeem us from the pathos of meaningless agony. When we are attuned to the pain of God, our suffering begins to speak the vernacular of hope. If we share in the passion of the wounded and suffering God, our wounds can become badges of discipleship rather the symptoms of despair.

Nearly every family I have served as pastor is acquainted with an emotional or physical scar from some rendezvous with a disease or natural disaster, the pain of a particular grief, or the impact of some brutal injustice. When we share our spiritual autobiographies in some of the more intimate support groups of the congregation, we reveal many stories of tarnished dreams and fragile hopes. We who are disciples of Christ only differ in the depths of our wounds. I concur with Stan Hauerwas in his observation that "the difference between happiness and suffering is that the latter creates a silence which is not easily shared."[4]

How can we who are wounded heal others? How can the community of faithful believers become a balm of healing when those who are most resilient and courageous in our midst also suffer in a silence which strains in vain for expression?

The Babylonian exile was the historical period of greatest humiliation for the people of Israel. It was during this time of enslavement that a voice of hope emerged from the Diaspora of a forlorn nation. The poetry that penetrated the gloom of this scattered and oppressed people described a certain symbolic suffering servant. He was not the model of a therapeutic personality. The graying strength of a heroic physician, like those featured on a television adventure series, was not depicted in these pulsating lines of Hebrew verse. The servant described by Deutero-Isaiah did not have it together either physically or emotionally. He was fraught with frailties. At the very sight of this non-hero, monarchs curled their lips in disgust. Why? Because "he had

---

2. Kitamori, *Theology of the Pain*, 46.
3. Rom 8:18–19 The New English Bible.
4. Hauerwas, *Naming the Silence*, 3.

no form or majesty that we should look at him, nothing in his appearance that we should desire him."⁵

I cannot read this line without prompting the memory of emotions I felt when attending in 1979 the Broadway production of Bernard Pomerance's drama, *The Elephant Man*. The dialogue illuminated the compassion of a London physician, Frederick Treves, upon discovering Joseph Carey Merrick, a disfigured cripple who suffered from neurofibromatosis, a rare neurological disorder marked by tumorous outgrowths over his skin and bone. Like some ancient Hebraic *elephant man*, the suffering servant of Israel was "as one from whom others hid their faces."⁶

With the incursion of Persian armies into the territory of Babylon, this poet/prophet envisioned the coming of a Hebrew deliverer who would come limping from the wounded household of Israel and emerge from the imprisoned survivors of the Babylonian holocaust. This servant/poet stretched his imagination in order to envision redemption coming through a person, a group of people, or a persistent remnant of the surviving faithful. We cannot be certain whether the poet anticipated the ironic arrival of an individual savior who would win by his weakness or whether he regarded Israel itself to be the redemptive nation whose anguish and struggle would become a light unto all other nations, but we do know that Deutero-Isaiah's heroic redeemer lacked all the features of a genuine, recognizable healer. This was no heartthrobbingly handsome hero from a television episode of *ER*.

How could this fragile one mend a people of broken dreams? How could a suffering slave liberate a captive nation? How could a wounded victim heal? Isaiah's poignant explanation shocks us with the theology of yet another biblical paradox:

> Surely he has borne our infirmities
> and carried our diseases;
> yet we accounted him stricken,
> struck down by God, and afflicted.⁷

Thus, the paradoxical message of the exiled Hebrew prophet articulated the restorative plan of God's rescuing love. The wounds of a distraught Israel were not to be healed through the vindication of the vanquished. A gallant, conquering military hero would not rectify the injustice of torture endured by the innocent. Israel's poet of the exile did not envision another Davidic monarch, waiting in history's wings with the armaments of vengeance. Redemption will come through the non-hero servant who would heal by suffering, conquer through weakness, and redeem through the anguish of love. Isaiah's poetry was unique, but it represented the maturation of Hebrew theology, as demonstrated by these incomparable lines:

> But he was wounded for our transgressions,

5. Isa 53:2 NRSV.
6. Isa 53:3 NRSV.
7. Isa 53:4 NRSV.

Part I: Paradox and the Doctrine of God

> crushed for our iniquities;
> upon him was the punishment that
> made us whole . . .[8]

According to Deutero-Isaiah, wholeness, healing, and hope will come to the world in no other way.

The early church always interpreted this poetic imagery in light of Jesus Christ. He was indeed the suffering servant who had been led "like a lamb that is led to the slaughter."[9] It was Dietrich Bonhoeffer who so accurately interpreted this ancient tradition when he asserted, from his prison cell in Tegel, Germany, "The Bible . . . directs us to the powerlessness and suffering of God; only a suffering God can help."[10] Yes, the fantastic hopes of Deutero-Isaiah were fulfilled just outside the gates of Herod's Jerusalem on a Friday afternoon during the Passover feast. It was the scourging of Jesus that is the source of our healing. The Man of Nazareth became the balm of healing for all humanity. Despite our sin, "the Lord has laid on him the iniquity of us all."[11]

The servant songs of the exiled poet present us with the Bible's most enduring paradox: Only a God of compassion who enters the arena of human anguish can help us amidst the absurdity of innocent suffering and inexplicable tragedy. Only the wounded healer can authentically heal us. Only he who has been despised and rejected has the power to rescue us in our loneliness and alienation. Only the Diseased One can really cure us. Only crucified love can transform death into eternal life. This is the paradox of God's movement through history and the mystery of God's advent in our personal lives.

Jürgen Moltmann observes that the Hellenistic theology of Plato and Aristotle insisted upon *apatheia* (inalterability, insensitivity, and freedom from emotional involvement) as a necessary divine attribute.[12] God knows neither anger nor love, sacrifice nor service. God is good and, consequently, cannot be the origin of evil, suffering, or punishment. God's role in the universe is to provide objective justice and infallible fairness in the affairs of humanity and the administration of the natural order. Both Judaism and Christianity have been influenced over the centuries by this understanding of an apathetic God. But a more authentic comprehension of Hebrew and Christian Scripture leads us to discover a *pathetic theology* at the Bible's core. Moltmann answers the question, "Why does God suffer?" by asserting that "He suffers from his *indwelling* [Hebrew: *shekinah*] in Israel, because through this *shekinah* he goes into exile with the people and is tortured with the martyrs."[13] Moltmann observes that this *pathetic theology* was unique to Judaism in the ancient world. Thus, it became the

8. Isa 53:5a NRSV.
9. Isaiah 53:7a NRSV.
10. Bonhoeffer, *Papers from Prison*, 122.
11. Isa 53:6b NRSV.
12. Moltmann, *Future of Creation*, 67–69.
13. Ibid., 71, emphasis Moltmann's.

central focus of the life of Jesus of Nazareth—the Jewish Messiah. Moltmann insists that the early church adopted this understanding of God, as shown by this revealing passage from the writings of Origen in the third century:

> The Redeemer descended to earth out of sympathy for the human race. He took our sufferings upon Himself before He endured the cross—indeed before He even deigned to take our flesh upon himself: if He had not felt these sufferings He would not have come to partake of our human life. What was this passion which He suffered for us beforehand? It was the passion of love. . . He suffers the sufferings of love.[14]

When Jesus called forth his new community, he did an extraordinary thing: He summoned a fellowship of sick, frail, wounded, and anxious followers. They were in some ways like frail patients within an intensive care ward. Simon Peter's very name was a mild joke. This *Petros* was a soft rock—spineless as a sponge when pushed to the wall on the night of Jesus' arrest. Matthew was chosen from among the collaborators with Rome—an untrustworthy tax collector. The other Simon was a Zealot, a card-carrying, dagger-toting terrorist. Even his reputation made Jesus' entourage suspect within the Roman establishment when the Nazarene teacher entered the East Gate of Jerusalem in a palm-branch parade. This motley crew of disciples jumped ship immediately upon Jesus' arrest. But these wounded ones ironically constituted the apostolic church! How did this happen? What transmuted them into passionate and powerful healers?

Recently, many admirers of the late Henri J. M. Nouwen (1932–1996) celebrated the fortieth anniversary of the publication of his classic, *The Wounded Healer*. At the time of its publication, some critics contended that Nouwen was a pop-psychologist who had theologically relinquished the power of God in favor of an impotent deity—a God so available and intimate that Nouwen's fragile deity forfeits all omnipotence. In the decades since Nouwen's popular treatise on practical theology and the care of the parish, the Roman Catholic Church has experienced much humiliation from sex-abuse scandals. Mainline Protestant churches that enthusiastically endorsed Nouwen's popular thesis have lost power, membership, political influence, and social relevance. Are these indications that Nouwen's critics were correct in perceiving an anemic theology and a disempowered church?

Four decades ago, Nouwen challenged leaders of the church to see the paradoxical, biblical understanding of power as the force of suffering love and volitional participation in the wounds of the world. Nouwen insisted that belief in the omnipotence of God does not set the believer above the hurts, sins, and sufferings of a fallen creation. When the church attempts to deny or cover up the sexual abuses of its apostate priests, it forfeits its authentic calling to share empathetically in the wounds of sexually abused children. When the Protestant Church gauges its strength by weighing its

---

14. Origen, *Homilies on Ezekiel*, 6.6, quoted in Moltmann, *Future of Creation*, 69.

political power or public esteem, it fails to embrace the paradoxical nature of its mission that was so clearly articulated and practiced by Henri Nouwen when he wrote, "A Christian community is . . . a healing community not because wounds are cured and pains are alleviated, but because wounds and pains become openings or occasions for a new vision. Mutual confession then becomes a mutual deepening of hope, and sharing weakness becomes a reminder to one and all of the coming strength."[15] For too long the church has shunned the paradoxical gospel of divine pain. It has all too often practiced an Easter without an authentic Lent, displayed a discipleship without discipline, and evolved into a counterfeit Christianity without a cross. The paradox of the church of wounded healers is that, through demonstrations of suffering love, authentic disciples discover a power that the world cannot give or take away.

Reggie McNeal has more recently attempted to change the scorecard for evaluating the church's faithfulness. He has called for a "missional renaissance" by which the church evaluates itself in terms of its measure of involvement with the hurting centers of humanity. "Our job is not to 'do church' well," he asserts, "but to be the people of God in an unmistakable way in the world. We are the aroma of Jesus in the cemetery of decaying flesh."[16] McNeal insists that the habitation of the missional church is within the "decaying flesh" of the powerless and suffering. The biblical mandate for radical mission forces the believer "to see the disparities between the kingdoms of this earth and the Kingdom of God, it [the Bible] becomes far more disruptive than informational. The Bible presents a call to action, not just a lesson to be studied."[17]

When we search the Scriptures diligently, we discover no Disney fairytale conclusion to the biblical narrative. The hardheaded hope of biblical realism is carried upon the back of this Messianic figure:

> He was oppressed and he was afflicted,
> yet he did not open his mouth;
> like a lamb that is led to the slaughter, and like a sheep that
> before its shearers is silent, so he did not open his mouth.[18]

The faithful parish serves as a microcosm of an alternative community that reflects the nature of a suffering God of passion and compassion. In each parish, some disciples are freshly acquainted with grief. Many have experienced catastrophic disappointments: the careless decisions of a rebellious child puncturing all those ballooned parental expectations, a career flattened by a persistent recession, or a marriage begun with imprudent idealism and ended in bitter alienation. We all have scars—past or present, deep or superficial. It was Scott Peck who, following his dramatic conversion to Christ, arrested our attention with a simple observation: "Life is difficult. This is a

---

15. Nouwen, *Wounded Healer*, 96.
16. McNeal, *Missional Renaissance*, 24.
17. Ibid., 27.
18. Isa 53:7 NRSV.

great truth, one of the greatest truths. It is a great truth because once we truly see this truth, we transcend it . . . Once it is accepted, the fact that life is difficult no longer matters."[19] Then Peck posits this astounding assertion: "The tendency to avoid problems and the emotional suffering inherent in them is the primary basis of all human mental illness."[20] The mission of the church is to confront the pain caused by systemic and personal evil, to bear a message of redemption, and to embody suffering love through activities that bring comfort, relief, healing, and hope.

From the cross, Jesus defined the church's mission. He entrusted the beloved disciple, John, with the care of his mother. But all his weak and wounded followers who witnessed the risen Christ soon discovered that their wounds were the sources of an emerging strength. Thus, Christians in every era have discovered that their scars are openings for an empathy that heals and the occasion for fresh vision.

I have participated in several small groups of conscientious believers whose hopes have matured by their confidentially sharing personal stories of pain, reminding everyone in the group of a coming strength. I especially give thanks for a grief support group in a parish I served that was started by the courageous impulse of a woman who had endured the sudden cardiac arrest and death of her middle-aged husband and was simultaneously coping with the spread of cancer within her own body. The bereaved are the most powerful witnesses to the paradox of God's peace amidst sorrow. There is a consoling Jewish legend that describes the angel of death as a creature with many eyes. If this angel comes to the bed of a person of faith who suffers and observes that he has arrived early, the angel gives the sick person one of these extra eyes. The wisdom of the legend is apparent: "A person who has been very close to death sees more than others."[21]

In one of his epic volumes on the Hebrew prophets, Rabbi Abraham Heschel writes, "the God of Israel is a God Who loves, a God Who is known to, and concerned with, man. He not only rules the world in majesty of His might and wisdom, but reacts intimately to the events of history . . . God does not stand outside the range of human suffering and sorrow. He is personally involved in, even stirred by, the conduct and fate of man."[22] Rabbi Heschel refers to this intimate involvement of the God of the Hebrews as "divine pathos," explaining, "The characteristic of the prophets is not foreknowledge of the future, but insight into the present pathos of God."[23] How did the ancient Hebrews have such certainty about the nature of divine Being? Heschel insists that "to the prophets, knowledge of God was fellowship with Him, not attained by syllogism, analysis, or induction, but by living together."[24]

19. Peck, *Road Less Traveled*, 15.
20. Ibid., 17.
21. Moise, *Ransom for Wurmbrand*, 50.
22. Heschel, *Prophets*, 4.
23. Ibid., 11.
24. Ibid., 3.

Part I: Paradox and the Doctrine of God

Within the pages of this book I have consistently paid a pastor's loving tribute to specific parishioners who were acutely aware of the pathos of God. Had these people not been convinced of God's intimate and compassionate presence amidst their plight, they would have abandoned all hope. If they had not lived together in the community of care and compassion, they would have existed in a state of sustained misery. These courageous parishioners have been shaped by their participation in corporate worship, the liturgy of paradox, the solidarity of shared prayers, and the experience of mystery in the act of worship.

In this chapter I honor the memory of Pete and Betty Yow of Greensboro's Hinshaw Memorial UMC. Betty served for decades as the church's highly competent secretary. Her joy and humor were contagious. She labored without financial compensation over those many years. She eagerly and willingly participated in each mission endeavor, and her husband, Pete, provided lay leadership in nearly every position of responsibility within the congregation. The two constantly gave sacrificial offerings of themselves upon the Eucharistic altar. They delivered the full measure of their devotion to such ministries as building Habitat for Humanity houses or sponsoring a child's education. Betty carefully prepared the bulletin for each worship service. But a severe stroke paralyzed Betty on a day of anguish for the entire congregation. She was confined to a bed for the rest of her life. Her speech was barely comprehensible, yet she was fully aware of everything about her. Thus, her active and visible ministry was abruptly restricted to acts of intercessory prayer and providing inspiration to visitors at her home. Even though Betty often felt the absence of God, she held fast to her trust in God's providential love and compassion amidst her wounds. Her trust was constantly galvanized by the constant kindness of a grateful, benevolent congregation and an adoring husband who stayed by her side until the moment of her death. She was courageously sustained by the worship of a God who did not hover above her, transcend her pitiful circumstances, or remain apathetic toward the reality of her colossal wounds.

Each parish appointment has introduced me to such noble disciples of Christ as Betty and Pete. These people have affirmed, with the fullness of their lives, the ever-present love of a compassionate deity that is acquainted intimately with their wounded identities. Carlyle Marney, whose prophetic legacy and personal friendship profoundly affected his many friends in a mountain parish I served, offered this insight into the servant songs of Hebrew literature: "The Healer himself will come on the floor. Israel's time of hurting is at an end. The old agony is passing away . . . Healing, the central business of God which he does in his appearing on our ward, is an aspect of his creation-redemption."[25]

The longest running off-Broadway play ever to be staged in New York is the musical *The Fantastics*, a drama our church groups often attended when we visited in the Big Apple to study current issues confronting the Unite Nations. This creative fantasy,

---

25. Marney, *Suffering Servant*, 44.

produced in an unpretentious little theater, is held together by a seemingly silly story concerning a mysterious lover, El Gallo. He causes young maidens to fall in love with him, then he breaks their hearts and abandons them forever. Why? El Gallo has a mission in life. He wishes to teach naive young girls a harsh reality: Real love emerges out of pain, emotional scars, and suffering. Only those who have been deeply hurt can know true love. So, in a dramatic exodus from a young girl whom he has deliberately hurt, El Gallo sings this haunting refrain:

> Deep in December, it's nice to remember,
> Although you know the snow will follow.
> Deep in December, it's nice to remember:
> Without a hurt, the heart is hollow.[26]

God-in-Christ has not come in some fraudulent or callous El Gallo fashion. The biblical narrative is not an account of the masochistic personality of a capricious, sadistic God. The suffering servant passages of the prophet Isaiah profoundly and directly articulate the language of biblical paradox. When we saturate ourselves with biblical story, we are transformed by a mysterious power that comes to us only through a God of pathos. Only this paradoxical power can fill our emptiness, heal our brokenness, and anoint us for the mission of healing.

---

26. Thomas Jones, *The Fantastics*. The off-Broadway production began May 3, 1960, and concluded January 13, 2002, becoming the longest consecutive running play in the history of theater in New York City.

7

The Tenderness of God's Tough Judgment

HOW CAN WE HOLD together with rational integrity and emotional health the belief in a God of unconditional love and a deity that firmly administers harsh judgment? Orthodox Christianity has boldly asserted since the Council of Nicaea in A.D. 325, that "for us and our salvation [Christ] came down from heaven," and that "he will come again in glory to judge the living and the dead." Every conscientious Sunday school child is prompt to recite among the lexicon of familiar biblical phrases, "God is love,"[1] and "Vengeance is mine, I will repay, says the Lord."[2] If we are to maintain our faith allegiance to the polarities of both of these proclamations, then we must explore the mystery of another prominent biblical paradox.

When the final episodes of the twentieth century were playing out, a myriad of doomsday prophets of gloom emerged. The resounding message of these alleged biblical fundamentalists was that Jesus' coming is imminent, and his wrath will soon consume this evil world with fire. Only the righteous will escape via the Rapture. These prophets used as a proof-text a curious portion of the Apostle Paul's First Letter to the Thessalonians, perhaps the oldest text in the New Testament, in which the writer anticipates the arrival of the risen Christ but never uses the term "Rapture." But most of their theological agenda of divine revenge emerged from the curious pages of John, the mysterious man of Patmos.

In anticipation of these fanatical trends, in 1999 novelist Gail Godwin published a delightful work entitled, *Evensong*. Her character Margaret Bonner, whom Godwin introduced in her earlier story, *Father Melancholy's Daughter*, is now a member of the clergy, married to a priest. Grace Munger, the daughter of a discredited Free Will Baptist preacher, obnoxiously pesters Margaret to promote and participate in a "Millennium March" parade in witness to the urgency of a coming cosmic catastrophe. As

---

1. 1 John 4:8 NRSV.
2. Deut 32:35; Rom 12:19; Heb 10:30 NRSV.

The Tenderness of God's Tough Judgment

Margaret emphatically dismisses Grace, she thinks of her seminary studies regarding Bishop Athanasius of the fourth century in Alexandria, who was visited by angels buzzing a report in his ear concerning "how much mischief the book of Revelation was capable of seeding in future generations."[3] Margaret muses, "If [Athanasius] had known his canon, originally meant only for the churches under his own guidance, would become *the* canon of Christianity at a later date, would he have had second thoughts and hidden John of Patmos's vision in a drawer, to be taken out only when he, the bishop, could be there in person to teach it and explain about levels of meaning? Handling the book of Revelation to a literal-minded person without any guidance was like presenting a child with a box of matches and telling him to go out and play."[4]

Yes, even the cynical D. H. Lawrence referred to the last book of the orthodox canon as the most un-Christian book in the Bible: "a gospel of hate in a gospel of love."[5] But while many mean-spirited agents of apocalyptic doom and global destruction misrepresent the fullness of the Christian message, a conscientious biblical theologian should embrace the wholeness of the sacred canon and explore why it accommodates both love and judgment in its multifaceted understanding of divine Being.

When I attempt to hold together these theological polarities, I am drawn to the writings and courageous work of Dietrich Bonhoeffer. If any Christian in modern history had reason to believe in a god of judgment and retribution, it was this remarkable pastoral theologian. His father, Karl Bonhoeffer, was the Director of the Neurological Clinic at the Friedrich Wilhelm University in Berlin and was considered to be the leading authority in psychology and neurology in all of Germany. When Dietrich was a teenager, Karl privately warned his family that Adolph Hitler possessed all the characteristics of a dangerous psychopath. Dietrich, who had publically denounced the sinister Nazi agenda, was offered an opportunity to stay in the safety of the United States as a professor and resident scholar at Union Theological Seminary in New York City. But he made the momentous decision to return to Germany, engage in the non-compliant agenda of the Confessing Church, and risk his own life in the process.

After experiencing the socially relevant preaching and emotionally charged worship at the Abyssinian Baptist Church in Harlem, New York, Bonhoeffer developed a new urgency and elevated enthusiasm in his proclamation upon returning to serve as a pastor in Germany. In July of 1937, he preached an extraordinary sermon at Finkenwalde in what is now Poland on Psalm 58, a Hebrew prayer calling for God's vengeance and retribution. The psalmist questions here the fairness of God. In the opinion of the Hebrew poet, the wicked "err from their birth,"[6] but violence comes to the righteous. The psalmist asks the Almighty, "Do you judge people fairly?"[7] The

---

3. Godwin, *Evensong*, 138.
4. Ibid.
5. Lawrence, *Apocalypse*, v–xli.
6. Ps 58:3 NRSV.
7. Ps 58:11 NRSV.

writer implores God to let the wicked "be like the snail that dissolves into slime, like the untimely birth that never sees the sun."[8] In response to this disturbing text, Bonhoeffer asked his congregation, "Is this frightful psalm of vengeance our prayer?"[9] The preacher then warned his congregation against the seductive temptation of evil Nazi hysteria and its anti-Semitic philosophy of hatred. He emphatically preached, "God himself in his anger has raised his hand against us to afflict us with our own sin, all our spiritual indolence, our open or inward disobedience, the profound lack of discipline in our everyday lives under his Word."[10] Thus, Bonhoeffer asserted that he and the congregation were not able to pray this psalm of vengeance. Nor was sinful King David, its purported author. Bonhoeffer rightly stated that this was an evil time in history, but the people of the church in Germany had silently allowed injustice to prevail. Furthermore, he boldly asserted that when his congregation cried out in distress for deliverance, evil would likely triumph due to their present silence in the face of such epidemic evil. Then Bonhoeffer said something astounding: He insisted that only Christ can pray this prayer for the church. Only his perfect innocence can look into the abyss of evil and pray the words of Psalm 58. Bonhoeffer prophetically asserted, "Above all let us learn here that faced with the enemies of God and his church all we can do is pray. Our own courage—no matter how great it may be—all our bravery is bound to snap in the presence of this enemy . . . Here the one who alone has power over Satan, God himself must take the matter into his own hands."[11]

Bonhoeffer insisted that the central focus of any Christian's faith must be a belief in and a commitment to the ultimate triumph of God's covenant of righteousness. God's plan of salvation is more important than one's own security and suffering. God's cause is the ultimate salvation of the human family. Thus, only Christ has the right to condemn and pray Psalm 58. So, what is the prayer of Christ through this psalm of retribution? "Father, forgive them; for they do not know what they do." Thus, Bonhoeffer brings together these two great polarities of biblical theology—love and vengeance—with these words to his astonished, but attentive, congregation: "The one who bore the vengeance, he alone was allowed to ask for the forgiveness of the godless."[12] Eight years before his own martyrdom, this German pastoral theologian preached that Christ bore God's vengeance for everyone. He assured his listeners that "God's wrath and vengeance will no longer strike anyone who comes to him, and stays on his side."[13] Thus, for Bonhoeffer, the central role of the church, especially in the midst of such horrific and systemic evil, is to pray in fervent supplication that God will bring all enemies of righteousness under the cross of Christ and grant them (and us) mercy.

8. Ps 58:8 NRSV.
9. Bonhoeffer, *Testament to Freedom*, 293.
10. Ibid.
11. Ibid., 295.
12. Ibid., 297.
13. Ibid.

The Tenderness of God's Tough Judgment

If both judgment and love have a place in Christian proclamation and worship, what then is the purpose and place of their inclusion? In the biblical narrative, the role of God's vengeance is consistently purging and cleansing. The message and context of Malachi is demonstrative of this purpose in the story of salvation history. It is important to note that Malachi is not a person, nor an obscure Hebrew prophet, but a nameless messenger. The Hebrew *malakhi* means "my messenger." The writer of this book did not declare his identity, but he or she described the environment and historical context so accurately that we know precisely when the messenger lived. The time was slightly before Nehemiah and Ezra, but after the conclusion of the Babylonian exile. The Jewish Temple had been restored. A minority of Jews had chosen to return to the land called Judah. But they were not able to recapture those thrilling days of yesteryear and the grandeur of Solomon's majestic Temple with its extravagant pageants and elaborate festivals. Sacred rituals were now anemic, routine, and boring. Minuscule Israel was hardly a light unto the nations; this vassal state was more like a wilderness lightening bug tolerated by a series of Persian potentates.

The book takes the literary form of a court scene in which God is on trial. The messenger lays two charges against YHWH: the Almighty has ceased to love his covenant people, and God has neglected to execute justice. Thus, the wicked prosper. Bad things happen to good people. Moreover, the oracle of Malachi, the last book of the Hebrew canon, questions the reliability of God's promise to Abraham and the covenant of love with the descendants of Abraham. In Malachi's time, the grand promises of Zechariah for an incomparable messianic Kingdom seemed as empty as a politician's platitudes the day after an election. The economy at the time of this writing was deplorable. Real estate in Judah was stagnant. Bare existence was a desperate struggle for the common man. Granted, the Hebrew people were not suffering under the fires of persecution as they had during the early phases of the Babylonian exile, but they faced the dullness of daily life and the distressing success of their unrighteous, pagan neighbors.

Thus, in the narrative of Malachi, God was on trial just as in Rolf Hochhuth's explosive contemporary drama, *The Deputy*. This modern play places Pope Pius XII and the conduct of the Roman Catholic Church on trial for the papal silence during the Nazi Holocaust and Hitler's "Final Solution." A brutal Fascist doctor in the play questions God's motivation by taunting Riccardo Fortama, the heroic victim of persecution who chose the way of voluntary martyrdom. "I took the vow to challenge the Old Gent," the doctor says in reference to the Almighty. He goes on to cynically taunt Riccardo with the theological question, "Do you find it more acceptable that God in person is turning the human race on the spit of history? . . . History: dust and altars, misery and rape, and all glory a mockery of its victims. The truth is, Auschwitz refutes creator, creation, and the creature."[14]

---

14. Hochhuth, *Deputy*, 247.

In contrast to Hochhuth's modern drama, the court scene in Malachi depicts a patient God who listens non-defensively to similar protests. But the court drama of Malachi suddenly shifts direction. God does not stay on trial. The messenger reports, "You have wearied the Lord with your words by saying, 'All who do evil are good in the sight of the Lord, and he delights in them,' or by asking, 'Where is the God of justice?'"[15]

The Jews who returned to the land of their ancestors in Judah at the time of the writing of Malachi had assumed their own innocence and aired these complaints to YHWH, but the writer announced that the messenger (the *malahki*) of God was about to appear. He would disclose that what some had called good was really evil. The messenger due to arrive would appear as a decisive, righteous judge described as a "refiner's fire" or a "fuller's soap" with the words: "He will sit as a refiner and purifier of silver, and he will purify the descendants of Levi and refine them like gold and silver, until they present offerings to the Lord in righteousness."[16]

The tribe of Levi assumed the role of priesthood in the reinstituted Jerusalem Temple. The messenger of the Hebrew poet made it clear that the priests—the acknowledged good guys, the holy ones of Israel—would be the first to be judged and found wanting. YHWH, the harsh judge, would purify, reform, and discipline the priests of Judah. Spiritual purification must start with the spiritual leaders of the congregation, as Bonhoeffer preached to his congregation in 1937. Judgment falls first in the book named Malachi upon those who have assumed their own purity while remaining silent in the atmosphere of brazen, insidious evil.

Thus, the fullness of the biblical witness consistently articulates a theology of God's judgment. But this judgment is never for the purpose of rejection or total destruction. God's judgment is always an act of grace that seeks purification and restoration. This purging activity is intended to produce nothing short of silver and gold—a redeemed people of inestimable worth. God's vengeance is for the purpose of granting abundant mercy.

Few biblical theologians have articulated this understanding of the paradoxical relationship of judgment to the fulfillment of covenant and the ultimate achievement of human atonement with greater clarity than N. T. Wright. In his insightful work, *Justification*, Wright consistently argues that throughout the Hebrew narrative, the teachings of Jesus, and the Letters of Paul, God steadfastly sticks to the task of maintaining covenant with Israel so that God's covenant blessing will ultimately extend to all nations and races. Divine judgment is a necessary part of the purification process leading to the redemption of the human race and the restored wholeness of all creation. This judgment is not for the purpose of creating double-decker chambers for the after-life—a heaven and hell. To the contrary: God's purifying judgment is for the purpose of saving earth and its inhabitants. Consistently, God will not tolerate the subjugation of the masses to hunger and abject poverty when the affluent of the world

---

15. Mal 2:17 NRSV.
16. Mal 3:3 NRSV.

hoard most of the earth's resources. YHWH chooses to punish for the sake of purification. The Almighty is harsh toward those who arrogantly discriminate on the basis of race, social class, or gender. But God's wrath and punishment are not a permanent condition for those who respond in contrition and reach out for the healing, forgiving mercy of God. The Almighty's punishment is never irrevocable. Because of the comprehensive salvation story of Israel that culminates in the death and resurrection of the Messiah, history is moving toward Christ, not chaos. Justification is the activity of God, consummated in the Christ event that brings about a new status for humanity. This new status is not a new character. Justification is the activity of God-in-Christ, who vindicates humanity in his court of law by declaring us *righteous* (a new status) but not yet *morally righteous*. While justification does not make us in an instant *morally righteous*, it does set us on course toward God's purification through a lifetime of spiritual growth in grace—the process of sanctification. This growth is the believer's response to both God's judgment and divine mercy. Through the activity of Christ, all people now have access to the covenant that God initiated with Abraham and Sarah. God's new, expanded community of the covenant (the *ecclesia* or "those called out" to be the congregation of the covenant) grows toward moral righteousness by following the way of Jesus, participating in the holy habits of the faithful community, and trusting in what N. T. Wright terms, "the single-plan-through-Israel-for-the-world [*sic*]."[17] God's judgment has the effect of "dealing-with-sin-and-rescuing-people-from-it" for the purpose of "bringing-Jews-and-Gentiles-together-into-a-single-family [*sic*]."[18] When divine judgment takes the function of purification, the Christian is not set upon a course of merely working out his or her private salvation. The Bible does not advocate a justification through good works. But N. T. Wright vehemently insists that "the things the Christian is commanded to *do* are not meant to be a grudging duty only, nor are they meant merely to bring us back into a zero balance before an unsmiling Judge. What the Christian is to do is *to please God*, to bring a smile to the Father's face, to give him delight, to gladden his heart."[19]

Thus, biblical references to future judgment are basically good tidings, not bad chidings. The one through whom God's justice will finally sweep the world is not a vengeful, hate-filled, arrogant tyrant, but rather the Man of Sorrows who loves the sinner and administers judgment in order to cleanse, renew, and redeem. N. T. Wright emphatically insists that "the final judgment . . . will be anticipated in the present world through the Spirit-led work and witness of Jesus' followers."[20] Thus, the church of Jesus Christ becomes an agent of God's cleansing by applying divine judgment to the conduct of its own mission and by confronting principalities and powers with the vision of a coming Kingdom. The church is called to proclaim and practice the

17. Wright, *Justification*, 98.
18. Ibid., 99.
19. Ibid., 187, emphasis Wright's.
20. Wright, *Surprised by Hope*, 142.

message of the God whose inclusive covenant comes not as a consuming fire, but as a refining flame, a cleansing lye ready to bleach white the dark stains of sin and injustice while inviting all people to participate in the glory of God's redeeming grace. This invitation is repeated again and again on every occasion in which the penitent people of God gather for corporate worship. When the faithful assemble in the humble posture of worship each week, obedient congregations speak the language of paradox, holding together both judgment and cleansing grace to articulate the vernacular of hope.

Peter Storey was a Methodist pastor in South Africa who resisted the evil of apartheid through his preaching and social engagement over several decades of ministry. One can only imagine his euphoria on February 2, 1990, when F. W. de Klerk, the seventh and last State President of apartheid-era South Africa, had just taken the oath of office in a nation beleaguered by economic sanctions and international isolation. On that day, de Klerk courageously addressed Parliament and announced the end of forty-two years of apartheid. Peter was overcome with emotion as he viewed the proceedings from his television at the parsonage in the South African community of Sophiatown. After the telecast, he stood at a window looking out upon the houses and remembered that this neighborhood had been a vibrant, albeit economically depressed, black community during the 1950s, when black residents were summarily commanded to leave. All their modest homes had been bulldozed in order to make room for white settlers. Peter's eyes were fixed upon the sight of a steeple in the distance—the steeple of the church once served by Trevor Huddleston, a courageous friend who defied these blatant injustices. When Rev. Huddleston's protests were ignored, this Church of England priest wrote a book that exposed the horrors of apartheid to the world.[21] The tumult resulted in Huddleston being recalled to England in hopes of calming his parish and pacifying the new affluent, Caucasian population of Sophiatown. Despite all the controversy this faithful priest had caused, he had profoundly influenced a young altar boy named Desmond Tutu, who had been transfixed by the vision and courage of his mentor and priest.

On that historic day, Peter Storey remembered the faithfulness of those who had been the voice of God's judgment throughout the crucible of South Africa's long pilgrimage of suffering. Thus, he observed, "It is as if God, grown suddenly impatient with our whoring after the false gods of totalitarianism, colonialism, and racial oppression, has dealt history a sudden blow to set whole segments of humanity off on a new course—away from madness."[22]

We all stand beneath the anvil of God's harsh hammer, but thank God for the grace within the firmness of his tough judgment.

---

21. Huddleston, *Naught for Your Comfort*.
22. Storey, *God in the Crucible*, 128.

8

Comforted by God's Tears

THE WHEREABOUTS OF GOD is our unrelenting concern. Rarely do we seriously question the existence of a divine, creative power. Our modern minds are far too sophisticated to assume that this infinitely expanding universe is the product of human creation or imagination. Earth's chauvinism was eclipsed centuries ago by the primitive discoveries of Copernicus. With each new telescopic exploration of the galaxies, we are even more surely convinced that this is an infinitely expanding universe in seemingly constant motion. Our most fundamental question concerns not the existence of God, but this inquiry into divine mystery: Does the Creator have compassion for the creation? Does God's creation have a destination? Is the universe friendly? Is there some guiding principle or destiny orchestrating the nature of things? Is there meaning within the motion? Such questions are best discussed when the scent of fresh lilac or yellow honeysuckle fills our senses and the rich tones of green landscape saturates our horizon. But these questions seem to inevitably arise during winter's deepest grief or amidst a sorrow that knows no season.

Back in 1983, a marvelously sensitive rabbi, Harold S. Kushner, probed such primal questions in the context of his existential pain. He had endured the excruciating distress of his young son's lingering illness and death. His book, *When Bad Things Happen to Good People*, tapped readers on the shoulder with its arresting relevance and theological candor. Kushner observed that a certain amount of suffering is universal. "Pain," he proposed, "is the price we pay for being alive."[1] But some forms of suffering are reprehensible, defying any collective consciousness of justice. Such was the suffering and death of his young son. Kushner concluded that either God is all-powerful, possessing the ability to cure his son but choosing not to, or God is all-loving but powerless to avert tragedy. He could not be both. "Forced to choose

---

1. Kushner, *When Bad Things Happen*, 64.

between a good God who is not totally powerful, or a powerful God who is not totally good," Kushner opted "to believe in God's goodness."[2]

If we follow this line of thinking, we are left with an impotent deity watching helplessly from the sidelines of human history. God's creation remains a victim of pain's chaos. The Almighty is incessantly caring and reliably loving, but impotent to change the nature of things. God's tears mingle with ours, but the Creator is powerless to interfere with nature's agonizing entropy. God grieves, but the Creator's grief does not amend injustices or console our bereaved spirits. Such a good but impotent god gives credence to the skepticism of comedian Woody Allen in his film parody of Dostoevsky, *Love and Death*. In the film's final scene, Allen faces the camera with the despondent look of a man who has been betrayed. He has been promised by a messenger of God that he would be saved from the fate of a firing squad, yet he was executed anyway. God did not come through on his behalf. Allen utters these final lines: "The important thing, I think, is not to be bitter. If it turns out that there is a God, I don't think that he's evil. The worst you can say about him is that basically he's an underachiever."[3]

Are these also our choices: A God of powerless goodness (an "underachiever") or a tyrannical deity of merciless power? A grieving God who refrains from protecting us, or a heroic, rescuing deity who is incapable of empathy? A weak, anemic God whose loving ways never threaten us, or a high-voltage God who strikes capriciously with his power and wrath? A sensitive, divine Being who weeps helplessly with us in our greatest anguish, or a dispassionate deity whose mighty presence protects all his faithful from tragedy and circumstances that might provoke empathetic tears of sorrow?

There is at least one book of the Bible that refuses to be caught on the horns of such a dilemma. It is the strange, apocalyptic little book we referenced in the last chapter's discussion of God's judgment, the Apocalypse of John, or simply, Revelation. This final book in the biblical canon gets its dubious name from a Greek word meaning "that which makes clear," or "a disclosure of something hidden." We can assume that the original readers comprehended the whole of this lengthy text's less-than-apparent message. Its message is anything but clear to the contemporary ear, as in my reference to Godwin's novel in the previous chapter. The last book of the Bible has become, therefore, the most abused book in the sacred literature of the church. Because of its mysterious symbolism, it has been used to support every form of hatred or personal vindictiveness one can imagine over the past eighteen centuries—from medieval crusades against the Islamic infidel in Palestine to the reckless violence of the Branch Davidians in Waco, Texas. How has a letter composed for clarification become so badly misunderstood?

The hope-filled message of John from the island of Patmos has been distorted primarily because its apocalyptic style is alien to the experience of most who read it.

---

2. Ibid., 42–43.
3. Commins, "Woody Allen's Theological Imagination," 244.

Its symbolic language is intriguing, but when read without reference to its original historical context, its message can become confusing at best or at worst, outright terrifying. Instead of an epistle of hope and deliverance, careless interpreters convolute its message into a crystal ball of inevitable, cosmic horror.

The author's literary task was to convey the radical political message that the oppressive Roman government will soon lose its evil power. Emperor Nero's days are numbered. The risen Christ (the Lamb) will soon establish an empire of his mercy and grace. If John had overtly written such an epistle, recipients of this message would have likely been arrested. Their very lives would have been vulnerable. Thus, the man of Patmos disguised his letter, comparable to a contemporary Boy Scout writing with milk as invisible ink. Held into the light of gospel faith, John's message becomes abundantly clear. Without that light, the scribbling is impossible to discern, as if it were white markings upon white paper.

In historical context, John of Patmos was a follower of the Way, held in cruel confinement under an oppressive rule of Caesar Nero. This persistent Christian partisan was no stranger to torture. John was exiled to a Romanesque, first-century Alcatraz Island in the Mediterranean Sea. The Appian Way was the pride of the Roman Empire and indeed one of the great achievements of the ancient world, but it was not formed by a rockslide. This sophisticated highway was gruelingly constructed by the sweat of slaves and conscripted prisoners like the mysterious John. Political and religious nonconformists crushed the rocks of Patmos in order to build broad highways for the Roman Empire's chariots.

Emperor Nero, that psychopathic tyrant, possessed absolute power. One written dictum from his hand could imprison, torture, or eliminate an entire faction of dissenters. Anyone who challenged his authority or refused to worship his image was likely to become a candidate for execution and fodder for his fires. Even a courageous follower of the Way who did not fear death by execution or torture would surely shrink in horror at thought of the anguishing death of a loved one in punishment for one's own disobedience to an imperial command. Pliny the Elder described Nero as "the destroyer of the human race" and "the poison of the world."[4] So it was with caution that John penned coded lines from the port city of Ephesus upon his release from years of forced labor. Because he cared about the fate of his loved ones in the churches of Asia, he composed his message in covert language with veiled symbolism. Authorities within Nero's oppressive military guard might have intercepted these mysterious communications from John, but could not possibly have known their meaning. The message, lacking a key to interpret the code, was assumed by government officials to be a benign letter written by a religious fanatic.

Today we can comprehend much of this enigmatic message, though some of it still remains obscure and speculative. Nonetheless, the central themes of the letter are crystal clear. The author confidently conveyed the expectation that the final coming of

---

4. Pliny the Elder, *Natural History*, 7.45, 22.92, quoted in Griffin, *Nero*, 15.

Part I: PARADOX AND THE DOCTRINE OF GOD

Christ was imminent and that victory over the forces of evil was at hand. Those who trusted in God in loyalty to Christ were eternally secure, but those who aligned with evil would perish. John of Patmos projected no anemic God—an "underachiever" with neither power nor authority over the affairs of humanity, nor an impotent deity who wallowed helplessly in the tears of human tragedy. The God we meet through the pen of this persecuted saint delivered a vision of the imminent time in which every tear shall be wiped from the eyes of the faithful. Here, in the apocalyptic Epistle of John, is a God of power before whom the entire Roman Empire is merely a fleeting phenomenon—a momentary obstacle to the ultimate triumph of divine righteousness, a weak bleep on God's radar of recorded history. John of Patmos was a realist who assumed that the faithful would continue to experience grueling times of horrendous anguish and sorrow. He admitted that a passing era of misery was imminent for all the churches of Asia. Nonetheless, John asserted that all faithful followers of Christ who remain pure amidst inevitable persecution will ultimately prevail. In the fullness of God's time, their sorrow will be transmuted into joy.

The letter was cleverly coded, addressed to wavering Christians in seven cities whose lives were on the verge of collapse amidst the threat of certain suffering and martyrdom. It was sealed by the tears of the sender, for John knew the probable fate of his persecuted friends. Seven congregations were addressed, a number representing completeness. Thus, the epistle was addressed to the whole church: Ephesus, a commercial center for the empire and place of mandatory worship of the emperor; Smyrna, central to the trade routes of the East; Pergamum, where the cults of Zeus, Athena, and Dionysus were obligatory; Thyatira, the garment and brass region; Sardis, center of wool trade; Philadelphia, a place where Dionysus was worshipped; and Laodicea, the "Wall Street" of the orient. The Christian movement was an anathema in each of these cities—disrupting commerce, challenging commonly accepted values, and defying idolatrous worship.

Under such dire circumstances, John shared his vision of power and hope with those who might be tempted to rescind belief and denounce their Christ: "Then I saw a new heaven and a new earth, for the first heaven and the first earth had passed away, and the sea was no more."[5] Professor J. M. Ford reminds us in the *Anchor Bible Commentary* that the sea is here a symbol of evil, danger, and distress. In this new reality God is bringing about, there shall one day be no more oppression, for the oppressors shall be obliterated. The voice of God speaks this therapeutic word from the throne of eternal power: "And I heard a loud voice from the throne saying, 'See, the home of God is among mortals. He will dwell with them; they will be his people, and God himself will be with them; he will wipe away every tear from their eyes. Death will be no more; mourning and crying and pain will be no more, for the first things have passed away.'"[6] John's amazing vision addressed leaders of seven influential churches

5. Rev 21:1 NRSV.
6. Rev 21:3–4 NRSV.

in Asia Minor. It fortified the readers with a sense of confidence in God's transforming power to alter fundamentally the direction of history. The divine voice announced, through John's letter, that it has already happened proleptically, for "I am the Alpha and the Omega."[7] In this epistle of hope, there is no abdication of God's power. Central to the message here is that the God who weeps with the persecuted is also a victorious deity with infinite power. Through the risen Christ, this strong and triumphant God makes his covenant-home among the persecuted faithful. The paradoxical presence of the God described by John of Patmos is powerful and good, omnipotent and loving, victorious and vulnerable, regal, yet acquainted with human grief.

How can this be? Is this not a logical contradiction? Not according to Canadian theologian Douglas John Hall. In his volume, *God and Human Suffering*, Hall rejects the conventional Christian interpretation of redemption that forces us to choose between a powerless God who is merciful and an omnipotent God who is indifferent to the plight of the innocent. There is a form of suffering that is not an expression of divine weakness, but is instead the positive choice of a God who displays infinite power by making a home among us. In God's ultimate display of power, the Almighty has chosen to heal history from within. Hall firmly asserts that God has come to share in our vulnerability. By making a home among us through Jesus Christ, God has come to our turf in the ultimate form of power—suffering love. In the book of Revelation we see a theological oneness of love, power, and justice in the very Being of God. This understanding of God, therefore, shapes the mission and worship of God's people. Hall, in a rebuttal to Kushner's courtship with cosmic dualism, writes, "The *mythos* of the suffering God—of the God who yearns parentally towards creation; of the God who is not powerless but whose power expresses itself unexpectedly in the weakness of love: this, I believe, is not only a more *profound* image of God than Kushner's limited deity, it is also more accessible to the human spirit. For every one of us knows, if we've lived and loved at all, something of the meaning of *that* yearning, *that* weak power, *that* powerful weakness."[8] Jürgen Moltmann points to this same paradox of God's power amidst sorrow and suffering in his classic, *The Crucified God*, in which he argues, "God is not greater than he is in his humiliation. God is not more glorious than he is in his self-surrender. God is not more powerful than he is in his helplessness. God is not more divine than he is in this humanity."[9]

The faith of the resilient saint of Patmos has inspired hope in human hearts throughout the ages. William Faulkner, the quintessential Southern novelist, profoundly comprehended the power of this bold faith when he wrote about the lives of oppressed blacks within his beloved homeland. In his novel, *The Sound and the Fury*, Faulkner describes the crumbling world of the Compson family, whose affluent lifestyle is shattered by the secret sins of their dysfunctional family. Only Dilsey, the

---

7. Rev 1:8a NRSV.
8. Hall, *God and Human Suffering*, 154–58, emphasis Hall's.
9. Moltmann, *Crucified God*, 205.

black maid who cares for the Compson children, appears to hold things together. In one memorable scene, she strides over a sandy road with tears streaming down her face. Her daughter, Frony, is by her side as Dilsey speaks of her strong faith in the message of the Apocalypse preached in that Sunday morning's sermon. She exclaims through tears of joy, "I sees de resurrection en de light . . . I sees de doom crack en hears de golden horns shoutin down de glory, en de arisen dead whut got de blood en de ricklickshun of de Lamb!"[10] This persecuted and abused woman weeps tears of ecstasy as she submits to the authoritative, apocalyptic message of John's Apocalypse. Frony attempts to hush her mother in case white folks might be passing, but nothing can restrain Dilsey's rapturous expression of faith as she shouts into the sunlight, "I've seed de first en de last . . . I seed de beginnin en now I sees de endin."[11]

The God who beholds the beginning of creation as well as the culmination of history dwells among us with the power of suffering love and empathizing tears. The God who presided over the elimination of the evil empire of Nero has made a home among us. The God who tossed the solar system into orbit and supervises the creation of new galaxies every few billion years also weeps over the hospital bed of a helpless, terminally ill child. The God who uproots empires—Egypt, Assyria, Babylon, Persia, Greece, Rome, the Third Reich, the Soviet Union—kneels beside the chained arms of a little man on the island of Patmos and whispers, "Dream the vision of the world's future and do not lose heart or hope." The same God who disbursed the nations at Babel and created our diversity of colors and tongues knelt down beside the tired body of a black man in Montgomery, Alabama, and said, "It is time that the nations and races of this world unite in the spirit of reconciliation and live out my eternal purpose initiated at Pentecost. Tell your people, 'I have a dream!'"

This God has, likewise, made a home within a special mission-project in Cape Town, South Africa, where hundreds of children are being fed both food and hope each day—a project enthusiastically supported by a congregation that I served. Over a decade ago a Methodist pastor, Abel Hendricks, and his wife, Frieda, observed scores of ghetto children scrambling for food in the city garbage dump. They were moved to tears—and action. Their Cape Town congregation initiated a feeding program for these desperate children. Through the years, they have been able to expand that program and invite Christians in North America to assist in order that many thousands may be fed. Tears have been transformed into tangible hope.

During the darkest days of racial apartheid in South Africa, Bishop Desmund Tutu (the altar boy who appears in the last chapter) visited the United States and was asked to appear before the House of Representatives Committee on Foreign Affairs' Subcommittee on Africa. Tutu had just received global recognition for winning the Nobel Peace Prize. The congressmen were debating the practicality of continuing

---

10. Faulkner, *Sound and the Fury*, 311.
11. Ibid., 313.

economic sanctions against the South African government. Politely, but forcefully, Bishop Tutu spoke from his theological standpoint:

> Mr. Chairman, we are talking about a moral issue. You are either for or against apartheid, and not by rhetoric. You are either in favor of evil or you are in favor of good. You are either on the side of the oppressed or on the side of the oppressor. You cannot be neutral. Apartheid is evil, is immoral, is un-Christian, without remainder . . . If you have supported the Nazis against the Jews, you would have been accused of adopting an immoral position. Apartheid is an evil as immoral and un-Christian in my view as Nazism, and in my view, the Reagan administration's support and collaboration with it is equally immoral, evil, and totally un-Christian, without remainder . . . Will you please, for a change, listen to victims of oppression. We shall be free, and will remember who helped us to become free.[12]

History is motivated by those who dream the dreams of God and are empowered by the fact that this Lord of tears, compassion, and power has made a home among us through the risen Christ. The liberating message of John of Patmos is as relevant today as the hour it was written. Our only source of redemption from the cycles of personal and global tragedy is that the earth is God's domicile. The Lord of Creation and infinite power weeps our tears, shares our sorrows, and dies our death. The fact that God has chosen to take the form of our weakness in order to destroy evil is the ultimate expression of his strength! This paradoxical reality prompted contemporary Christian Kazōh Kitamori, who suffered under political oppression during the era of imperial Japanese expansion, to describe the pain of God as "the essence of God," and indeed, "the heart of God."[13]

Luís Espinal likewise experienced this paradoxical truth when he labored as a priest among the poorest peasants in Bolivia. He was brutally murdered shortly after leading one of his most sensitive prayers in a service of corporate worship, ending with these words of sacrificial commitment: "We want to go on giving ourselves, because you [O God] continue hoping amid the night and weeping tears through a thousand human eyes."[14]

These faithful servants have embodied the theology of John. The concept of the pain of God was especially driven home to me in 1985. The ecumenical arm of the Protestant Church, with headquarters in Berlin, sponsored a visit of several clergy from the United States to observe, along with German pastors and parishioners, the fortieth anniversary of peace in Europe. On one of those sunny days in May, we somberly toured the memorial at Plötzensee. The compound had been a prison for political opponents of the Nazi regime. Here thousands of resisters had been executed following

---

12. "Hearing before the Subcommittee on Africa," 8–9.
13. Kitamori, *Theology of the Pain*, 46.
14. Gutiérrez, *On Job*, 92.

the mockery of justice in Berlin's kangaroo court. When we visited Plötzensee Prison, mounds of lovely flowers designated this as a place of death. A steel beam hung with large hooks remained screwed into the ceiling, inviting visitors to imagine the gruesome sights of tortuous and painful hangings that had occurred within these depressing walls. This had been Berlin's Patmos. The tragedy of Plötzensee Prison, moreover, had happened in the heart of a *Christian* Germany. Christians in the surrounding neighborhood have lived in the haunting post-war shadow of this memorial to their bloody national heritage ever since. This neighborhood of surviving Christians was a modern Laodicea. A few bold martyrs from the Plötzensee community had protested the plight of the innocent during the Holocaust. But their bodies were merely added to the number of victims laid upon the altar of courageous martyrs. The unmerciful executions did not stop until bombs had leveled Berlin.

The German Christians, on this pensive anniversary in May of 1985, painfully remembered the shame of those infamous years. They invited dialogue and worship with fellow Christians from the US. Just a twenty-minute walk from Plötzensee Prison, the Roman Catholic Church had constructed a commemorative place of worship, Mary Queen of Martyrs of the German Catholics in Honor of the Martyrs for Freedom of Religion and Conscience in the Years 1933 to 1945. Remorseful, contemporary congregants have refused to forget the transgressions of their horrific past. The courtyard of the sanctuary, completed in 1963, is designed to resemble a prison with barbed wire—not aesthetically pleasing. The sanctuary also contains architectural reminders of the nearby prison. But this place of memorial and worship does not invite a wallowing in sorrow, guilt, or vindictive self-righteousness. Above the giant Eucharistic altar is a mural encompassing the entire chancel wall of the church. Faces of anguish have been painted upon the canvas that engulfs the table. The artist has depicted tortured bodies swinging upon ugly iron hooks of execution. But, as one is seated in worship at a distance, the artist's concept becomes apparent: This arresting sight of despicable human suffering has been drenched in a gigantic tear. The tear of God falls upon his Eucharistic table of redemption when the people of God kneel at the altar of the church near the infamous prison. The memory of the congregation's shame is also the acknowledgment of God's mercy and the paradoxical power of God's redemption.

When any faithful congregation gathers for worship, the liturgy should remind all the prayerful and penitent that they are swimming in the salty context of God's tears. In this reality is our hope. This paradox of God's weakness and power is experienced only through authentic acts of worship and the liturgy of paradox that permeates these holy moments. Through habits of worship, we fortify our comprehension of and commitment to a God of tears and power. This God is our only hope for redemption! For the power of God is revealed through divine tears that shall wash us and the bloody stains of human history with the baptism of God's sorrow and the healing power of God's pain.

9

Chosen by Rejection

As we discovered in chapter 4, some of our most intriguing biblical narratives are grandparent stories. An idyllic portion of the oral tradition in Genesis describes Jacob as a model of the Abrahamic faith. Other strands of ancient tradition, however, candidly disclose that this father of the twelve tribal identities of Israel was a scandalous trickster. The story in Genesis straightforwardly chronicles the captivating account Jacob's rival brides, Leah and Rachel. This is one of the Bible's most outrageous grandparent stories. Like many grandparent legends, this one is outrageously funny, sprinkled with pungent humor. It is embarrassingly honest, startling us with the most shocking notions about God's dealings with his chosen people. Like the deity we meet upon Mount Moriah who forced the knife-clutching hand of Abraham to choose between his love for a son and his trust in a divine promise, YHWH's paradoxical nature shines through this legend of Jacob's brides.

In this chapter we shall focus upon a fascinating biblical narrative that announces a paradoxical theme as if from the lips of one of our own revered grandparents. Parental stories are usually pious and evasive. Grandparent stories, however, are unpretentious and unadulterated. Parental narratives are neat and moralistic. They refrain from revealing the whole story in order to preserve family propriety. Grandparent stories acknowledge the ambiguity of the human condition. Their characters are unpredictable. These stories do not moralize with punch line endings. Their truth is held in paradoxical tension, as are indeed the narratives of some of the most arresting, subtle stories of the Bible.

A friend told me about a time when his son sheepishly entered the house at midnight, reporting a dented fender. My friend immediately exploded into a tirade, expounding upon his own pristine record as a teenage driver and detailing the fastidious care he had taken with his hard-earned '57 Chevy throughout his college years. The son went to bed depressed and guilt-ridden. At breakfast, however, his grandfather dropped by. Surprisingly, he laughed when he heard about the fender bender episode. With a compassionate arm over his grandson's shoulder and a twinkle in his eyes, Grandpa put this whole matter into a broader perspective. "Did I ever tell you about the time your dad crashed into a State Patrol vehicle at an intersection?" he began. "It was just after the Duke-Carolina game of '65. It wouldn't have been so bad if he hadn't stashed all those six-packs in the back seat. Your dad was on probation until graduation. He graduated from that school *Laude how cum* instead of *Magnum cum laude*. I've still got the receipts from our attorney. Want to see a copy of the court proceedings?"

Grandparent stories call a spade a "spade" instead of an "agricultural implement." According to the Old Testament scholar Terence Fretheim, this is precisely what the inclusion of the YHWHist tradition within the narrative of Genesis accomplishes. The scandalous side of the ancient Jacob saga is told with all its warts in full view. If we listen to these stories with the ears of those for whom they were first written, we begin to hear the biblical message with far more relevance. Most of those for whom Genesis was originally composed were Hebrew descendants of Leah and Jacob. Chapter 29 of Genesis was their grandparent story. They traced their lineage through Leah, Jacob's second choice, instead of fair Rebecca, the favorite and beloved wife of the patriarch from whom Israel received its name and identity.

This story should be rated "R" for its unapologetically explicit humor. No Hollywood screenwriter could match its intrigue. It is sandwiched between two theophanies: Jacob's dream of a descending ladder and his wrestling with an angel at the river Jabbok. It is an excursion from the larger narrative, but integral to the big picture of God's covenant with Jacob. Despite Jacob's unwillingness to accept responsibility and his tendency toward deceit, God blessed Jacob and promised him that he would become the father of a nation of descendants. But from where would such fertility originate? Jacob had not chosen a wife. He was not getting any younger. He was a nomadic herdsman and could not offer either impressive financial security or the promise of a favorable future. Thus, he traveled east in search of a wife as he fled his brother Essau, whom he had tricked out of an inheritance. At the well of Haran, he encountered men who knew his kinsman Laban. These men introduced Jacob to Rachel, the radiant daughter of Laban who had come to gather water for the family's flock of sheep. Jacob's mother, Rebekah, was sister to Laban, and Jacob's personality was largely influenced by his mother's guile. Apparently deceit had become a family talent. Jacob rolled aside a stone from the mouth of the well so that Rachel's flock could drink, then asked the girl to summon her father. When Jacob embraced Laban under the hot sun of Haran, it was a rendezvous of two rascals. Jacob the trickster had met his match in Uncle Laban, the premier flimflam artist of Haran.

Jacob was smitten with the unparalleled beauty of his uncle's ravishing daughter. From that first encounter at the well, Jacob would have paid any price to have this woman as his bride. Laban, seeing Jacob's vulnerability, demanded a dowry that exacted the full measure of Jacob's commitment. Laban was not going to lose his stunning daughter, the prize beauty of Haran, to some vagabond nephew without a hefty return on his investment. Jacob agreed, therefore, to labor as Laban's herdsman for seven years in order to win Rachel's hand in marriage.

Laban conveniently failed to mention one minor detail in his contract with Jacob: He *forgot* to tell his nephew that, in this culture, it was obligatory to marry off the oldest daughter before the younger sisters could be wed. No parade of wealthy, eligible men had formed outside Laban's home to court the unexceptional Leah. When the time finally arrived for the wedding ritual that was to consummate the union of Laban's gorgeous daughter to his enterprising nephew, Jacob pledged himself to the woman who stood behind a veil at his side. He had arduously labored seven sweaty years for this reward. The nuptial night passed in ecstasy, and as the sunlight of dawn broke into the couple's wedding chamber, Jacob found himself gazing into the timid eyes of Leah—Rachael's older, mediocre sister. He was horrified!

The biblical text does not report that Leah face or figure were repulsive, only that "Leah had weak eyes" (Gen 29:17a NIV). This description may be tantamount to the line often used to describe a blind date, "She has a great personality." Although the narrative of Genesis does not provide a physical description of Leah, the Hebrew text quickly asserts, "Rachel was graceful and beautiful." The Hebrew name *Leah* literally means, "wild cow" or "gazelle"—not exactly the most flattering feminine analogy. Laban and his wife had set the stage for some fierce sibling rivalry merely by their choice of names, for *Rachel* was the Hebrew name for a cute, cuddly "ewe lamb." Regardless of her looks, Leah was known throughout the town of Haran as Rachel's old-maid sister. Leah was, at best, Jacob's second choice and clearly a shocking disappointment to a passion-filled groom, as she must surely have seen the morning after this deceptive nuptial night!

Being a second choice always leaves wounds. In our culture, we only honor winners. A few years ago a young woman wept profusely in Atlantic City, sinking into weeks of severe depression. Why? She had been declared runner-up in the Miss America contest. No one wasted pity on her. We adore beauty, but we worship winners. Even the holy term "Madonna" has become a convoluted icon in a culture that worships a sensuous voice and a voluptuous figure.

The spotlight of this intriguing biblical story now turns quickly away from Leah's unexceptional physical appearance to illuminate her exceptionally beautiful sister. Jacob promised Laban he would not return to Canaan for another seven years if his uncle would promise Rachel as his wife. Their agreement was a sort of marry-now-pay-later plan. The elaborate wedding festival in Haran lasted a full week. Just as soon as the union between Leah and Jacob was achieved through Laban's deceitful scheme, Jacob also married his true love, Rachel. The YHWHist author is blatantly honest in reporting, "So Jacob went in to Rachel also, and he loved Rachel more than Leah. He served Laban for another seven years."[1]

If there was ever a patron saint for the loser, it is Leah. She is the heroine of anyone who has ever been second choice. One's wedding is supposed to be the most magnificent moment in one's life. But by week's end, Leah's new groom was in the arms of her rival sister—her parents' favorite. Sometimes we feel authentic pity even for a bride, and Leah is our prototype for provoking such empathetic emotions.

The contemporary crown prince of losers in popular culture is the playwright and actor, Woody Allen. He is the modern equivalent to Charlie Chaplin's little vagabond, for the audience always finds humor and pity in the fictitious characters he projects on the screen. In *Broadway Danny Rose*, Allen creates a pathetic caricature of himself in the title character. Danny Rose had an affinity for losers. He was a talent agent who always picked the worst acts in show business: a one-legged tap dancer, a one-armed juggler, a blind xylophone player, and a parrot that sang, "I Gotta Be Me." When some of Danny Rose's acts became famous, they deserted him for fear of associating with a loser. He was constantly being victimized by victims. In this film, Woody Allen may have revealed his earnest desire to be rescued by the grace of some figure like Danny Rose, who would offer unconditional acceptance to a perpetual and incurable loser.

Leah's story suggests just this sort of grace. She is like a Danielle Rose—a touch of grace for those who are perpetually confirmed as second choice. Nonetheless, Leah became a primary matriarch of Israel. The children that were born into the covenant of Abraham through her union with Jacob paradoxically became a great nation. These descendants truly lived up to the meaning of Jacob's new covenant identity—*Israel*, meaning "he who struggles." Descendants of Jacob's twelve sons became slaves in Egypt. They were despised by the affluent cultures of the ancient world. The descendants of the Leah-Jacob union especially became *a nation of losers*. The biblical image of Leah became a subtle and profound reminder, for this biblical grandparent text makes it clear that God's promise to bless Jacob would have been made null and void had it not been for this *loser*, Leah. This woman gave birth to six of Jacob's sons, plus one daughter. The text of Genesis, moreover, became the genealogical source book for the whole nation of Israel. Of the four sons born to Leah, three were named with references to YHWH. Reuben literally meant, "The Lord has looked upon my affliction." All the descendants of the tribe of Reuben throughout the centuries have worn with pride this badge of their identity. Simeon, son of Leah, was given a name that literally meant, "The Lord has heard that I am hated." When the people of Israel have been persecuted and treated as outcasts, the descendants of Simeon have remembered with pride the tradition of Leah. A third child was named Judah, or "I will praise the Lord." Thus, the honored delineations "Judaism," "Jewish," and "Jew" emerge from Leah's offspring. Judah was the father of the tribe that presumably settled in Jerusalem and produced the southern kingdom. A fourth son, Levi, founded the house of Levitical

---

1. Gen 29:30 NRSV.

traditions that defined and cultivated all temple worship. Leah also gave birth to Issachar, Zebulun, and Dinah. Most of the people who would be known as Israelites, therefore, have claimed to emerge from this sacred lineage. Leah provided the genealogical heritage that saved Israel. Thus Leah, the seeming loser, is the often-overlooked paradoxical figure within the story of Israel's salvation history.

The saga of Leah is a magnificent grandparent narrative. It requires a mature mind to comprehend and appreciate. The fertility of Rachel, according to the YHWHist author of Genesis, was due to an agreement between the two sisters. It was commonly believed that the mandrake, a potato-like plant, possessed an aphrodisiac property that stimulated conception. Through a bargain with Leah, Rachel was given mandrakes gathered by Leah's son Reuben. God guided this decision. God gave new life to Rachel's womb, and Rachel finally gave birth to a child—Joseph. God's promise to Jacob was thereby fulfilled and exceeded, but Leah played the essential role in this consummation.

Jacob always loved Rachel more. But she died early giving birth to her second son, Benjamin, whose very name meant "child of sorrow." Rachael was buried in an unceremonious spot near Bethlehem. Leah grew in Jacob's favor throughout their long lives together. She was finally buried with highest honors in Hebron, near Jerusalem. This place was the tomb of several hallowed patriarchs and became an everlasting shrine visited by thousands of contemporary Jews annually at *Bar Mitzvah* and *Bat Mitzvah* ceremonies. Entombed here together are Abraham and Sarah, Isaac and Rebecca, Jacob and Leah. The place is also a site of holy pilgrimage for Jews, Muslims, and Christians alike. Through Leah the loser, all the peoples of the earth have indeed been blessed!

This is truly a biblical grandparent story with paradoxical import. Descendants of Leah—that is, most Jews throughout the world—look upon her with gratitude and admiration. In the saga of this meek, patient matriarch there emerges a theology of hope for a world of lost causes. The doors of history are opened through a promise and a future fulfillment for all losers who patiently persist in covenant faith. Leah is the patron saint for countless women who inhabit pews and chairs in the sacred space of sanctuaries for worship in each congregation that I have served. She is perhaps an inadvertent patron saint for mainline denominations that have been on the losing side of competing popularity struggles in a culture of civil religion. The future of us all is being shaped by a providential God who sees beyond our limitations toward the horizon of divine possibilities. Yes, God's magnificent plan is being fulfilled through some of history's losers like Leah. Each of us is integral to God's glorious purpose. God takes initiative in the lives of both winners and losers. To be second choice is also to be chosen.

Bishop Goodrich of Texas told the story of a certain couple that wanted to have a baby. They tried to adopt a child, but their age was prohibitive. However, about the time they had reached a condition of despair, the wife became pregnant. She exercised extreme caution throughout her fragile pregnancy. When the doctor delivered the baby, he quickly summoned the father for advice. The infant was a baby girl. The mother was doing fine, but the baby was deformed, having a stump where the right arm should have been. The father and doctor conferred. They wrapped the child so that the mother, in this initial moment, would see only the infant's face. When the long-awaited child was handed to her eager mother, she immediately pulled away the blanket and saw the truth. This baby was not a pretty sight. After a brief silence, the mother spoke gently with conviction, "God knew how much we needed her, and He must have known how much she needed us."[2]

As we read this chapter together, we may be thinking of ourselves as a winner, a loser, or a mixture of positive fate and negative fortune. We are fashioned by our creator with vast differences in physical beauty, innate intelligence, or natural talents. But whether we are at the top of the list or at the bottom of the heap, we are all chosen by God. The divine plan cannot work without us. We are integral to the fulfillment of God's ultimate purpose. This is the gospel message, according to the paradoxical Hebrew story of Leah.

By the way, there emerged from the tribe of Judah (one of Leah's offspring) a very special child. He was born in the tiny Judean village called Bethlehem, near the place of Leah's burial, and, according to the paradoxical narrative of the biblical text, this direct descendant of Leah the loser became the savior of the whole cosmos.

---

2. Goodrich, Robert E., Jr., "Dear God, Where Are You?" sermon preached on *Protestant Hour Radio*, PRTVC, Atlanta, GA, March 23, 1969.

10

Paradox and the Mathematics of Mystery

As suggested in the previous chapter, the Story of salvation history is cosmic in scope. God's choices are surprising. But God guides the movement of time and the human saga with initiatives of grace that emerge within the natural order of an ever-expanding creation. The more humanity discovers about the evolving and infinite breadth of the universe, the breathtaking beauty of mathematical axioms and theorems upon which the universe is constituted, and the wisdom of natural selection in the evolutionary process, the greater and more majestic is our concept of God. When the Hubble telescope discovers a new planet or previously unverified galaxies or a nova beyond anyone's imagination, God's grandeur is further magnified. Our little box of brains can never encompass the infinite expanses of the Creator's creation or the comprehensiveness of divine love for that which God has brought into being. New discoveries in the disciplines of science and mathematics only magnify the believer's sense of awe and wonder.

For several decades, a regimented pattern was repeated nearly each afternoon as sundown approached in suburban New Jersey. Two men strolled down a familiar path with their hands clasped behind their backs as they engaged in intense conversation. A thick canopy of trees sheltered their walk through a community of stately homes near the lush green carpet of a nearby golf course. These creatures of habit had become intimate friends due to their mutual absorption into topics of passionate interest. The neighborhood through which they walked, however, was not a typical American community. This was Princeton, New Jersey. The two strollers usually conversed in German. One of the men was almost forty years younger than his walking companion. In temperate weather, he usually dressed in a dapper white linen suit with a matching white fedora. He was slimmer with a gaunt, frail appearance, wearing thick glasses. The older friend usually wore unkempt, baggy pants held in place by antiquated

Part I: Paradox and the Doctrine of God

suspenders. Despite their differences in age, the two men experienced a delightful intellectual synergy upon their engaging daily walk through this suburban landscape.

When *Time* magazine placed upon its cover the long-awaited choice of the single most influential living citizen in the twentieth century, the older man's face was splashed across a special edition at the inception of a new millennium. He was a nuclear physicist and mathematician named Albert Einstein. When that same newsweekly devoted a special issue to the one hundred greatest minds of the last century in commemoration of the end of the millennium, Einstein's young walking companion, Kurt Gödel, was cited as the century's greatest mathematician.

Even though Gödel was a member of the esteemed faculty of the prestigious Institute for Advanced Study near the Princeton campus, his name was hardly a household reference except among a small community of philosophical mathematicians. Employees of the Institute such as Einstein and Gödel were products of Abraham Flexner's dream to collect in one place the most creative scientific and mathematical minds on the planet with a single mission and dedication "to the usefulness of useless knowledge."[1] Oskar Morgenstern, a world-renowned economist and friend of both Einstein and Gödel, disclosed in a letter that Einstein had told him that the only reason he remained a resident of Princeton and an employee of the Institute was "in order to have the privilege of walking home with Gödel."[2]

Both Einstein and Gödel remained at painful odds with a majority of the international community of thinkers. Both men had revolutionized conventional scientific thought at an early age. Einstein was best known for his theory of relativity and Gödel for his "proof of incompleteness," or simply, "Gödel's paradox." In a concise presentation at the University of Vienna at the age of twenty-four on October 7, 1930, Gödel provided a clever proof for "the incompleteness of arithmetic," using a creative and complex numbering system. We shall return to a discussion Gödel's paradox later in this chapter, for any comprehensive and relevant doctrine of God is compelled to consider the wondrous beauty of mathematics and especially the profound revolutionary discoveries of Kurt Gödel.

The dominant cultures of Babylon, Egypt, and Greece that were prominent during the exile of the Hebrew people (587–515 B.C.) employed mathematics in order to unlock the mysteries of celestial movement. Mathematical formulas influenced philosophers of the ancient world, and many believed that celestial deities controlld human fate. The exiled Jews were certainly exposed to these new understandings in mathematics, but they consistently maintained their allegiance to the one God of their Abrahamic heritage and never accepted the notion that celestial gods controlled the destiny of mankind. Even though most Jews of the exile remained in Babylon and absorbed a more sophisticated understanding of mathematics and astronomy, they also learned to sing the Lord's song in this foreign land. Since the second millennium

1. Goldstein, *Incompleteness*, 14–15.
2. Quoted in ibid., 33.

B.C., this empire had developed a form of mathematics that was far superior to the Egyptian comprehension. Some historians of ancient cultures observe that the Babylonians dominated the field of mathematics from 1700 B.C. to 300 B.C., greatly influencing the Greek philosophers and mathematicians.[3] By the time they had conquered much of the Mesopotamian region, including Judah, the Babylonians had developed a sexagesimal system that later influenced Hellenistic and Arab astronomers and philosophers.[4]

Hebrew theology forbade participation in astrology and any suggestion that celestial constellations are remotely relevant to human destiny. Wisdom literature consistently articulated the doctrine that God alone guides human destiny. But the sacred literature that took form during the exilic period was greatly influenced by exposure to a Babylonian intellectual climate informed by an advanced understanding of the mathematical laws that govern the movement of celestial constellations. The authors of wisdom literature, while categorically rejecting the philosophy that stars and planets control or influence human affairs, vigorously articulated the notion that God's law brings harmony to the cosmos. The Hebrews had learned the beauty of Babylonian mathematics and had concluded that the Author of covenant, the Provider of Torah, the Initiator of unconditional grace, and the Mind behind the mathematics was Israel's Creator-God.

The poet that composed Psalm 8 was likely acquainted with Babylonian theories related to the mathematics of celestial movements. Instead of adopting a philosophy of determinism inherent within the Babylonian and Hellenistic belief systems, which worshipped a variety of celestial beings, the author of this psalm merely broadened the panorama of his praise through his covenant commitment to the single Lord and Creator of the entire universe.

Our last chapter illustrated that the story of salvation in the Hebrew canon is much larger in import than the narrative of an obscure racial and ethnic tribe in the ancient world. The intriguing saga of Abraham and Sara's descendants, including the lowly Leah, is a story about the salvation of the entire cosmos, and the substance of this audacious claim is paradoxical. The message is that God uses what is rejected in the progression of nations and tribes in order to bring about the ultimate salvation of a fallen cosmos.

No passage more lucidly illustrates the breadth of divine grace than the unrestrained scope of God's redemption celebrated within the Eighth Psalm—a seminal representation of Hebrew wisdom from the exilic period. This remarkable poetry was composed to be sung at an anticipated future occasion when worshipers would parade into the reconstructed Jerusalem Temple during harvest festivals. This compelling poem was a prophetic form of liturgy, for it was likely composed before the days of Ezra and Nehemiah and the actual construction of the Second Temple. Psalm

---

3. Davis and Hersh, *Mathematical Experience*, 9–11.
4. See Goetz et al., "History of Mathematics," *New Encyclopedia Britannica Macropaedia*, 23:603–33.

Part I: Paradox and the Doctrine of God

8 provides a liturgy of hope and realized expectations. The Hebrew God was about to reconstitute Israel as a people eager to obey the Torah in a newly inhabited city with an unpretentious place of worship rising out of the ashes of previous punishment and deserved destruction. The words and music hold together two antithetical human emotions—fear and joy. This paradoxical tension draws on the profoundest elements of Hebrew worship, and it is instructive to the contemporary church in the form and content of its worship. The tension betwwen fear and joy, awe and ecstasy, was to be felt when Hebrew worshipers and refugees from a generation's captivity in Babylon entered the new Temple. Thus, with the Eighth Psalm as its theological script, throngs of the faithful would dance and sing to a melody inspired by the captivating sound of *shophar* (ram's horns) and *khatsotsrah* (trumpets). The cadence of their song was sustained by the charming rhythmic resonance of the *toph* (a small tambourine). The sweet ecstasy of harmonic choral voices brought joy to the redeemed upon their entry into the abode of divine presence.

Religions of the ancient world were usually regarded as tribal expressions of the folk beliefs of specific racial, ethnic, and national identities. But the boldness of this poem emerges from a theology that crystallized during the Babylonian exile—namely, the notion that the Hebrew God is the sovereign of all nations and all people. "O Lord, our Sovereign, how majestic is your name in all the earth!"[5] The sphere of influence for YHWH, according to the psalm's author, was not restricted by national boundaries. God's glory is experienced throughout the entire cosmos. From birth, awe and reverence are intuitive. It is only human, therefore, to bow in fear and joy before the Creator of the celestial canopy: "Out of the mouths of babes and infants you have founded a bulwark because of your foes, to silence the enemy and the avenger."[6]

Nearly every child has gazed in wonder at the endless expanses of the celestial canvass. During the exile, Hebrew parents regarded it their sacred duty to explore the constellations after dark with their children, not because the stars had magical powers or influence over their child's future, as was believed by their pagan neighbors, but because the Creator God is the provider of this infinite cosmos of incredible beauty. Thus, Hebrew children were taught just how majestic this limitless, incalculable universe is. Each child intuitively experiences both the fear and ecstasy of that intimate, loving moment with parents out under the stars.

Thus, each of us from childhood experiences an emotional smallness and insignificance beneath the stars. We are nothing in the great scheme of things, it seems. Thus, this ancient poetry of worship shouts to the accompaniment of a vibrating *shophar*, "What are human beings that you are mindful of them, mortals that you care for them?"[7] In the equation of God's arithmetic, under more stars than can be calculated, who are we humans that the Creator would take notice of us?

   5. Ps 8:1 NRSV.
   6. Ps 8:2 NRSV.
   7. Ps 8:4 NRSV.

It is essential to note that the psalmist's answer to this crucial question is articulated exclusively for acts of sacred worship. Only in corporate worship can a question that provokes the terror of perceived insignificance be transformed into an affirmation of grace. Only in worship does divine Torah—the product of covenant love—come as a gift through the paradoxical revelation that, even though we humans are like tiny molecules within the eco-system of cosmic reality, we are made "a little lower than God, and crowned . . . with glory and honor."[8]

Artur Weiser, that conscientious scholar of Hebrew literature, contrasts the profound insights of Jewish wisdom literature with Hellenistic philosophy during the period of this psalm's composition. Weiser cites Sophocles' famous assertion in *Antigone* (429 B.C.), "Wonders are many, and none is more wonderful than man," and adds this astute observation: "The difference between the Greek and biblical estimates of man is demonstrated by the very fact that in the Old Testament human dignity has no value of its own, but has value only because it is a gift from God."[9]

Thus, in the music and language of worship, this paradoxical affirmation can be intuitively comprehended and celebrated—namely, that we lowly human beings have been installed by the Ruler of the universe as stewards of this earth: "You have given them dominion over the works of your hands; you have put all things under their feet."[10] This dominion is not a license for exploitation. On the contrary, the Creator has established humans for the purpose of worship, and the act of worship defines the human mission of caring for the created order. We are commissioned through covenant, renewed through worship, and appointed to a responsibility for the earth's protection, nurture, and preservation. Therefore, in Hebrew mythology humans have not gained power over nature by means of some rebellion against the deity. On the contrary, humans have received, as a commission from God, the task of dominion, or stewardship. The Hebrew Psalter makes it clear that God wants the natural world to be subjected to human care only insofar as humans are subservient to the authority of the Creator who loves and desires to sustain his creation. The engaging harmony of Hebrew music and the orderly rhythm of the psalmist's poetry hold together within the act of worship the polarities of a great paradox: Humans are a small particle in the cosmos, but humanity is the crown of creation. This paradox only makes sense in the context of worship because this reality is contingent upon covenant loyalty. Without the covenant story of Abraham, Moses, the prophets, and Jesus the Messiah, the human story is indeed "a tale / Told by an idiot, full of sound and fury, / Signifying nothing."[11] In the context of worship and the singing of these remarkable affirmations, the finite is confronted with the infinite, the transient with the eternal, and the psychology of the pathos of human insignificance with the grandeur of covenant and mission. Only through wor-

---

8. Ps 8:5 NRSV.
9. Weiser, *Psalms*, 144.
10. Ps 8:6 NRSV.
11. Shakespeare, *Macbeth*, Act 5, Scene 5, lines 26–28.

ship can humans begin to see the vision of a transformed future in which this earth and all the celestial bodies are moving toward the full realization of a potential, ideal being defined by God. Worship's metaphorical reference to "Kingdom" articulates a special language of expectation and promise. Thus, Psalm 8 eloquently communicates an elevated anthropology while affirming divine omnipotence. The God of covenant loyalty honors humanity and crowns humans with a role in the inevitable progress of nature and human history toward fulfillment and the cosmic destination—the ideal of Kingdom. This psalm celebrates the mathematics of God's mercy and the symmetry of a created order that makes sense.

Thus, the affirmations of this poignant poem bring us back to our discussion of the obscure but essential figure of Kurt Gödel. The mathematician's great rival in the philosophical world was Ludwig Wittgenstein, who was adamant in denying paradoxes as being "trivial epiphenomena" of the ways in which language works. Wittgenstein had to "by-pass" Gödel's proofs, acting as if Gödel's intricate mathematical postulates did not even exist.[12] What Gödel had demonstrated was that certain mathematical equations, while true, cannot be proven to be so. Their proofs are forever incomplete because these mathematical realities or formulas exist *a priori*—that is, without dependence upon the mind of man. If humans did not exist, these mathematical equations would still be an ideal reality. Literally, Gödel's first theorem revealed to an unsuspecting, exclusive community of intellectuals on that crisp day in Vienna during the fall of 1930 a shocking realization. Gödel carefully stated his famous theorem in this way: "In any formal system adequate for number theory there exists an undecidable formula—that is, a formula that is not provable and whose negation is not provable."[13] This brief "incompleteness theorem," and Gödel's twelve pages of accompanying "proofs," dealt a devastating blow to the prevailing philosophy of the twentieth century—namely, the "logical positivism" espoused as dogma by the Vienna Circle of philosophers. This concept dominated the entire post-Enlightenment world of science and mathematics and was also termed "radical empiricism." As the Scottish philosopher David Hume (1711–1776) argued, *a priori* reasoning is to be discarded as having no ontological import. Truth and reality can only be established through empirical evidence. For Hume, *a priori* reasoning (presumptive thinking lacking empirical experiment or evidence) could tell us how concepts relate to one another but cannot tell us anything of substance about the world beyond empirical disclosure. That is, things like mathematical postulates and theorems can all be proven by experimentation and observation. For example, the scientific world was not quick to endorse Albert Einstein's theory of relativity until photographic plates recording an eclipse of the sun tested its mathematical underpinnings.[14]

12. Goldstein, *Incompleteness*, 189.

13. Goldstein, *Incompleteness*, 23.

14. The first experiment was attempted in the Crimean in preparation for the eclipse of August 21, 1914. But this effort was premature due to Einstein's miscalculations and the beginning of the First

Paradox and the Mathematics of Mystery

"Logical positivism" especially discounted any discussion of the concept of God. Postulations regarding the existence of a Being whose existence is the cause of all other beings cannot be observed, quantified, or reported with accuracy. Theology is irrelevant to the concern of science, according to the philosophers of logical positivism. They assumed, therefore, that if something could not be demonstrated through empirical evidence in the laboratory of human experience, it could not be accepted as a true reality. Thus, all mathematical equations must be subjected to some observable criteria. Logical positivists taught that all mathematical formulas must be proven through observable experimentation. Bertrand Russell of Oxford University had spent a lifetime writing his monumental three-volume *Principia Mathematica*, carefully explaining to mathematicians throughout the world how all formulas can be subjected to rules for empirical proof. When Russell was asked what he would say if he were to find himself standing before God at the pearly gates, he humorously and sardonically quipped, "Oh Lord, why did you not provide more evidence?"[15]

In the years following the publication of Gödel's "incompleteness theorem," Bertrand Russell abandoned his colossal project, *Principia Mathematica*, and churned out several fascinating volumes that chronicle the history of philosophical and cultural thought in the Western world. Russell virtually abandoned his role as a philosopher of mathematics because of Gödel's theorem, while Wittgenstein closed his eyes and ears to Gödel's "proofs" and continued his flawed theories of language and mathematics until his death in 1951.

The two men who became intellectual friends through their conversations at Princeton were essentially Platonists. Einstein's fascination with Gödel's view of the universe was related to his young friend's courageous defiance of radical empiricism. They both came to understand that there are mathematical truths that simply exist, dictating the movement of celestial beings as well as subatomic particles. Man is not the measure of all things! Some realities exist *a priori*, regardless of whether we humans exist as thinking minds. These mathematical realities are true despite the incompleteness of human effort to test and prove them. Gödel's mathematical paradox holds together mathematical truths that can be validated by empiricism as well as even more profound mathematical axioms and postulates that are not contingent upon human experimental proof. Such truths merely exist, independent of the human mind or empirical disclosure.

Gödel's corollary theorem states that "the consistency of a formal system adequate for number theory cannot be proved within the system."[16] His language is indeed Platonic. In Plato's philosophy there exists an ideal reality that cannot be ob-

---

World War. But a highly successful experiment was conducted on May 29, 1919, when another eclipse was viewed from the tiny island of Principe, a Portuguese colony north of the equator off the Atlantic coast of Africa. See Isaacson, *Einstein*, 202–205, 255–62.

15. Quoted in Goldstein, *Incompleteness*, 78.
16. Ibid., 23.

served by human perception. These ideals exist independently of the mind of man. But these ideals can be proleptically experienced in an incomplete world that is striving toward becoming its ideal self. We can receive a foretaste of the ideal that is to be fully disclosed in an ever-expanding future.

Gödel's wife was a common *hausfrau* who knew absolutely nothing about mathematics and the professional work of her frail, brilliant husband. Gödel's mother in Austria comprehended her son's profession even less. But her loyal son devotedly corresponded with her, revealing some of his most intimate thoughts and feelings. On October 20, 1963 (fifteen years before his death at age seventy-two), Kurt Gödel wrote his mother that his incompleteness theorems had consequences in the mystical and religious sphere. She had sent him an article that had recently been published in Europe about the implications of his famous theorems. Confessing to his mother that he had not read the article, Gödel confided in this affectionate letter, "It was something to be expected that sooner or later my proof will be made useful for religion, since that is doubtless also justified in a certain sense."[17] Indeed, Gödel's theorems supported Platonism's insistence on the existence of the domain of eternal verities that transcend human perception. His philosophical point of reference supporting *a priori* knowledge entertains the notion that certain paradoxical realities transcend empirical verification.

Einstein's death in 1957 was emotionally devastating to Gödel. The great physicist was his only true friend who shared his Platonist philosophy of mathematics. Perhaps these two were the first to comprehend that the way humans understand themselves in relationship to the universe would be transformed by the three jarring theories of the twentieth century: Einstein's relativity, Heisenberg's uncertainty, and Gödel's paradox of incompleteness. According to biographer Walter Isaacson, Einstein spent his final years at Princeton's Institute pursuing his "white whale"—namely, the quest for a "unified field theory." When he died of an aneurysm at age seventy-six, he left by his bedside several pages of tightly written mathematical equations riddled with cross-outs and corrections. As Isaacson notes, "To the very end, he struggled to find his elusive unified field theory."[18] As early as 1951, due to Gödel's influence upon his thinking, Einstein almost abandoned his pursuit of the theory, confessing, "It is so difficult to employ mathematically that I have not been able to verify it. This state of affairs will last for many more years, mainly because physicists have no understanding of logical and philosophical arguments."[19] Due to Gödel's paradox, Einstein pursued a unified field theory regardless of his inability to verify it, for the two men understood that the universe is held together by absolute mathematical realities that transcend verification. Thus, Einstein said of himself, "I am a deeply religious nonbeliever."[20]

---

17. Ibid., 192.
18. Isaacson, *Einstein*, 536.
19. Ibid., 514.
20. Ibid., 536.

Hebrew wisdom literature that includes the Psalter was compiled by a redactor who pulled together a vast assortment of Hebrew poetry and aphorisms. The redactor worked during a period of great anxiety in the life of an exiled Israel. The Psalter, therefore, later became the poetry of paradox and mystery, pointing to a Creator God busy constructing an ever-expanding cosmos. This poetry affirms a God whose glory radiates above the heavens. This is the God that brings order out of chaos through the mathematics of mercy, the wisdom of axioms and theorems, the beauty of the Torah, and the intrigue of paradox.

Perhaps no one has comprehended the cosmic implications of Hebrew salvation history and poetry better than the Apostle Paul. In a letter attributed to him by the early church, he told followers of the Way in Colossae that the life-death-and-resurrection of Christ makes sense of cosmic reality. He assured neophyte disciples in Colossae that "[Christ] is the image of the invisible God, the firstborn of all creation, for in him all things in heaven and on earth were created, things visible and invisible, whether thrones or dominions or rulers or powers—all things have been created through him and for him. He himself is before all things, and in him all things hold together."[21]

In these ten chapters we have explored various facets of a biblical theme that glitters like a diamond in the narrative of the Bible. Paradox is one of several significant themes that draw us closer to experiencing holy mystery. It is certainly not a singular or superior theological concept that claims to explain the nature of all things or unlock the great enigmas of existence. The paralyzing problem of theodicy is one among several issues that will forever befuddle our minds and cripple our arrogant spirits. The devastating alarm of the silence of God is not explained away by the paradoxical fashion of God's self-disclosure. But the theme of paradox in Hebrew wisdom literature does point us to the second person of the Trinity. In these next chapters, therefore, we shall explore the paradoxical teachings of the Man of Nazareth and discover the power of his paradoxical life. He is not only the fulfillment of Hebrew hope that mirrors the paradoxical themes of Hebrew Scripture, he is also the one in whom "all things hold together."

---

21. Col 1:15–17 NRSV.

Part II

Paradox and Christology

11

The Blessing of Misfortune

IN THE INITIAL TEN chapters I have proposed that a major theological theme within the biblical canons of the Judeo-Christian tradition is the paradoxical nature of God's disclosure. The significance of paradoxical themes within the biblical narrative may, of course, be cited along with other salient orthodox teachings related to the being of God. Many portions of wisdom literature, in particular, articulate a theology of paradox. This book does not suggest that God always divulges divine nature through paradoxical self-disclosure or that paradoxical teachings unlock the mammoth mysteries of divine Being. But the content of these initial chapters has provided an argument for a merciful God amidst life's perplexing unfairness. We are led to discover the most profound dimensions of wisdom through the foolishness of God. In the bleakest of personal circumstances, we intuitively experience hope in the comfort of divine presence. The incomplete context of bad news need not obscure our comprehensive vision of the majestic tapestry of good news woven into the vast panorama of the cosmic carpet. Fear and love need not be conflicting responses to our experience of God. The God of our tradition reveals the essence of authentic power that takes the form of divine weakness through God's wounds and tears. This paradoxical deity disciplines those whom he loves and chooses to use nobly those whom he rejects. The laws of science and mathematics especially glorify God, and their most profound truths are grounded in a paradoxical reality that transcends human proof.

The most astounding assertion of the Christian faith is that this God, so paradoxically disclosed in the Hebrew Bible, is most vividly and clearly revealed through the life and teachings of the Jesus of history. In these next ten chapters we shall more intensely explore paradoxical dimensions within the second persona of the Trinity. If one of the salient orthodox teachings of Christian tradition is the paradoxical revelation of God, how does the Jesus of history and Christ of faith embody that reality?

Part II: Paradox and Christology

In this chapter we shall explore one succinct, pithy component of Jesus' teachings that is paradigmatic of all his life and teachings—namely, the Beatitudes. These eight paradoxical blessings introduce the so-called Sermon on the Mount in the First Gospel narrative. The account of Jesus' life and teachings that initiates the Christian New Testament is attributed to Matthew, one of the twelve apostles. This gospel record was written in order to answer the many questions of the author's congregation. A sub-theme of this volume relates to the influence of paradoxical theology upon the worship and mission of the contemporary church. Thus, it is important to explore the nature and historical circumstance of Matthew's congregation and the people for whom he wrote this narrative. The Sermon on the Mount was the first of five sets of teachings articulated in this preliminary volume of the four-Gospel witness. Thus, the early church, on the recommendation of Bishop Athanasius in the fourth century, began its written proclamation and record of the life and teachings of the Messiah with the message of this book. Even though the narrative was composed some fifty years after the crucifixion of Jesus, its content was attributed to the former tax collector who Jesus chose for his entourage of disciples. The book was to serve as a catechism for Jewish converts to the Way of Christ. Matthew wrote his narrative in order to instruct the congregation that was formed by his leadership, but he relied upon other resources for his chronicle of the Jesus' life. Over 90 percent of the content of an earlier document—the Gospel of Mark—formed the narrative fabric of this written witness introducing the New Testament message. Mark's Gospel was composed before A.D. 70 and the first major Jewish revolt that triggered Rome's destruction of Herod's Temple and the annihilation of nearly all rebel factions. Matthew, as one of the chosen twelve and an eyewitness to the ministry of Jesus, would hardly have needed to draw on the testimony of Mark. He could have easily provided the authentic primary source material for a highly personal narrative. Thus, this account of the life of Jesus was likely composed by a scribe-like person who was probably a Jewish convert in Matthew's congregation. Thus, he developed his composition a generation after the crucifixion. His primary purpose was to answer questions that had arisen in the minds of fellow converts to the faith. We cannot be certain today about the place of his parish, but the most likely location is Antioch of Syria. This late first-century church was likely centered in a sizeable metropolis with a diverse ethnic culture. The author was steeped in Hebrew language and culture, but he wrote in the predominant tongue of a cosmopolitan culture of that era—Greek. About thirty years after the composition of this narrative, Ignatius was Bishop of Antioch. This highly influential Episcopal leader of the emerging church wrote affirmative references to this gospel in his own messages to churches within his administrative responsibility.

Whereas many specifics about the parish in which this gospel was composed are uncertain, we can be confident that the writer answered many relevant existential questions through this six-segment narrative interlaced with five sets of Jesus' teachings. The congregation wanted to know how this new faith in Jesus the Messiah of

Israel fit in with the traditions of Jewish heritage and the faith backgrounds of the Antioch congregation's converts. They wanted to know if they must discard their Jewish customs and ancient legacies. How were they to conduct their lives and be faithful to Judaism's festivals and rituals? What was to be their relationship with the powerful and well-established synagogue in Antioch? Who was Jesus, what did he teach, and what were the primary events in his life? By what authority did he teach, heal, and conduct his ministry?

The setting of the Beatitudes, therefore, addresses this issue of authority. The young peasant teacher from the nearby village of Nazareth ascended the Galilean hillside much as Moses had received the Decalogue at Mount Sinai. The writer of this catechismal curriculum wanted to make it clear that someone greater than Moses had now arrived. Jesus began his teachings, therefore, in the fashion of a pious peasant-Cynic profoundly influenced by the Hebrew wisdom tradition. The Beatitudes are eight paradoxical statements (or nine if the foci of the final blessing are separated) that appear to be contrary to reality or common sense, overtly turning worldly values upside down. This was the preamble to the first of Jesus' five blocks of teachings in Matthew's catechism. Even though Christian tradition has tagged chapters 5 through 7 as the Sermon on the Mount, this accumulation of teachings is really not a sermon. In all likelihood, this collection of oral traditions is a compilation of remembered sayings and ethical reflections that were first articulated by Jesus in the nearby village of Capernaum, where he conducted a school of discipleship from the home of Peter's mother-in-law. This village was a placid fishing community that could probably be glimpsed from the Galilean mountaintop upon which the crowd had gathered to hear the young revolutionary teacher.

It is important to note the nature of his audience: "When Jesus saw the crowds, he went up the mountain; and after he sat down, his disciples came to him."[1] The author's implication here is that Jesus offered his instructions primarily for the immediate benefit of his closest disciples, who had already left their jobs and families to follow him. But these instructions were also *overheard* by a larger assembly of the curious.

Not all of Jesus' carefully selected apostles had emerged from poverty in order to follow this itinerate rabbi. Four of the twelve were sons of fishermen, holding a position of distinction and security within a successful merchant class. Even Matthew the Apostle was wealthy before leaving his position of collaboration with the Roman tax office. But the multitude from Galilean farms and villages constituted the poorest of the poor at the bottom of Rome's economic pyramid. Galilean culture, according to biblical scholar John P. Meier, contained a vague middle group that differed greatly from the contemporary American middle class. This middle group was made up of village craftsmen and farmers who possessed fair-sized plots of land. Such small farmers led a precarious life due to the vagaries of weather, grasping rulers like Herod Antipas, and heavy taxation (both civil and religious). Further down the ladder were hired

---

1. Matt 5:1 NRSV.

servants, traveling craftsmen, and dispossessed farmers. At the bottom of the pyramid were the many slaves who did much of the labor on large agricultural estates.[2] Thus, the great majority of those who heard the paradoxical Beatitudes would have lived in abject poverty. These were the *anawim*—a Hebrew reference to the poor who were literally crushed by their condition, those who suffered from hunger and cried out to heaven for release from their misery.

The New Moses sat down, as was the custom for a rabbi engaged in teaching. The standing throng eagerly awaited his first utterance, for his appearance suggested an aura of authority. Analogous to the cornerstone assertion of Mosaic law—the *Shema*, "Hear, O Israel: The Lord is our God, the Lord alone"[3]—Jesus' opening blessing captures the essence of all the other Beatitudes and provided a fitting preamble to this entire set of teachings. This initial blessing was a liberating message to a subjugated class of Galilean people among an already enslaved nation, a crowd of hopeless, hungry outcasts of a despised race at the bottom of Caesar's pyramid of oppression. The first paradoxical assertion was, therefore, astounding: "Blessed are the poor in spirit, for theirs is the kingdom of heaven."[4] The new kingdom that is now coming into reality with the advent of Jesus exists for the purpose of liberating the radically poor. On that day, Jesus made eye contact with a crowd of the *anawim* that felt the pain of their intense poverty and political hopelessness. This first and primary blessing was not a spiritualized pronouncement that disregarded the economic reality of these oppressed ones. Jesus had not risen above the condition of his audience. He was one of them. He did not pull rank when he addressed the *anawim*. He smelled the stench of their unwashed bodies and soiled garments. They came to the mountaintop with bleeding sores from relentless toil and the cruel lashes of their taskmasters. These who heard the opening chord of his first symphony of teachings suffered from cruel oppression.

They and their ancestors had perhaps climbed to the summit of this same stony peak on several previous occasions, for these Galilean people had been hungry for hope over numerous generations. They had listened to earlier teachers, self-proclaimed prophets, and pseudo-Messiahs who had articulated defiant messages of liberation through violent revolution. These mountains in Galilee had provided cover for many militant terrorists desperate to disrupt the *Pax Romana*. This was familiar turf for the *Sicarii*—literally the "dagger holders," assassins who terrorized fellow Hebrews thought to be collaborators with the Roman hegemony. Roman military might had brutally crushed the first Jewish rebellion shortly after the composition of Matthew's text, and the second revolt was routed in the early second century when a militaristic messiah named Bar Kokhba and his spiritual proponent, Rabbi Akiba, were executed in A.D. 135. Many among the *anawim* were hoping that this Man of Nazareth was another militant revolutionary. But on this day, Jesus' audience heard a startling message

---

2. Meier, *Marginal Jew*, 282.
3. Deut 6:4 NRSV.
4. Matt 5:3 NRSV.

The Blessing of Misfortune

that neutralized their passion for revenge and their desire to establish a restored Jewish state.

Jesus began his ministry upon this mountain by blessing the poor in spirit as if his listeners were already living in the reality of a Hebrew Jubilee. The advent of Jesus has ushered in the beginning of a new, hopeful economic and political reality. In the Kingdom of God Jesus was initiating, these destitute people would experience the fullness of God's blessing. Their descendants would experience liberation from oppression. The poverty of the cross, not a revolution wrought by violence, would be the means for accomplishing this liberation.[5]

Dietrich Bonhoeffer, surrounded by the evils of Nazi despotism, warned in 1937 that "the Antichrist also calls the poor blessed, but not for the sake of the cross, which embraces all poverty and transforms it into a source of blessing. He fights the cross with political and sociological ideology."[6] Jesus did not bless the *anawim* in order to dismiss the least of these, or to disregard the severity of their pain, or to make of them implements of his political power. Unless one acknowledges the authority of the speaker, this initial Beatitude is a nonsensical, whimsical utterance by a delusionary fool. Matthew's Gospel boldly presents Jesus as the embodiment of God's being and the fulfillment of Israel's messianic promise. His eyes penetrated the hopelessness felt by impoverished Galileans. He alone perceived the coming future that was set into motion on that day as he spoke upon the mountain. The kingdom had arrived with his first utterance on this Galilean hillside: "Blessed *are* . . ." The series of eight blessings are stated in the present tense! Those whom Jesus blessed were joyful now, for in the eyes of Jesus, they began to see an arriving future. In that moment, through these ethical instructions, Jesus was bringing into being a new community of people who would bear one another's burdens and sacrificially share their meager financial resources in order that all could have the assurance of daily bread and a faith family. Thus, the source of their present joy was not that the *anowin* would live easy lives in a happy world, or that things would inevitably get better every day, or that a heavenly reward would be waiting for them after their miserable deaths. Their happiness arrived in the moment of Jesus' proclamation of the Beatitudes because the multitude of potential followers saw within him a prolepsis[7] of God's coming kingdom—a *shalom* reality, the

---

5. Jas H. Charlesworth offers insights into the early church's referral to its identity among the poor. Jesus may have had some acquaintance with the community of Essenes at Qumran. "It is apparent that the Essenes referred to themselves as 'the Poor in spirit' and 'the Poor.' The terms signified that they had renounced all worldly possessions and dreams so that they might be members of God's lot, and the remnant of God's chosen elect. The Qumran community—and no other group, according to our extant sources—used 'the poor' as a technical term to refer to itself . . . It is conceivable; therefore, that Jesus could have been positively influenced by the Essenes' dedication. Perhaps the first Beatitude originally meant something like the following: 'Blessed are you Poor—who like the Essenes live only for God—for you already possess God's Kingdom'" (Charlesworth, *Jesus within Judaism*, 70).

6. Bonhoeffer, *Cost of Discipleship*, 120–21.

7. Webster's Dictionary defines "prolepsis" [Greek, *pro*, "before" + *lambunein*, "to take"] as the description of "an event that takes place before it could have done so" or "the treating of a future event

promised Jubilee Year,[8] and the promise of an everlasting mercy and restitution for all of Israel.

This contextual understanding of the first Beatitude is essential, for it is the source of fervor and vitality in early Christian worship and the sustaining power for the mission and social action agenda within the community of disciples that Jesus formed and has sustained through the ages. Thomas G. Long, in reference to the Beatitudes, has asserted that "if God's promise of the kingdom of heaven is an empty promise, then a life of seeking justice and showing mercy is a fool's illusion."[9] This blessing of the first Beatitude foreshadows all the ethical teachings that follow in Jesus' Sermon on the Mount.

The paradoxical blessings of the Beatitudes are not impractical depictions of an impossible, irrelevant ethic. Jesus intended the new community of his followers to be formed in accordance with these behavioral expectations and thus become the people of the Beatitudes. Stanley Hauerwas shares this understanding of the ethical teachings of Matthew's Gospel: "What cannot be forgotten is that the one who preaches the sermon is the Son of God, that is, he is the Messiah, making all things new. The sermon is the reality of the new age made possible in time."[10]

It is little wonder that, in the initial stages of the twenty-first century, the church of Jesus Christ is growing at a pace comparable to the population growth across the continent of Africa, in many portions of Latin America, among the numerous islands of the Pacific, and within the People's Republic of China. In Europe and North America, the church has become too affluent and alienated from the lives of the poor in spirit. We have lost sight of the eschatological character of Jesus' proclamation and have largely disregarded his paradoxical teachings, applying them only to some ethereal, heavenly reality and overlooking their power to transform the history of humanity. But Jürgen Moltmann argues that the gospel message is a conversion to the future. When God's people begin to act in the present as if the future has already arrived, human history is radically transformed. Moltmann argues that "the church loses its fellowship with the messianic mission of Jesus if it is not 'the people of the Beatitudes' and does not consist of the poor, the mourners, the meek, those who hunger for righteousness, the pure in heart and the persecuted."[11] In reality, the Beatitudes were not addressed to individuals but to the new community that Jesus portended through the gathering of his disciples and expanded by preaching to the multitudes of the poor that assembled upon the mountaintop. No one can live the ethics of the sermon alone. But one can grow toward a life of holy habits that reflect the spirit of all that Jesus

---

as if it had already happened" (*Webster's New Twentieth Century Dictionary of the English Language: Unabridged*, 2nd ed., s.v. "prolepsis," 1,439).

8. See Lev 25:8–17; 25:23–55, 27:16–25; Num 37:4 NRSV.
9. Long, *Matthew*, 48.
10. Hauerwas, *Matthew*, 60.
11. Moltmann, *Church in the Power*, 81.

taught. This can only happen with a faith community's support through corporate worship, prayer, encouragement, and accountability. We are invited to become a part of "the people of the Beatitudes" gathered around the life and teachings of Jesus. As Hauerwas asserts, "The Sermon [on the Mount], therefore, is not a list of requirements, but rather a description of the life of a people gathered by and around Jesus. To be saved is to be so gathered. That is why the Beatitudes are the interpretive key to the whole sermon—precisely because they are not recommendations."[12]

Every church I have pastored has been, in part, an aggregate of the poor, the grieving, the meek, those who hunger and thirst in pursuit of righteousness, the merciful, the peacemakers, and some despised and persecuted. These worshippers serve among the affluent, the arrogant, and the honored whose suffering is primarily vicarious. Perhaps none fit all eight facets of the Beatitudinal blessings, but collectively, this is the posture of the paradoxical church. We are blessed through the eternal *kairotic now*[13] of corporate worship. We are acquainted with the vicarious pain and collective joy of our mission. The "people of the Beatitudes" touch the poor with empathy. They comfort those in grief, feed the hungry, dig wells of hope for the thirsty, advocate on behalf of the persecuted and powerless, and join ranks with the peacemakers.

The salty tears of the church contain power because Jesus announced the coming of a reality in which there will be no more cause for sorrow. We mourn now with Jesus' blessing. We experience paradoxical joy because our eyes have seen the ending. As a result of the life of the One who spoke the Beatitudes, we now know that history is moving toward Christ and not a chaotic, senseless future. We weep at the sight of Syrian tanks destroying homes and the lives of civilians in the cities of Idlib and Homs. We anguish upon watching video evidence of malicious machetes slicing the flesh of children soldiers in Uganda at the cruel orders of Joseph Kony. But we envision the time already initiated by Jesus in which these atrocities will have ended.

---

12. Hauerwas, *Matthew*, 61.

13. From the Greek word *Kairós*. This specific reference in the language of the New Testament points to "the appointed time in the purpose of God" (Richardson and Bowden, *The Westminster Dictionary of Christian Theology*, s.v. "kairos," 316). A *kairotic* moment is a time of fulfillment. Paul Tillich used the word to refer to times of crisis or turning points in history that demand specific existential decisions while the opportunity is still present. The advent of Christ was the unique example for the early church of such a *kairotic* moment. See Alan Richardson's article in *The Westminster Dictionary of Christian Theology*, 316. Jürgen Moltmann further illuminates the term in the Gifford Lectures, explaining its origin in Hebraic theology: "Israel was familiar first of all with the *kairological* understanding of time. Concepts about an endless, linear, temporal continuum, and ideas about time in the absolute sense, were alien to her. On the contrary, every happening had 'its own time.' There is seedtime, and the time of harvest; the time to give birth, and the time to die (Eccl 3:1–8). Every event has its particular moment in time, and this moment in time is the event's own, proper setting . . . That is why Israel talked about 'times' in the plural. She was not conscious of time as unity, because she did not see world events as homogeneous. Time is determined by happening, not happening by time. The time of the event is the appropriate, the favorable time—the only time in which it can take place . . . It is God's covenant with his creation, conferred once and for all, which establishes the times of created being" (Moltmann, *God in Creation*, 118–19).

We envision a time when the meek will inherit the real estate on this earth, not because the meek within the church are greedy for plunder and revenge, but because we believe in the triumph of God's grace and Jesus' affinity with the meek. Those within the church community who engage in missions of mercy experience these blessings. A man who completed a year of guiding a class of Disciple Bible students in a local prison told me that he intends to continue in this ministry for the rest of his life. He confessed that he had never felt such joy and liberation in his spiritual life until he began this didactic ministry among prisoners.

I have often witnessed the solemn resolve among the lives of Stephen Ministers who bring mercy and empathy through active listening to care-receivers, one person at a time. As Thomas G. Long reminds us, "True mercy grows not out of intrinsic human goodness, but from the grateful awareness that God is merciful; those who discern that God is merciful are freed themselves to be merciful."[14]

The "people of the Beatitudes"—the people of Jesus' paradoxical blessings—are affirmed without seeking either affirmation or reward. They trust in the authority of the author of the Beatitudes, the Man of Nazareth who embodied the paradoxical nature of God. They remember that not even Moses could approach divine presence to view the face of God. The Galilean peasants who gathered on this mountaintop long ago understood that divine Being is mysterious, remote, and transcendent. But they suddenly perceived the face of God in the countenance of Jesus. They saw absolute purity within the person of Jesus. Then they heard him utter the astonishing words, "Blessed are the pure in heart, for they shall see God."[15] Joy came to the "people of the Beatitudes," for happiness is Jesus' gift to all who grow toward a life shaped by the ethics and spirit of this Galilean teacher. He empowers us to grow toward purity of heart and perfection in love through supportive communities of faith and the assurance of his grace.

Wright Spears is an integral member of the congregation I now attend in retirement. I encounter him attending regular worship services each Sunday. He vigorously participates in the instructional fellowship activities of the faith community on Wednesday evenings. For over thirty-five years, Dr. Spears served as President of Columbia College in South Carolina, bringing about early racial integration and pioneering social reforms. At the time of this writing, he is in the midst of his hundredth year. During all of his decades of faithfulness, he has been a prophetic, persistent peacemaker. In recent years, he has helped initiate an annual Lake Junaluska Peace Conference that brings together hundreds of participants from the congregation, surrounding communities, and across the nation. All these interreligious events have been keenly focused upon the essential role of faith communities in the task of peacemaking. Participants have included Leymah Gbowee of Liberia, a recent recipient of the Nobel Peace Award, and attendees from peace-advocacy agencies like Common

14. Long, *Matthew*, 49.
15. Matt 5:8 NRSV.

Cause, Bread for the World, and Amnesty International. I have rarely encountered a person more humble, affirming of others, and self-sacrificial than Dr. Spears. He is an embodiment of the Beatitudes because he is constantly being shaped by the habits of an authentic faith community—the paradoxical church, the "people of the Beatitudes," blessed through participation in the suffering love of Jesus.

We need not believe and teach, as did John Calvin, that those who possess earthly real estate through greed and disregard for the poor will lose it in God's judicial punishment. We are, however, drawn to the arresting authority Jesus' gracious teaching, as was Bonhoeffer, who witnessed the unmerciful confiscation of property by Nazi violence but still insisted that "when the kingdom of heaven descends, the face of the earth will be renewed, and it will belong to the flock of Jesus."[16]

Why am I so emphatic that the Beatitudes' affirmations be applied to the here and now of human history, instead of being reserved for rewards in heaven? Jesus constantly taught his disciples that God had not forsaken the earth. He instructed his followers to pray daily, "Your kingdom come, your will be done, on earth as it is in heaven." God created the earth and all its inhabitants, sending his son to build his church upon it. The powerless have an ample share in the Kingdom of God because these have an integral place within the life of the church of Jesus Christ—its restorative fellowship, its generous offerings, its supportive family of faith, and its shelter amidst persecution. Thus, when the church authentically becomes the "people of the Beatitudes," the meek are blessed during their life on earth with a joy that the world can neither give nor take away. They are both *recipients of* and *participants in* the loving ministries of an authentic, Christ-centered church.

Perhaps the paradoxical Beatitudes have been pushed to the periphery by the church in North America and Europe because we have made so many compromises with the powers of this world that we are no longer a persecuted people centered upon the ethics and example of Christ. We have become an aggregate of chameleon congregations, ready to classify Jesus' blessings as tentative suggestions or irrelevant platitudes relegated to some ethereal, heavenly reality.

The Montagnard people of Vietnam have lived under oppressive Communist domination since Ho Chi Minh drove the French from colonial rule at the battle of Dien Bien Phu in 1954. These suffering people merely traded taskmasters in this violent revolution. Many of mountain people of Vietnam had accepted the Christian message and practiced a pure, disciplined ethic in a culture that did not tolerate religious expression. They were terrorized and tortured by their new taskmasters. When the US military engaged in a futile attempt to liberate this land from its repressive government, many of these Christian converts collaborated with the American military. After the Marines departed the region in 1973, villages were burned and Montagnard Christians were imprisoned, tortured, and murdered.

---

16. Bonhoeffer, *Cost of Discipleship*, 123.

Part II: Paradox and Christology

For several years I provided administrative guidance for a colony of Montagnard refugees who had responded to the hospitality of Covenant United Methodist Church in Charlotte. Approximately twenty-five newly baptized Montagnard refugees attended an annual business session in which the church's mission is reported and celebrated, concluding with Eucharistic worship. During the business session, the pastor introduced a middle-aged man who had spent seventeen years in the mountainous jungles of Vietnam as a fugitive from tyrannical military officials who sought to imprison him or take his life. He hid in caves and slept in clearings with his wife and three children. The Communist authorities were in constant pursuit. Finally, they were able to escape to the safety of a refugee camp in Thailand. Only he was able to secure a visa to the United States. He labored at a minimum wage position in Charlotte for several years. The pastor of Covenant UMC and leaders of the congregation advocated on his behalf and provided church sponsorship for his family's immigration. On the week of the Charge Conference, his family had finally arrived to be reunited with their joyous husband and father. Each family member was introduced that evening to the ovation of an emotionally charged congregation. When the Montagnard families knelt around the sanctuary's altar-table at the Eucharist celebration, they lifted their eyes to behold a large, elevated cross. They held high their outstretched hands like beggars and received the Bread of Life from their district superintendent host. That night, a grateful and awe-filled congregation experienced the spiritual presence of Christ when these weathered, amber-skinned refugees knelt at that sacred altar and saw within the Eucharistic symbols the very face of God.

12

The Resilient Power of Failure

FAILURE EVENTUALLY VISITS EACH of us. One of the saddest moments to cross the contemporary stage is the requiem scene from Arthur Miller's *Death of a Salesman*. Willy Lowman has failed as a businessman, a father, and a husband. Biff, his cynical son, offers a cursory epitaph as he reflects upon his father's devastating suicide, "He had the wrong dreams. He never knew who he was," while Willy's other son, Charley, offers this far more sensitive observation: "Willy was a salesman. And for a salesman, there is no rock bottom to the life . . . He's a man way out there in the blue, riding on a smile and a shoeshine."[1] Poor Willy Lowman's dreams were entirely quixotic. He never made the fortuitous sale or climbed the ladder of success as an entrepreneur. Linda, his patient and perplexed wife, speaks one of the most haunting lines in modern American drama when she stands center stage and laments, "I can't understand it, Willy. I made the last payment on the house today. Today, dear. And there'll be nobody home."[2]

Failure is a word we try to strip from our vocabulary. It has no place in a society that only acknowledges winners. We want to be identified with leaders who have made it to the top, teams that win the Super Bowl, charismatic religious leaders who rescue us from a life of meaningless despair, and a religious movement that assures us of a happy and successful ending. We are drawn toward self-help, pop-psychology solutions to life's enigmas and scriptural aphorisms that dissolve doubt, resolve theological ambiguities, guarantee winning outcomes, and abolish troubling paradoxes.

But can everyone be a winner? Where is the gospel message for poor Willy Lowman, his distraught family, and the many that experience his burdensome plight? Moreover, is the authentic goal of the Christian pilgrimage a life of incremental success? If the vocation of each disciple of Jesus is to follow his example, should we

---

1. Miller, *Death of a Salesman*, 138.
2. Ibid., 139.

Part II: Paradox and Christology

anticipate the assurance of a profitable, triumphant outcome? Back in 1897, Charles Sheldon published *In His Steps*, a fictional book now among the world's bestselling titles. The main character is the Reverend Henry Maxwell, pastor of First Church in the town of Raymond, who challenges his congregation not to do anything for a whole year without first asking, "What would Jesus do?" Perhaps the plot and theme of this popular Christian classic is a bit naive or antiquated, but in order to be faithful in the formidable task of following Jesus, one must be attentive to the narrative of the Master's life.

In order to follow in his steps, we shall need to immerse ourselves into the pattern and activity of his life. In this chapter we shall, therefore, examine the exemplary life of Jesus through the fascinating lens of Luke. We shall discover in the Jesus of the Third Gospel the prototype for our success, the model for life's management, and the power of personality we can imitate along our road toward successful achievement of our goals. We may be surprised, however, to discover that the writer discloses the serendipitous nature of success through the events of Jesus' life. A careful reading of our Master's life demonstrates that the path to ultimate success requires failure. The route to fulfillment leads us through abandonment and rejection. Success in the Christian pilgrimage is paradoxical, as is especially clear in the narrative of the Third Gospel. Consequently, Luke does not begin his biography of Jesus with a tender nativity narrative. The congregation that first heard this intriguing account of the life of Jesus was introduced to the controversial figure of John of the Wilderness. All within Luke's initial congregation would have been acutely aware that this kinsman of Jesus was a loser in the history of failed Hebrew prophets. After all, Herod Antipas had cruelly beheaded this outspoken critic of his personal life, and many of Luke's Christian converts would have known his tragic fate. But Luke insisted that John the Baptizer was not only the last of the prophets, but also the greatest of all Hebrew prophets—more important than Isaiah, Jeremiah, or even Elijah. Luke, then, held a radically different view of this seeming loser. He records that a messenger from God revealed to a frightened priest named Zechariah that his barren wife, Elizabeth, would conceive in her old age. The messenger insisted that the child must be named John—a name meaning "God shows favor." The birth of this child was indeed a heralded event, "for he will be great in the sight of the Lord."[3] Luke's careful wording communicated encouragement to a congregation of marginal, persecuted people who suffered for their belief in the Messiahship of Christ. Here in the opening stanza of his written witness, Luke names John the Baptizer—a failed revolutionary—as the most important of all Hebrew prophets because he was of maximum importance "in the sight of the Lord." For only God has the perception to see success in failure, greatness within extinguished hope, and triumph amidst acts of injustice and defeat.

When the divine messenger told a peasant teenager of Nazareth named Mary that she would bear a son after the Holy Spirit came upon her, he then revealed that

---

3. Luke 1:14 NRSV.

her child would be the very Son of God, "for nothing will be impossible with God."[4] Thus, a peasant child and offspring of a lowly Jewish girl would be the one who "will [bring] down the powerful from their thrones, and [lift] up the lowly, [fill] the hungry with good things, and [send] the rich away empty."[5] Mary's language, as conveyed by Luke, is subtly coercive and politically explosive. Jesus' young mother is shown to be neither meek nor mild. The revolution about to be ushered in by the son of a Palestinian peasant teen is paradoxical because it would be achieved by one whose ministry would end in an agonizing death and abandonment by his closest allies. Luke discloses the fate of the Messiah even in his enchanting depiction of the humble birth in a cave within Joseph's ancestral village of Bethlehem. When the righteous man Simeon came into the Jerusalem Temple upon the occasion of the circumcision of Jesus, he frankly told the child's young mother, "This child is destined for the falling and the rising of many in Israel, and to be a sign that will be opposed so that the inner thoughts of many will be revealed . . . and a sword will pierce your own soul too."[6]

Luke's congregation was obviously asking, "Will the incarnation of God's being actually experience failure through an ignominious death? How can a true Messiah experience a futile mission? Moreover, shall we followers of his Way experience similar disappointments and unfulfilled hopes if we imitate Jesus' way of life and remain obedient to his teachings?"

Luke's answer to these festering objections was his subtle depiction of a paradoxical figure whose very failure was the seed of a resilient hope. When Jesus articulated his mission by reading the words of Isaiah in his hometown synagogue, the initial response was approval. These poor men from an obscure, isolated, and economically deprived village were ready to welcome the proclamation of any good news, the merciful release of relatives from a Roman prison, the recovery of sight among the blind of the village, or the arrival of the elusive Levitical promise of a Jubilee Year.[7] But their moods suddenly shifted to rigid opposition when their hometown hero began to apply this gospel of liberation to Gentiles, even the pagans in nearby Sidon and Syria. These pious men were acquainted with Jesus' family, but they were so enraged by his inclusive interpretation of sacred Scripture that they threatened to murder him by tossing him down a steep cliff just outside this tiny village.

When Jesus subsequently departed into the wilderness in preparation for his ministry, he was tempted to worship the Evil One in trade for political authority over the kingdoms of the earth. Since there was, in reality, only one political king (the Roman Caesar), Jesus was being offered the option of replacing Emperor Tiberius. Such power would come at an enormous price, for according to the theological perspective of Luke, the suffering servant Messiah would have to abandon his tactics and scuttle

4. Luke 1:37 NRSV.
5. Luke 1: 52–53 NRSV.
6. Luke 2:34–35 NRSV.
7. See Luke 4:18–19 and Lev 25:10–12 NRSV.

his mission. In the wilderness of temptation Jesus decided to remain the paradoxical prophet who would achieve God's purpose through his failure. In Luke's interpretation of history, the only force dominant enough to topple tyranny is a servant Messiah who reflects the mystery and paradox of God's forgiving love. Only the paradoxical figure of majestic failure could redeem human history from its destruction.

This paradoxical message was at the core of the teachings of the itinerate rabbi of Galilee. In his Sermon on the Plain, he blessed the poor and hungry while warning the rich and healthy fed that they faced an inevitable ruin. He taught that only those who loved their enemies would succeed in abolishing their adversaries. Only in failure would the righteous poor and powerless attain the power of an ultimate victory. Jesus insisted that authentic prophets never appear as expected. When asked about the reliability of the message of his kinsman, John of the Wilderness, he reminded the curious that they should not have anticipated seeing in that remote, arid place "someone dressed in soft robes."[8] While John was the last and primary Hebrew prophet, the least inhabitant in the coming Kingdom of God would be greater than he.[9]

In the agenda of this world, financial resources define one's value. But Jesus' humble movement was clandestinely financed by female followers, including Joanna, the wife of Herod's steward Chuza.[10] The austerity of his ministry was intentional. When Jesus assembled his disciples in Galilee, he warned them, "Foxes have holes, and birds of the air have nests; but the Son of Man has nowhere to lay his head."[11] Thus, when Jesus organized his evangelical campaign in the Galilee region, he instructed the seventy to travel light. They were certainly not told to dress for success. Jesus cautioned that they were being sent as lambs amidst wolves. Thus, Luke's narrative was as much an instructional manual for his struggling, persecuted congregation as it was a record of the historical Jesus' evangelical mandate. Followers of the Way were instructed to "carry no purse, no bag, no sandals."[12] One did not join the Jesus movement in the initial years of the church's existence to win success, social status, or acclaim. Thus, Luke preserved the oral tradition of Jesus' admonition, "For those who want to save their life will lose it, and those who lose their life for my sake will save it."[13] Thus, the writer of the Third Gospel succinctly and systematically articulated the language of paradox that characterized the content and form of Jesus' ministry.

This is why he treated little children with such dignity and honor. In their innocence and total dependence upon others, children are models for this paradoxical life. Thus, when his disciples argued among themselves about who was the most significant in the movement, Jesus placed by his side in a place of prominence a little

---

8. Luke 7:25 NRSV.
9. See Luke 7:28 NRSV.
10. See Luke 8:3 NRSV.
11. Luke 8:58 NRSV.
12. Luke 10:4 NRSV.
13. Luke 9:24 NRSV.

child and asserted, "Whoever welcomes this child in my name welcomes me, and whoever welcomes me welcomes the one who sent me; for the least among all of you is the greatest."[14]

In a culture of greed, bigger is better. Whether one is a farmer in first-century Galilee or a contemporary executive at Enron or Lehman Brothers, expansion is the name of the game. The paradoxical prophet of Nazareth provided an insightful parable about a successful farmer who was set upon expanding his agricultural inventory by tearing down his old barns and building new, more elaborate ones. But the voice of God shattered his self-absorbed dream of inevitable achievement: "You fool! This very night your life is being demanded of you. And the things you have prepared, whose will they be? So it is with those who store up treasures for themselves but are not rich toward God."[15]

Luke was providing both an insightful record of Jesus' paradoxical teaching as well as nurturing a generous sacrificial community of new disciples eager to be agents for transformation in the world. The Jesus of Luke's narrative succeeds by his failure. He refused to be defined by others. He embodied the divine purpose and never strayed from his God-defined mission. In so doing, he possessed God's peace. By giving his life away, he achieved perfect security. Although Jesus attracted some adherents that were materially blessed, he did not want their lingering guilt but instead welcomed their amended spirit of sacrifice and self-giving. "From everyone to whom much has been given, much will be required; and from the one to whom much has been entrusted, even more will be demanded."[16] In the new community initiated by Jesus' raising from the dead as the crucified servant of Nazareth, disciples are drawn to the paradoxical pattern of their Lord and the instructions that he exemplified: "When you are invited [to a banquet], go and sit down at the lowest place, so that when your host comes, he may say to you, 'Friend, move up higher'; then you will be honored in the presence of all who sit at the table with you."[17] In the Kingdom of God, the mathematics that monitors achievement is a radically new *modus operandi* articulated by a resolute prophet who had no pillow to lay his head upon: "Indeed, some are last who will be first, and some are first who will be last."[18]

In the Kingdom of God, priorities and price tags are reversed. The criteria for achieving a durable success are redefined. A poor beggar named Lazareth is transported by angels to the abundant banquet table of father Abraham. The rich man, during his time in the land of the living, had only shared small scraps of food that had fallen from his table with sore-infested Lazareth. In the afterlife, he became a pitiful, tortured man in Hades, crying to God for mercy. The Abraham of Jesus' parable

14. Luke 9:48 NRSV.
15. Luke 12:20–21 NRSV.
16. Luke 12:48 NRSV.
17. Luke 14:10 NRSV.
18. Luke 13:30 NRSV.

reminds the wealthy, callous man that he had received an abundance of good things during his lifetime and had been regarded as successful and prosperous. Lazarus had been treated as a loser. But the roles were ultimately reversed: "But now [Lazarus] is comforted here, and you are in agony."[19]

Luke portrays a Jesus who personified all that he taught. On that final, fateful week, Jesus orchestrated a demonstration by mounting a diminutive colt instead of a horse worthy of an aggressive military leader. The Messiah that entered the East Gate of Jerusalem at the beginning of Passover was vulnerable and doomed to failure. After all, the parade of palms began in Bethany—a village of Judah's poor. During the defining moment of his final meal with the apostles, a foolish dispute arose among them over their visions of grandeur for the new political administration they assumed to be imminent in the successful political ascendancy of Jesus. Each apostle jockeyed for the primary position. But Jesus rebuked all of them with this admonition: "the greatest among you must become like the youngest, and the leader like one who serves. For who is greater, the one who is at the table or the one who serves? Is it not the one at the table? But I am among you as one who serves."[20]

The crucifixion was the ultimate paradoxical event. The mission announced at his hometown synagogue was blatantly unfulfilled. This Passover celebration in Jerusalem was not a Jubilee moment in which the ideals of a godly Kingdom mysteriously became a reality. Before that fateful evening had ended, the drama of Luke's narrative moves to Gethsemane, a clandestine arrest, and a mock trial. All the apostles had tucked tail and run for their own security. Peter, the most dependable of the lot, denied even knowing Jesus of Nazareth. Only a few humble women from Galilee stood at a distance to witness the horrendous events at Golgotha—Jerusalem's garbage dump. They alone among the many followers from Galilee remained near the cross. A member of the Sanhedrin named Joseph from the nearby village of Arimathea provided a burial cave. He was a secret admirer of Jesus. These courageous women, who had witnessed the incomparable humiliation of Jesus' crucifixion, came to the tomb where his body had been laid out. It was the first day of the week. They came to administer spices and ointments in their grief. They came in a state of unmitigated despair. They came in dismal hopelessness. They approached the tomb of their fallen leader fearfully. They came in devotion to a man who had embodied all the attributes of the Hebrew God in whom they trusted. They came despite the obvious evidence that their beloved hero had been a failure. They came because they loved him, believed in his teachings, and trusted in a God whose ways they did not understand. They came not because they wanted to be identified with a winning cause. The stories of their lives were accounts of recurring defeat. They came as fragile losers desperately longing for the daylight of an elusive hope. They came, by the grace of God, on the day the world would be changed forever.

19. Luke 16:25 NRSV.
20. Luke 22:26–27 NRSV.

Luke's resurrection narrative contains the unique record of the risen Christ's appearance to disciples in an obscure village called Emmaus. Luke alone tells the story of the ascension of the risen Christ. According to his theology, the Lord would no longer remain on earth in visible form, for he sent his Holy Spirit to reside in the community of his disciples. The new community was given the power to transform the world. But the ascension of the crucified God occurred not in Jerusalem or even some Mosaic-like mountain in Galilee, but at Bethany—the village of poor losers. He ascended while surrounded by all those loser-disciples who would soon begin the process of transforming the world by the power of a paradoxical God.

Our minds and hearts are, therefore, confronted with the paradox of success. It is difficult for those who have always been winners to hear this dynamic biblical interpretation of reality. Those "masters of the universe" described so vividly by novelist Tom Wolfe in *The Bonfire of the Vanities*[21] grow deaf to this paradoxical message of warning within Scripture. They consider a religion for losers offensive. Yet all of us will ultimately taste the bitterness of failure, like the pilgrim in Morris West's novel who confesses that "the juices which feed his dreaming had dried up."[22] Sooner or later we become thirsty for the wondrous word that speaks the whole biblical message: God has made his abode among us. In so doing, the Crucified God who is acquainted with our grief and has experienced our failures has also accomplished his ultimate triumph for all of us. The magnificent defeat of the cross is our victory. The wounds of our failure are healed by the One who staggered on broken feet out of a borrowed tomb on resurrection morning, "bearing on his body the proud insignia of the defeat which is victory."[23]

Martin Buber was a revered Jewish seer whose voice has spoken profoundly to our contemporary plight. He revived an old Hasidic tale about an angel who wanted to alleviate all human suffering. This angel had observed that an inordinate amount of pain and sickness had swept the earth. He rebelled against the God who had allowed such death and deprivation. The angel confronted God and begged that the entire administration of the earth be placed in his hands for a year's time. The angelic bands trembled at such audacity. But then the heavens grew bright with the radiance of God's smile. The angel, feeling the approval of God, began to rule the earth and, consequently, brought forth a year of joy and sweetness for every living creature. The groans of the sick and dying were quieted. There was bounty and prosperity for everyone. Then on one cold winter's day there was a cry of anguish from earth. The angel, disguised as a pilgrim, rushed down to see what possibly could be the matter. There he found that there was plenty of bread for all, but the loaves were unpalatable. They were like clay in the stomach. People were lying everywhere in agony, cursing God for sending a false blessing. The angel immediately flew to the Almighty and collapsed at

---

21. Wolfe, *Bonfire of the Vanities*, 73.
22. West, *Summer of the Red Wolf*, 2.
23. Buechner, *Magnificent Defeat*, 18.

Part II: Paradox and Christology

God's feet. He begged to know where his power had failed and why he was unable to effect a lasting transformation of the world. God answered with a truth too deep for the angel, saying, "the earth must be nourished with decay and covered with shadows that its seeds may bring forth—and it is this, that souls must be made fertile with flood and sorrow, that through them the Great Work may be born."[24]

This Hasidic parable is indeed close to the theology of the New Testament. The cross of Christ holds together the great paradox of victory through defeat and success out of failure. Jesus' blood is the present seed of our future success. His broken body is bread for our pilgrimage toward victory. The cross' shadow is the source of our light in the despair of our present plight. Upon the cross hung a preacher who had no reliable followers. All his disciples had fled. Only traumatized and faithful women remained. His mission ended outside the gates of Jerusalem in failure. But God the Redeemer, who through Jesus has fully entered the pain of human failure, has guaranteed the successful fulfillment of the Kingdom of his beloved son. The Eucharistic bread we eat is our foretaste of God's victory banquet. Through the joy of faithful discipleship, we proleptically participate in the ultimate success of our Lord. The God of the crucified One has, therefore, not called us to be successful, but to be faithful. The main purpose of God's invitation to us is to drive us from our absorption into the importance of our own success and to draw us unto him. When we are so absorbed into God's love through faithfulness, we receive a righteousness and joyful liberation we would otherwise be helpless to achieve. We are granted a success that offers glory to God alone. This is the paradox of Christian discipleship: Those who accomplish nothing more than faithfulness to God are truly the transformers of history. It is they who are most likely to profess, "It was not I, but the grace of God that was within me." Such success is achieved in the words of Tennyson, as "men rise on stepping-stones / Of their dead selves to higher things."[25]

This chapter has focused on the Third Gospel's account of Jesus' life in order to provide biblical evidence for a paradoxical understanding of success. We are, consequently, invited by the message of Luke's Gospel to look back over our personal pilgrimage of faith and remember painful failures. Perhaps we have worked hard toward the goal of reconciliation in a marriage, yet our covenant of matrimony has ended in failure. Perhaps we have labored arduously for peace, but war continues unabated. We may have given an incalculable amount of time toward the nurture of children and instruction of youth within a congregation, but our efforts may not show in their behavior. We may have even flung ourselves into some program of authentic Christian evangelism, communicating the gospel message of hope to those in sullen despair. Yet the harvest continues to be barren. Failure faces many of us in the mirror. Our path is cluttered with decaying dreams like brown winter leaves in the path of our faith pilgrimage. Many of us have served Christ faithfully through the servant ministries of

---

24. Buber, *Tales of Angels, Spirits and Demons*, 11, quoted in Palmer, *Active Life*, 81.
25. Tennyson, "In Memoriam A. H. H.," 242, lines 3–4.

mainline denominations and witnessed the evaporation of membership and financial resources. But it is imperative to remember our Lord's promise that our labors are never in vain. Parker Palmer has wisely asserted that "failure is life's ballast."[26] We can float on our bloated egos, thinking that our efforts may save the world, or at least a small corner of it. But compassion begins when we realize that it is not our work that brings about earth's transformation; it is not our goodness that truly redeems. Yet we can still affirm the dignity of failing in a worthy cause. We can confidently embrace the grace that meets us in our failures. As Palmer reminds us, "The paradox is that failure may turn to growth, while success can turn to self-satisfaction and closure."[27] Our failures, therefore, enable us to trust more radically in the providential grace of God. When we are down for the count and depleted of all our resources, we may lift up our heads. Our redemption truly draws near!

---

26. Palmer, *Active Life*, 87.
27. Ibid., 89.

13

Christ as Servant Leader

OVER A FIVE-DAY PERIOD in 1997, the world grieved the deaths of arguably the two most admired and famous women on earth. One was a statuesque princess. She defined fashion and style throughout the Western world. The other was short and bent by an osteoporosis stoop. She wore a white and blue servant's sari as her diminutive form leaned over the dying bodies of Calcutta's starving. The lovely princess lived a life of ironic contradiction: a caring mother, a coquettish symbol of royal promiscuity, a considerate public servant who championed altruistic causes, a self-indulgent celebrity with a flamboyant lifestyle. The lady of Calcutta, in contrast, was consistent and disciplined. But the world was in love with both of these women whose contrasting legacies had already achieved mythical proportions. The iconic Princess of Wales was known as "the people's princess." The aged, wrinkled nun, originally from Albania, was being called a saint years before her death in September of that year. Her baptismal name, Agnes Gonxha Bojaxhiu, had long been forgotten. The world knew this eighty-seven-year-old servant to the outcasts of India simply as "Mother Teresa."

Daniel Schorr of National Public Radio, always laconic, gave this penetrating assessment of these legendary women: "There is a difference between a noble life well-lived and a media image of a nobility well-cultivated."[1] If we were given the task of choosing our top-ten list of people who have most indelibly influenced our lives, we would likely select only those individuals who fit such a description: either a noble life lived lowly or a lowly life lived nobly.

Jesus is the prototype for authentic leadership. Even intellectual skeptics and cynical enemies of the church admit that Jesus of Nazareth has had an incomparable impact upon human history. He is the primary model of a lowly life lived nobly. His life defies the commonly accepted assumption that leadership is contingent upon financial power, political prowess, and military might. Many subscribe to the Machiavellian

---

1. Schorr, Daniel, *National Public Radio*, 88.5 WFDD, Greensboro, NC, September 5, 1997.

view of leadership: In order to be a successful leader, one must adhere to political realism. Deceit, despotism, and political manipulation have all been accepted tactics of successful post-Renaissance leaders. When *Time* magazine recently announced their choice of the one hundred most influential people from around the world for 2012, the magazine did not primarily choose the lives of lowly persons living nobly. The theme of the *Time* gala's keynote address delivered by Hillary Clinton, who was then US Secretary of State, focused upon a new paradigm for American power "that must be earned by each successive generation."[2] Pop culture seems to define leadership through the shallow philosophy of a Donald Trump reality television program. The words "servant leadership" have become an anathema in the evaluation of many modern Machiavellians and contemporary realists.

But the gospel narratives consistently depict Jesus as a paradoxical leader who pursued a life of costly service. None of the stories about Jesus contradict this quintessential image. He taught his disciples to follow a path toward sacrifice and self-surrender rather than power and self-aggrandizement. He modeled his teachings with every moment of his existence as a humble servant of God. There is no more profound example of Jesus as a servant leader, however, than the one we discover in the thirteenth chapter of John's Gospel. This is the fulcrum story in the Fourth Gospel. Theologian C. H. Dodd called the twelve chapters preceding this narrative "The Book of Signs." Jesus performs seven symbolic acts that point to the reality of his Messiahship. He predicts his passion and cruel death. But this pericope describes a pivotal event immediately preceding John's account of Jesus' arrest and crucifixion. Chapters 13 through 21 of the Fourth Gospel are consequently known among most scholars of Scripture as "The Book of His Glory," for Jesus is glorified through his subservient obedience to suffering and death.

In John's Gospel, this Thursday evening supper was a pre-Passover meal. Jerusalem was somewhat like the contemporary city of Mecca celebrating a joyous Eid al-Adha at the end of Ramadan. The metropolis of the Jewish Temple was flush with thousands of excited pilgrims from faraway places. Reservations were tight. Jesus, as host, planned the evening in advance and was extravagant in providing accommodations for his disciples. According to the Evangelist's account, this was no Spartan meal. The twelve were generously fed as they reclined around a sumptuous pallet, talking profusely. They were filled with anxiety over the political implications of Jesus' presence in Jerusalem amidst throngs of faithful followers from Galilee. These common farmers and fisherfolk were suddenly thrust into an environment of urban sophistication ruled by Roman military authorities. Passover week would become a defining moment, and the disciples knew it. They wondered which of them Jesus would choose to help execute his political revolution and lead the expectant Jewish multitudes. They were especially confused that night because Judas was seated at the place of honor, sharing with Jesus a dish containing a Passover delicacy. He was likely from Karioth

---

2. Stengel, "*Time* Gala," 3.

and thus the only disciple from Judea. Perhaps his accent and apparel set him apart from the others and prompted their jealous worries. Was he the one Jesus loved and trusted most? Peter, who had jockeyed for first place in the entourage, was miffed by the seating arrangement. He reclined at the far end of the pallet, stewing in angry resentment.

Then Jesus did an astonishing thing at this pre-Passover, Eucharistic meal. He "got up from the table, took off his outer robe, and tied a towel around himself. Then he poured water into a basin and began to wash the disciples' feet and to wipe them with the towel that was tied around him."[3] This was a shocking move. Leaders did not act like slaves. The washing of men's feet was a job relegated to wretched women slaves—the people lowest on the social pyramid. No self-respecting male would stoop to such an indignity. The room grew silent. The festive atmosphere of pre-Passover vanished. The twelve were horrified, then embarrassed. Judas, who had hoped Jesus would become the leader of militant Zealots and ignite a violent revolution against Roman authorities, was confirmed in his suspicion that this man lacked the grit of a real revolutionary leader. At last, Jesus reached the end of the pallet, where Peter reclined. The indignant fisherman said, "You will never wish my feet."[4] At this point, Jesus realized that none of the twelve had understood his mission. So he replied to a stubborn, imprudent Peter, "Unless I wash you, you have no share with me."[5]

Perhaps John the Evangelist was invoking another baptismal symbol in telling the story of the foot washing. But I suspect that much more is at stake here. I surmise that Jesus was here modeling the form of leadership he expected of Peter and his other disciples. I contend that our Master was demonstrating servant leadership for the entire church. Thus, he explained his actions by saying, "If I, your Lord and Teacher, have washed your feet, you also ought to wash one another's feet. For I have set you an example, that you also should do as I have done to you."[6]

Back in 1927, *Time* magazine was launched as a popular newsweekly and initiated the tradition of choosing a Man of the Year to be revealed on its final December cover. If the publication's founder, Henry Luce, had been let loose in the first century, surely he would have chosen among the obvious candidates for universal recognition: Herod the Great, the unrivaled builder; Caesar Tiberius, whose autocratic power sustained a *Pax Romana* through the oppressive violence of his conquering army; or Titus, Vespasian's clever son who suppressed the first Jewish revolt by pulverizing the Jerusalem Temple and sending the Hebrew masses into permanent exile. These were the movers and shakers of history slightly before the writing of the Fourth Gospel. Surely a first- or early second-century Roman version of *Time* would have features one of these powerful luminaries.

3. John 13:4–5 NRSV.
4. John 13:8a NRSV.
5. John 13:8b NRSV.
6. John 13:14–15 NRSV.

Christ as Servant Leader

On a bookshelf in the missionary home of my friend Gordy Graner in Cochabamba, Bolivia, I spied a book of essays by Robert Greenleaf titled *The Servant as Leader*. I soon learned that Greenleaf's philosophy had profoundly influenced my missionary friend. That Sunday afternoon I perused the thoughts of the author, a senior executive of AT&T. In his retirement, Greenleaf began analyzing the decades he had spent in corporate management. To his horror, he came to the realization that industrial America had devolved into a dehumanized, competitive structure based upon intimidation and abuse of power. Leadership had become an art of manipulation. Greenleaf came to see that he had been a part of a violent industrial era that was now dying stubbornly and painfully. Until his death in 1990, Greenleaf championed the concept of "servant leadership."[7] In 1982, he joined with a creative and visionary Episcopal bishop, Bennett Sims, to form the Institute for Servant Leadership. The model for the leadership style he fostered was the Man of Nazareth who picked up the towel and washbasin in that Jerusalem dining room. Bishop Sims insists that success in business must be measured in terms of serving the greater good: "Winning becomes the creation of community through collaboration, rather than the conquest of others by competition."[8]

Who have been the movers and shakers of history in our own era? Howard Hughes, J. Paul Getty, Aristotle Onassis, and Rupert Murdock have been among the richest and most powerful leaders in the previous century. Ghandi and Mother Teresa were among the poorest and least powerful. Which American president actually accomplished more for the cause of freedom than a vulnerable preacher in Montgomery, Alabama, named King? Will history honor President P. W. Botha of South Africa or his most famous political prisoner, Nelson Mandela?

The Man of Nazareth with the washbasin is history's prototype for effective leadership. But since the Renaissance, the Western world has endorsed a Machiavellian *modus operandi*. Now, at the close of the industrial age and the rise of the informational era, surely our children deserve a more compassionate, promising future. After all, the twentieth century was arguably the most violent in the history of humanity. A future filled with hope must be forged by the church modeling servanthood for a culture that is longing for a more perfect way. When Jesus washed the feet of his disciples, he was telling them that costly service and self-giving is the identity of God. The One with the washbasin embodied God. Jesus, the quintessential servant leader, provides us with a vision for a new, hope-filled future aligned with his coming Kingdom.

William D. Cohan's *House of Cards: A Tale of Hubris and Wretched Excess on Wall Street* is one of the most thorough and insightful accounts of this economic catastrophe of 2007 and 2008.[9] The author tells one story after another about how titans of finance allowed greed and arrogance to bring about a global economic calamity in

---

7. Greenleaf, *Servant as Leader*, 1.
8. Sims, *Servanthood*, 13.
9. Cohan, *House of Cards*, 269–450.

Part II: Paradox and Christology

2007 and 2008. The current political gridlock in Washington related to entitlements, deficit spending, increased military funding, and resistance to tax increases for the rich is a relevant agenda for theological analysis. When economic priorities are established in the context of servanthood principles, budgets (personal, corporate, or governmental) are radically altered. Thomas Mann and Norman Ornstein's volume on how the American constitutional system has been diverted by political extremism has convinced many of us that *It's Even Worse Than It Looks*.

Senator Mark Hatfield is a devout American Baptist who gained political power early in his career as the youngest governor in Oregon's history. When he won his senatorial seat, he came to Washington, DC, full of political idealism. But he quickly learned that he had little power to change much of anything. He was often the only senator to vote in opposition to funding the war in Vietnam. In his reflective, confessional book titled *Between a Rock and a Hard Place*, Hatfield observes that he came to the realization that "service to others, solely for their own behalf and even entailing deep sacrifice, is the true essence of leadership and the ultimate form of power. There is a power in servanthood which transcends all notions of power sought after so avidly in the secular political sphere of life."[10] Even though Hatfield sought to model servant leadership in Washington, he marshaled few proponents of this profound paradoxical concept among his congressional colleagues. Still today, the only way out of the misery caused by the politics of systemic greed is to follow the leadership of the One who said, "Whoever wishes to become great among you must be your servant, and whoever wishes to be first among you must be slave of all."[11]

Efrain Agosto, Director of Hispanic Ministries at Hartford Seminary, contends that following Jesus always requires a radically different form of leadership. Agosto insists:

> The key to the leadership of Jesus was that he carried out his mission in direct contrast to the established leadership of his day . . . Therefore, anytime Christians ask themselves what kind of religious leadership they want, especially in times of crisis, like those faced now in the aftermath of September 11, 2001, a Christological question needs to be asked: Who is attending to the poor and oppressed? What in our actions and policies is creating more or less justice, or injustice? . . . To invoke the name of God and not call for justice to the neglected masses is to shortchange a Christological definition of leadership.[12]

Through my years of pastoral ministry I have had the privilege of learning about leadership from many humble practitioners of Christ-like servanthood—from laity who have transformed communities by their compassionate acts of self-giving and

---

10. Hatfield, *Between a Rock*, 26.
11. Mark 10:44 NRSV.
12. Agosto, *Servant Leadership*, 200.

Christ as Servant Leader

pastors who never enter the limelight but "live by the grace of daily obligation."[13] These have been lowly servants leading a noble life.

The pastor's role is to model servant leadership in the administration, mission, and worship experiences of the church. No one can be a pastoral servant apart from the encouragement and accountability of a congregation and pastoral colleagues. A servant leader of a parish flock will especially need the inspiration of colleagues who have demonstrated years of costly, sacrificial service. Servant leadership is not merely a theological concept or ideal; it is a practical reality that has sustained the church of Jesus Christ throughout the centuries.

Among the several model leaders that have shaped the posture of my pastoral role is Gordon Cosby, the founding pastor of the Church of the Saviour in Washington, DC. I first learned of him through teachings within my hometown church during my college years, which introduced me to Elizabeth O'Connor's classic chronicling the story of Gordon Cosby's ministry, *Call to Commitment*. Throughout the formative years of my theological education, I was inspired and instructed by Rev. Cosby's exemplary servant leadership. The mission groups within a tiny parish in our nation's capitol had a profound impact upon the identity and evolving faithfulness of my hometown congregation. I shall not use these pages to enumerate the many of servant ministries that Cosby's leadership launched in impoverished neighborhoods in Washington. They have been described extensively by O'Connor, who served as the parish's theological interpreter and scribe through her several volumes: *Journey Inward, Journey Outward, The Eighth Day of Creation, The New Community, Search for Silence, Our Many Selves*, and other titles. Fully a half-century before Reggie McNeal's writings and avant-garde articulations, the Church of the Saviour was a "missional renaissance"[14] congregation.

Upon my first visit to Dayspring, the Church of the Saviour's retreat center in a rustic forest setting in rural Maryland, Gordon told us that no community would ever be transformed by well-intended socio-economic ministries apart from the spiritual empowerment of a worshipping faith community. Later in the week, we encountered Gordon in an abandoned rental housing unit in the so-called "riot corridor" of the city's poorest and most dangerous neighborhood. One of the church's mission groups had purchased the apartments to transform them into affordable housing. Gordon, hard at work, climbed down from a ladder, paintbrush in hand, to greet his guests from North Carolina.

At the close of 2008, this iconic pastor retired at ninety-one. During his sixty years of servant leadership, he had never controlled or manipulated his flock. He was the facilitator of an extraordinary array of effective ministries that brought hope, harmony, and healing in neighborhoods of neglect in our nation's capitol. One mission group found jobs for over eight hundred people during the last year of Gordon's official

---

13. Godwin, *Father Melancholy's Daughter*, 209.
14. McNeal, *Missional Renaissance*, 24.

Part II: Paradox and Christology

pastorate. Another provided 325 units of affordable housing. This small community of resolute disciples had launched Columbia Road Health Services, Christ House medical clinic for the homeless, and Miriam's House for women living with HIV/AIDS. The list of spiritually nurturing ministries fostered by this congregation to touch the lives of "the least of these" in Washington is astonishing! Moreover, in every parish to which I have been appointed, there is visible evidence of Gordon Cosby's influence in the faith-based activism his teachings and example have inspired. Schools of Christian Discipleship akin to the didactic program of the Church of the Saviour are at the core of effective ecumenical urban ministry centers in Greensboro and Charlotte—cities where I pastored for over a quarter of a century.

On March 20, 2013, Gordon died at the age of ninety-five. His legacy remains invisible to the broader society, for he was an authentic biblical prophet who never sought public adoration. He consistently irritated political leaders in Washington who ignored their responsibility for the poor and powerless. He authentically lived a lowly life nobly and inspired a legion of servant leaders throughout the world.

Within each of the seven parishes to which I was appointed as a pastor, I consistently discovered a cadre of authentic servant leaders. For several weeks each year, Harold Pitts of Greensboro wore a pair of sneakers draped over his neck by their shoelaces to acquaint people with the challenges of the annual CROP Walk—a ministry of Church World Service addressing the issue of global and local hunger. He was so respected as one who consistently practiced his faith that he motivated the city to become a national leader for this crucial humanitarian concern. Harold's coworkers told me how this modest, ethically-principled man's presence at corporate meetings ended the use of racist and sexist language. No one questioned the moral authority of his leadership in the business world or at church. After Harold returned from an exploratory mission trip to Bolivia, he instigated his congregation's thirty-year involvement with the Methodist Church mission center, Thiu Rancho, in Cochabama. The congregation helped construct a building to house its multi-faceted education program for local farmers and a spiritual life retreat center for religious leaders throughout the region.

I was privileged to serve on the Board of Trustees of Pfeiffer University upon the occasion of an historic trustee retreat and weekend of vision-casting for a more focused future. After analyzing carefully the heritage and core values of this United Methodist-related institution, the trustees crafted this vision statement: "Pfeiffer University will be recognized as the model church-related institution preparing servant leaders for lifelong learning."[15] The entire curriculum of the school was henceforth directed toward this vision. Community and church service became an integral part

---

15. This vision statement was developed through the efforts of a planning retreat held at Appalachian State University in November 1999, at which time a strategic planning effort redefined Pfeiffer University's vision and clearly defined its strengths, weaknesses, and core values. See Pfeiffer University, "The Pfeiffer Initiative: The Strategic Plan for the Future of Pfeiffer University," brochure, 2000.

of the student experience, and young adults began to choose this university precisely for the purpose of pursuing vocations in medicine, business, teaching, ministry, and other avenues toward a life of service. The University recruited a new dean and faculty members for their expertise in this philosophy. Even with the departure of Dr. Charles Ambrose, the university's visionary president and administrative guide to the formation of this clarity of purpose, the school continues to produce new generations of authentic servant leaders at a crucial time in our nation's history.

It is difficult to erase a first impression. Thus, the initial service of worship can be a daunting task for a pastor preparing liturgy and sermon. When that moment came in my final pastorate, I preached a sermon based on John's pivotal thirteenth chapter in an effort to challenge the congregation to amplify and mature its identity as a servant community in accordance with John's description of the Son of God with towel and washbasin. At the sermon's conclusion, I proceeded to wash the feet of a child, an elderly woman, and a chosen leader of the laity. Months later, a gifted layman and sculptor (with whom we shall become better acquainted in chapter 29) crafted in clay the scene of Jesus washing the feet of Peter. This sculpture was mounted for display at the atrium entrance of this urban church. It gradually became an acknowledged symbol of what that congregation is and aspires to become.

14

Emptied to Be Filled

WEBSTER'S UNABRIDGED DICTIONARY DEFINES *kenosis*, an Anglicized derivation from Greek *kenos*, as "an emptying," alluding to Philippians 2:7 in noting that this word is used in theology to refer to "Jesus humbling Himself by taking on the form of man."[1] Perhaps the most scandalous proposition among the major religions of the world is orthodox Christianity's unique assertion that the omnipotent Creator who presides over the universe emptied God's self of all power, taking human form to become a Galilean peasant identified as Jesus of Nazareth. This theological belief is the ultimate paradox. The humble servant who experienced death upon a Roman cross emptied himself of power and thus refused to rescue himself from this horrific fate. He forfeited his opportunity to establish a dominion of fairness, refused to destroy his cruel torturers, and rejected Messianic authority to liberate the besieged sons and daughters of his Abrahamic heritage. Moreover, this amazing paradoxical doctrine of *kenosis* claims that fulfillment within the lives of Jesus' disciples is contingent upon the faith community's willingness to follow the pattern of emptying one's self of prominence, power, or position. A disciple is filled by emptying, empowered by the disposal of power, satisfied by self-denial, blessed through humiliation, and elevated through descent.

Kenosis was not a sophisticated doctrine developed by a persecuted church after several decades of theological reflection amidst the humiliating era of tyrannical Roman rule. To the contrary, this affirmation was clearly articulated long before any of the gospels had been written, perhaps even prior to the conversion of the Apostle Paul, and certainly before the composition of his early epistles such as his First Letter to the Thessalonians. This familiar, poetic assertion was the central theme of a Christological hymn that Paul inserted into a letter he wrote to the house church in Philippi while he

---

1. *Webster's New Twentieth Century Dictionary of the English Language: Unabridged*, 2nd ed., s.v. "kenosis."

awaited release from prison. Canticles and hymns that were already part of rituals of worship in the house churches of an emerging Christian movement in Galilee made their way into texts that were eventually canonized during later decades. John of Patmos inserted early apocalyptic hymns that envisioned the joy of the coming Kingdom into his coded messages to the congregations in Asia Minor.[2] The melodic canticles of Luke's infancy narratives had an earlier origin within the poetry of praise sung within house churches of the early first century in celebration of the incarnation. Even the Johannine Prologue was a poetic oracle used in worship as a Christian Midrash, or reflection upon the Genesis narrative in light of the coming of the Messiah. But clearly the magnetic rhythms and memorable poetry of Philippians 2:6–11, according to renowned New Testament scholar Raymond Brown, constitute "a prepauline hymn that the Philippians knew and that Paul may have taught them at the time of his first visit."[3] Professor Brown, furthermore, finds it plausible that the original composition of this hymn was not in Greek, but in Aramaic, the dialect of Jesus' first disciples.

The hymn makes no effort to answer some of the following Christological issues in a systematic or comprehensible fashion. If Jesus was in the form (*morphe*) of God, is this the same as being equal to God? Thus, was Jesus the uncreated Creator, or does this hymn suggest that Jesus was the creation of the Father-God? Was he "begotten" but not "made" by the father? Does this hymn suggest that the historical being, Jesus, was in the image and likeness of God as a second Adam, as in the Genesis 1:27 assertion that "God created Adam in His image"? If so, does this imply that Jesus was not equal to God, but only similar to God? Does the hymn imply that Jesus was equal to God, but chose not to cling to that position of ultimate power and authority? Or was he offered the possibility of becoming equal to God (as was Adam) and declined the offer, as suggested by the Synoptic witness concerning three episodes of temptation in the wilderness? The language of the simple hymn remains paradoxical rather than doctrinal and systematic. This captivating hymn is an early Church expression of the poetry of paradox and mystery. Its beauty defies rational analysis, but its message has edified Christian worship through the centuries.

This hymn was likely part of the oral tradition of house churches in Galilee and Judea as early as the 30s of the first century. Even though its original language was likely Aramaic, and although it was sung by disciples in house churches long before the sophisticated incarnational theology of the Johannine Prologue penned several decades later, the hymn offers the highest expression of New Testament Christology. From the very origins of Christian community, a paradoxical Christology was upon the tongues of joyous disciples in acts of worship. This magnificent poetry of earliest Christian praise contrasts the Adam of Genesis (who was made in the image of God but ambitiously tried to rise higher) with the historical Jesus (who was made in the image of God but chose to go lower). This primitive hymn affirms that God ultimately

2. See Rev 4:8; 4:10–11; 5:9 NRSV.
3. Brown, *Introduction to the New Testament*, 491.

Part II: Paradox and Christology

exalts the One who emptied himself. Without answering all the complexities implied by this assertion, the hymn celebrates a paradoxical mystery. This renowned hymn announces to the world that the authentic nature of God is uniquely revealed through a lowly servant who emptied himself in order that the world might be filled by the lavish love of a compassionate, forgiving Creator.

What enabled Jesus to be the fulfillment of God's salvation for the cosmos was that YHWH's Spirit (Hebrew: *ruach*, Greek: *pneuma*) dwelt fully within him. This Spirit was the energy behind all his mighty works. This was the same *ruach* that brought about the original creation. This creative energy was given to Jesus at his baptism and the launch of his public ministry. Through this energy of creation, Jesus announced the true beginning of the Kingdom of God and its transformation of the world. This same Spirit led Jesus into the wilderness of temptation immediately following his baptism. According to Matthew and Luke' testimonies, the Tempter assailed Jesus' Sonship/Messiahship by saying, "If you are the Son of God, command . . ."[4] In a triad of temptations, Jesus was enticed to grasp the magical power to turn stone into bread, leap from the Temple and not be harmed, and worship the Tempter in exchange for unlimited political power. The Spirit that led him into this wilderness of temptation provided him with the courage to drain him of all these implements of power, to deny himself, and to remain faithful to the divine vision for his existence. Because Jesus was filled with the Holy Spirit (*ruach*), he was intent upon emptying himself in complete obedience to a more perfect way—the paradoxical path to the cross. His strength was made perfect in his weakness. The story of the temptations is the gospel's prelude to crucifixion. The power of Jesus was manifested in acts of self-giving. Thus, he healed the sick and fed the multitudes. Even legions of the Roman army and the intimidation of an inhuman execution were powerless to obstruct the movement toward fulfillment within God's coming Kingdom that Jesus' life inspired and his resurrection made inevitable. His self-emptying life was the prolepsis of existence within God's anticipated future.

We have seen how the early church celebrated the paradox of the *kenosis* of Christ through a victorious hymn. Jürgen Moltmann suggests that the empowerment to lead a self-emptying way of life was God's great gift to his son. At the moment of his baptism, Jesus received a *kenosis* of the Spirit, for Moltmann maintains that "if we talk about a 'condescending' of the Spirit, we have also to talk about *kenosis of the Holy Spirit*, which emptied itself and descended from the eternity of God, taking up its dwelling in this vulnerable and mortal human being Jesus. The Spirit does indeed fill Jesus with authority and healing power, but it does not make him a superman; it participates in his weakness, his suffering, and his death on the cross."[5]

Within the house churches in Galilee where the original Christological hymn was first sung by the tiny community of followers Paul founded in Philippi, or even

---

4. Matt 4:3b; Luke 4:3b NRSV.
5. Moltmann, *Way of Jesus Christ*, 93, emphasis Moltmann's.

within elaborate Gothic cathedrals of the modern era, there is not the innate strength of will to live the *kenotic* life of Christ. Apart from God's gift of "a *kenosis* of the Holy Spirit," all aspiring disciples fail to be authentic followers of his way, but through this gift, all followers of the Way may discover an incomparable joy through acts of self-emptying. We find that the more we give away God's love, the more we have. Its source is infinite. The more we forgive others, and especially our enemies, the more we receive the forgiveness of a merciful God. The more inclusive our love becomes, widening the door of hospitality and grace to our persecutors and enemies, the more complete will be our quality of *koinonía*—the fellowship of self-giving love within the Church. Without the gift of "a *kenosis* of the Holy Spirit," the church grasps for power, wealth, stately buildings, entitlements for professional clergy, and prestigious places among the institutions of influence and political dominance. The more the church clings to these implements of self-preservation, the more rapidly it dies. This is the paradox of *kenosis* revealed in the life of the Man of Nazareth, who emptied himself in order that we may be filled with a new quality of existence. Garnishing the things of this world cannot fill human emptiness. The artificial powers of this world cannot procure fulfillment. But God's gift of "a *kenosis* of the Holy Spirit" can truly satiate human hungers and fill human emptiness.

To its detriment and demise, the church of Jesus Christ has resisted taking the form of *kenosis*. Sören Kierkegaard, that Danish gadfly of the church during the nineteenth century, provided a parable that suggested that the church of that era had attempted to reduce the story of Christ's passion into an innocuous, Docetic fairy tale. Through efforts of pastors and theologians to make the Christian message blend with cultural norms, the church pretended that the real Jesus story was something like a child's tale about a handsome prince who disguises himself to dwell among common people. Thus, according to Kierkegaard's analogy, the converted were like the unsuspecting young maiden who falls in love with the prince, thinking that he too is a pauper. In this fairy tale version of the gospel, converts are taught like children that the prince (Christ) has come in order to take us to the heavenly castle where we shall live happily ever after. This misunderstanding of Christian faith has little to do with this world of flagrant injustices. Under this warped gospel message, the task of faith is not to transform the world or address the injustices of an apathetic culture. Kierkegaard chided the complacent church of Europe for this appalling distortion. He insisted that the historical Jesus truly emptied himself of all power and authority. He died on the cross and experienced the radical abandonment of God, crying from the cross the words of desertion—the initial words of Psalm 22 in Aramaic. As with the theology of the Psalter's poetry of lament, Jesus died trusting in the ultimate triumph of God's mercy and the prevailing ascendency of divine grace. In the moment of death, Jesus experienced radical abandonment, assuming that his mission had ended in failure but still believing that God's coming Kingdom would prevail despite his futile efforts. The paradoxical context of the good news within the gospel's Passion Narrative is that the prince (Christ) has forever forsaken his regal identity. The *kenosis* of his Spirit dwells now amidst the hovels of city slums, the anguish of oppressed masses, and cries of diseased or emaciated human bodies. The church's mission is to take the form (*morphe*) of a servant, emptying itself of station or status and following the lead of a *kenotic* Spirit. Consistently, the four Gospels demonstrate that the prince has suffered, is suffering, and will suffer for the sins of the world. The Son of God has refused to pull rank on us, for as Kierkegaard concludes his sobering parable, "this is the unfathomable nature of love, that it desires equality with the beloved, not in jest merely, but in earnest and truth."[6]

The church of any era is powerless to exert the courage and trust required to lead a self-emptying existence unless it is endowed with the gift of a *kenosis* of the Spirit. Surely Saint Athanasius comprehended this when he argued against the heresy of Arius by asserting, "He, indeed, assumed humanity that we might become God. He manifested Himself by means of a body in order that we might perceive the Mind of the unseen Father."[7] Only as we receive God's gift of the Holy Spirit can any of Christ's followers be empowered to lead the paradoxical life of *kenosis*, but this luminous level of living is available to all. Moreover, it is the only hope for a world bent upon self-destruction through self-aggrandizement, greed, and violence. This "*kenosis* of the Holy Spirit" is the sacred self-emptying that guides humanity's progression toward history's fulfillment.

Revitalization within the church occurs when spiritual leaders and communities of faith discover the joy of a *kenotic* life. When the church of the thirteenth century needed a renewed impetus in its spiritual vitality and integrity in its mission to the poor, along came Francis, the son of a wealthy merchant in the Italian town of Assisi. A converted Francis took literally his pilgrimage of imitating Christ and conducting his affairs in accordance with the Sermon on the Mount. He and his entourage of monks gave their possessions to the poor. When he experienced a vision of Jesus telling him "to rebuild my church," he journeyed to the dilapidated remains of San Damiano and began reconstructing the church stone by stone. He did the same at Rivo Torto and Santo Maria. His generosity with the poor and diseased spread contagiously among his admirers. Small communities of faith-centered servants began to imitate the actions of this man from Assisi. Such cooperatives and communes emerged all over Europe with the formation of a new ecclesiastical order—the Franciscans. The joy of unselfish service began to spread like the spiritual fires of a new Pentecost. Small, unpretentious chapels in villages were filled with parishioners of poverty, assisted through the generous sharing of resources by the wealthy. The rule that governed this movement, in the simple language penned by Saint Francis, was "to live in obedience, in chastity, and without anything of their own and to follow the teachings and the footprints of

---

6. Kierkegaard, *Parables of Kierkegaard*, 44–45.

7. Saint Athanasius, *On the Incarnation* 54:3. See also Catholic Church, *Catechism*, 129; Weigel, *Truth of Catholicism*, 9.

Our Lord Jesus Christ."[8] It is imperative that Christians around the world pray that the newly consecrated Pope Francis, the former Argentine priest born Jorge Mario Bergoglio, will indeed lead modern Catholicism toward a recovery of the *kenotic* spirit of the saint from Assisi from whom he takes his papal name.

The movement that swept England in the eighteenth century and helped evangelize a burgeoning American continent was catapulted into being by a *kenotic* spiritual reformer. The Reverend John Wesley gave away his earthly possessions almost as rapidly as he received them. In a letter to a friend, he dictated the essence of his last will and testament: "If I leave behind me ten pounds (above my debts, and my books, or what may happen to be due on account of them) you and all mankind bear witness against me, that I live and died a thief and a robber."[9]

This same self-emptying spirit defined the ministry of Wesley's best known emissary to the new world—Francis Asbury. This first bishop of an emerging denomination threw himself into the work of evangelism and the administration of churches throughout the thirteen colonies and the expanding American frontier to the effect that he substantially emptied his existence. Vast multitudes in the new nation came to know the gospel largely through the sacrifices of circuit riders and itinerant proclaimers of the salvation message who followed the self-emptying example of Asbury. The first bishop of the Methodist movement rode by horseback over 650 miles per month in order to convene conferences, ordain clergy, establish new congregations, and administer a burgeoning Methodism. He often reported being "tired down with fatigue and labor," but was relentless in proclamation and service.[10] A friend of Asbury remarked toward the end of the bishop's ministry, "It was a living death, a perpetual martyrdom."[11] Because physicians of the early nineteenth century treated fevered patients with bloodletting, Asbury submitted himself to this antiquated medical care to address his pain and fever, as well as the excessive fluid buildup of congestive heart disease. He rode to the smallest of hamlets to spread the good news, traveling by horse about six thousand miles annually and preaching approximately three to five hundred sermons per year.[12] Through Asbury's sacrificial leadership, a generation of self-giving pastors emerged to foster the movement's exponential growth. John Wigger, in a recent biography of Asbury, described these ecclesiastical leaders as "driven men, but their ambition expressed itself as a desire to excel at Christian charity and forbearance."[13] In this frontier period of national expansion, a self-emptying church, with the help of enthusiastic laity and clergy leadership, spread the authentic message of the gospel to found communities of altruism and sacrifice. They fit Reggie McNeal's

8. Robson, *Saint Francis of Assisi*, 64.
9. "A Letter to Walter Churchey," in Wesley, *Works of the Reverend*, 12:419.
10. Wigger, *American Saint*, 223.
11. Ibid., 394.
12. Ibid., 277.
13. Ibid., 261.

Part II: Paradox and Christology

contemporary description of a "missional renaissance people." In an attempt to recover the dynamics of the Franciscan and Wesleyan movements, McNeal insists that "People don't go to church; they are the church. They don't bring people to church; they bring the church to people."[14] A growing evangelical church does not require showy buildings or mammoth budgets, only a willingness to empty itself in order to respond compassionately to human hurt.

The Danish priest, social activist, and professor of pastoral psychology Henri J. M. Nouwen lived just such a life of Christ-centered *kenosis*. He possessed a paradoxical personality, for his profoundly contemplative heart was at odds with his unharnessed energy. About the time he attained authorial fame, he departed from secure academic positions on Ivy League faculties in order to live among peasants in Latin America or communities of celibate monks in a cloister of silence at Genesee. Toward the end of his remarkable life, he had become a famous author and lecturer at Harvard University but was restless once again. He felt called by God to live and serve as chaplain at L'Arche Daybreak Community, a residence for young adults with disabilities. Several of the community's administrators recognized the prophetic nature of his calling and wrote this affirmation of his inimitable choice: "For [Henri] to make the journey of his heart and come to live among us in L'Arche was very prophetic. Our society goes against such choices. People strive to get into universities, to make a name for themselves, to have status and success. He had that, but he chose another way."[15] His more abundant way was to accept his L'Arche assignment to assist Adam Arnett, a twenty-five-year-old man who could not speak or move without help and experienced frequent seizures. Henri assumed the responsibility of waking Adam in the morning, bathing him, preparing his breakfast, brushing his teeth, placing him in his wheelchair, and attending to all his basic physical needs. Soon Henri discovered that in performing these menial duties at Daybreak, he was actually meeting his own greater needs. Perhaps for the first time he discovered his own emptiness—his need to be loved, appreciated, and accepted in a caring environment. He had wisely chosen to leave Harvard's community of competition in order to enter L'Arche as a place of compassion. He unwittingly came to this *kenotic* community as an extremely insecure and fragile person. By emptying himself, he was filled with a life of purpose. He was nurtured by a community of compassion. None of his days at L'Arche were wasted, although his readers were perhaps deprived of his engaging writing.

Through the centuries of church worship, the official lectionaries have designated that the reading of the Philippian hymn in the letter's second chapter be reserved for Passion Sunday. This *kenotic* hymn introduces the theology of Holy Week, the gospel accounts of the last fateful week in the life of our Lord, and his gruesome crucifixion. How appropriate to choose this text to be at central focus for contemplation and inspiration on the most holy of all weeks of the liturgical year! Every disciple enters this

14. McNeal, *Missional Renaissance*, 45.
15. Ford, *Wounded Prophet*, 158.

week with a mandate to adopt the mind of Christ and to become like the One who emptied himself in humble obedience and trust.

Perhaps the world regards self-emptying acts of love as a waste of intellect and human potential. In a real sense, the paradoxical life implied by the mind of Christ is a waste of time in this competitive, achievement-coerced culture. But from the perspective of the church, *kenotic* activity is a form of worship—a royal waste of time[16] and the only source of salvation for a world bent on competitive violence. Perhaps the church's paradoxical message concerning self-emptying love, contained in an ancient hymn of the first century church, offers our only hope for survival and the attainment of authentic peace and fulfillment within the course of human history.

---

16. Dawn, *Royal "Waste" of Time*, 1.

15

The Sacrament of Jesus' Suffering

THE ENIGMA OF HUMAN suffering has perplexed philosophers and theologians of every mode of thought and religious tradition. Every attempt to be systematic and rational concerning a doctrine of God must pass through the theodicy gauntlet.

In *The Blood of the Lamb*, a riveting story of emotional tragedy by Peter DeVries, we enter the pensive pilgrimage of Don Wanderhope, a young man whose intellectual journey has led him away from his austere Calvinistic past with its theological certainties. He has become an agnostic with a tendency to fall in love with troubled women. He meets Rena Baker who is pious, but physically sick. Before the relationship has time to mature, Rena succumbs to disease and dies. Don then meets and marries Greta Wigbaldy, who has kept it a secret from him that she had once given birth to a child out of wedlock and had given the infant up for adoption. Greta develops such feelings of guilt and desperate need for sensitivity from her husband that she commits suicide to end her troubled life. Wanderhope becomes increasingly cynical, confessing that "there seems to be little support in reality for the popular belief that we are mellowed by suffering. Happiness mellows us, not troubles; pleasure, perhaps, even more than happiness."[1] But Don never considers his tragic marriage to have been futile, for it resulted in his most treasured pleasure—an affectionate, adorable daughter named Carol.

But this resilient father's world begins to crumble upon the discovery that his precious daughter has fallen victim to a vicious form of leukemia. On Carol's birthday, the anxious father races eagerly to the hospital for an intimate celebration of her disease's remission. He briefly stops by the hospital's chapel at the shrine to Saint Jude, "Patron of Lost Causes and Hopeless Cases," where he is interrupted by a nurse who reports a serious infection in Carol's lungs.[2] Don rushes to his daughter's side in time

---

1. DeVries, *Blood of the Lamb*, 120.
2. Ibid., 228.

to witness her final moments. Upon leaving Saint Catherine's Hospital in anguish, he remembers that he had departed the chapel in such haste that his daughter's birthday cake remained on a pew. When he retrieves the cake and walks outside onto the steps beneath a crucifix mounted on the central doorway, he impulsively flings the cake at the form of a suffering Jesus. Wanderhope's voice describes the poignant scene:

> Then through scalded eyes I seemed to see the hands free themselves of the nail and move slowly toward the soiled face. Very slowly, very deliberately, with infinite patience, the icing was wiped from the eyes and flung away. I could see it fall in clumps to the porch steps. Then the cheeks were wiped down with the same sense of grave and gentle ritual, with all the kind sobriety of one whose voice could be heard saying, "Suffer the little children to come unto me . . . for of such is the kingdom of heaven."[3]

Novelists, philosophers, theologians, and poets have all addressed the enigma of a God of goodness tolerating and even proliferating the prominence of such a deplorable circumstance as this. But like DeVries, most writers have returned to the biblical figure mounted above the doorway of that hospital in order to probe the mysteries of theodicy. No attempt to address the rational contradictions of the horrendous human suffering tolerated by a God of goodness has exceeded the profundity of the four narratives contained in the canonical Gospels. In this chapter we shall examine separately and collectively the Passion Narratives and their subtle responses to the theodicy dilemma.

The narrative of Mark is the briefest biblical account of Jesus' life, but this initial gospel narrative is essentially the story of Jesus' painful death extended backwards with a cryptic summary of the Man of Nazareth's ministry and teachings. Mark's account of Jesus' excruciating suffering upon the cross casts a shadow over the entire text. The execution of John the Baptist (Mark 1:14) suggests the looming fate of the Galilean teacher who immediately announced that the Kingdom of God had now come near through his arrival and ministry. Even before Mark describes the scene of Jesus' triumphant entry into Jerusalem and the final week of his earthly existence, he records several predictions by Jesus of his imminent passion. The episode with Jesus' disciples in Caesarea Philippi is decisive. Peter, standing amidst cascades of water flowing into the upper Jordan River, impulsively responds to Jesus' inquiry about his identity by asserting that their Galilean rabbi is the promised Jewish Messiah. In nearby grottos were shining statues dedicated to prominent Roman gods. But Jesus responds to his disciple's enthusiastic endorsement of his identity by sternly telling Peter and his followers that "the Son of Man must undergo great suffering, and be rejected by the elders, the chief priests, and the scribes, and be killed."[4] Even considering the glorious account of Jesus' transfiguration in a mysterious moment upon a mountain

---

3. Ibid., 237.
4. Mark 8:31 NRSV.

Part II: Paradox and Christology

and the spiritual endorsement of Moses and Elijah, the Messiah Peter had identified declared that the Son of Man will "go through many sufferings and be treated with contempt."[5] According to Mark, when Jesus sojourned from Galilee into Judea, he rendered a surprising ethical teaching about divorce, shocked his disciples by giving prominence to little children, and challenged the wealthy and possessive pietists by articulating clearly the requirements for receiving eternal life. Sensing the insecurity of his ambitious apostles and their contentious political rivalries, he candidly announced as they neared Jerusalem's walls, "See, we are going up to Jerusalem, and the Son of Man will be handed over to the chief priests and the scribes, and they will condemn him to death."[6] Mark emphasizes that Jesus must travel this road of suffering alone. Gethsemane is symbolic of his radical abandonment by his disciples and the God that had called him to the messianic role. When Jesus was arrested, Mark states that a young man "wearing nothing but a linen cloth" was among the entourage of followers. But, even he fearfully raced away naked in order to avoid a similar horrific fate. It is a reasonable assumption that this mysterious reference is to John Mark, the Evangelist himself, publically confessing his shameful abandonment of the innocent Messiah. This was, likewise, the confession of all who constituted the nascent church for whom Mark penned his Gospel.

Mark's account of the resurrection of the crucified One is amazingly brief in contrast with the author's thorough and specific account of Jesus' passion. The original ending of this initial biography of the Messiah is abrupt and underwhelming, with the female disciples fleeing the empty tomb in terror.[7]

In Matthew, the emphasis is strongly upon Jesus' choice to take upon himself the pain and agony of the crucifixion by fulfilling the Messianic expectations of the Hebrew Scriptures. The Matthean Jesus has the power to avoid the humiliation of the passion. But his power is paradoxically revealed in an exaltation that requires suffering. Matthew insists that Jesus had twelve legions of protective angels at his disposal and could have escaped the torture, but he remained obedient and unwavering in his resolve to redeem the world through submission to suffering.[8]

Luke's two-volume story meets the description of a Passion Narrative extended both backwards and forward into the narrative. The idyllic nativity scene in David's town of Bethlehem is immediately followed by the child's circumcision. The righteous and devout Simeon, after witnessing this Hebrew ritual, looked into Mary's innocent eyes and warned her that "a sword will pierce your soul too."[9] The Third Evangelist's narrative follows the general chronology of Mark; therefore, Jesus consistently predicts his passionate death. Luke, however, provides a literature of martyrdom by which a

5. Mark 9:12 NRSV.
6. Mark 10:33 NRSV.
7. See Mark 16:8 NRSV.
8. See Matt 26:53 NRSV.
9. Luke 2:35a NRSV.

suffering Messiah is necessary for salvation history to reach fulfillment. Discipleship is defined by the follower's willingness to suffer for righteous principles of a coming Kingdom. Thus, Jesus told his unsuspecting, ambitious disciples, "If any want to become my followers, let them deny themselves and take up their cross daily and follow me."[10] It comes as no surprise to the reader of the Third Gospel that Luke's second volume renders a detailed account of the stoning of Stephen, an early church deacon. In his dying moment, the martyr linked his fate with the many faithful descendants of Abraham who were enslaved for four hundred years in Egypt and treated as strangers and foreigners.[11] Thus, for Luke, the suffering of the Son of Man and his followers is a necessary component of the drama of God's salvation and redemption of the world as a result of the sufferings of Jesus on the cross. Choosing to follow Jesus is an invitation to experience both the suffering of persecution and the joy of a spirit-filled life.

The Fourth Gospel, acknowledging that suffering is indeed the plight of all and that sin exacerbates the intensity of human suffering, proclaims in the prologue that the being of God (*logos*) became flesh and abides with us. Moreover, it is through Jesus' particular suffering that "we have seen his glory."[12] The Messiah's exaltation and glorification (central themes of the Johannine narrative) is the result of his suffering for the sins of humanity. Jesus is, consequently, crucified on the day of preparation for the Passover meal. His torture is necessary for human redemption, for he has become the Passover Lamb of God. He does not answer Pilate's mock-interrogation. He even accepts scourging with metal whips that tear his flesh in an even more excruciating death. He was complicit with the divine plan that required the Son of God to suffer so excessively. Thus, when all had been accomplished in these hours of incalculable pain, he announced the completion of God's purpose with a final agonizing utterance, "It is finished."[13] Thus, in the last of the canonical Gospels, Jesus is exalted in his obedience to God's ultimate will requiring his suffering and death. Perhaps the theologians Gerstenberger and Schrage have best captured the Johannine theology of the Christ's passion by observing that "the paradox that the Suffering One is the Son of God is interpreted to mean that his humiliation is at once also exaltation, and his pathway of suffering is a way of victory."[14]

It is little wonder why the early church considered the suffering of Jesus to be sacramental. If we considered Luke to be the first historian of the church, his account of the day of Pentecost reveals that a ritual of remembrance and anticipation began immediately: "Day by day, as they spent much time together in the temple, they broke bread at home and ate their food with glad and generous hearts, praising God and

---

10. Luke 9:23 NRSV.
11. Heb 11:13b NRSV.
12. John 1:14a NRSV.
13. John 19:30 NRSV.
14. Gerstenberger and Schrage, *Suffering*, 171.

having the good will of all the people."[15] The ritual of "breaking of bread" as a remembrance of Jesus' sacrificial suffering became immediately emblematic of the new community. Even though followers of the Way were often misunderstood by a pagan culture that accused them of practicing cannibalistic rituals, the primitive Christian movement was guided by the instructions of the Apostle Paul to the community in Corinth: "The cup of blessing that we bless, is it not a sharing in the blood of Christ? The bread that we break, is it not a sharing in the body of Christ?"[16] From its inception, therefore, the followers of the Way who constituted the nascent church glorified in the suffering of Christ and accepted persecution and sacrificial suffering as their inevitable plight in the path toward glorification. Paul was apparently the first to refer to the ritual within the *agape* meal as "the Lord's Supper." John of Patmos chose a coded phrase to confuse Emperor Nero's Roman agents when he made reference to "the marriage supper of the Lamb."[17] By the second century, the sacred meal had been dubbed "the Eucharist" by Didache, Ignatius, Justin, and Irenaeus. The sacramental ritual of sharing bread and wine as symbols of Christ's suffering and glorification was, consequently, separated from the social fellowship of the agape meal. When communities began to accept the delay of Jesus' *parousía*, the devout moved away from daily observances and reserved the first day of the week to gather to celebrate the risen Lord's victory over the power of sin, suffering, and death.

In the previous chapter, we explored the paradoxical nature of Christ, who experienced fulfillment through self-emptying. In this corollary chapter, I have made the case that Christ's choice of suffering is a paramount theme that casts a long shadow over these four canonical narratives. But both chapters invite the question: Where is the joy and fulfillment in discipleship if following the Way leads to a path of pain? Are not self-protection, survival, and avoidance of suffering human nature? How is the volitional act of self-emptying and acceptance of unjust suffering different from masochism? The way of discipleship appears to be neither natural nor the recommended practice for sound mental health. What aspect of the gospel message prompted the post-Pentecost community of faith to experience such vast increases[18] in the ranks of the saved?

Back in the era of the Vietnam War, when some Christians chose to suffer social rejection and imprisonment rather than participate in the violence of war, the theologian Dorothee Söelle raised questions about the anti-war devout's choice of suffering. She noted the tone of Christian masochism within a deprived faith tradition and warned against embracing its neurotic implications. She cited a prayer by the reformer John Calvin as indicative of a Protestant tradition that borders upon masochism. Calvin's prayer sanctioned severe forms of punishment for the devout,

15. Acts 2:46–47a NRSV.
16. 1 Cor 10:16 NRSV.
17. Rev 19:9 NRSV.
18. See Acts 2:47 NRSV.

saying in his petition, "we are worthy of them and have merited them by our crimes."[19] Söelle delineated three dimensions of suffering: physical, psychological, and social. She insisted that all three forms are present in true suffering, and that when Christians choose the route of voluntary suffering as a means of repenting for their sins, these devout disciples have inadvertently misunderstood the role of Christ's suffering and lost sight of the eschatological vision of the Christian faith. Söelle warns that the explanation that God sends affliction as punishment or that all suffering carries out some exalted purpose of God can be the theological equivalent of masochism. The passion of Christ created a faith community committed to the elimination of cruel and unjust human suffering. Söelle identified a contemporary expression of Calvin's theology of Christian suffering by recounting the hellish life endured by a woman of faith in a Bavarian village who tolerated all three dimension of humiliating torture from a violent husband in order to practice forgiving love. But her restraint failed to alter his abuse. Rather than a demonstration of sacrificial, redemptive suffering, Söelle suggested that this pious woman's actions constituted an expression of neurotic masochism masquerading as exemplary Christian behavior.

For Söelle, the masochism of the pious is a sick theological phenomenon. But the theological companion of such a demented expression of religious piety is belief in a sadistic God. When the wrath of God is one's essential theological motif, the sacrament of Christ's suffering is desecrated indeed! When God is viewed as the Almighty ruler who always acts fairly in sending suffering, one many conclude that all suffering is punishment for human sin. This turns God into a sadist who takes pleasure in human suffering and punishment for the unrighteous. If the torture of Jesus was the intentional will of God for his beloved son, what does that say about the nature of the Creator?

A theology of Christian paradox avoids the ethical dilemmas implied by these questions. When we maintain the orthodox belief of a paradoxical unity within Father, Son, and Holy Spirit, we do not find in the gospel narratives either a sadistic God or a community of masochists brought unknowingly into a bizarre, manic fellowship. On the contrary, the four Evangelists make it clear that where the Son goes, the Father goes as well. God was upon that cross outside the gates of Jerusalem. The pain of the Son was the pain of the Father. The self-emptying of the Son expressed the self-giving of the Creator God. This God accompanied the Son to Golgotha. The forsakenness of Jesus in the opening lines of Psalm 22 expresses the forsakenness of the Father himself in the Creator's abandonment by the creation. Jesus, the Son, does not "suffer" death, for suffering always implies life. But the Father suffers the agony of grief in the Son's death because of his infinite love of the Son. This paradoxical understanding of the passion rejects the notion of a dominating Almighty Father who feels no pain but causes pain in another. The paradox of God's indwelling (Greek: *perichoresis*) and the

---

19. Calvin, "Forms of Prayer for the Church," *Tracts and Treatises on the Doctrine and Worship of the Church*, 2:108, quoted in Söelle, *Suffering*, 9.

inseparability of Father from the Son makes Jesus' suffering sacramental, redemptive, and the ground of human hope.

The God who experienced the fullness of human suffering in Jesus is also the God whose intention is to abolish all human suffering, eliminate the sting of death, and establish a kingdom community of joyous self-giving disciples committed to the realization of this coming reality. The early church clearly avoided practicing a psychosis of masochism and the sickness of belief in a sadistic God. The orthodox church found it imperative to denounce the Docetic theology by which the Creator God refrained from inhabiting the Galilean on the cross. The paradoxical identity of the triune God does not tolerate an apathetic God who refuses to bleed or surrender to powerlessness. This paradoxical teaching is truly the scandal of the cross. The suffering of Jesus and the suffering of God are a singular phenomenon by which God demonstrates his identity with the plight of Christ and his solidarity with human beings and his tormented creation. Thus, the sufferings of Christ are likewise God's sufferings, and this is a source of hope and joy for those who imitate the way of Jesus. Resurrection is the endorsement of this union of suffering by both Father and Son. The Holy Spirit has initiated a community whose work is to abolish pain caused by human insensitivity, to prevent the anguish of war, to heal horrific diseases, to cushion the sorrow of natural disaster, and to proclaim the victory of the crucified God over the forces of death and injustice. Such a community is the embodiment of God's joy. This community, gathered in celebration of the sacrament of Jesus' suffering, is "steadfast, immovable, always excelling in the work of the Lord, because [it knows] that in the Lord [its] labor is not in vain."[20]

When the community of those who suffer vicariously for others gathers around a table fellowship in order to celebrate the sacrament of Jesus' suffering, it experiences a *kairotic* moment. In the earliest rendition of the sacrament, the Apostle Paul refers to Jesus' initiation of a ritual of remembrance with these words upon giving thanks and breaking bread: "This is my body that is for you. Do this in remembrance of me."[21] But this sacramental act is more than an act of remembrance. Such a limited sacrament would be an expression of masochism in tribute to a sadistic God. The sacrament of Jesus' suffering is a remembrance in order to be empowered by hope through a meal within the present moment. In the *kairotic* moment of receiving the broken bread and wine that recalls Jesus' passionate suffering and death, the community also receives the power of hope informed by this memory. In the mystical moment of biblical memory, the worshiping community recalls the promise of the authoritative host as he shared the cup with his disciples and said, "This is my blood of the covenant, which is poured out for many. Truly I tell you, I will never again drink of the fruit of the vine until that day when I drink it new in the kingdom of God."[22]

20. 1 Cor 15:58 NRSV.
21. 1 Cor 11:24b NRSV.
22. Mark 14:24–25 NRSV.

The Sacrament of Jesus' Suffering

Worship is that *kairotic* experience in which past, present, and future converge through the living presence of the suffering Christ. When the sacrament of Jesus' suffering is observed in earnest, the worshipper is surrounded by a crowd of witnesses: those who have unjustly suffered and died in agony due to their uncompromising commitment to Christ, those who have courageously remained faithful to the vision of Jesus' promised Kingdom, the church community of the present moment whose members are sustained by scriptural memory and the heritage of martyrdom, and the yet unborn who will join the unending procession of faithful witnesses.

Père Jean-Pierre de Caussade, an eighteenth-century Jesuit priest in France, articulated the theology of this paradoxical reality in a brief treatise titled *The Sacrament of the Present Moment*. In a section affirming the reality of the living Christ, he provides this significant insight:

> Jesus lives and works among us, throughout our lives, from the beginning of time to the end, which is but one day. He has lived and lives still. The life he began continues in his saints forever . . . They will continue till the end of time, since, in fact, time is but the history of divine action. The Holy Spirit has picked out in clear and unmistakable characters a few moments of that vast duration of time, preserved in the Scriptures a few drops of that ocean, revealed the secret and mysterious way in which Jesus appeared on earth. We can trace through the arteries and veins and confused mixture of the children of men, the origin, race, genealogy of that first born . . . The Holy Spirit is writing a living gospel with the pen of action, which we will only be able to read on the day of glory when, fresh from the presses of life, it will be published.[23]

We live in a culture that attempts to overlook suffering by escaping into the excessive consumption of food, sex, and entertainment. Modern escapist cinematic themes are dominated by the pornography of violence whereby pain is experienced by fictional victims or surrogates of real evil. The dream of modern society is a painlessly happy perpetual Disneyworld. Since this dream is unattainable, we attempt to anesthetize pain with a plethora of pharmaceutical products. We avoid being confronted with the reality of hunger in Ethiopia, typhoid epidemics in Tajikistan, the spread of HIV/AIDS in sub-Saharan Africa, or cholera in post-earthquake Haiti. When we are baptized into Christian community, we vicariously enter the suffering of "the least of these." Because of our belief in a triune God, we do not embrace suffering as a result of deserved divine punishment. This is the posture of a demented Christian masochism or modern Docetic interpretations of the gospel message. Instead, we enter into another's pain because we follow a compassionate God who experiences the pain of his Son and thus the pain of all the children of his creation. Moreover, because of the resurrection of the crucified Messiah, God's sufferings are apocalyptic and thus fruitful, like labor pains suggested by Jesus in John's Gospel: "Very truly, I tell you, you

---

23. de Caussade, *Sacrament of the Present Moment*, 100–101.

will weep and mourn, but the world will rejoice; you will have pain, but your pain will turn into joy. When a woman is in labor, she has pain, because her hour has come. But when her child is born, she no longer remembers the anguish because of the joy of having brought a human being into the world. So you have pain now; but I will see you again, and your hearts will rejoice, and no one will take your joy from you."[24]

The sufferings of Christ are not his alone because the compassionate being of God was within Christ. Thus, the Holy being of God suffered with Christ and suffers with the community of Christ's followers. God's pain anticipates the coming reality in which there will be no pain or suffering or sorrow. The anguish of many among Christ's followers is *apostolic suffering* due to persecution, imprisonment, poverty and hunger. We vicariously enter those sufferings in the modern church because they are the birth pangs of a new order, a new creation. Because of the sufferings of Jesus and his resurrection, this world of suffering is passing away. Those who gather around the sacrament of Jesus' suffering through Holy Communion willingly enter the arena of global agony. We hear with acute empathy the cries of starving and abused children around the world. We are present with the poor and powerless in arenas of political oppression. We are aggressive advocates for peace in lands tormented by civil war and military aggression. The community gathered around the table of the sacrament of Jesus' suffering is not masochistic or neurotic, for we pursue the vision of a coming reality in which all suffering and injustice shall be abolished. Until that day, we shall share the Passion of Christ for life through compassion for those who suffer. Pascal, the seventeenth-century mystic philosopher, was right in saying that "Jesus will be in agony even to the end of the world."[25] But Jürgen Moltmann was quick to observe that the opposite is likewise true: "In the agony of Christ this world finds its end."[26] The sacrament of Jesus' suffering is a perpetual reminder to the disciples of the crucified One that the day will ultimately arrive in which suffering will be abolished. Thus, the suffering of the Man of Nazareth upon a Roman cross is the revelation of a paradoxical Messiah, for "he did not redeem his people through powerful signs and wonders of liberation. He redeemed them, if at all, through suffering and through hope."[27]

How can a simple symbolic act—the Eucharist—stand against the powerful sources of suffering in the modern world? Sam Well, currently the Vicar at Saint Martin in the Fields, introduces us to William Cavanaugh's account of the church's resistance to the oppression of Chilean peasants after a military junta seized power and began systematically murdering political enemies, church activists, and those who resisted the imposed authority.[28] After seven years of silence living in the shadows of fear, the bishops of Chile issued a defiant document that challenged this tyrannical

24. John 16:20–22 NRSV.
25. Pascal, *Pensées*, No. 553," 268.
26. Moltmann, *Way of Jesus Christ*, 157.
27. Ibid., 164.
28. Wells, *Improvisation*, 157–68.

police state. They entitled their 1980 prophetic statement, "I Am Jesus, Whom You Are Persecuting." Cavanaugh's research showed that Catholic theology had so spiritualized and individualized the Christian faith that the visible body of Christ had disappeared before the eyes of oppressive government leaders. In reality, the state was left to impersonate God. In his *Torture and Eucharist*, Cavanaugh described the emergence of a new theological understanding articulated by courageous bishops who sparked revolutionary changes. These bishops came to the realization that the church's "own disciplinary resources—Eucharist, penance, virtue, works of mercy, martyrdom—are not matters of the soul which must somehow 'animate' the 'real world' of bodies, but are rather body/soul disciplines meant to produce actions, practices, habits that are visible in the world."[29]

As the church in Chile began to participate more visibly in the sufferings of the poor, the military junta began to take notice. The bishops endorsed self-employment workshops, financed nutrition programs, initiated neighborhood organizations, and expanded soup kitchens. The church's renewed image of radical hospitality extended to the poor, becoming an eschatological sign of hope and that sanctioned the gathering of God's people around the Eucharistic table. Holy Communion began to make the church dramatically visible as the body of Christ in defiance of torture, human rights violations, injustices in the penal system, and the assassination of political opposition. The existing political climate was radically altered, and positive changes began to occur when the Eucharist became a visible symbol of a new courageous resolve. Cavanaugh described this as a shift to a new understanding of Christ's suffering and the suffering of the church: "Christ adopted the form of a servant. His gift of self to humanity, his complete *kenosis*, is such that he gives over his very identity to the community of his followers . . . so that we become what is offered on the altar."[30]

For each follower of the Way of Jesus, suffering is not only an endemic part of life, it is integral to one's spiritual journey and mission. Redemptive pain is the pathway to joy. Each time the believer kneels at the table of Eucharist and celebrates the sacrament of Jesus' suffering, he or she sees a vision of a reality that God is bringing about through the ministries of the church. Thus, the recipient of the grace of Communion also receives a profound sense of joy that the world cannot give or take away.

I have written the initial draft of this chapter, and a considerable portion of this book, while conducting a labor of love. During the first months of our retirement, my wife and I willingly accepted the privilege and responsibility for the care of her dying mother, Sarah. This saintly woman suffered from the spread of an ovarian cancer that infested her lungs. She was known in her small town's community and church as a simple, independent-minded widow with a gentle, generous spirit. After nearly nine decades of excellent health, she was losing her fight for survival against a painful, aggressive disease. But Sarah was a woman of uncommon tenacity. Born on a farm

29. Cavanaugh, *Torture and Eucharist*, 197.
30. Ibid., 229–30.

Part II: Paradox and Christology

during the First World War, she was accustomed to hardship. Her father suddenly died during her high school years, and it became necessary for her to enter the labor force to help her mother and siblings to cope with the economic challenges of the Great Depression. She became acquainted with the arduous toil of operating a loom in a heated textile mill on a summer's day for a single dollar's pay. She survived the anxiety of the Second World War, and in the same modest farmhouse where she grew up, had painfully given birth to the child who became my wife. Now she required her daughter's compassionate care in order to cope with the encroaching threat of an excruciating disease. After a brief period of remission due to cyber-knife radiation, the vicious disease metastasized into her abdomen, threatening all her vital organs. By Ash Wednesday we requested hospice care so that Sarah's final months could be spent in our home.

It is difficult to witness someone you love endure constant pain. We learned the art of palliative care from the hospice professionals who visited our home. Our daily mission was to administer just enough medicine and food to balance consciousness against chemically induced sleep to sustain quality of life for this dear woman. Our efforts were never to eliminate her suffering, but to monitor and control its severity to maintain awareness and a meaningful existence until her dying moment.

Our days began with morning devotions and prayers of thanksgiving. During daily periods of cognitive awareness and moderate pain, we shared some of our most satisfying conversations about memories and life experiences. We asked her questions regarding the gaps in our knowledge of family events, heritage, and stories. We learned about her life in rural North Carolina during an era of hardship and communal generosity. We heard her reasons for purchasing property near the elementary school with her husband so that their only child would have a good education and a better life. We learned about the centrality of church life to her family's survival and her congregation's role in good times and bad. We discovered deeper levels of tenacity within a woman who labored for over a quarter of a century as supervisor of that elementary school's cafeteria, missing only one day of work in order to attend her own mother's funeral. We learned much through these conversations about a woman who had always regarded suffering as intrinsic to a life of meaningful accomplishments and abundant joy.

Over these months of home hospice care, we observed the ritual of verbal blessings each evening. Sarah successfully attempted to articulate at least one daily blessing. She would give thanks for a personal card, a phone message offering intercessory support, a song sung by the musical therapist, a visit from a member of her hometown church, the positive effects of a pain-reducing medicine, or a word of encouragement from the hospice doctor. Sarah never failed to name at least one such daily blessing. Every evening, the three of us shared prayers of gratitude. During her final weeks, Sarah's prayers probed deeper into the realm of intimacy with God. She always thanked her Creator for such a fulfilling life, the love of a supportive family, the grace of sins forgiven, and the love of church friends near and far. Then she voiced the earnest petition to be taken by death to another reality where there would be no more pain or tears of anguish. Often she concluded with this plea, "If I awaken tomorrow, please spare me the severity of suffering." Our prayers were always followed by the kiss of peace, even when our nights were far from peaceful.

Sarah died according to her wishes on a placid Sunday morning with her daughter at her side, softly stroking her white locks and the fair skin of her cheeks. She died as she had lived: at peace with God and the world about her.

It was a magnificent gift of grace for the three of us to experience this degree of spiritual intimacy within the confines of our home. Only her final four days were spent at Homestead, the county's hospice center. This was one of the most spiritual periods of our lives together. The powerful presence of a Creator God who suffers with his creation was palpable. The obedient presence of the Man of Nazareth upon a cross of horror was felt each time we were tempted to think that we had been abandoned by an omnipotent God. We acknowledged the presence of the Holy Spirit in the daily gift of serenity and joy amidst our periods of greatest bewilderment. We felt greater affinity with anguishing martyrs, suffering parishioners we had served during our decades of parish ministry, historic saints of distinction, unnamed and obscure people of faith among the poor, victims of the Holocaust in Europe, and the familiar lives of deceased family members. We were comforted by the daily scriptural remembrances of the paradoxical Messiah who redeemed all of us through his redemptive suffering and triumphant grace.

16

The Sword of Peace

JESUS WAS A PACIFIST. This fact comes as a considerable embarrassment to many within the contemporary church, especially those of us who proclaim the Lordship of Christ through the ethos of mainline denominations within the United States. While the struggle of the church to resist militarism has existed since the ascendency of Emperor Constantine in the fourth century, accommodation of the prevailing culture of violence has especially defined the contradictory character of the church throughout the American experience.

A small community of Quakers located in North Carolina was acutely aware of pacifism as a defining issue for the church during a time when congregations played a prominent role in the initial stages of the unfolding American story. Each summer, members of the charming rural community of Snow Camp, North Carolina, enact an outdoor drama written by William Hardy titled *The Sword of Peace*. The narrative depicts the ethical struggles of a pacifist Christian community—the ancestors of current Snow Camp citizens—during the two decades prior to the Revolutionary War battle of Guilford Courthouse fought in nearby Greensboro on March 15, 1781. The drama tells the story of spiritual ambiguity in the life of Simon Dixon, a Quaker miller who wanted to end the despotic rule of British King George III but was prevented from taking up arms due to his deeply embedded faith in a pacifist Jesus. The script depicts the defiant spirit of General Nathanael Greene, for whom the city of Greensboro was named, and the arrogance of Lord Cornwallis, commander of the British forces in America. Quaker compatriots repeatedly remind Simon Dixon of scriptural admonitions—especially the teachings of Jesus' Sermon on the Mount—requiring the devout disciple to renounce violence. This theatrical presentation is a useful reminder for a contemporary generation that has long dismissed the memory of a time when Christians struggled with the moral ambiguities of participation in the violence of any war, even for the patriotic purpose of defending liberty. Many followers of Christ in

America have long since adopted the cultural assumptions that justify warfare in the defense of national self-interest. But many of our ancestors in the American colonies were torn between their commitment to the authority of Scripture, especially the pacifist witness of Jesus, and the allure of noble nationalistic ideals.

This is for good reason. One becomes an authentic disciple of Jesus by pursuing the way of the Man of Nazareth as revealed in the four canonical Gospels. We are not called by his message to become a clone of Jesus, but we are invited by the gospel message to enter by baptism into a transformed community of those who live in accordance with the instructions of Jesus. Seasoned disciples of the early church, therefore, fashioned an aberrant community composed of believers modeled in the likeness of Jesus.

Before Jesus chose his initial apostolic followers, he was beguiled by the Tempter to receive all the powers of this world by giving allegiance to him rather than the God of Abraham, Moses, and the prophets of Israel. He was tempted to receive the power of materialism (bread), command over nature (transcendence of natural laws) and absolute political domination (rule over the kingdoms of this world). The Jesus of the gospels rejected all of these temptations, including their implied militaristic command. The Jesus of Scripture was firmly convinced that pursuing the will of a merciful Creator God of the Abrahamic covenant would result in the ultimate establishment of a peaceable kingdom. But the ascendance of this Kingdom would require his death through the violence of a resistant world. Thus, his disciples would not need supernatural forces or militaristic intervention. The power for the transformation of this earth to such a dominion of mercy, grace, and peace would come about through the movement of the Holy Spirit in the hearts of humanity and the nurture of a community of nonviolent followers committed to modeling their lives after the Way of Jesus.

Thus, the Galilean teacher explicitly instructed those who desired to follow him, "You have heard that it was said to those of ancient times, 'You shall not murder'; 'whoever murders shall be liable to judgment.' But I say to you that if you are angry with a brother or sister, you will be liable to judgment; and if you insult a brother or sister, you will be liable to the council; and if you say, 'You fool,' you will be liable to the hell of fire."[1] These teachings upon a hillside above the Galilean lake were likely a synopsis of the comprehensive instructions Jesus had developed in his school of discipleship in the home of Peter's mother-in-law at Capernaum. But these were not peripheral instructions, nor did they come with the caveat that they were inapplicable to the oppressive Roman government, or that such instructions were a spiritualized, idealistic ethic not feasible within the real geopolitical world of military power. Instead, Jesus boldly added to his ethical idealism, "Love your enemies and pray for those who persecute you so that you may be children of your Father in heaven . . . For if you love those who love you, what reward do you have?"[2]

1. Matt 5:21–22 NRSV.
2. Matt 5:44–46a NRSV.

Part II: Paradox and Christology

It is extremely important to note that there is no incongruity between these teachings and the progression of the events within Jesus' life. More than any person in history, his teachings were embodied in the conduct of his existence. His authentic life of pacifism and non-retaliation was truly an affront to the imperial powers. The Roman authorities strictly controlled Jerusalem and all of Judea. Rome knew how to deal with any form of opposition, and Jesus' references to his manifestation of a *kingdom* were an implicit threat to absolute imperial authority. Thus, by the command of Pilate, the emperor's emissary in Jerusalem, Jesus was imprisoned, tortured, humiliated, and crucified even though he was clearly not a Zealot or an advocate of violent revolution. Justification for the use of violence to maintain the civility of the polis was abundantly available in the ethical writings of the Greek philosopher Aristotle (384–322 B.C.),[3] whose ideas greatly influenced the ethos of Roman law in preserving the *Pax Romana*. The immensely influential oratory of Cicero (106–143 B.C.) helped consolidate the ethics of retaliation in Rome's punitive justice.[4]

Pilate forcefully brought Jesus into the Praetorium at the center of Roman authority in Jerusalem. He had an ethical dilemma standing before him in the form of a nonviolent, nonresistant Jesus. His prisoner was obviously not a physical threat. He had uttered nothing suggestive of armed rebellion, as did the *Sicarii* (the "dagger holders") of upper Galilee. Pilate could not sufficiently wash his hands from guilt for his condemnation and execution of an innocent, nonviolent, but defiant, Jesus. The falsely condemned Galilean peasant/prophet broke his silence at the mock trial by telling a bewildered Pilate, "My kingdom is not from this world. If my kingdom were from this world, my followers would be fighting to keep me from being handed over to the Jews. But as it is, my kingdom is not from here."[5]

Jesus' pacifism was paradoxical. He was indeed confrontational, aggressive, and divisive. The new community that formed around his life and teachings was also intensely controversial due to the apostles' rejection of the violent ways of the world. The politics of power, as demonstrated by Pilate, only knew a repressive response to nonviolence. Thus, Jesus knew that his followers would suffer brutal opposition, so he warned them by saying, "I came to bring fire on the earth, and how I wish it were

---

3. The Greek philosopher Aristotle wrote, "Happiness is thought to stand in perfect rest; for we toil that we may rest, and war that we may be at peace. Now all the Practical Virtues require either society or war for their Working, and the actions regarding these are thought to exclude rest; those of war entirely, because no one chooses war, nor prepares for war, for war's sake: He would indeed be thought a bloodthirsty villain who should make enemies of his friends to secure the existence of fighting and bloodshed. The Working also of the statesman excludes the idea of rest, and, beside the actual work of government, seeks for power and dignities or at least Happiness for the man himself and his fellow-citizens: Happiness distinct from the national Happiness which we evidently seek as being different and distinct" (Aristotle, *Nicomachean Ethics*, Bk. 10, in Frost, *Masterworks of Philosophy*, 166).

4. Cicero asserted, "The only excuse, therefore, for going to war is that we may live in peace unharmed; and when the victory is won, we should spare those who have not been blood-thirsty and barbarous in their warfare" (Cicero, *De Officiis*, 37).

5. John 18:36 NRSV.

already kindled!"⁶ It is certain that following Jesus can literally divide families, as in William Hardy's drama concerning Quaker pacifists' struggles during the American Revolution. Thus, it should come as no surprise or logical contradiction to read the words of Jesus in Luke's Gospel, "Do you think that I have come to bring peace to the earth? No, I tell you, but rather division! From now on five in one household will be divided, three against two and two against three; they will be divided: father against son and son against father, mother against daughter and daughter against mother."⁷

Some youth in parishes I served during the Vietnam era refused to fight in that conflict because of their faith in a nonviolent Jesus. These conscientious objectors often experienced the scorn, hostility, and sometimes violence of the community, but they were always embraced and encouraged by the remnant of faithful believers within the congregations drawn to the image of a nonviolent Lord. The peace that Jesus brings within the church is paradoxical. Congregations become divided over the issues surrounding war, nationalism, patriotism, and justice. Jesus' peace is assertive, but is does not seek to achieve political power or control. It rejects attitudes of retribution and revenge, in stark contrast to the core government values. Followers of Jesus in every era who have chosen not to kill have also been willing to surrender their very lives in faithfulness to the fundamental teachings and example of their non-retaliatory deliverer.

The common people of Galilee who had known the origins of their homegrown rabbi and prophet insisted that Jesus provide some sign to interpret his central mission. Both Matthew and Luke note that Jesus was quick to respond by saying, "This generation is an evil generation; it asks for a sign, but no sign will be given to it except the sign of Jonah."⁸ That generation addressed by Jesus was evil because the people who had grown up in the nurture of the synagogue had still not recognized in Jesus the true essence of Judaism—the fulfillment of all the law and prophets, as was clearly disclosed in the message and theology of the book of Jonah. This reluctant prophet of Hebrew tradition was like the people of Jesus' Galilee: holding onto their intense hatreds for over seven centuries, remembering the horrible atrocities committed long ago by the Assyrian oppressors (the Nazis of the ancient world). The name Jonah in Hebrew literally meant "dove," a symbol of Israel. Jesus had come to manifest the theology of that pivotal book. Jonah had been written in a period after the Babylonian exile as a culmination of the evolving revelation of YHWH as a God of unconditional forgiveness and mercy whose grace extended toward even the vilest of offenders, including nations and races beyond the scope of Jewish heritage. By choosing the sign of Jonah, Jesus became the embodiment of the true Israel of the Abrahamic covenant, and his theology was the culmination of the sanctifying historical pilgrimage of a suffering nation. By embodying mercy and forgiveness, Jesus' Israel would truly become

---

6. Luke 12:49 NRSV.
7. Luke 12:51–53 NRSV.
8. Luke 11:29 NRSV. See also Matt 12:39 NRSV.

Part II: Paradox and Christology

a light to the nations, and Jesus saw his role as bringing that light through his obedient acts of nonviolent mercy. Just as the God revealed in the book of Jonah provided redemption to a repentant Nineveh, so did Jesus come to bring the message of salvation to all those who would respond through contrition, obedience, instruction, and entrance (through baptism) into the new community of covenant love and nonviolent conduct.

Historians have discovered few, if any, examples of acknowledged Christians advocating or participating in war or other overt acts of violence prior to the ascendency of Emperor Constantine. Following the death of Galerius in May of A.D. 311, four rivals fought for control of the Roman Empire. By October 28 of A.D. 312, only a bridge over the river Tiber north of Rome separated the armies of Constantine from his rival Maxentius. The night before the battle, Constantine had a vision in which he saw the Latin letters, *Chi Rho*, the church's symbol for Jesus the Christ, with this mandate: "Conquer by this."[9] Constantine was firmly convinced that the Christian God had given him the victory at the Tiber River on the end of that fateful day. Within a year, the Edict of Milan had redefined the policy of the empire toward the Christian faith. Persecution was abolished, even though Christianity was not yet proclaimed to be the one official religion. Constantine had not yet been baptized nor had he relinquished belief in other gods. But this warrior monarch had taken political control of the church and, in effect, *baptized* his army as defenders of a faith into which he had never been nurtured. Emperor Constantine, in fact, knew very little about the teachings of Jesus, the Messiah's context in Hebrew heritage and theology, and the events within the Galilean's life. Nor did he care much about knowing anything about these things. These matters were not relevant to his political agenda of "Christianizing" the empire.

The story of Constantine's dream quickly took on legendary status and was embellished by the emperor himself through his correspondence with Eusebius, bishop of the metropolitan see of Palestine and historian of the church. These exaggerated accounts became the authorized record of church officials who rejoiced in their newly-sanctioned freedom from persecution. Even though Constantine's mother was a convert to the new religion, she had not nurtured her son in the faith, nor had he participated in activities of corporate worship. He had not read the gospels, nor did he ever show any interest in the historical life and teachings of Jesus. Eusebius, who wrote his *Life of Constantine* in A.D. 337, met with the emperor only twice at Nicaea in A.D. 325 and ten years later at the thirtieth anniversary of the emperor's accession. But Eusebius used his relationship with Constantine to promulgate a Christian theory of empire, teaching that the emperor ruled by God's grace and was analogous to earlier deified rulers in history. Because Eusebius also articulated his support of Arius in the controversies that led to the Council of Nicaea, he was a dubious interpreter of Christian theology for this new Christian convert and ruler of the Roman Empire. The

---

9. Latourette, *History of Christianity*, 92.

historian Michael Grant bluntly states that Constantine "revered the Christian God, as a God of power, as *the* God of power. He was the God who had given Constantine power, and had enabled him at the Milvian Bridge, to defeat Maxentius (who, for this purpose, was made out to be more anti-Christian than he really was)."[10]

Just as post-Enlightenment liberal Protestant theology developed Christologies without considering the authority of Scripture and the canonical records of how Jesus lived and what he taught, the Constantinian church was brought into being by an emperor who knew little or nothing about the Man of Nazareth and his teachings. And even more damaging, this defender of the faith thought such records were irrelevant to his purpose. Thus, the emperor ordered the creation of a *labarum*—a long spear covered with gold and joined by a transverse bar to create the insignia of a cross. This standard supported a wreath of precious stones surrounding the emblem, *Chi Rho*. The emperor believed that this *labarum* had magical powers to subdue his enemies. An apostate church—a convoluted version of the community envisioned and established by the historical Jesus through the activity of the Holy Spirit—was promulgated by a man who maintained belief in the sun deity and presented sacrificial offerings at the temple of Apollo in order to hedge his bets and assuage the strong opposition of Roman aristocrats to his endorsement of Christianity.

Biographer Michael Grant notes that Constantine "hardly ever mentions the theology which proclaimed and explained the Crucifixion, and he saw the Cross not so much as an emblem of suffering as a magic totem confirming his own victoriousness."[11] What little he learned about his newly adopted faith had no visible effect upon his ethical and theological assumptions. His allegiance to a sun god made his transition to quasi-Christianity ever more acceptable, for he thought of the risen Christ as the unconquered sun god. It came as no surprise that the emperor named the Christian Sunday after the sun god, and believers prayed toward the east and the rising sun. The sun god's birthday upon the winter solstice (December 25) was set by the militant emperor as the official date of the birth of Christ.

A century later Augustine, Bishop of Hippo in northern Africa (A.D. 354–430), developed a rationale for Christian support for a just war. He wrote in the historical context of an empire disintegrating amid the aggressive advancements of pagan hordes from northern Europe. This philosophical bishop systematically and rationally considered the practical issue of defense. How should a Christian empire defend itself against the barbarism of the nomadic warriors then bringing chaos to the sophisticated but vulnerable Roman culture? Augustine spiritualized the Sermon on the Mount by writing, "What is here required is not a bodily action, but an inward disposition. The sacred seat of virtue is the heart."[12] Augustine is credited with conceiving of "just war" in his monumental *The City of God*, in which he wrote:

10. Grant, *Constantine the Great*, 147.
11. Ibid., 149.
12. Quoted in Holmes, "Time for War?" http://www.christianitytoday.com/ct/2001/

Part II: Paradox and Christology

> Yea but a wise man, say they, will wage none but just war. He will not! As if the very remembrance that himself is man, ought not to procure his greater sorrow in that he has cause of just war, and must needs wage them, which if they were not just, were not for him to deal in, so that a wise man should never have war; for it is the other men's wickedness that works his cause just that he ought to deplore, whether ever it produce wars or not."[13]

Augustine taught that no war is just that is preemptive, non-defensive, or fails to have as its objective the restoration of peace. Through the centuries the official Roman Catholic doctrine has maintained the essence of Augustine's teachings, insisting that "governments cannot be denied the right of lawful self-defense, once all peace efforts have failed."[14] The following conditions for the moral legitimacy of war must be consistently applied: (1) the potential damage inflicted by the aggressor must be lasting, grave, and certain; (2) all other means for avoiding war must be shown to be "impractical or ineffective"; (3) the war must have a serious prospect of success; (4) "the use of arms must not produce evils and disorders graver than the evil to be eliminated";[15] (5) "non-combatants, wounded soldiers, and prisoners must be respected and treated humanely"; (6) indiscriminate destruction of whole cities and their inhabitants is "a crime against God and man"; economic injustice, envy and pride should be resisted for these "threaten peace and cause war."[16]

Throughout the centuries since Augustine's time, only minority faith communities have resisted a spiritualized or metaphorical interpretation of Jesus' nonviolent life and pacifist teachings. Chief of among these are Anabaptists, Quakers, Mennonites, Hutterites, Brethren in Christ, Moravians, Shakers, and some Pentecostal sects. These have become paradoxical communities, preaching and practicing peace while accepting the scorn, ridicule, and violence of a hostile "Christian" culture. The Fellowship of Reconciliation was established after the First World War in order to bring together the efforts of these and other historic peace churches. Advocates of Christian pacifism, however, have never attained a dominant role in a post-Constantine world.

The most influential voice during the twentieth century championing the reconsideration of just war as a preferable Christian choice was Reinhold Niebuhr, a former pacifist pastor and professor of Christian ethics. With the abrupt rise of Stalin's Communism and the racist extremes of Hitler's Nazi Party in post-war Europe, Niebuhr pensively reflected upon humanity's propensity toward evil and violence. He became a proponent of a "Christian realism" that interpreted the context of Jesus' ideals, including his pacifistic teachings and admonition to love one's enemies, to be metaphorical and, consequently, not applicable to geopolitical reality. Niebuhr endorsed with slight

---

septemberweb-only/9-17-55.0.html?paging=off.

13. Augustine, *City of God*, 221.
14. Catholic Church, *Catechism*, 615.
15. Ibid.
16. Ibid., 617.

modifications the Catholic consensus regarding Christian justification for war. But he warned, "Not all wars are equally just and not all contestants are equally right."[17] Niebuhr further cautioned, "Even a war which is judged by neutral opinion to be wholly defensive cannot be waged with completely good conscience because the situations out of which wars arise are charged with memories of previous acts of aggression on the part of those in defense."[18] Thus, Niebuhr recognized the moral ambiguities of participating in the violence of war. Combatants' objectives are never likely to be absolutely pure, but Niebuhr insisted that violence is sometimes necessary in order to prevent the triumph of evil. The philosophical structure of his arguments was elevated in popular acceptance during the Second World War and was read with enthusiastic acceptance during decades of the Cold War by both leaders of the church and intellectuals within the US Department of State. David Brooks, editorial writer for the *New York Times*, asked President Obama whether he had read Reinhold Niebuhr, to which Obama replied, "I love him. He's one of my favorite philosophers."[19]

The long shadow of Niebuhr's consideration of the ethics of Christian assent to war went largely unchallenged by acclaimed theologians until the 1972 publication of John Howard Yoder's *The Politics of Jesus*. This obscure Mennonite professor was profoundly influenced by Karl Barth's insistence that the church is a clearly defined community modeled after the Jesus of Scripture. Yoder made the strong case that the authentic church must take upon itself the very nature of Jesus Christ, it must nurture its disciples in the radical ways of the Man of Nazareth, and it is called to become a counter-cultural witness in a world of extreme violence. Yoder was writing at a time when young Christians were questioning the justice and rationalization for war in Southeast Asia. Thus, Yoder demonstrated that the "politics of Jesus" was a noncoercive form of redemption, and his crucifixion was his politics.

Shortly after the publication of *The Politics of Jesus*, I became a member of a small ecumenical group initiated by Greensboro Urban Ministry that read Yoder's compelling work. Our group of six laypeople and two clergy members had taken the name *Dunamis*, the New Testament Greek word for "power." We were seeking authentic ways for the church to speak to power without being seduced by the desire for political empowerment. We were inspired by a small group by that name in Washington's Church of the Saviour. During that period, a young United Methodist professor of religion and ethics at Notre Dame University, Stanley Hauerwas, serendipitously encountered a little pamphlet titled "Peace without Eschatology?" The author was John Howard Yoder. Hauerwas was not a pacifist, but when he travelled the short distance to the Mennonite seminary where Yoder taught, a personal and academic friendship began that would challenge the Niebuhrian theological consensus regarding just war.

17. Niebuhr, *Nature and Destiny of Man*, 283.

18. Ibid.

19. Brooks, "Obama, Gospel and Verse," *New York Times*, April 26, 2007, http://www.nytimes.com/2007/04/26/opinion/26brooks.html?_r=1&.

Part II: Paradox and Christology

Stanley Hauerwas' acceptance of pacifism was not immediate, but his philosophical roots had prepared him for such a conversion. He rejected the notion that peace is some philosophical ideal formulated by human rationale, as with Kantian ethics. Rather, "the peace Christians embody, and which they offer to the world, is based on a kingdom that has become present in the life of Jesus of Nazareth."[20] Thus, there is an integral and necessary connection between the authentic church's ethical stance regarding violence and the actual historical being of the Man of Nazareth—both his life and teachings. Christian ethics, in Hauerwas' view, cannot make Christology (the idea and systematic interpretation of Christ) its starting point. Just as theologians throughout centuries of Christian tradition have attempted to justify the amalgamation of political power with the church's agenda, the church of the twenty-first century, with its enthusiasm for a post-9/11 "war on terrorism," has failed to grapple with the reality of the historical Jesus and the gospel records of this aggressively nonviolent peacemaker. Thus, Hauerwas contends that "the life of the man whom God made his representative is ignored or used selectively."[21] Moreover, in addressing high-profile contemporary theologians, Hauerwas vehemently insists that "some have placed such great emphasis on Jesus' death and resurrection as the source of salvation that there is almost no recognition of him as the teacher of righteousness."[22]

A growing remnant within congregations across Christendom is being drawn toward the paradoxical posture of Jesus Christ as both the teacher of righteousness and the nonviolent, self-sacrificing savior who rendered a consistent, but aggressive, witness to a pacifistic life. A significant number of baptized members are refusing to participate in promulgating violence or participating in war. These few are willing to endure insults, ostracism, and even violence directed toward them and their families. Their courageous stance takes a variety of forms, and historic peace churches continue to provide theological maturity and guidance to this pursuit of authenticity. John Howard Yoder has provided helpful insights by describing at least twenty expressions of historic Christian pacifism and imparting his theological assessments of each as demonstrations of faithfulness to Jesus.[23] In Yoder's assessment, Christian pacifism may take many legitimate forms, and all communities that center upon the life and teachings of Christ and diligently seek a more authentic pattern of faithfulness are indeed part of the global network of Christian pacifism. Yoder and his Mennonite sect have historically practiced pacifism as an absolute principle. But this may not be the starting point for many congregations and denominations that are now gravitating toward a more perfect way. Many congregations have, for example, been so inspired by the civil rights movement and the theology of Martin Luther King Jr. that their pacifism is directed towards effecting social change. Still others may be drawn to the

20. Hauerwas, *Peaceable Kingdom*, 6.
21. Ibid., 72.
22. Ibid.
23. See Yoder, *Nevertheless*.

example of what Yoder terms "the pacifism of the virtuous minority."[24] These faithful do not leave their "just war" denominations, but are inspired by such aberrant activity as the ministry of Catholic lay leader Dorothy Day, who worked within a remnant community and labored nonjudgmentally alongside fellow pacifists and just war adherents in order to witness the lifestyle and message of Jesus. An ancient tradition within the Roman Catholic Church was the establishment of "evangelical counsels" by which many generations of congregants have responded to the call to participate in a level of morality distinct from mere observance of church law or covenants of membership. Taking on a life of poverty or loving one's enemies or refusing to participate in war were not thought to be standard expectations for all, and certainly not novice Christians. But the Roman Catholic Church has always provided a place of blessing for those whom God has invited to deeper level of faithfulness. Maryknolls and other collective communities within the global witness of the Catholic Church carry out mission-directed imperatives. Thus, small groups within Roman Catholic congregations are empowered to witness and work aggressively as peacemakers witnessing to "pacifism of the virtuous minority." Protestant mainline denominations would be prudent and increasingly faithful to the Bible's depiction of Jesus if they developed a similar pacifistic tradition.

Within my own denominational identity—the United Methodist Church and Wesleyan theological tradition—I adhere to the historic emphasis on the doctrine of sanctification. Methodists who are faithful to our historic roots pursue Jesus' expectation to follow in a pilgrimage leading toward Christian perfection. Our aspiration is to become perfect in love during our lifetime. After all, our Master concluded his pivotal set of teachings on pacifism with this admonition: "Be perfect, therefore, as your heavenly Father is perfect."[25] To provide for the formation of courageous groups within a congregation that practices "pacifism of the virtuous minority" is not a strategy for creating a divisive form of arrogant spiritual elitism. It is a nonjudgmental means of providing an honest option for those who are called to a ministry of peace advocacy. These people of special sensitivity and conscience will, consequently, have a place and platform by which they may abide within a diverse community of Christian pilgrims, all of whom are peacemakers if not pacifists.

I have discovered several options among John Howard Yoder's catalogue of varieties of religious pacifism that are both viable and pragmatic in a traditional mainline denominational setting. This gives me hope and encouragement, for I do not wish to separate myself from my many faithful friends who maintain a "just war" perspective. If a disciple of Jesus is convinced by the paradox of our Lord's vision for a kingdom of peace to enter a ministry of confrontation, challenge, and political opposition to war, that person needs not to abandon his or her denomination if that faith community provides a place of blessing for these who are called forth by Jesus to do his costly

24. Ibid., 77.
25. Matt 5:48 NRSV.

Part II: Paradox and Christology

work of peacemaking. But all within the household of faith who affirm the lordship of Jesus must renounce the idolatry of a patriotism that blesses wars of aggression and gives supreme priority to national self-interest.

In each of the seven parish appointments I have served, I have found avenues for expressing my witness to a nonviolent Christ. During my initial pastoral appointment, my faith community was in the center of a vibrant campus community. One of our members was drafted and sent to Vietnam, where he flew a helicopter and became the most decorated soldier in the Vietnam War at that time in the state of North Carolina. He returned home to advocate against the drafting of his younger brother. The conflict in Southeast Asia profoundly divided the campus community, families, and the church. Much discussion about the ethics of war was elicited when we placed *Life Magazine* pictures of soldiers who had died in one week of combat in the sanctuary. I provided biblical instruction to college students who conscientiously resisted the local draft board. This congregation never spoke with one voice on the issue, but the Social Principles[26] of our denomination gave ample space for affirming those who pursued the path of pacifism and resistance to war. Our congregation maintained its profound ministry to young adults in the community who went off obediently to war, praying for their safety and a swift conclusion to the violence. Pacifists were treated with increasing respect, and the congregation learned from the pulpit that nonviolence is a way of life in accordance with the proclamation and mission of Jesus.

When I joined several in my congregation during the 1980s in opposition to American foreign policy in Nicaragua and its support of an oppressive military regime in El Salvador, we found alliances within a vast ecumenical array of Christian pacifists in the city of Greensboro. Yet I was grateful for the courage and candor of a prominent church member who entered the pastor's study, placed an envelope upon my desk, and declared, "I have written an editorial for the *Greensboro Daily News* expressing my opposition to your sermons and activities around town related to political matters in Latin America." Then he firmly and emotionally added, "But I will give my life fighting for your right to express your convictions from the pulpit of this church." He remained long enough for me to hear his perspective so I could discover the agony and ambiguity that prompted his visit. Many years later, this same veteran approached me at the graveside funeral of a mutual friend to remind me of this emotional occasion. Then he confessed, "On the issues related to those military actions in Central America, I was wrong and now recognize your reasons for advocating on behalf of peace."

During an era when nuclear weapons were being stockpiled by the US and USSR at unprecedented levels, our bishop appointed me to the task of giving leadership to a conference-wide study of a document written and endorsed by the Council of Bishops titled "In Defense of Creation." The problem with this carefully constructed theological composition was not its factual analysis of the dangers posed by the arms

---

26. United Methodist Church, "Social Principles of the United Methodist Church," in *Book of Discipline of the United Methodist Church*, 103–42.

race or its biblical references, but its failure to confess and address the violence within the United Methodist Church. Since the Enlightenment, the church has felt more and more comfortable advising the culture and its governing authorities on how to run their affairs. But as we have demonstrated in this chapter, since the days of Emperor Constantine the church has rarely acknowledged that it has itself become an extension of a violent, materialistic culture. But when members of the church refuse to comply with military service, leave well-paying jobs at factories that produce armaments or chemicals of warfare, or nurture their children in nonviolent behavior, the world will truly take notice of the church and what it has to say to government about the arms race or other matters of political policy.

This chapter, which has given clearer focus to the paradox of a pacifistic Jesus (who died a violent death because of his nonviolent witness), is really a discourse on evangelism. When the church increasingly reflects with authenticity the likeness of Jesus, many more seekers will be drawn to this strange community whose eschatological vision of a Kingdom of peace is the source of its passion and the content of its mission.

17

King Upon a Cross

Royalty is not all that royal these days. The monarchy of Britain has tottered on the brink of collapse on several occasions over the past two decades, due in part to the exploits of a prince whose unsavory behavior hinted at a subconscious desire to abdicate the throne long before his coronation was likely. Restoration of the esteem of Queen Elizabeth II has required her surviving the outcry of popular opinion surrounding the tragic death of Princess Diana, the arrival of her sixtieth Jubilee Year, and the probability of her becoming the longest reigning monarch in the British Empire's illustrious history. But global television audiences realized that the monarchy had truly taken a comedic turn when Her Majesty participated in a James Bond film fantasy at the opening ceremonies of the Thirtieth Olympiad in London by entering the athletic arena via as her stunt-double parachuted in from a helicopter.

Who in their right mind would really want to be a reigning monarch at the opening of the twenty-first century of the Christian era? The sun now sets upon the British Empire. The task of parliamentary rule over the British Isles alone is more than enough for a commonwealth with a cosmetic monarchy. After all, it is dangerous to be a queen or king these days. The Arab Spring of 2011 sent shock waves throughout the Middle East. As a powerful dictator was angrily executed in Libya and another autocratic ruler deposed in Egypt, King Abdullah bin Abdulaziz of Saudi Arabia and President Khalifa of the United Arab Emirates began to beef up their entourage of security guards. The hereditary President of the Syrian Arab Republic, Bashar al-Assad, launched a brutal war of aggression against his own people. The comedian Mel Brooks, in his satirical cinematic sketch on Louis XIV of France, had it wrong: It is *not* so good to be king. Thirty years ago, the hereditary king of Iran died a broken man in ignominious exile from a country that loathed his legacy of political oppression. Iranians were even willing to replace his absolute monarchy with a government of religious tyranny under the Ayatollah Khomeini. The few remaining potentates in the global community must fear the dubious fate of King Abdullah II of Jordan, a prisoner of a volatile political environment. On the whole, we do not seem to think well of kings. Except for a few benevolent despots whose memory has been entombed in the hearts of grateful peasants, the monarchs of history are largely despised and occasionally pitied much like Shakespeare's Lear.

It seems strange indeed that the orthodox affirmation of the Christian faith proclaims that Jesus of Nazareth is King of kings and Lord of lords. This belief seems out of place in a democratic society and even sounds offensive to people whose human rights have been usurped by royal decree. Few Americans would entertain the notion of living under the authority of a king of any sort. The main reason my Scottish peasant ancestors, James and Nancy Thompson, packed all their meager belongings in the 1770s and came down from their native highlands to take ship to a new life in a colony called North Carolina was to escape the injustices suffered under the rule of England's King George III.

In the time of Jesus' ministry, the pyramid of imperial power was invincible. Only foolish Zealots in Galilee, detached from political reality, considered a strategy of armed rebellion. Informed Hebrew religious leaders, however, remembered that only six decades earlier, General Pompey's legions had defeated a massive slave rebellion in southern Italy and crucified over six thousand rebels, lining the Appian Way with bodies nailed to crosses. No one had successfully challenged Roman authority, and the quickest way to destroy an itinerant preacher from Galilee was to convince Roman judicial authorities that Jesus has proclaimed himself to be the true King of the Jews. Thus, Jesus was brought before Pilate because it was reported that this Galilean teacher had made precisely such an assertion. If Pilate could prove that Jesus had promoted himself as a rival king eager to depose Herod Antipas, Jesus' actions would be declared a treasonable offense deserving Roman execution. Jesus did not say to Pilate that he was a king, nor did he deny the title. He merely offered this mysterious explanation: "My kingdom is not from this world."[1] Jesus' enigmatic assertion indicated that he regarded himself to be a very different sort of sovereign. His parables had been filled with references to a Kingdom that was being inaugurated through his own teaching and acts of miraculous healing. If Jesus had indeed claimed to be the legitimate successor to Herod Antipas, then all of his disciples and many Galilean supporters would have been accomplices in a treasonous plot.

The mere scene of Jesus before Pilate offers a dramatic paradox related to the mystery of the incarnation and the true meaning of the gospel. It appears that a powerless Jesus is being judged by the potentate Pilate, but in reality, an insignificant Pilate is being judged by Christ—the true spiritual Messiah of Israel. The mystery of the incarnation is symbolized in this crucial slice from the life of Jesus. This scenario discloses the paradoxical nature of political power in the theology of John's Gospel. When John's Gospel depicts the showdown between Jesus and Pilate, the Evangelist

1. John 18:36 NRSV.

describes this logically incompatible scene. Pilate seemed to hold the fragile fate of Jesus under his political command, yet in reality, Jesus is the one really in complete control. Pilate's ultimate fate and his infamous legacy in human history were being defined in this decisive moment.

A paradoxical interpretation of the incarnation must be derived from the evidence of the faith community out of which the theology of the gospel witness emerged. D. M. Baille, in his classical statement on the incarnation, warns us that "since a paradox is a self-contradictory statement, we simply do not know what it means or what we mean by it unless it has that direct connection with the faith which it attempts to express."[2] John's Gospel, therefore, describes the paradox of a King upon a cross. This symbol emerges from scriptural testimony that dominates the narrative of all four Gospels. Only in the language of worship does the paradox of a King upon a cross receive dignity and transformational power. To embrace the cross and crown of thorns as interpretative symbols of redemption and the core of the Christian faith is equivalent to contemporary disciples wearing necklaces sporting miniature electric chairs.

The logical contradiction of an omnipotent King upon a cross did not emerge from John the Evangelist's imagination. The whole life of Jesus embodied this paradoxical situation. His actions within history established the reality of this divine mystery. His Kingdom was *in* this world, but not *of* this world. This King defined the nature of his dominion by what he did, what he taught, and the faith he invoked in his community of followers. Jürgen Moltmann has written extensively about the Kingdom of God and wisely observes that "it is not the term [Kingdom of God] which must be allowed to define the experience. The experience must define the term."[3] The actual life of Jesus experienced by the apostles gave substance to John the Evangelist's paradoxical depiction of the Lord's trial. His teachings and compassionate ministry among the poor defined the nature of his Kingdom.

Jesus taught his disciples parables that reversed the value systems of this world. They knew, therefore, that their King was the sort of monarch who threw banquets in honor of those despised by society. This ruler pays maximum attention to the lost and the lowly in his kingdom. Jesus also defined his role as King by what he did: He healed the sick and regarded their illnesses not as punishment for their sins, but as a vulnerable opening by which they might be restored to wholeness. In action surprising for a king, Jesus defined his regal authority through intimate companionship with the community of the twelve. He ate and drank with sinners—the sort of people conventional monarchs would avoid at all cost. King Jesus gave first rank in his court to the poor, who received his most encompassing Beatitude: They shall be citizens in the Kingdom of heaven. He even placed children upon his knee and said that each

---

2. Baillie, *God Was in Christ*, 110.
3. Moltmann, *Christ for Today's World*, 9.

adult must become like these little ones before he or she may be received into God's blessed domain.

The surprising activity of this extraordinary King paradoxically defined his Kingdom. The paradoxical theology of the early church did not emerge from a vacuum of abstract analysis. Jesus demonstrated by word and deed that, in his Kingdom, the last shall be first and the first last, the weakest shall be the strongest, and the forsaken shall be welcomed. Jesus, as seen through the eyes of John the Evangelist, is the paradoxical King: a monarch on his knees washing the feet of his subjects, royalty wearing the robe of condemnation, the King of kings donning a crown of thorns. The story of King Jesus before Pontius Pilate, therefore, poignantly illustrates the unique nature of his sovereignty. We know that Jesus' arrest occurred in the dead of night. According to John's Gospel, our Master was taken first to the dwelling of Caiaphas, who was high priest that year. In compliance with Roman authority, he was then transferred at an early hour to Pilate's headquarters. It can be assumed that Jesus was interrogated by Annas, the father-in-law of Caiaphas, before three in the morning—the hour of the cockcrow. During the period between three and six in the morning, he was cross-examined by the high priest himself. Toward sunrise, he was led before Pilate, who continued the interrogation and sentenced him to die by the Roman form of execution—crucifixion. Pilate's headquarters during the feast of Passover was the Praetorium. Normally the governor's Praetorium in Palestine was at Caesarea, along the picturesque Mediterranean Sea. Jerusalem was out of the way—not a strategic military city. But the sacred city of David contained a palatial residence for the governor to use during the volatile period of religious feasts or other times of tension.

I vividly recall standing with fellow pilgrims from our Greensboro church upon the excavation beneath the Convent of the Sisters of Zion, or Church of Ecce Homo—the traditional site for Pilate's Praetorium. It was here, upon a stone pavement dating to the time of our Lord that, according to tradition, Jesus was ushered into the presence of the cautious governor. At this pilgrim's shrine, we examined markings etched in the cobbled stone. These ancient chiseled lines indicated how the Roman soldiers played a cruel game of mockery. After a judicial decision of conviction was announced, the soldiers often cast dice in order to win the authority to dress the condemned criminal for his execution. This grotesque charade was called "the game of kings." The winner placed the condemned prisoner in the marked area upon the cobbled stone, draped a royal robe around the humiliated prisoner's shoulders, and simulated a mock crown. These ancient stones beneath a Jerusalem church were an archaeological reminder of Roman cruelty and the irrevocable authority of imperial justice.

Who was this Pilate, before whose seat Jesus was thrust? One ancient Jewish source (Philo) described him as one who committed rape, murder, and violations of every human dignity. Josephus, an eyewitness to Jewish history of the first century, described the many times in which this governor forcibly put down popular insurrections. During his oppressive term, the Roman authorities had taken money from the

Part II: Paradox and Christology

temple treasury in order to construct an elaborate aqueduct. When Jewish protests arose, Pilate viciously squelched the opposition. On another occasion Pilate savagely executed Samaritan rebels near Mount Gerizim. Due to all this unrest, Rome finally decided to remove Pilate from his jurisdiction. There are no reliable records concerning his subsequent fate.

Yet, throughout the ages, this man will be remembered in the church's recitation of its most ancient and revered creed, which recalls that our Master "suffered under Pontius Pilate." Ironically, the writer of the Fourth Gospel described this hollow man as an indecisive, passive potentate. At first he declined even to see the teacher from Galilee. He did not want to be entangled in Jewish religious disputes. In the English narrative it would be more accurate to insert "Judean religious leaders" wherever there is a reference to "the Jews" in the Fourth Gospel's account of the arrest and trial of Jesus. The Judean rulers of the Sanhedrin and the Temple participated in this mock trial—not the collective people called "Jews." In Galilee, Jewish throngs had followed and admired Jesus, their homegrown teacher and miraculous healer. He was not executed by the Jews. Had this been the case, a stone would now be placed on our church altars instead of a cross. The Man of Nazareth indeed "suffered under Pontius Pilate," a Roman official. This governor literally had the power of life or death over Jesus. The Fourth Gospel discloses that the Judean religious leaders even reminded Pilate that it was illegal for their Sanhedrin to put to death anyone without prior imperial approval. Pilate was acting in collaboration with Herod Antipas, King of the Judeans and puppet potentate answerable to the Emperor of Rome.

Thus the scene in John's narrative quickly shifts from the spectacle in the public courtyard. Pilate brought Jesus into the Praetorium, asking him privately, "Are you the King of the Jews?" Our Lord responded obliquely, "Do you ask this on your own, or did others tell you about me?"[4] Pilate, perceiving Jesus' question as insolence, defensively replied that he was not a Jew and would rather not be entangled in Jewish controversy. Thus, Jesus told this governor who possessed the power of the emperor by proxy that his Kingdom was different from anything Pilate had ever seen: "If my kingdom were from this world, my followers would be fighting to keep me from being handed over to the Jews. But as it is, my kingdom is not from here."[5] When Jesus testified that his central role in life was to reveal the truth, Pilate dispassionately asked Jesus the philosophical question, "What is truth?" Threatened by the confident silence of the Galilean teacher, Pilate stalked out to the Praetorium's court and asked the Judean leaders what they wished to do with this alleged King of the Jews. Thus, Pilate became history's symbol of all who sustain political power by passing the buck! He granted the Judean leaders a choice between Barabbas, a violent Zealot, and Jesus, a prophet of nonviolence.

---

4. John 18:34 NRSV.
5. John 18:36 NRSV.

Pilate, despite his feigned innocence and non-complicity in this trial, was not a passive observer of Jesus' condemnation. It was he alone who ordered the scourging of our Lord. Contemporary students of Roman justice have recently discovered the intensity of torture experienced by the victims of scourging. Sharp iron nails and pieces of pointed glass protruded through the threads of the whips used in scourging. These lashes literally tore the flesh. Scholars now assume that Jesus' early death upon the cross was due to severe physical shock from this mutilation of his flesh. The Scriptures tell us that Pilate ordered this cruel scourging.

While Pilate assumed judgmental authority over Jesus, the King on a cross was the ultimate judge of Pilate. Several interesting legends suggest what might have become of this wicked man who played a bit part in cosmic history. The Orthodox Church preserves the legend that Pilate's wife, acquiring the name of Procula, became a Christian along with her penitent husband. The Coptic Church celebrates Pilate's memory to this day, declaring him a saint and martyr. The church of the fourth century even developed a curious manuscript known as *The Acts of Pilate*, an account of the passion and death of Jesus, as well as the contrition and conversion of Pilate. All this is speculation. Pilate left no footprints in the sands of time after the crucifixion. This mighty ruler of Palestine is instead remembered as an unwitting personification of irresponsibility and human sin.

Only Luke reports that Pilate, remembering that Herod Antipas was in Jerusalem for the Passover feast, sent Jesus to the king. Pilate was already dubious about taking authority to order the crucifixion of apparently an innocent man. But, if the Galilean followers of Jesus saw within the Nazarene the true "King of the Jews," then Caesar's proxy monarch, Herod Antipas, needed to encounter Jesus and take responsibility for his fate as a potential insurrectionist. Pilate's sending Jesus to Herod's jurisdiction was an acknowledgement that all of the rabbi's teachings had taken place in Galilee. Moreover, the Roman Emperor had given Antipas authority over this region as the "King of the Jews." This term was never applied to Jesus until the morning of the trial. Pilate, desiring to wash his hands of the matter and learning that Jesus, as a Galilean, was from Herod's sphere of jurisdiction, sent Jesus to Antipas in Luke's narrative, hoping that his political nemesis would make the difficult ruling on the Galilean's fate.

Why was Pilate slow to acknowledge that Jesus' center of operation and school of discipleship was in Caesarea of Galilee and not in Judea? Each of the Synoptic Gospels consistently report that the inscription over the wounded head of Jesus read, "This is Jesus, King of the Jews" (Matthew), "This is the King of the Jews" (Luke), or merely "the King of the Jews" (Mark). But John's Gospel has the inscription read in three languages, "Jesus of Nazareth, the King of the Jews." Herod Antipas was son of King Herod the Great by Malthace, his Samaritan wife. He and his older brother Archelaus and their half brother Philip were heirs of the subdivisions of their father's larger dominion. When the Romans removed Archelaus from ruling Judea, Herod Antipas remained the ruler of Galilee and Perea (Transjordan) until six years after

Jesus' crucifixion, when he was deposed by Emperor Caligula and exiled to Lyons in Gaul. At the time of the crucifixion, this puppet king was lusting after more power and desired to receive from the emperor the same authority as his father, who had built the massive Temple in Jerusalem as a symbol of his architectural genius and political favoritism from Emperor Tiberius. So it was that King Herod Antipas' authority was entirely contingent upon satisfying imperial expectations. Thus, Herod's primary mission was to maintain the peace and please the emperor at all costs. He had demonstrated his loyalty by building the prosperous city of Tiberias on the Galilean bank in the emperor's honor. Antipas aimed to please—and he succeeded. Raymond Brown observes that "during four decades of the reign of Augustus and Tiberius, Galilee under Antipas saw no revolt against the Romans."[6] Technically he was not a king, but rather a puppet of Roman power. Ironically, he was deposed for his overambitious attempts to reclaim his father's territorial jurisdiction.

Luke did not miss the irony of Pilate trying to hand over a peaceful Galilean teacher who would be crucified as "the King of the Jews" to a paranoid Herod Antipas. But Antipas had no desire to take responsibility for Jesus' fate. This itinerant preacher was technically a citizen of his province, but he knew that the supposed "crime" (claiming to be ruler of the Jews) was committed in Judea and that he had been apprehended in Jerusalem. Thus, while enjoying the Passover feast in the city, Antipas conveniently saw himself as a private citizen without the responsibility of jurisdiction. The governor had merely followed Roman judicial procedure by conducting a preliminary investigation (*anakrisis*) of Jesus. He had complete authority and needed no other judicial opinion. Luke reports that Pilate and Antipas had been enemies for some time. Raymond Brown reminds us that "Pilate had seen Herodian princes place themselves at the head of a mob during a feast to make protest against him."[7] Thus, the governor's disingenuous gesture requesting Antipas to render a second opinion (another *anakrisis*) was a political move appealing to Herod Antipas' ego and his royal desire for recognition in a region that remained under the absolute authority of the Roman Emperor. Once Herod had that acknowledgment, he returned Jesus to Pilate's jurisdiction, winning in the game of passing the buck. Luke's narrative makes a mockery of the whole administrative structure of a kingdom that would eventually evaporate before the glow of Jesus' ultimate reign. Emperor Augustus is a footnote in Luke's birth narrative (Luke 2:1). Tiberius is only worth noting because, during the fifteenth year of his dominion, John of the Wilderness began his ministry in preparation for the Messiah's coming. The city that carried his name is not even mentioned in Luke's careful geographical depiction of events in Galilee. Luke reports that pitiful Antipas was threatened and perplexed by news of all the miracles in this region of his kingly rule. When some Pharisees told Jesus that King Herod Antipas wanted to kill him, he replied, "Go and tell that fox for me, 'Listen, I am casting out

---

6. Brown, *Death of the Messiah*, 763.
7. Ibid., 767.

demons and performing cures today and tomorrow, and the next day I must be on my way, because it is impossible for a prophet to be killed outside of Jerusalem.'"[8] In Luke's narrative, Antipas remained upset throughout Jesus' ministry. When Pilate invited him to weigh in on Jesus' fate, his wounded ego was restored. The fox and the snake made peace. But Antipas lacked the courage to act like a king. He took no responsibility for the condemnation and execution of the Nazarene, and Luke's story reveals the fraudulence and insecurity of both Pilate and Herod. Only the man with the crown of thorns acted like the authentic King that he indeed was.

When the Evangelist John told the story of the trial of Jesus, he addressed the issue of authority. The community of the beloved disciple (the church of John the Evangelist) was shown in the writer's description of the trial scene that Jesus rules from the cross. His disciples could give allegiance to no other king than the Man of Nazareth, who was crucified by Pilate. Since each of the canonical gospels was written in order to impart the climax of Israel's cosmic Story of redemption, the paradoxical portrait of the Messiah nailed to a Roman cross with a crown of thorns was indeed a fulfillment of YHWH's design for the redemption of Israel and all humankind. *Israel*—literally meaning in Hebrew, "he strives [*yisra*] with God [*el*]"—is embodied by this King upon a cross. Each of the gospel narratives describes Jesus' fate as the personification of the enigmatic symbol contained in Isaiah (Isa 52:12–13) discussed more thoroughly in chapter 6 of this volume. The paradoxical reality of Israel's Messiah as this suffering King was manifested in the image of his crown of thorns on a Roman cross. God rules through God's suffering presence in a world of abhorrent injustice and human misery. Moreover, humanity's injustices shall be eradicated from this earth, and redemption shall come to a suffering world through the activity of the Holy Spirit within the life of the paradoxical church that truly embodies the compassionate and self-giving love of Jesus. God's kingly rule is the fulfillment of Israel's hope to draw all races and nations into alliance with YHWH in a covenant of grace. King Jesus is aligned with the previously unfulfilled heritage of Israel that began with King David and was diverted by subsequent wicked monarchs of Israel and Judah in defiance of the Hebrew prophets of righteousness. This King on a cross felt the pain of his fellow Jews, who had been crushed by conquering pagan nations during centuries of foreign oppression. The object of this King on a cross' love was his own people—citizens of Galilee, Judea, and Jerusalem. This King wept for the plight of a Jewish people who would soon lose their sacred Temple and be scattered to the winds for another nineteen centuries of exile.

But this King on a cross was not a political Messiah. He made it clear in the Garden of Gethsemane on the night of his arrest when he rebuked a disciple who had drawn a sword in his defense, "Put your sword back into its place; for all who take the sword will perish by the sword. Do you think that I cannot appeal to my Father, and he will at once send me more than twelve legions of angels? But how then would the

---

8. Luke 13:32–33 NRSV.

Part II: Paradox and Christology

Scriptures be fulfilled, which says it must happen in this way?"[9] "This way" was the way of the King-on-the-cross, the servant envisioned by Isaiah the prophet. All other kings and kingdoms of the world become dust and ashes. Only the King-on-the-cross his survived the ravages of time.

When the Romantic poet Percy Bysshe Shelley visited Egypt in December of 1818, he visited a colossal marble-carved statue nearly covered by sands of the desert. He was so stuck by the irony of the moment that he composed these striking words as a fitting epithet for the figure in the sand:

> Half sunk, a shattered visage lies, whose frown,
> And wrinkled lip, and sneer of cold command,
> Tell that its sculptor well those passions read
> Which yet survive, stamped on these lifeless things,
> The hand that mocked them, and the heart that fed:
> And on that pedestal these words appear:
> 'My name is Ozymandias, King of Kings:
> Look on my works, ye Mighty, and despair!'
> Nothing beside remains. Round the decay
> Of that colossal wreck, boundless and bare
> The lone and level sands stretch far away.[10]

Through the ages the church has been confronted with the temptation to renounce the paradoxical authority of the nonviolent, suffering King on a cross and succumb to the apostasy of national idolatry. Churches have even wrapped the American flag around Jesus, giving that symbol of patriotism a prominent place near the altar. When national and political agendas conflict with the teachings of Jesus, churches are enticed to endorse the posture of capitulation.

On August 1, 1990, Iraq invaded its oil-rich neighbor to the south, Kuwait. The aggression was instigated by Iraq's repressive president, Saddam Hussein. President George H. W. Bush condemned the invasion and began marshalling support for military intervention. Iraq made attempts to negotiate a deal that would allow the country to take control of half of Kuwait. In my sermons I advocated for a posture of patience and a negotiated peace. A member of the church that was scheduled to be deployed to Kuwait began to question the ethics and wisdom of the invasion. He articulated his objections before the local Army Reserve Office armed with a manuscript of a recent sermon from his church's pulpit. The young man left his position as a volunteer soldier, relinquished all financial benefits, and followed his conscience. He felt compelled to follow the command of an eternal, nonviolent authority.

The brave clergy and theologians who drafted the Barman Declaration in defiance of Nazi bigotry stood in opposition to Pilate in order to register their allegiance

---

9. Matt 26:52–54 NRSV.
10. Shelley, "Ozymandias," 802, lines 4–14.

to King Jesus. Many of them suffered the cruel fate of execution under the dominion of a twisted cross. Of such is the Kingdom of heaven. Rosa Parks was a devout member of an African Methodist Episcopal Church working in a downtown department store in Montgomery, Alabama, when she was ordered to sit in the back of a segregated bus. But she answered to a more exalted authority than the Jim Crow laws of Alabama. Of such is the Kingdom of God. Nelson Mandela was forbidden to organize black African workers under apartheid laws, but he was obedient to divine authority. Each week he was in prison, a cadre of Methodist pastors, including Rev. Peter Storey, brought to him the grace and power of Holy Communion in defiance of an unjust, racist government. Of such is the Kingdom of our Lord. Elias Chacour, a Maronite priest serving a congregation near the village of Jesus' childhood, suffered the indignity of his family's forced removal from their ancestral lands. Even though he has been urged to advocate violent retaliation, he continues to preach forgiveness of his enemies and an adherence to the principles of the Sermon on the Mount. Of such is the Kingdom of the King on a cross.

A dear friend tearfully told me the story of his eight-year-old grandchild, a leukemia patient at the university hospital. Instead of expressing self-pity, this remarkable child prayed prayers of thanksgiving until the day of her death. She consistently testified to the loving presence of Jesus in her pain. This little child had been nurtured in the love of a community of resurrection faith, and she remained under the authority of the risen King until her dying moment. She felt the power of the wounded monarch who had held little children in his arms and by whose stripes she has been made whole. Of such is truly the Kingdom of heaven!

A comrade pastor and close friend of mine was under constant pressure to dilute the gospel of his conviction so that the people of his congregation would feel more comfortable with their affluence. During a crucial Sunday service of worship, he humbly confessed to them, "I am your servant and pastor." Then he added with firmness of voice, "But you are not my Master." Of such is the Kingdom of Christ.

G. A. Studdert-Kennedy, an influential preacher and poet of the previous century, penned a fitting benediction for these faithful disciples who, in each generation, have embodied such courageous confrontational faith in defiance of principalities and powers:

> Blessed are the eyes that see
> The Agony of God,
> Blessed are the feet that tread
> The paths His feet have trod.
> Blessed are the souls that solve
> The paradox of Pain,
> And find the path that, piercing it,
> Leads through Peace again.[11]

11. Studdert-Kennedy, "My Peace I Give Unto You," 441, lines 5–11.

Part II: Paradox and Christology

Jesus' trial before Pilate points us toward the paradox of political power. This episode reminds us that the real power is not invested in Washington or other national capitols. American presidents often complain that the first thing they discover upon occupying the Oval Office is the limitation of their power to produce substantial change. A few decades ago the historian Arthur Schlesinger Jr. rightly observed that the wisest of our presidents have recognized the limitations of their power by exemplifying a "constitutional Presidency" (leadership based upon shared power) instead of an "imperial Presidency" (the usurpation of power).[12]

I served a congregation that maintained the tradition of a choral performance of Gian Carlo Menotti's opera, *Amahl and the Night Visitors*, during Epiphany. The three oriental kings in the story enter the simple dwelling of an impoverished mother and her crippled son. These kings tell them of the monarch whose humble birth has inspired their journey. The mother responds to their announcement by saying enthusiastically, "For such a King I've been waiting all my life."[13]

We live under the authority of a King on a cross who defined his royal identity by wearing a crown of thorns. His paradoxical identity invites us to sing in grateful moments of corporate worship the lines of Cleveland Coxe as a confident affirmation of faith:

> O where are kings and empires now,
> Of old that went and came?
> But, Lord, thy Church is praying yet,
> A thousand years the same.[14]

A King born in a cave, a monarch riding on an unpretentious ass, a ruler with a cross as his scepter and a circle of thorns for his crown—this is Christ the King to whom we offer our most fervent prayers.

---

12. Schlesinger, *Imperial Presidency*, viii.
13. Menotti et al., *Amahl and the Night Visitors*, score.
14. Coxe, "O Where Are Kings and Empires Now," 308, lines 1–4.

18

Starting to Live by Stopping for Death

THE MANNER IN WHICH Jesus faced his own death has always been a crucial consideration in the faith development of his followers. He is the model for all who contemplate their own mortality. After all, the Passion Narratives describe Jesus in Gethsemane dealing with the apparent abandonment of his heavenly Father who allowed and orchestrated this cruel, inhumane ending. How could Jesus proceed toward Golgotha ardently believing in the goodness of a deity who appeared to have forsaken him? What does his obedience unto death say to a disciple living in any historical circumstance of persecution, disease, violence, warfare, or natural disaster? What was the source of Jesus' incomparable courage as he lived out his entire ministry with a consciousness of his mission to perform God's design for cosmic redemption through his sacrificial death?

Jesus is our role model for grappling with the dilemma of death because he lived each day of his ministry with a consciousness of a divine purpose through his sacrificial ending. With this awareness, he lived with urgency. He truly considered each moment, each relationship, and each conversation to be sacred. The church did not inherit a reliable oral tradition narrating Jesus' childhood and adolescence. But if we accept the validity of Matthew's nativity narrative, we can only imagine his conversation with Mary when she presented him with a container of myrrh—a substance for anointing the bodies of the dead—and told her son about the mysterious visitors who offered this gift in tribute to his birth. From childhood, Jesus was acutely aware that he was to die for an exalted purpose.

Paradoxically, Jesus demonstrated to his followers the joy and incomparable vitality of a liberated life by his constant references to his impending death. Because of his perpetual awareness of his divinely appointed pilgrimage toward death, Jesus was fully alive with zeal, purpose, and enthusiasm. He was at peace with his role in performing God's redemptive purpose. He did not avoid discussion of his anticipated fate in his many conversations with the apostles. The other synoptic writers follow Mark's lead in remembering that Jesus described his imminent death as soon as Peter in Caesarea Philippi identified him as the Messiah of Israel. It seems ironic that as soon as this impetuous disciple articulated this bold profession of faith, Jesus immediately "began to teach them that the Son of Man must undergo great suffering, and be rejected by the elders, the chief priests, and the scribes, and be killed, and after three days rise again."[1] Matthew and Luke did not alter this sequence of events in their narratives. The Johannine Jesus, however, spoke more obliquely about the matter of the Messiah's death. The Fourth Gospel describes Jesus confronting priestly leaders by announcing, "Destroy this temple, and in three days I will raise it up."[2] None of them could have known that his veiled reference was to the temple of his own body and that he was portending his own death.

Yet Jesus' demeanor in the Galilean ministry was one of laughter, joyous surprises, affirmation of life, spectacular healings, and raucous playfulness. He and his apostles were even falsely accused of being gluttonous drunkards.[3] Jesus referred to those who made such accusations when he said, "They are like children sitting in the marketplace and calling to one another, 'We played the flute for you, and you did not dance; we wailed, and you did not weep.'"[4] Jesus was absorbed into the wisdom of the prophet who pensively declared that "the grass withers, the flower fades; but the word of our God will stand forever."[5] He acknowledged with every fiber of his being that life is transitory; therefore, he constantly encouraged his apostles to savor every moment they shared with him. This is why he commended reflective Mary of Bethany "who sat at the Lord's feet and listened to what he was saying," and reprimanded her sister, Martha the industrious host, who "was distracted by her many tasks."[6]

Jesus' fixation upon his own movement toward a costly death, however, was neither macabre nor depressing. It was a clarion call to celebrate the temporary—to savor each opportunity to be with the Messiah of Israel while there was still time. It was, likewise, a message to the community of his ardent followers: *Carpe diem*, relish each sacred moment in relationships of love within the community of faith.

This was the subtle theme of a sobering Swedish film titled, *She Danced Only One Summer*, in which two lovers are pictured in a meadow of daisies. He picks one lovely yellow flower and hands it to her as a gesture of his affection. She says, "Isn't it a pity that this flower will never live again?" He replies, "But why! There are thousands of

---

1. Mark 8:31 NRSV.
2. John 2:19 NRSV.
3. See Luke 7:34 NRSV.
4. Luke 7:32 NRSV.
5. Isa 40:8 NRSV.
6. Luke 10:39–40 NRSV.

them! The others will grow up in their places next spring!" She somberly responds, "But this one will never live again."[7]

Jesus was teaching his church to savor moments together, especially loving moments within the household of faith. Treat the living as though they are dying and the dead as if they are yet alive. Celebrate the sacredness and transient nature of all relationships in life and in death!

Even though Jesus maintained a consistent focus upon his pilgrimage toward a sacrificial, redemptive death, he did not use this circumstance to pry open the paradoxical knot of *theodicy*.[8] This theological term refers to the believer's defense of the justice and righteousness of God in face of the reality of evil. Theodicy has a twofold task: seek to justify the ways of God to humanity, or to justify the sinful ways of humanity to God. Theodicy, in short, asks the question of the ages: If God is good, whence evil? If God is righteous, why is there flagrant inequity in the suffering and death of innocents?

Instead of rationally or philosophically resolving this ineffable mystery, Jesus chose to prepare his disciples for death with clear accountability, courage, and trust in the providence of an enigmatic deity. Instead of dissolving the paradox of theodicy, he held the notions of a good Creator and an evil creation in unresolved tension. Just before he approached the time of his passion, Jesus was confronted by a cadre of disturbed Galileans who had witnessed the brutal slaying of their close friends at the hands of Pontius Pilate. Their devout Hebrew friends had made pilgrimage to Jerusalem for the Passover. But upon their arrival, they were cut down near the Temple Mount in the forecourt of the priests by decree of Pilate. This was the very place where lambs were slaughtered for Judaism's most sacred feast, so the blood of these pilgrims mingled with that of the paschal lambs. These martyred Galileans may well have been militant Zealots carrying weapons into the city of David or peaceful pilgrims who merely refused to honor the images of Caesar erected in Jerusalem by an arrogant, pagan Pilate. Luke does not give the full context of this tragic incident, but the group confronting Jesus wanted to know how God would rectify this horrendous injustice. Was it not time for YHWH to strike with vengeance those who had transgressed against the sons and daughters of Abraham? We know from the writings of Josephus that Pilate had sent infantrymen into a Samaritan village and massacred citizens who had vowed to reinstitute the rituals of animal sacrifice to YHWH upon Mount Gerizim. It was this same Pilate who had ordered effigies of Roman emperors to be brought into the sacred city of the Jews. Only the civil disobedience of thousands later prevented another massacre. Emperor Augustus, after all, had removed Archelaus from his rule of Judea

---

7. Quoted in Michalson, *Faith for Personal Crises*, 176.

8. This is not a biblical word, but its origin is commonly attributed to the philosopher Gottfried Wilhelm von Leibniz (1646–1716) who first used the term in a letter dated 1697. He combined the Greek word for "God," *Theós*, and the term for "justice," *díke*, to coin a shorthand expression regarding a technical theological contradiction.

Part II: Paradox and Christology

when Jesus was still a child in Nazareth for using excessive violence against the Jews. This predecessor of Pilate had slaughtered some three thousand faithful Jews at about the time of Passover.[9] Jesus fully comprehended the legitimacy of these intensely personal theological concerns as the Galileans asked if their martyred comrades had died because of their great sins. Their question was an attempt to draw Jesus into a political denunciation of Pilate and the Roman bureaucracy. They were eager to hear from the lips of their kinsman an endorsement of their lust for revenge. But Jesus circumvented the political implications of this horrible incident, using their concern as an opportunity to speak of the divine judgment all must face in dying.

Instead of attempting to resolve the ineffable mystery of theodicy, Jesus chose to talk about the reality of death and the moral accountability that must be reckoned by the devout as well as the devilish. Thus, Jesus did not respond with a theological explanation. He did not dissolve the mysterious paradox that holds in creative, unresolved tension the notions of a good Creator and an evil creation. Instead, he merely told a story—a simple parable about a fig tree.[10] His story told of a man who planted a fig tree in his vineyard. He soon discovered that the tree was nonproductive. Patiently, he gave it three years to produce fruit. Then he instructed his gardener to cut it down, for the unproductive tree was wasting soil. This prompted the gardener to plead for the tree's survival. He argued that if he were given a chance to dig around it, nourish and water it, then the tree would blossom and abound in sweet fruit. The vineyard's owner allowed himself to be convinced to allow the fig tree one year's probation.

My initial response to the parable was disappointment. Jesus, who was always so empathetic toward victims of oppression, told these distraught people that they should use this tragic occasion to repent their own evils. Jesus appears to have been listening with callous ears. Perhaps the reason that Jesus' response appears harsh to me and other contemporary disciples is that we have been hearing the parable with Western ears. We desire a logical answer to life's greatest enigmas. Instead, Jesus told a parable of Eastern wisdom about a farmer and a fig tree. His Hebraic response is more akin to the thinking of modern Jewish writer Elie Wiesel. Wiesel contends that justice eludes human grasp. History always provides a Pontius Pilate to rule with cruel impunity. The perpetrators of evil stand backstage in every era's drama, awaiting a cue to enter. Good people suffer in every generation. The most noble among us suffer death by martyrdom, but everyone must eventually face an ending. In his biographical account of his death camp experiences,[11] Wiesel reports that he was present at the public hanging of a tiny youth whose crime was stealing of a crust of bread. His *offense* was likely committed to keep a parent alive. In face of this atrocious evil, Wiesel perceived only one ray of hope. All shall die: this innocent child, his parents whom he sought to save, the SS guard who sentenced him to the gallows, Eichmann of the "Final Solu-

---

9. Fitzmyer, *Gospel According to Luke*, 1,003–1,009.
10. See Luke 13:6–9 NRSV.
11. See Wiesel, *Night*.

tion," the Nazi High Command, and Adolph Hitler himself. Each individual death reminds us that all will die. All will face accountability before the God of the Mosaic covenant. For Elie Wiesel, this is a hardheaded hope amidst the tragedies of history. In the death camp, he came to believe that if only one Jew survived and maintained faithfulness to YHWH, the ancient pilgrimage of salvation history would be preserved and ultimate victory over the oppressor would become a reality.

Jesus' parable suggests a similar theology. Like Wiesel, Jesus refused to condone wrath toward the oppressor. Hatred transforms the righteous person into the same demonic form as the object of his or her hate. Instead, Jesus offered a parable of mercy showing that each death, whether caused by a tragic evil or a natural disaster, is a reminder to all that we have a fleeting opportunity for repentance. The tree was given the grace of one more year in order to produce. In like manner, every tragedy is a sobering reminder that we have one more chance at aligning ourselves with God's righteous covenant. Thus, Jesus' parable makes no attempt to dissolve the paradox of theodicy. Instead, he trusted in the providential love of a merciful God whose ways remain mysterious. This God of tender mercy and tough judgment holds all people accountable for the conduct of their lives.

A culture of violence propagates the notion that a redemptive death is heroism upon the field of battle. Role models of courageous soldiers are paraded before children and youth with the implication that dying a violent death for one's country is the quintessential redemptive act. A culture that renders supreme value to those who have paid the ultimate price by dying for their country merely sustains the cycle of violence that is exacerbated by this honored core value of civil religion.

Some of the most popular Protestant hymns in America related to death, heaven, and life after death were written during the Civil War and the decades immediately following this nation's most violent era. Moreover, some of the most flagrant violations of scriptural teaching related to these matters of theology emerged during this influential period. Believers were encouraged to consider that the essence of the Christian faith is a rescue of people from this world of sin, suffering, injustice, and warfare—not a mission to rescue the world from itself. Salvation exclusively came to mean "going to heaven when you die"—not the reality of Christ's kingdom of *shalom* being established on earth, as in the petition of the Lord's Prayer. Over 750,000 people died in that protracted period of carnage. In the South, this meant 20 percent of all men of military age were killed, especially in my home state of North Carolina, which sent by far the highest percentage of its male population to fields of armed conflict.[12]

Subsequent generations of Americans, especially those devoutly engaged in the worship and missional life of the church, have tried to make sense of all of this. If each fallen ancestor died a redemptive death and is gathered with the saints in glory, for what exalted purpose did they die in battle? Is the story of their valor a narrative of our redemption? Is dying for the preservation of the institution of slavery a redemptive

---

12. See Hilderman, *They Went into the Fight*.

Part II: Paradox and Christology

act? No wonder Southern revisionists concocted lengthy essays and volumes of research in order to justify states rights and other political abstractions in order to validate humanity's violent ways before God. The chiseled statues that dot the vast shrine of Gettysburg on the 150th anniversary of that battle are impressive artistic attempts to articulate a gospel of redemption through that righteousness military conflict.

In 2008, historian Drew Gilpin Faust, President of Harvard University, published her engaging study, *This Republic of Suffering: Death and the American Civil War*. A crucial portion of Dr. Faust's research centers on how the dying and bereaved appropriated their understanding of Jesus' dying and a Christian interpretation of life beyond death. She supplies numerous stories of dying soldiers, abandoned in open battlefields, managing to scribble on note paper a brief prayer or personal testimony of faith in their last moments of earthly existence. Amid the carnage of so many unidentified bodies, life seemed cheap. Devout Christian soldiers on both sides of the conflict were asking, "Where is God in all of this?" Did the redemptive death of Christ somehow bless the blood-soaked soil and sacrifices on the battlefields of an anguished nation? President Lincoln's immortal words upon the dedication of the cemetery at Gettysburg expressed the nation's yearning for a sense of meaning in the aftermath of such slaughter as he pledged the corporate resolve "that these dead shall not have died in vain."[13] But how could death on such a colossal scale be the source of national redemption? Christian families in both the North and South asked how the death and resurrection of Jesus could bring them comfort and transform this seemingly senseless conflict into a noble saga of glorious purpose, valor, and redemption.

In November of 1861, Julia Ward Howe and her husband Samuel visited President Lincoln at the White House. That week, she was inspired to write "The Battle Hymn of the Republic." The hymn was set to the tune of a popular ballad (viz., "John Brown's Body") and quickly became one of the Union's most popular songs of the throughout the war:

> In the beauty of the lilies Christ was born across the sea,
> With a glory in his bosom that transfigured you and me;
> As he died to make men holy,
> Let us die to make men free,
> While God marching on.[14]

Even the eloquence of Lincoln and the poetic fervor of the abolitionist Julia Howe failed to grasp the reality that, according to the gospel witness in Scripture, only one death had the power of universal redemption. Stanley Hauerwas, reflecting upon the horrors of that conflict, observed, "If the Civil War teaches us anything, it is that when Christians no longer believe that Christ's sacrifice is sufficient for the salvation

---

13. Lincoln, Abraham, "The Gettysburg Address," at Soldiers' National Cemetery, Gettysburg, PA, November 19, 1863.

14. Howe, "Battle Hymn of the Republic," 717.

of the world, we will find other forms of sacrificial behaviors that are as compelling as they are idolatrous. In the process, Christians confuse the sacrifice of war with the sacrifice of Christ."[15]

During the Civil War, death and its aftermath became an obsession. Clergy and popular writers articulated elaborate theological conjectures surrounding the dying soldier's reunion with deceased family members. Dr. Faust observes that "in the Civil War death was hardly hidden, but it was nevertheless, seemingly paradoxically denied—not through silence and invisibility, but through an active and concerted work of reconceptualization that rendered it a cultural preoccupation."[16] Many popular religious authors felt it incumbent to comment upon the geography and furniture of heaven, implying that the mission of Jesus was to come to earth ever so briefly, die on a cruel cross, and return to heaven in order to provide an anteroom paradise for all believers—especially those who have fought for such noble causes as Southern independence or the liberation of slaves. Over fifty volumes on the subject of heaven were written between 1830 and 1875.[17] Many well-intended, devout believers turned toward a distorted Christian form of spiritualism by which the bereaved were encouraged to conduct séances with their dead kindred. Mary Todd Lincoln famously conducted such spiritual rituals at the White House in an attempt to assuage her grief by communicating with her deceased son, Willie. One of the most popular writings during the war years was *The Gates Ajar*, a journey of fantasy written by Elizabeth Stuart Phelps in which the protagonist, Mary Cabot, learns of the death of her beloved brother in the anguish of battle. She is comforted by an aunt who provides an elaborate scheme of how heaven is constituted as a perfected replica of earth. This was one of the most popular religious writings during the era surrounding the war.[18]

Enthusiastic worship within every faithful parish will give joyous testimony to the fact that Christ's sacrificial death is sufficient for the salvation of the world! Yes, worshipers are compelled to honor and give thanks for the lives of courageous men and women who have died sacrificially. But only the death of Jesus the Christ is the source of human redemption. Thus, Christ-centered worship must refrain from glorifying war and comparing sacrifice in battle to our Savior's unique role in cosmic redemption.

Jesus came and died in order that we may have life in abundance. He came to establish his glorious Kingdom of *shalom* and to abolish all warfare. His parable of the Fig Tree is an utterance of grace—not a story of harsh, unmitigated judgment. The twist of the story occurs when the gardener pleads on behalf of the unproductive tree, beseeching the owner for another year's reprieve to bear fruit. So it is that God does not come to us like some sadistic night policeman, eager to arrest and convict. The

---

15. Hauerwas, *War and the American Difference*, 34.
16. Faust, *Republic of Suffering*, 177.
17. Ibid., 179.
18. Ibid., 186–97.

Part II: Paradox and Christology

Lord does not always explain the rationale or timing of his arrival, but God comes, as surely as death, even our death. There is still time for reconciliation with an enemy or family member. There is ample time to communicate our love to someone. There is still time to set things right with one another and with God. Yet this gracious God always sounds a sober warning. Life has its inevitable ending. Do not wait until it is too late. Let us experience abundant life while we remain within the land of the living, for the joy of this abundant life in Christ will indeed accompany us to the other side of death.

Dostoevsky's story, *The Dream of a Ridiculous Man*, communicates a similar message. A foolish man is so depressed that he holds a revolver to his temple. He sees his existence as nothing more than pain and suffering. Yet in a state of indecision, he falls asleep. He dreams that he indeed pulled the trigger. He sees himself laying in a coffin, cold and motionless. To his utter consternation, death did not produce his non-being. His conscious thoughts transcended his dead body. Suddenly he realizes that his life on earth had not been despised. He begins repenting of past evils, especially his cruel treatment of a young girl. He even embraces times of excruciating suffering in his life. He cries out, "On our earth we can truly love only with suffering and through suffering. We know not how to love otherwise. We know no other love. I want suffering in order to love."[19] The ridiculous man finally awakens from his dream, immediately realizing that he had not committed suicide. Through this transforming experience, he becomes (for the first time) truly alive. He eagerly goes forth proclaiming, "The main thing is to love your neighbor as yourself—that is the main thing, and that is everything, for nothing else matters."[20]

During the years following the tragedy of September 11, 2001, attendance at Ash Wednesday worship services has increased dramatically. At that service, we place ashes in the form of the cross upon the forehead of each worshiper. The pastor looks into the eyes of each person kneeling at the altar and says, "As in Adam all must die, so also in Christ shall all be made alive." With these sobering words of judgment and grace, we are all invited to face the fact that we shall die. Christ's sacrificial death is our source of salvation unto eternal life. Only by embracing this reality through the living Lord are we made truly alive. In so doing, we shall discover the solemnity and wisdom of Emily Dickinson when she wrote during the year of the Battle of Gettysburg,

> Because I could not stop for Death—
> He kindly stopped for me—
> The Carriage held but just Ourselves—
> And Immortality.[21]

---

19. Dostoevsky, "The Dream of a Ridiculous Man," in Kamen, *Great Russian Stories*, 146.
20. Ibid., 155.
21. Dickinson, "Because I Could Not Stop for Death," 350, lines 1–4.

19

Resisting Resurrection

THE SUNDAY NEAREST TO All Saints' Day has become an emotionally sensitive time in my worship experience. For decades I have presided over a liturgical experience in which the names of those who have died since the last observance are called individually, followed by a poignant pause, the lighting of a candle upon the altar, and the sharp ringing of a bell. A sermon follows theses sobering, reflective moments, and the congregation of relatives and intimate friends remain exceptionally attentive. The pastor of the church I now attend began his sermon at this year's All Saints' service with an absorbing account of a young adult parishioner who had recently lost his wife to an aggressive brain tumor. Standing before her casket with his arms enfolding his three-year-old daughter, the bereaved father nodded to his pastor and said to his daughter, "Darling, Reverend Giles is going to tell you where your mother is now."

Reverend Giles' sensitive sermon correlated resurrection faith and the congregation's memory of the authentic Christians who had died during the year. His proclamation was followed by an offertory transition preceding the morning Eucharist. During these reflective moments, I saw that one of the elementary children in the Sunday school class I teach had left the pew where he had been seated with his grandparents and was racing toward the narthex. This child lives with his grandparents because of the recent death of his mother. He was alone with his mother when she died. The All Saints' service had likely evoked vivid memories of his traumatic experience. Since I was seated at an inconspicuous place in the nave and could make an unobtrusive exit from the gathered worshippers, I quickly joined the grandparents at the church's entrance to discover the disconsolate child weeping uncontrollably. What does one say to a child to bring comfort, assurance, and hope amidst such a stark reality?

In the first ten chapters of this book we explored various facets of the proposition that the nature of God's being is revealed paradoxically. In this second section, we examine the corollary concept within the biblical presentation of the Messiah of

Part II: Paradox and Christology

Israel as the human embodiment of that divine paradox. Jesus of Nazareth comes to us through Scripture as a paradoxical reality bringing blessing through his misfortune, power through his failure, the essence of revolutionary leadership through his costly service, fulfillment through the emptying of his life, sacredness through his suffering, peace through confrontation, kingly rule through his crucifixion, and abundant life through his acceptance of a gruesome death.

But the construct of this theology of God's complete and mysterious dwelling within the life of the Man of Nazareth is contingent upon the clarion acclaim of Scripture that this paradoxical man of history was indeed raised by God from the dead. This whole theological construct crumbles unless the crucified Jesus has been raised from the dead. Unless this is a reality, the whole pronouncement of faith is a house of cards. The Apostle Paul risked the credibility of his entire theological paradigm when he wrote this message to a skeptical community of newly converted Christians in Corinth: "Now if Christ is proclaimed as raised from the dead, how can some of you say there is no resurrection of dead? If there is no resurrection of the dead, then Christ has not been raised; and if Christ has not been raised then our proclamation has been in vain and your faith has been in vain."[1]

In this chapter I shall argue that the resurrection of Jesus of Nazareth was an unprecedented historical event because, through this occurrence, God brought new life and divine endorsement to the authentic paradoxical man whose very existence uniquely embodied the being of God. The good news of resurrection, however, has been resisted in every era of the church's history. This crucial proclamation has been regarded as irrational and mysterious, as with the appearance of "strange things" (*paradoxa*) in Luke 5:26. We resist the doctrine of the resurrection of the crucified God for the same reasons we view with skepticism the paradoxical disclosures of God and the paradoxical teachings and events in the life of Jesus.

Resurrection has been resisted by followers of the Way from the time of Paul's ministry in Corinth until the present moment. Why is the good news so contested by both ancient and modern Christians? Jewish converts to the Way, as evidenced by Paul's First Epistle to the Corinthians, did not inherit the expectation of a risen Messiah. Most rabbinic Jews of the first century, however, did believe in a general resurrection at the culmination of history with a reconstructed, resurrected Israel, as reflected in the scroll of Daniel: "The kingship and dominion and the greatness of the kingdom under the whole heaven shall be given to the people of the holy ones of the Most High."[2] Pharisaic Judaism during Jesus' life embraced both the concept of the personal hope of righteous individuals as well as the national hope for faithful Israel through a general resurrection. When Judas Maccabaeus prayed for departed warriors in their struggles against infidel Greeks, the author of 2 Maccabees reported, "For if [Judas Maccabee] were not expecting that those who had fallen would rise

1. 1 Cor 15:12–14 NRSV.
2. Dan 7:27 NRSV.

again, it would have been superfluous and foolish to pray for the dead."³ Most Hebrew converts to the Way already believed that God's climactic act in history would be a rising of all the dead, but prior to the Easter event, no Jew anticipated the resurrection of God's Messiah.

Each canonical gospel was written from the perspective of belief in the resurrection of the crucified Messiah. The paradoxical nature of Jesus' existence—his strange teachings, mysterious parables, astounding healings, and revolutionary ministry—is rendered plausible by this essential belief. But it is amazing how little documentation the four Evangelists give to the resurrection story. They all include a narration of the empty tomb of Jesus. Except for the early and authentic version of Mark, the gospels contain accounts of Jesus appearing alive before his followers. But none provide an eyewitness account of the actual event itself. It could certainly be argued that the Jesus of the gospels went to Jerusalem knowing that he would be arrested and executed. But is it, likewise, plausible that he also trusted that Israel's God would raise him from the dead, vindicating faithfulness after such a horrendous death?

The gospel writers and the Apostle Paul articulated a belief in the bodily resurrection of Jesus. N. T. Wright, examining the whole corpus of the Pauline Letters, states that "for Paul, the resurrection of Jesus of Nazareth is the heart of the gospel (not to the exclusion of the cross, of course, but not least as the event which gives the cross its meaning); it is the object of faith, the ground of justification, the basis for obedient Christian living, the motivation for unity, and not least, the challenge to the principalities and powers."⁴ So why has the church through the ages been so resistant to this pivotal proclamation? Why has this resistance been especially articulated by followers of the Way throughout the centuries of Christian witness, beginning with the communities of faith surrounding the Apostle Paul and each of the gospel writers?

The Evangelist Matthew reported that the chief priests and Pharisees implored Pilate to guard the tomb in the likelihood that Jesus' disciples would steal the body and spread the falsehood that he had been raised from the dead.⁵ Resurrection was resisted from the start because dead people do not come out of their tombs alive. John's Gospel alone tells the story of Jesus' raising of Lazarus as a precursor to the empty tomb narrative. But Lazarus' raising was resuscitation. He would eventually experience another death. The early church proclaimed the uniqueness of what God did with the body of Jesus. This inimitable event was, in fact, a prolepsis of what God will do upon the culmination of human history. The resurrection of Jesus, moreover, makes possible in this life a new existence for all that believe in the gospel message. It provides in the present moment a foretaste, or *earnest*, of what God will ultimately procure in human history—namely, the advent of a new heaven and a new earth. The Apostle Paul used the metaphor of a seed to explain the impact of Jesus' resurrection

---

3. 2 Macc 12:44 NRSV.
4. Wright, *Resurrection of the Son of God*, 266.
5. See Matt 27:62–66 NRSV.

as "the first fruits of those who have died," reminding the Corinthians that "what you sow does not come to life unless it dies."[6]

Just as many in each era of church history have been reticent to accept the paradoxical teachings and extraordinary activities of Christ, so too have many insisted upon a faith that removes mystery, requires empirical evidence, and resolves paradox. Many modern Christians, therefore, resist the notion of a bodily resurrection. They simply remind the church that dead people do not come out of graves. Resuscitation, yes; resurrection, no. Many devout Christians take pride in a post-Enlightenment view of reality, assuming that belief in a bodily resurrection requires returning to a pre-seventeenth-century, non-scientific, irrational world view.

Throughout most of the twentieth century, biblical scholarship has utilized form criticism and analytical methods developed in part by the German theologian Ernst Troeltsch (1865–1923). This University of Heidelberg professor wanted the church to remain relevant during an emerging era of unprecedented scientific advancement and social change. Troeltsch came to understand history as a study of human beings interacting within a complex web of forces. But objective history excludes consideration of metaphysics, ultimate reality, or the concept of God. Historical method cannot, therefore, employ resources that deny empirical evidence. In short, an objective study of religion and biblical literature must be congruent with a modern scientific and rational methodology. Interpretations of biblical texts must, therefore, subscribe to the cause-and-effect realities within the natural world. Central to Troeltsch's philosophy of historical method was the principle of analogy. Historical judgments presuppose an essential similarity between what humans now experience and what people have experienced in past time periods. This requires an analytical, critical exploration of all Scripture, because these revered ancient texts have their origins many centuries before the Enlightenment and the emergence of a scientific, cause-and-effect worldview.

Troeltsch's methodology for exploring and analyzing Scripture has dominated the works of biblical scholars through most of the last century. Rudolf Bultmann, for example, utilized this method of analysis, coupled with an existential interpretation influenced by the philosopher Martin Heidegger. In his discussion concerning the Pauline argument for resurrection, Bultmann asserts in a matter-of-fact way, "For the resurrection, of course, simply cannot be a visible fact in the realm of human history."[7] Those elements of the Bible that defy analogy were deemed to be non-historical, or mythological. But the mythological stories may indeed have a life-altering impact on the believer and great value within the faith community, even though these texts may not have their origin in an historical event. These pericopes from the Bible may indeed have a legitimate and existential impact upon the individual Christian and the believing community. Bultmann regarded the story of the empty tomb and other such texts to be mythological, but sacred. He insisted that the gospel accounts of

---

6. 1 Cor 15:33 NRSV.
7. Bultmann, *Theology of the New Testament*, 295.

the resurrection are best appropriated through rational process. Later practitioners of Bultmann's methodology, especially those among the Jesus Seminar, began to use the designations "authentic" and "inauthentic."[8] Thus, anyone using Bultmann's methodology will likely assume that if the bones of the dead Jesus were discovered today in a Palestinian tomb by some enterprising archaeologist, all the essentials of the Christian faith would still remain unchanged.

Marcus Borg has popularized the insights of Bultmann in an attempt to make the Christian faith plausible to modern skeptics. He too attempts to address the sophisticated person sitting on a church pew who assumes that a molecular, protoplasmic, corpuscular being could not rise from the dead. Borg is evangelical in affirming the validity of Christ's ethical teachings, his formation of a new community built upon those teachings, his courageous confrontation of racial and ethnic barriers, and the inspiration of his redemptive death. Resurrection, for Marcus Borg, is the symbolic expression of the living presence of this God-centered life within the lives of his followers. Thus, Borg maintains his identity as a follower of the Way of Jesus, but insists that belief in a bodily resurrection is a violation of a rational view of historical reality.

H. Richard Niebuhr was a highly influential Yale Divinity School professor during the mid-twentieth century. He wrote his doctoral dissertation on the typological method of Ernst Troeltsch. Niebuhr then meticulously employed this analytical method in his most famous work, *Christ and Culture*, published in 1951. In 1957, he published a volume that received little notice titled *Resurrection and Historical Reason*, in which he maintianed his commitment to Troeltsch's analytical methodology. But Niebuhr observed in this volume that the New Testament witness consistently asserts that the resurrection of Israel's Messiah is a unique event. It has only one analogy—namely, original creation. Through the resurrection of Jesus as the Christ of faith, God has created that which is truly new. This new reality, which had its origins in the physical resurrection of the crucified Man of Nazareth, will have its fulfillment, analogy, and consummation within the culmination of human history through the arrival of the Kingdom of God. Jesus' life embodied this coming Kingdom and his resurrection was the guarantee of its ultimate arrival. Niebuhr, thus, finds it unnecessary to abandon form criticism and an analytical or historical critique of biblical literature in general and the resurrection narrative in particular. He insists that resurrection can be compared only with the event of original creation—*creatio ex nihilo*. But it differs from original creation in that it "draws upon the past and evokes the historical possibilities of the future."[9] Thus, Niebuhr's assertion here has extensive implications for the methodology of form criticism that insists upon the demythologization of the Easter proclamation. Form critics, according to Niebuhr, have clothed the central message of the Christian faith in the strait jacket of natural law and discarded the textual witness to a unique occurrence as irrational. Niebuhr further argues that "all laws

8. Ibid.
9. Niebuhr, *Resurrection and Historical Reason*, 171.

Part II: Paradox and Christology

of nature are highly abstract, because they have to do only with aspects of total events, but never with the totality of a single event."[10] I find H. Richard Niebuhr's argument to be a highly plausible explanation that maintains the mystery of Christ's resurrection without discarding analytical methods of historical assessment.

In a massive volume titled *The Resurrection of the Son of God*, N. T. Wright carefully examines the resurrection theme in the entire biblical corpus—the Letters of Paul, documents of the early church apart from Paul, including the early Christian Apocrypha, works of early church theologians, and the Nag Hammadi texts. He gives particular attention to the Easter stories within the four canonical gospels and summarizes their theological import. He refrains from claiming that his comprehensive study proves the historicity of the bodily resurrection of Jesus, but he considers that his efforts provide a rational ground for the contemporary, scientific-method-oriented skeptic to believe with fervor in the physical resurrection of Jesus. He makes a convincing case, offering exhaustive textual evidence that the New Testament authors did not imagine the resurrection event or invent this article of faith. Wright makes a compelling argument for uniqueness when he writes,

> The early Christian understanding of Easter was not that this sort of thing was always likely to happen sooner or later, and finally it did . . . This was not a special favour performed for Jesus because his god liked him more than anyone else. *The fact that dead people do not ordinarily rise is itself part of early Christian belief*, not an objection to it. The early Christians insisted that what had happened to Jesus was precisely something new; was, indeed, the start of a whole new mode of existence, a new creation. The fact that Jesus' resurrection was, and remains, without analogy is not an objection to the early Christian claim. It is part of the claim itself.[11]

Each of the four gospels was written from the perspective of their narratives' endings. Resurrection is their gospel. Thus, it comes as no surprise that John the Evangelist began his account with a curious prologue of eighteen verses that serve as a *Midrash* related to the first creation story in the initial chapter of Genesis. "In the beginning was the Word, and the Word was with God, and the Word was God."[12] John's central message was that this Word "became flesh and lived among us, and we have seen his glory, the glory as of a father's only son, full of grace and truth."[13] The prologue is not only a *Midrash* that relates Israel's Messiah to the Hebraic theology of creation, but is also a prelude and interpreter of the narrative of John's story. None of the disciples recognized Jesus' true glory until the event of resurrection. The prologue's central message is, therefore, really about resurrection. God's raising Jesus

---

10. Ibid., 166.
11. Wright, *Resurrection of the Son of God*, 711–12, emphasis Wright's.
12. John 1:1 NRSV.
13. John 1:14 NRSV.

unto glory is compared in John's *Midrash* to the unique event of original creation. John's astonishingly profound narrative about this inimitable, paradoxical life of Jesus can only be told in the context of this commentary on original creation. Thus, the seven paradoxical signs of the Messiah's lordship that hold together John's mesmerizing story move toward the recognition of his glorification through the resurrection. Glorification of the paradoxical being, Jesus of Nazareth, can only be compared to the event of original creation. The spiritual presence of this unique being—the embodiment of the being of God—has been let loose into the world through the power of the resurrection, and history is, consequently, moving toward the Kingdom reality that he proleptically revealed. All things are made new through his spiritual presence in the life of the church. A new creation has occurred through the resurrection of the paradoxical being of God, who has come in the flesh and body of the Man of Nazareth.

Even though disciples have resisted the proclamation of Jesus' resurrection in every era, including new Christians in the community Paul established in Corinth, the message of the empty tomb forces the disciples to deal with the life of Jesus. Due to the resurrection, this prophet from Nazareth was more than a figure in history, soon to be forgotten. The original followers of the Way professed that this man who had lived among them with such compassion was alive once more, and his return now redefined the meaning of their lives. They could no longer nurse their hurts, wallow in their grief, and seek revenge upon those who had crucified their Lord. Christ had been let loose into their world! No gravestone had been strong enough to keep him down. Resurrection came as God's protest against their resignation at the sight of Jesus' death. Mighty Rome had erected a stone to anchor his death. Resurrection was an act of civil disobedience! The risen Christ has forever been released into the world in order to bring new vitality, meaning, and hope to all of his disciples, lifting them from graves of despair and attitudes of sullen resignation. Through the resurrection, the community of his followers has become the hands and feet of the living, risen Christ.

Throughout Mark's Gospel there runs the theme of the hidden Messiah—the secret presence of God in the ministry of Jesus. The Messiah's identity was not apparent to his disciples. Mark concluded his story with an empty tomb, an angel, and a promise. The empty tomb released the secret of God's paradoxical truth: In dying, Christ was made truly alive. Why, then, did the oldest manuscript of Mark (the great fourth-century codices Sinaiticus and Vaticanus) end the story on a note of dread and terror? "So they went out and fled from the tomb, for terror and amazement had seized them; and they said nothing to anyone, for they were afraid."[14] I am not convinced by N. T. Wright's argument that the original manuscript of Mark contained an extended conclusion which is now lost and for which the two extra endings that were thrown into the mix are inadequate substitutes.[15] I find it entirely credulous that the apostles

---

14. Mark 16:8 NRSV.

15. See Wright's *New Testament and the People of God* and chapter 14 of *Resurrection of the Son of God*.

Part II: Paradox and Christology

were fearful in the face of this unprecedented mystery. Hugh Anderson, formerly a Professor of New Testament at the University of Edinburgh, wisely surmises, "Again the silent dread with which the record closes can be taken as a sign of the awe and reverence of those for who the old world has run its course and the new day of God is actualized through the living Jesus who is on the move toward encountering men."[16] I find a great profundity within Mark's laconic Gospel narrative, which ends the story with the sober observation, "for they were afraid." The period at the end of this climactic sentence sustains the awe and reverence inherent in the astounding message of resurrection. The fear of the God that raised Jesus is the beginning of wisdom and understanding. This cryptic ending provokes skeptical resistance, but it also invites deep-seated trust and faith's reliance upon awe, reverence, and paradox.

Peter, who had denied Jesus and fled in self-defense, was told that this is not the end of the story. Because of the resurrection, Peter experienced forgiveness, restoration, Pentecost, and a glorious mission. Because of the resurrection, Peter encountered persecution. Ultimately he was crucified upside-down. "Go and tell Peter that it's not over quite yet," the messenger said at the empty tomb.

When we are confronted with God's direct intervention into history that defied the finality of Jesus' crucifixion, we too are afraid. Mark understood this fear as a natural and immediate response. The empty tomb was a soul-shaking reality. Jesus, therefore, cannot be studied like some archaeological bone from an ancient grave. We must deal with the risen Lord in our present moment. The risen Christ requires each of us to become new beings, transformed by the power of his unconquerable love. We may resist the good news of his resurrection, but its message will no longer allow us to wallow in our own pity. We are not allowed to become too comfortable with our own grief. The future is now open, and we are responsible for living courageously in the power and hope that resurrection faith offers in our present moment. Resurrection faith sends us in mission to transform a world of corruption, suffering, alienation, sin, and death.

A Jewish rabbi, greatly disturbed by all the prejudice and persecution suffered by his people in the tragic 1930s, wrote an appeal to all Christendom to be printed in newspapers on the eve of another Easter. It stated in part, "I challenge the Christian world to measure itself by the standards of Christ. As long as any group is judged by its creed or color or country in place of its character, Christianity is a sacrilege rather than sanctity. To this end I summon Christians everywhere to make this Easter to signify Christ realized and not merely Christ risen."[17]

Easter faith jolts us into a new awareness that the paradoxical ethic that Jesus taught upon the hillsides of Galilee is not an impossible ideal, that loving one's enemies is the expected stance of a disciple, that the peaceable kingdom of reconciled enemies is not merely a utopian concept, and that the followers of Jesus are truly called to imitate his paradoxical ways. Easter forbids us from admiring a dead prophet

16. Anderson, *Gospel of Mark*, 354.
17. Elmore, *Inexhaustible Christ*, 121.

and invites us to follow a living Lord! The mission of Christ to bring unto fruition a world in which all people are united through covenant love is not a quixotic ethical ideal; it is the ultimate destination of salvation history. We cannot return to business as usual if our business is resurrection faith. We are called to proclaim the message of *Christ realized*. His love is not merely an ideal; it is a reality that takes hold of our entire existence. His capacity for compassion is not merely a legacy of remembrance contained in the four gospel reports; it is his call for us to imitate his example. His tenderness and forgiving spirit is, therefore, a present reality through the living witness of his caring community, the church.

Theologian Robert McAfee Brown once wrote a meditation in which he depicted the Easter event. After the crucifixion, all the apostles had gone back to their fishing business and other trades. Bartholomew, in the imagination of Dr. Brown, raced over the hill to meet them with the Easter news. This was their response: "If he's risen that means he was right all along. It wasn't just a dream. And that means back to the road, back into the midst of trouble. Why couldn't he have stayed dead? Just when I'm beginning to get my life together again, this has to happen."[18] Resurrection faith challenges us to abandon our fears and take charge of our lives. History is not a cylindrical squirrel cage. We are not trapped by incessant cycles of tragedy. Hope presides over each sunrise. God has given each of us a future worth living! Likewise, grief can no longer be our crutch. At the risk of sounding callous, I contend that resurrection faith does not countenance protracted grief. Grieve we shall. Grieve we must. But we shall not grieve devoid of hope! Resurrection faith holds in dynamic tension both grief and humor. The Eastern Orthodox tradition of setting aside a Sunday in Eastertide for telling jokes about death and dying during the act of worship is poignant. I am particularly fond of Halford Luccock's reflections upon famous last words. He writes that when Samuel Upham of Drew Theological Seminary was in mortal struggle, his family gathered about his bedside. One announced that the professor appeared to have expired. Another protested, saying, "Feel his feet. No one ever died with warm feet." Dr. Upham opened his eyes for a moment and said, "Joan of Arc did." These were his last words.[19] Resurrection faith enables the believer to laugh in the face of death.

John Wesley's final words were the assuring, "The best of all is, God is with us." Eberhard Bethge, relative and dear friend of Dietrich Bonhoeffer, gives an account of this pastor and theologian's final moments. When the Nazi guard escorted him to the place of his execution, he told his British friend Payne Best, "This is the end—for me the beginning of life."[20] But the final word from the cross is the source of our most profound inspiration, for our Lord merely quoted the Psalter, "Father, into your hands I commend my spirit."[21] Hebrew children in the time of Jesus were taught the lines of

---

18. Brown, "Easter: The Demand and the Promise," 75.
19. Quoted in Luccock, *Unfinished Business*, 26.
20. Bethge, *Dietrich Bonhoeffer*, 830.
21. Luke 23:46 NRSV.

Psalm 31 as a bedtime prayer, therefore, his reassurance in his dying moment was the equivalent of "Now I Lay Me Down to Sleep." Such childlike trust truly belongs to the Kingdom of heaven. When we accept for ourselves this Christ-inspired trust in the providential power of God, we cannot sink into the quagmire of hopelessness and unabated grief. Increasingly we are drawn, therefore, to the lives of those who have approached their dying with the resurrection faith shown by Malcolm Muggeridge, that yeasty British journalist who lived to be eighty-seven. In his final months, he wrote this autobiographical reflection as he contemplated the fact of his finitude:

> So, like a prisoner awaiting his release, like a schoolboy when the end of term is near, like a migrant bird ready to fly south, like a patient in hospital anxiously scanning the doctor's face to see whether a discharge may be expected, I long to be gone. Extricating myself from the flesh I have too long inhabited, hearing the key turn in the lock of Time so that the great doors of Eternity swing open, disengaging my tired mind from its interminable conundrums and my tired ego from its wearisome insistencies. Such is the prospect of death.[22]

The Jesus of John's Gospel has promised the holy comforter in order that our fear of both resurrection and death may dissolve. I observed and participated in the power of that tranquility each Easter morning during my ministry at Shady Grove UMC—a rural congregation near Winston-Salem. A throng of the faithful eagerly gathered in the cemetery adjacent to the church, standing above the graves of their spouses, parents, and ancestors. As the first rays of sunlight penetrated the gentle fog and damp mist, the liturgy of hope emerged from depths of emotion: "Christ is risen. *Christ is risen indeed.*"

I likewise experienced for several years each Easter morning a delightful tradition at Harrison UMC, the oldest church of this denomination in Mecklenburg County, founded by Bishop Francis Asbury himself in the early months of 1785. At Easter sunrise, a gifted female pastor performed a role-play of Mary Magdalene, reminding congregants, "This is no idle tale. Come with me. Come and see." The congregation followed the barefooted evangelist into the cemetery, where the liturgy of Easter celebration was concluded. This Easter sunrise drama held together the emotions of fear and joy, skepticism and belief, weeping and elation, mystery and assurance. Biblical paradox is experienced most existentially in the act of meaningful worship.

Thus, we return to a corner of a church narthex on All Saints' Sunday with a tearful child gasping for breath and hope at the memory of his mother's startling death. In those precious moments when he was surrounded by two loving grandparents and enfolded by the arms of his Sunday school teacher, hearing the congregation singing a resurrection hymn minutes before the breaking of sacred bread, I prayed that this beloved little one might feel the living presence of a risen Christ who would raise his mother by grace and forever cover mother and child with abundant and undying love.

22. Muggeridge, *Twentieth-Century Pilgrim*, 3:149–50.

20

In Christ the Future Is Present

TIME IS BOTH OUR great obsession and our most perplexing mystery. The recent havoc wrought by Hurricane Sandy in the northeastern United States resulted in the loss of electrical power, the disruption of the whole transportation system, and a state of panic in a population defined by incremental calculations of time. Flight schedules, fixed work patterns, and reliance upon time-oriented computers were all jeopardized. Any natural disaster that disrupts these patterns produces a colossal crisis. With our accelerated dependence on sophisticated technology, the quality of our lives is increasingly measured in shrinking blocks of time that ironically provide less leisure and fewer qualitative periods of relaxation with family and friends.

Part of our problem is that we have failed to honor the sacred mystery of time and to reflect upon the wisdom of our biblical heritage regarding its passage. In his *Confessions*, Saint Augustine, Bishop of Hippo, candidly asked, "What, then, is time? If no one asks me, I know what it is. If I wish to explain it to him who asks me, I do not know."[1] Through many centuries, the prevailing concept of time's movement has been dictated by solar and lunar calendars established during periods of the Greco-Roman dominance. Few philosophers challenged the commonsensical wisdom of Heraclitus (535–475 B.C.) and his observation that all things move and nothing remains the same. He is remembered by his famous analogy, "Upon those who step into the same rivers different and ever different waters flow down."[2] That is, no one can step into the same river twice. All this makes perfect sense to even the youngest child playing barefoot on the edge of a flowing mountain stream. It resonates with a grieving widow, gazing with nostalgia at the pages of a family album and reflecting upon days of bliss preserved in photographs of a family picnic beside that same moving mountain stream. She acknowledges through her tears that memory is a poor substitute for

---

1. Augustine, *Confessions*, Bk. 11, 162.
2. Goetz et al., "Heraclitus," *New Encyclopedia Britannica*, 5:860.

real presence. Since the era of Heraclitus, we have assumed that we cannot accurately retrieve or reconstruct the past. Thus, we grasp wistfully for the resolve of William Wordsworth, who counseled,

> What though the radiance which was once so bright
> Be now for ever taken from my sight,
> Though nothing can bring back the hour
> Of splendor in the grass, of glory in the flower;
> We will grieve not, rather find
> Strength in what remains behind . . .[3]

The process of grief is inescapable. Photography becomes a hobby for many of us because it is our frail attempt to freeze and preserve the present.

The Hellenistic notion that time moves in cyclical repetition has dominated Western thought about the nature of things. Thus, time's flow follows patterns dictated by the earth's rotation around the sun and the moon's movement about the earth. The cycle of a year, the calibration of 365 days, the necessity of a leap year's additional day, the mathematical standardization of hours within a day or seconds within an hour—all are expressions of our human desire to make sense of time. All of this is predicated upon the uncontested validity of Heraclitus' logic and the predictable patterns of earth's solar system. These constructs provide the hooks upon which we hang history and enable us to calculate time's advancement with precision. Moreover, objective history is scrutinized by the rational process of analogy that records or discards evidence of unusual events. Thus, in Western civilization, we have come to assume that time can serve the purposes of humanity. It can be organized, evaluated, recorded, calculated, predicted, and controlled with precision.

There was, however, a rival school of philosophical thought regarding time's movement that emerged in Hellenistic culture one generation prior to Heraclitus. Parmenides (540–515 B.C.) resided in the remote Greek colony of Elea, where he adamantly declared that existence is timeless. Parmenides stressed the fixity and permanence of things. Moreover, he taught that reality consists of the unity of past, present, and future. Thus, for Parmenides, the flow of time is illusory. His counterintuitive assertions were pushed aside by most of his contemporaries during this pre-Socratic period, but his views eventually influenced Plato (427–347 B.C.), who arrived at the conclusion that there are certain realities that transcend time and change. These exist in their ideal, perfected form outside of human mind and memory. Plato, therefore, argued that reality is more than just our memory and the record of events within time's flow. He contended that there are timeless truths and unchanging realities that define the authentic nature of things. This insight by the Greek father of philosophy was greatly appreciated by Gödel in his mathematical Platonism, as we discovered

---

3. Wordsworth, "Ode: Intimations of Immortality from Recollections of Early Childhood," 704, lines 174–81.

in chapter 10. Neither the sacred canon of Hebrew literature nor the New Testament proclamation of the gospel of Christ was significantly influenced by any of these Hellenistic abstractions surrounding the nature of time. Biblical theology, however, has more in common with the teachings of Parmenides than the assumptions of Heraclitus. Hebraic references to time emerge from the story of a covenant people's relationship with a God who is understood to be timeless. Thus, Hebrew Scripture taught that God the Creator breathed life into the world before the existence of time. The Old Testament has no general word for "time." There are no specific Hebrew words that delineate the categories of "past," "present," and "future." The Hebrew word most commonly translated into the English language as "time" (*ayt*) refers to the instant during which something occurs, as in the observation that there is "a time to love, and a time to hate; a time for war, and a time for peace."[4] But the Hebrew word *olam* refers to immeasurable time, whether past or future. This word indicates an immense portion of time that is beyond human comprehension, although it is not the same concept as the English word "eternity." Thus, the prophet Micah articulated this consoling vision of hope: "The lame I will make the remnant, and those who were cast off, a strong nation; and the Lord will reign over them in Mount Zion now and forevermore [*olam*]."[5] The prophetic "forevermore" does not suggest an unending period, but Micah here implies a condition of extremely long duration. The common Hebrew word *moed* is a designation for a fixed time. It is often used to cite specific allusions to festivals of Judaism. "These are the appointed festivals of the Lord, the holy convocations, which you shall celebrate at the time appointed [*moed*] for them."[6] Consistently, throughout all Hebrew Scripture, God is the creator and master of time.

Followers of Jesus who proclaimed him to be the Son of God, consequently, affirmed that the divine Being is the one "who is and who was and who is to come."[7] Thus, the Apostle Paul uniquely referred to the divine Creator as "the eternal God."[8] The Hebrew and Aramaic languages spoken by Jesus offered no special term for past, present, or future categories of time. In nearly three hundred references to time in the Old Testament, none imply time's measurable duration. The word points to some revelatory event within time. In point of fact, the biblical text describes a deity who speaks in the language of events; thus, authors of the narratives were rarely precise regarding the duration of an event or time period. The prophetic voice of Deutero-Isaiah issues a semi-consoling word of comfort: "For a brief moment I abandoned you, but with great compassion I will gather you. In overflowing wrath for a moment I hid my face from you."[9] That "brief moment" lasted from the Babylonian invasion

4. Eccl 3:8 NRSV.
5. Mic 4:7 NRSV.
6. Lev 23:4 NRSV.
7. Rev 1:4 NRSV.
8. Rom 16:26 NRSV, "tou aiōníou theou."
9. Isa 54:7–8a NRSV.

Part II: Paradox and Christology

of Jerusalem in 586 B.C. until the Edict of King Cyrus authorized the Hebrew slaves in the Diaspora to return to Judah in 538 B.C.—a humiliating period of forty-eight years spent in horrific captivity! The prophet consolidated his message of promise in a hymn of triumphant joy in which YHWH promised, "I will make with you an everlasting covenant, my steadfast, sure love for David."[10] The Abrahamic covenant with the sons and daughters of Israel and the renewed covenant with the spiritual descendants of King David are not subject to chronology or change. It is an eternal promise that will never be broken from God's side.

Lengths of time are not absolute or fixed in biblical narrative. Forty days or forty years are mere aphorisms for "a long time," as in the epic of the flood or wilderness wanderings of Moses and the liberated slaves. Even the chronicles of the kings make little attempt to provide an accurate, objective chronology. Certain happenings that occur over the course of a single day may dominate the narrative for several chapters, while decades of a ruler's regime may be summarized with a cursory reference like "Joash did what was right in the sight of the Lord all the days of the priest Jehoiada."[11] The chronicler reports that this good king's reign lasted forty years. Righteous rulers tended to stay on the throne for a long time, and devious ones sometimes experienced a sudden ending after brief governance. A chronicler of Israel reports that Menahem reigned ten years in Samaria, and "He did what was evil in the sight of the Lord; he did not depart all of his days from any of the sins of Jeroboam son of Nebat, which he caused Israel to sin."[12] The prophet Joel announces, "Alas for the Day! For the day of the Lord is near and as destruction from the Almighty it comes."[13] These vague references to the time of an imminent event were sufficient for the author.

When the prophets referred to the future, they did not develop a pure concept of chronological reference. Thus, the voice of Jeremiah, whose final days were spent in Egyptian exile, offered no transparent timetable for this divine promise: "For surely I know the plans I have for you, says the Lord, plans for your welfare and not for harm, to give you a future with hope."[14] The prophet Amos, who was a cultivator of sycamore trees and attuned to the rhythms of the seasons, reminds me of the many farmers in a parish I served in North Carolina. This cultivator from Tekoa projected the coming of an abundant harvest but offered no specific predications regarding its arrival, saying only, "On that day I will raise up the booth of David that is fallen, and repair its breaches, and raise up its ruins, and rebuild it as in the days of old."[15] Historians completing their dissertations would not dare make reference to a specific historical period as "the days of old." When did the day predicted by Amos actually arrive? The

10. Isa 55:3 NRSV.
11. 2 Chr 24:2 NRSV.
12. 2 Kgs 15:18 NRSV.
13. Joel 1:15 NRSV.
14. Jer 29:11 NRSV.
15. Amos 9:11 NRSV.

question is irrelevant to the redactor of the prophetic text. In Amos' scheme of things, God will act in God's own good time.

The New Testament references to "eternal" (*aiōníou*) do not significantly deviate from the Hebraic concept of time. *Eternal* can mean "long, distant, or uninterrupted time" in the past or in the future. This adjective makes no real distinction between limited or unlimited durations of time. In all biblical narrative, individual events are arranged according to their content, not necessarily their chronological order. Events vastly separated by chronological time may coincide in content and, thus, be identified as being simultaneous. The linear scale of time is not as important as the rhythms of time. Thus, a Hebrew prophet would likely tie together the stories of original creation, the promise to Noah, the call of Abraham, and the covenant tablets of Moses at Mount Sinai when calling Israel to engage in renewal of this everlasting relationship with the Lord of the covenant.

The Hebrew concept of time is linear, even though precise reference to its duration is not essential. The corpus of wisdom within *Qoheleth* expresses cynicism regarding the destination of time. Mortals have precious little time under the sun, and it is expedient to make the most of it by performing appropriate tasks within God's gift of time. There is a proper time for nearly every human activity. Wisdom is in knowing when to act in order to render glory to YHWH: "a time to be born, and a time to die; a time to plant, and a time to pluck up what is planted."[16] In Hebrew thought, the river of Heraclitus remains a mystery. Time cannot be comprehended, much less managed and controlled; it moves inexorably toward God, who graciously gives it for his covenant people to use wisely.

This was indeed the faith of Jesus. He invited his followers to receive God's gracious gift of "eternal life" (*zōē aiōnious*) in keeping with his Hebraic tradition and the central theological themes of wisdom literature. Thus, he referred to a quality of time, not the calculable dimensions of a quantitative period, when he invited his hearers to receive this incomparable gift. "Eternal life" was, therefore, a reference to a quality of existence that is a present reality but not limited in duration or gauged numerically. The context of time in the qualitative state of eternity (*aionious*) is contrasted with measurable time (*kairos*). When the Hebrews recited the shepherd's psalm in the Temple liturgy, they did not pledge to YHWH that they would "dwell in the house of the Lord [the Temple in Jerusalem] *forever.*" Through this liturgical poem, they rejoiced that as long as they continued in the land of the living, they would experience the ecstasy of worship in YHWH's special house on Mount Zion. "Eternity" has no beginning or ending. It is a quality of existence that transcends chronological measurement. It is more akin to Parmenides' unitary concept of a stationary block of time than to Heraclitus' ever-flowing stream of measurable time.

The four gospel writers each depict Jesus as the fulfillment of the Hebrew Story of salvation history. The river of God's time has moved toward this omega event—the

16. Eccl 3:2 NRSV.

advent of the Messiah of Galilee. John the Baptizer was seen as the end of the prophetic era. Jesus' arrival marked a new, incomparable historical moment. When he gave his mission statement at his hometown synagogue, Jesus declared that the long-awaited Jubilee Year, described in the Levitical laws of Moses and further elucidated by the prophet Trito-Isaiah, had arrived through him. He then rolled up the scroll of Isaiah and announced, "Today this Scripture has been fulfilled in your hearing."[17] But how could this be? The poor had not yet heard good news. Zealots in Roman prisons had not yet been released. The blind of Galilee remained sightless. Masses of oppressed Jews languished in miserable subjection in Judah, Galilee, and the vast Roman Diaspora. How could these ideals be a present reality as the local boy of Nazareth read the Jubilee Scripture? All the Lucan Beatitudes are articulated in the present tense: "Blessed *are* you who are poor, for yours *is* the kingdom of God."[18] Had Jesus, speaking upon a level surface somewhere in Galilee, failed to level with his impoverished and oppressed kindred? Within a generation from when he articulated his mission in Nazareth, the Temple would be pulverized by Roman armies, Zealots would commit mass suicide at Masada, and Jews would enter two millennia of a seemingly fathomless Diaspora.

In this chapter I have strongly urged that we resist the temptation to read the Hebrew Bible with a Hellenistic worldview, for to do so is to miss the profound depths of its message of hardheaded hope. Likewise, we risk forfeiting the paradoxical theology of time in the New Testament if we contaminate the early church's message of hope with Hellenistic categories of time. In Grecian thought, time is an endless flow of ceaseless cycle and recurring events. The ancient Hellenists vehemently resisted belief in a Creator God who enters the arena of human history and participates in the suffering of those whom God loves. Hellenistic philosophers did not conceive of a loving Creator who penetrates this fractured creation for the purpose of healing it from within. The Greeks devised methods of escaping time and the messy matters of this world. Most Hellenistic philosophers taught that our bodies have a soul substance that escapes this imperfect world upon our death. The philosophic mind should, therefore, remain attuned to trans-earth ideals during this life and escape to a place of perfection as a saved and safe soul after the body's death. This system of belief infiltrated the minds of many in the Greco-Roman world of the early Christian era and dominated the lifestyle and practices of the Gnostics.

Hellenistic language about the immortality of the soul, however, was alien to Jesus and the disciples of the early church. His incarnation implied precisely the opposite of escapist Hellenistic and Gnostic philosophies. The Evangelist John was writing in Greek and thereby addressed Hellenistic minds when he audaciously proclaimed that the very essence of God's Being (*logos*) had become flesh in Jesus. To what end? John's answer was the antithesis of an "immortality of the soul" message of renunciation of

17. Luke 4:21 NRSV.
18. Luke 6:20 NRSV.

this world. Boldly he pronounced to a culture dominated by Hellenistic ideas, "For God so loved the world that he give his only Son, so that everyone who believes in him may not perish but may have eternal life."[19] Incarnational theology could only have arisen from the covenant heritage of Judaism and its theology of time. Only in the fullness of time was it possible that God's Being became completely manifested in the flesh of this Man of Nazareth. He came at a most propitious time—a unique, qualitative, and unrepeatable moment. Only in God's time could such an incomparable event occur. John the Evangelist spoke clearly to the erroneous soul-substance escapists and the Gnostic philosophers of that day when he wrote, "Indeed, God did not send the Son into the world to condemn the world, but in order that the world might be saved through him."[20]

Incarnation occurred in the fullness of time—a Hebraic concept that permeates the Old Testament. The Passion Narrative encompasses more than a Passover meal in Jerusalem (a linear designation), a mock trial, and a Roman-style crucifixion thirty-three years after the death of Herod the Great in the sixteenth year of the rule of Emperor Tiberius. The passion of Christ and the fulfillment of Israel's salvation history is a distinctive moment that draws together all other moments in time, giving meaning and momentum to the human saga. The Greek word that the gospel writers used to convey the significance of this unique moment is *kairos*. This word speaks of a quality of time, not a period or length of time, as in *chronos*. It refers to a limited slice of time marked by a suitable or unique circumstance. It marks a fitting season characterized by remarkable opportunity. In Mark's Gospel, for example, the propitious moment arrived when Jesus' cousin John was arrested. Jesus then began to proclaim the message of the good news and the arrival of Jubilee, saying, "The time [*kairos*] is fulfilled, and the Kingdom of God has come near, repent, and believe in the good news."[21] Thus, Jesus compared the kingdom of heaven to a harvest time [*kairos*] in which weeds are burned and productive grain is gathered into bundles.[22] When he was asked by the Sadducees and Pharisees to show a sign from heaven, he retorted, "You know how to interpret the appearance of the sky, but you cannot interpret the signs of the time [*kairos*]."[23]

The New Testament's understanding of time emerged from the context of Hebrew Scripture—the Bible of Jesus. It is a cosmic view in which God enters time and history in order to redeem the cosmos, not to rescue humans from the dreadful earth or to deliver the soul from the sinful body. God has come in the flesh of Jesus to make home with humanity. The theology of incarnation emerges from the Hebrew concept of *Shekinah*—YHWH making a home among the covenant people. The

19. John 3:16 NRSV.
20. John 3:17 NRSV.
21. Mark 1:15 NRSV.
22. See Matt 13:30 NRSV.
23. Matt 16:3b NRSV.

divine dwelling place is with the people of God's creation. As the theologian Jürgen Moltmann explains, "In the eschatological *Shekinah*, the new creation takes the whole of the first creation into itself, as its own harbinger and prelude, and completes it. Creation begins with time and is completed in space . . . For the Easter community of Christians, God already 'dwells' in this godless world in the form of the crucified Christ, while in the form of the risen One he anticipates through the presence of his Spirit his universal *Shekinah* in the new creation."[24] The eternal has invaded temporal in order to redeem it. Moltmann addresses the impact of the Jesus event upon God's relationship with time when he writes, "It is the presence of God in the time of those he has created or, to put it more precisely, the dynamic presence of eternity in time, which links beginning and end, thus awakening remembrance and hope."[25]

The language of worship, especially the liturgy of the Eucharist, is the vernacular of *kairotic time* and the interpreter of resurrection hope. In Luke's account of the Passover meal with his disciples, Jesus speaks of his imminent suffering and tells them, "I will not eat it [the Passover supper] until it is fulfilled in the Kingdom of God."[26] After giving thanks over the cup of wine, he told his followers, "Take this and divide it among yourselves; for I tell you from now on I will not drink of the fruit of the vine until the Kingdom of God comes."[27] Thus, from the earliest expressions of Christian worship until the present, disciples have experience the paradox of the Jesus of history at the Jerusalem meal with his disciples and the presence of the risen Christ of the future with contemporary worshipers through the breaking of the bread and sharing of the wine. This is the universal, paradoxical presence surrounding the celebration of Eucharist throughout the world. Every day over the course of two millennia, this act of thanksgiving has taken place somewhere. Through this sacred act of adoration, the past and future meet in worship's eternal now. After all, in the words of Moltmann, "simultaneity is one of the attributes of eternity."[28]

One of the privileges I have experienced as a pastor has been leading for twenty years the thirty-four sessions of Disciple Bible. With each new fall class of disciples, I have felt the spiritual intimacy of twelve or so laypeople meeting weekly to engage in dialogue over a comprehensive survey of the Scriptures. The final session was always Eucharistic. After a late spring meal on a rhododendron-covered mountaintop, I administered the sacrament to a cluster of disciples who gazed upon the golden horizon of a grace-filled sunset. In that mystical moment in our collective memory, the Christ of the past and future was powerfully present among us.

On an especially memorable Christmas Eve in Charlotte's Providence United Methodist Church, I administered the Eucharistic sacrament at three consecutive and

24. Moltmann, *Coming of God*, 266–67.
25. Ibid., 266.
26. Luke 22:16 NRSV.
27. Luke 22:17–18 NRSV.
28. Moltmann, *Coming of God*, 287.

crowded services. I was exhausted from the week's schedule, the balancing of congregational and family commitments, and the emotional energy of consecutive services filled with nostalgic music and lofty expectations. I had momentarily forgotten that on this special night our church hosted a shelter for the homeless of the city in an ecumenical ministry appropriately termed "Room in the Inn." Thus, I eagerly departed a warm sanctuary filled with the aroma of extinguished candles and wilting evergreen wreaths. As I made my way into the catacomb-like basement of the building in anticipation of a quick drive home and an uninterrupted night's sleep, I passed through a dimly lit space filled with rows of blanketed cots providing hospitality to our homeless guests on that cold night. One of the volunteers in this ministry eagerly called me to the bedside of a woman who had just been released from the Presbyterian Hospital. She was tenderly holding the infant child whose birth had prompted her brief hospital stay. Despite my inattentiveness to his advent during the formal liturgy, Jesus had truly arrived during the Eucharist at that church on this hallowed night.

When I was a pastor at First UMC in Waynesville, North Carolina, many guests of the Lake Junaluska Assembly visited our congregation for worship between their responsibilities of leading workshops and educational events. A frequent guest and popular speaker at the Assembly during those years was Bishop Peter Storey of South Africa. For a considerable time, he was a prophetic voice among white citizens of that beleaguered land—a population that had become dependent upon the privileges of apartheid. He had always spoken the truth in love, even though he was ostracized and rejected by most of his parishioners. At regular intervals throughout these years of confrontation, he continued to visit the local prison, bringing the grace of Eucharist to a prisoner named Nelson Mandela. Several years after his dramatic and unanticipated release, Mandela initiated a political process through a policy of "truth and reconciliation" by which the Christ of the future brought healing and hope into a broken and pain-inflicted nation. Through this agonizing process, victims and those who had perpetuated the evils of apartheid met face to face. When the truth was confessed, pardon was automatically administered. Only a man who had experienced the risen Christ of the future through weekly Eucharist in prison could lead a nation in this activity of redemption and grace.

Christ UMC in Greensboro has a remarkable sanctuary with a huge Eucharistic table in the form of a marble cross. An encompassing altar wraps around this massive table. A creative artist and member designed cushioned kneelers after she saw a vision of beauty while seated in the balcony during a worship service. A dozen members working over a period of approximately ten years transposed her design into the reality of a unique needlepoint creation. This congregation was also resourceful in providing sponsorship for a large community of Montagnard refugees who had migrated into the city. I always trembled with emotion when I watched these humble disciples of Jesus fall upon their knees on the needlepoint cushions. Here they communed with their comrades several thousand miles away in the jungles of Vietnam and also with

Part II: Paradox and Christology

the Montagnard Christians who had lost their lives in affirmation of Christ amidst an oppressive Communist culture. I always sensed in those sacred moments the presence of the Jesus of the Last Supper in Jerusalem and the Christ of his coming future.

The theological constructs within the biblical narrative bring together the dimensions of past, present, and future in the personhood of Jesus Christ. But biblical assertions regarding the nature of time appear counterintuitive in the post-Enlightenment era. When Isaac Newton published his massive *Mathematical Principles of Natural Philosophy* in 1687, he systematically provided reliable calculations for the relationship of time to the movement of planets and stars, and the role of entropy in the predictable patterns of time's movement. The impressive work of this Cambridge University genius dominated the field of physical science for over two centuries. Newton provided indisputable evidence that absolute and true measures of time, distance, and the movement of matter flow equably without relation to anything external. Newton's neat, unchallenged mathematical assumptions governing the progression of time were especially valid when applied to calculations within the context of the solar system.

All of that changed during what historians now call the "miracle year" of 1905, when an assistant clerk in a Swiss patent office was riding home on a train from downtown Bern. His view was dominated by the massive, ancient clock tower that was the pride and emblem of the city. As he gazed at the giant hands of the clock now receding from his vision, Albert Einstein imagined the vehicle racing down that same track at the speed of light. Over the coming months, Einstein calculated that the time on his imaginary train would remain constant while traveling at the speed of light even as the time registered by Bern's beloved clock tower would progress at anticipated precise increments. By summer of that amazingly creative year, this young mathematician had formalized a Specific Theory of Relativity with calculations related to the constant speed of light. Later he developed a General Theory of Relativity that challenged the world of physical science and the commonsense explanation of time. From Euclid to Newton, scientists and mathematicians assumed that space has three simple, calculable dimensions: length, width, and height. Einstein's theories introduced the concept of spacetime, which combines space and time into a single continuum. In the relativistic context of Einstein's calculations, time cannot be separated from the three dimensions of space. The observed rate at which time passes during the movement of an object depends upon that object's velocity. Both velocity and the strength of gravitational fields can slow the passage of time. Such slowing came to be called "time dilation" and is explained by Einstein's Special Theory of Relativity. It is certainly understandable that Karl Popper, the best-known philosopher of science in the twentieth century, referred to the advent of Einstein's theories of relativity as the reemergence of Parmenides,[29] the ancient Greek philosopher who (against Heraclitus) insisted that time and motion are an illusion.

---

29. Popper, *Unended Quest*, 127.

Julian Barbour, a renowned contemporary theoretical physicist, has made the astounding assertion that "unification of general relativity and quantum mechanics may well spell *the end of time*."[30] Barbour spent four decades in the disciplines of physics and astronomy in order to propose a radically alternative view of the universe and to prove the nonexistence of time. Barbour's thesis is intricately explicated in his provocative volume, *The End of Time*, a book that may require some background in the discipline of quantum physics.[31] I reference his groundbreaking thoughts on the subject of time here not because his views testify to a biblical perspective, but because they have much in common with the paradoxical unity of time professed by the New Testament Evangelists. It is not a violation of human reason, therefore, for a conscientious physicist to claim that all facets of time converge. But it is, likewise, a reasonable and bold step of faith for a conscientious student of Judeo-Christian Scripture to assert that this convergence takes place in the event of Jesus Christ—time's omega point.

A thesis similar to Barbour's is expounded by contemporary physicist Sean Carroll in his intriguing volume, *From Eternity to Here: The Quest for the Ultimate Theory of Time*. One cannot imagine a more cosmic perspective than this comprehensive work, which raises questions about the relevance of time in the context of timespace, the observable existence of black holes, the probability of parallel universes, existence before the Big Bang, string theory, and the possibility of a multiverse reality. What is the nature of simultaneity in such an inexhaustible, expansive universe? Carroll postulates a reality that likely holds together more than one universe with comparable planets—earth and its cohort—separated by thousands of light-years in space. This physicist's reflections are not merely relevant to philosophers of physical science. In looking through the astronomer's telescope, Professor Carroll broadens the horizon of the theologian's concept of God. His challenge to the customary interpretation of time gives further credence to the Bible's wisdom literature and enables us to proclaim with renewed confidence the doctrine of a ubiquitous Christ.

Adolf von Harnack successfully used form criticism in the nineteenth century to question the historical reliability of the gospel narratives. A subsequent generation led by Rudolf Bultmann and his host of disciples applied the same scrutiny to the texts of the Christian canon to uncover the existential relevance and power of Jesus' inspirational life. Robert Funk and Markus Borg fine-tuned a historical-critical hermeneutic of the Christian message in order to make it more palatable for sophisticated twenty-first-century skeptics. But no significant post-Newtonian interpretation of time has influenced a single page of the voluminous research emerging from these post-Enlightenment interpreters of Christ. I am reminded of Kierkegaard's analysis of the impact of the most influential Christians theologians of his era, by which he

---

30. Barbour, *End of Time*, 14.

31. In preparation for an engaging reading of Julian Barbour's challenging work cited here, I recommend his presentation of a succinct synopsis of this theme in an appealing and comprehensible lecture available at http://pirsa.org/12060007/.

remarked that they had succeeded in performing a miracle greater than that of Christ, for they had turned wine in to water. When contemporary pastors and theologians remain oblivious to the phenomenal discoveries of astrophysics and the breathtaking beauty of mathematics in an ever-expanding universe, they settle for a limited concept of God and an earth-chauvinist concept of time. Doing theology in such an intellectual vacuum is comparable to doing astronomy without a telescope.

Hebrew wisdom literature imparts an enchantingly poetic description of the mystery of time. The Jewish authors encouraged devout worshipers to make the most of time's elusive passage. *Qoheleth* sounded much like a gloomy Parmenides in observing, "What has been is what will be, and what has been done is what will be done; there is nothing new under the sun."[32] Various biblical sources contain conflicting theological insights regarding the mystery of time. But biblical theology consistently proclaims that time is consolidated in the being of a timeless God. Thus, the Temple liturgist who wrote these words invoked an act of worship, "O give thanks to the Lord, for he is good; for his steadfast love endures forever."[33] This affirmation articulated the faith of Jesus in whom all facets of time paradoxically meet, and the divine love that he embodies is truly the Alpha and Omega.

---

32. Eccl 1:9 NRSV.
33. Ps 106:1 NRSV.

Part III

PARADOX AND THE HOLY SPIRIT AS AN EXTENSION OF THE INCARNATION

21

Ship of Fools

THE FABRIC OF THIS book is Trinitarian; thus, each of its three components is interrelated to form a unified affirmation of the Judeo-Christian God whose mysterious disclosure is paradoxical in nature. These three segments weave a unified pattern. The Son is like unto the Father and of one substance with the Father. Thus, we have carefully utilized a broad range of scriptural evidence from both the Hebraic tradition and early church proclamation in order to depict a God of mercy who guides the destiny of humanity toward a future that God defines, despite life's apparent unfairness. The wisdom of this God's activity in our lives appears as foolishness. God's presence is profoundly apparent in moments of God's anguishing absence. The message of reliable hope usually arrives in the context of bad news. We tremble in fear before the splendor of this God's unconditional love. By God's wounds, we are healed. Through God's callous judgments, we experience the tenderness of the Creator's mercy. The tears of God are ultimately our only source of comfort in grief and our sole release from bondage to despair. God's grace is cosmic in scope, for the Creator God uses those he has rejected in order to accomplish his ultimate objective. God's incalculably expanding universe is held together by perfect, inscrutable mathematical laws that become more mysterious and paradoxical as we probe their amazing depths and experience their breathtaking beauty.

The paradoxical revelation of God's being occurred through the life, death, and resurrection of Jesus of Nazareth. Consequently, we have presented ten corollary chapters dealing with the second persona of the Trinity. Through Jesus, we experience the paradoxical being of God with authenticity and completeness. The Son of Man indeed embodied all the facets of God's paradoxical self-disclosure. In these ten chapters, we have probed the depths of Jesus' Beatitudes in order to discover his message of present and future blessing amidst the saga of human misfortune. In the failure of his mission to inaugurate a Jubilee reality and establish a dominion of righteousness

Part III: Paradox and the Holy Spirit as an Extension of the Incarnation

in Israel, he makes available the resilient power for accomplishing a far more comprehensive, successful mission. Thus, Jesus came as the prototype for servant leadership, revealing the ultimate form of power that is only released through acts of emptying one's self of all political might. By his *kenosis* are we filled and fulfilled. His suffering is the sacrament of our salvation. His aggressive confrontation of evil and injustice is the only source of humanity's peace. He rules earth from the cross. By confronting us with the fact of our finitude, the risen Christ has opened for us a renewed quality of life that begins in the moment of decisive trust and is impervious to death's destruction. Belief in his mystifying resurrection is essential for all who experience the reality of the paradoxical God. The gospel witness to Jesus as the quintessential paradoxical Being transforms our understanding of time, for in him, the future is present.

Any systematic theology becomes a house of cards and an intellectual exercise in ethereal thinking if the theologian fails to ground these assertions in the reality of human experience. Thus, we must see evidence of the essence of a Christ who continues to exist in the life of the church through his Holy Spirit. When this evidence becomes visible and palpable, the rubbery substance of theological jargon hits the empirical road. The ancient biblical witness becomes a present reality. The Story invades and interprets our little stories. The risen Christ becomes a living reality within the life, mission, and worship experiences of the contemporary church. The theological construct of this book shall appear as a sandcastle, with chapters that fragilely hold together ethereal shadows, unless there is evidence in the life of the church of lives modeled after the paradoxical nature of Christ. Thus, in this section of the book, we shall explore various facets of the life of the church in the hopes of illustrating with tangible evidence the authentic community that has been formed by the example of Christ.

There are many eloquent definitions of the Holy Spirit, and massive volumes have provided a plethora of evolving explanations and applications of this doctrine. But for the purpose of this discussion, we shall employ the functional language of the theologian John Macquarie, who laconically described the church as "an extension of the incarnation."[1] It is the activity of the Holy Spirit within the church that enables a congregation of Christ-followers to grow toward the image and likeness of his paradoxical Being. A lifestyle of paradoxical activity requires a supportive community; it is not something that develops instantaneously. Only as Jesus gave himself in death upon the cross did the self-giving love of God reach its full consummation. The Holy Spirit is the power of God that extends the life of Christ into each new generation, but as Macquarrie vehemently warns, "the church has not achieved this consummation of the incarnation—if it had, then it would have utterly given itself up, and would have disappeared as this earthly entity which we know."[2] The story of the church is an ongoing saga concerning God's people that has not yet attained "the measure of the

---

1. Macquarrie, *Principles of Christian Theology*, 348.
2. Ibid.

stature of the fullness of Christ."[3] While the authentic church may be called an extension of the incarnation, it remains acutely aware of its imperfections and its distance from this unique, paradoxical Being who was fully absorbed into the love and mercy of God. The Apostle Paul instructed his congregation in Corinth that they were the "body of Christ," but he made it abundantly clear that Christ is the head of that body. The activity of the Holy Spirit within the life of the church, therefore, is the energy of sanctification, enabling the church to become more faithfully a gradual extension of God's incarnate love.

But how, when, and where is the church ever truly an extension of the life and teachings of its Messiah? When those outside the church press their noses against the stained-glass windows of our sanctuaries to gaze within, they often see the opposite of the paradoxical Being described in the pages of holy writ. They view a people with diminishing influence grasping for power. They behold impressive, carefully preserved real estate locked like museums housing treasures in neighborhoods of poverty and human squalor. They overhear sanctimonious sermons that bash the poor, condemn gays and others outside the church fellowship, wrap Jesus in an American flag, and endorse wars of national aggression. Rather than the paradoxical church of self-emptying generosity, they witness congregations with bloated budgets reserved for projects of self-aggrandizement. They read in the newspapers summaries of resolutions written by conscientious church committees that are directed to government authorities and legislative bodies when such an exercise in futility is an avoidance of dealing with the myriad of unjust practices within the polity of the church.

Nonetheless, we have here made a convincing, but not exhaustive, biblical argument for the reality of a surprising Creator God whose essence clearly resides as a community formed in the likeness of Jesus Christ. Where is the evidence of this reality?

I write as a pastoral theologian who has served seven parish appointments over a period of thirty-five years. I have lived among devoted laity and planned ministries with extraordinary servant leaders in campus communities, rural environments, small county-seat villages, and bustling cities. By Episcopal appointment, I have administered the connectional mission of a district cluster of over seventy United Methodist parishes in the metropolitan area of Charlotte, North Carolina. I have had the privilege of serving with common, ordinary people who have engaged in extraordinary missions with inspiring enthusiasm. Does the paradoxical church, formed by the character of Jesus, actually exist? If so, where? Evidence is essential. Otherwise, this theological tent should be folded and discarded as gibberish.

With passionate conviction I write this testimony of encouragement to my pastoral colleagues who have witnessed the numerical decline and political irrelevance of their denominations. Through the years I have merely grown in my conviction that the calling of clergy and leaders among the laity is to remain faithful to the vision

---

3. Eph 4:13 NRSV.

Part III: Paradox and the Holy Spirit as an Extension of the Incarnation

of this paradoxical God and to imitate the biblical image of Christ—his paradoxical teachings and resolute example.

During the Babylonian exile, when the Jerusalem Temple lay in ruins, the synagogue was formed as an institution and tradition in the Diaspora. Jesus' own comprehension of Hebrew Scripture was apparently influenced by the teachings of that tiny synagogue in Nazareth, the instruction and example of his parents, and his occasional pilgrimages to Jerusalem's Temple. The Hebrew prophets realized that very few people would believe their words or respond to their urgent instructions during their lifetime. The experience of Elijah is especially instructive. After his bold witness upon Mount Carmel and his humiliation of King Ahab, this courageous prophet knew that he would be the object of Queen Jezebel's retaliatory anger. In escaping to the wilderness, he collapsed with exhaustion beside a solitary broom tree and fell asleep, but was prompted by a nocturnal messenger to abandon this place of fearful hiding. When the word of the Lord challenged him to return to aggressive confrontation of an evil political administration, Elijah answered with reluctance and defeat, "I have been very zealous for the Lord, the God of hosts; for the Israelites have forsaken your covenant, thrown down your altars, and killed your prophets with the sword. I alone am left, and they are seeking my life, to take it away."[4]

I cannot count the times during my own ministry that I have made my abode in the cave of Elijah's resignation and mimicked his capitulation to failure. But at those times when I ignored the fact that God is still in charge and that the Holy Spirit is an enabling presence, I have felt the arresting presence of a God who visits in moments of God's most austere absence. Amidst the most depressing circumstances in the life of an average parish, this deity paradoxically speaks a defiant command: "Go out and stand on the mountain before the Lord, for the Lord is about to pass by."[5] Divine presence, through the inspiration of the Holy Spirit, provides the majestic power to sustain the incarnation within the life of the parish. The Holy Spirit enables the Jesus of the past to become present with relevance and authority. Paradoxically, the power of the Holy Spirit does not come through the dramatic force of hurricane winds. It need not pulverize rocks, defeat mighty armies in spectacular battles, or initiate natural disasters with the import of a fiery judgment. Amidst the eclipse of God's presence, when we are prone to resign from confrontational engagement, to relinquish our clerical ordination, and to escape into some pension-secure retirement, the paradoxical disclosure of God happens like "a sound of sheer silence."[6] The paradoxical God has zero tolerance for a church-initiated pity party. The Holy Spirit speaks to the contemporary mainline church as it spoke to Elijah. Our marching orders are unambiguous. Elijah was commanded to become politically subversive by anointing a new King to rule over Israel in deposition of King Ahab. Elijah's retirement plans were scuttled. He

---

4. 1 Kgs 19:10 NRSV.
5. 1 Kgs 19:11 NRSV.
6. 1 Kgs 19:12 NRSV.

spent the rest of his days in preparation for passing the torch of prophetic authority to Elisha—a young servant leader in need of intensive mentoring. Bringing down a corrupt and powerful monarchy was no easy assignment, but this was precisely the mission of the aging Elijah. Even the gates of hell could not prevail against the accomplishment of this divine imperative. Moreover, Israel's feisty prophet received this consoling divine promise: "I will leave seven thousand in Israel, all the knees that have not bowed to Baal, and every mouth that has not kissed him."[7]

The biblical witness is consistent: The Holy Spirit always sustains a remnant of the faithful who consistently live the paradoxical life, refusing to kiss the ass of Baal or any other false God. This renewing and transforming Holy Spirit carries each new generation onto the path that leads to God's future of righteousness, reconciliation, forgiveness, peace, and joy.

I have rarely discovered a church that is so small, so contaminated by fear, or so toxic with hatred that it does not contain a small remnant of those who are faithful to the biblical vision of God's coming kingdom. Moreover, it is clearly the principle role of the pastoral theologian to nurture, through pulpit proclamations and the adventure of small group dynamics, a cadre of servant leaders who are bathed in scriptural holiness and remain faithful to the imperative mission of Christ. When a pastor experiences vicious toxicity of spirit and the absence of even a single group who will commit to the disciplines of holy habits (intercessory prayer, fasting, sacrificial giving, concentrated biblical studies, witnessing, serving the poor, providing advocacy for the powerless, and working on behalf of justice), the administrative authorities should have the courage to terminate that apostate church.

A young woman in the Charlotte District was appointed to a congregation of inflexible, chauvinistic members in a neighborhood of growing diversity of race and lifestyles. She was enthusiastic about her mission and asked to receive only a partial salary in order to sustain a ministry of outreach in that challenging community. She diligently attempted to engage her members in ministries of care and compassion to families with young children living in the vicinity of that historic church. She elicited the assistance of volunteers from other congregations of the district. Many neighborhood families came to a Saturday book-bag gathering to receive free school supplies and the hospitality of the pastor and an assortment of volunteers. Very few members of the sponsoring congregation bothered to attend this outreach effort. When nearly twenty-five first-time guests appeared in worship on the following morning, all of the regular attendees huddled together on one side of that dignified sanctuary. As regular members entered, they abandoned their usual places to sit opposite from the forlorn visitors. These neighborhood guests were greeted only by the pastor, who struggled to restrain her embarrassment and humiliation.

When I learned about this despicable behavior, I requested a Charge Conference assemblage of the leadership. After confronting those in attendance with their

---

7. 1 Kgs 19:18 NRSV.

Part III: Paradox and the Holy Spirit as an Extension of the Incarnation

pastor's report, no one denied the accuracy of her description. I asked, "Why did you not enthusiastically greet the people of your neighborhood?" Silence ensued. Then one of the men spoke for the congregation with this devastating response: "They were the wrong kind of people." Upon hearing this candid expression of intolerance, I announced to that stunned assemblage, "At the next session of the Cabinet, I shall recommend to the bishop and Conference that Duncan Memorial cease to exist as a church." I turned to their distraught pastor as we departed and resolutely said, "With that man's unchallenged testimony, Jesus exited this church."

Yet in all my years of active ministry, evidence of this intensity of venomous spirit has been extremely rare. I have nearly always discovered an eager remnant of people intensely committed to the exhilarating mission of the paradoxical Christ. Within each congregation, intimate spiritual relationships have been nurtured through small disciple group experiences. Laypeople have eagerly engaged in both the inner journey of theological exploration and the outward journey of sacrificial service. Churches that are completely devoid of such serious engagement with the paradoxical message of the Scriptures have little reason to exist as a representative of the Christian message. The tolerance of their toxicity is harmful to the promulgation of the gospel. The church that claims to be an extension of the incarnation is always meant to become an aberrant community, challenging the mores and values of the prevailing culture. But no one enters the family of redeemed sinners without needing the enduring and endearing nurture of a conscientious pastoral theologian who empathetically shepherds the flock.

An early ecclesiastical tradition adopted the image of the ship as an appropriate symbol of the church. As towns and cities of the post-Constantinian Roman Empire began to embrace these rapidly expanding Christian communities, sacred space for corporate worship took the architectural form of a cross with a central aisle leading toward the altar at the conjunction of the crossbeam contour of the chancel. Worshiping laity assembled in that spacious aisle, appropriately named the "nave." All who stood or sat in that sacred space imagined that they were passengers in the hull of a great ship. Here they received the nourishment of word and sacrament in their voyage to a heavenly destination.

In 1494, Sebastian Brant, a conservative German theologian living in Basel, Switzerland, wrote a scathing satire on the abhorrent vices of the church of his city. He entitled his poetic satire *Das* Narrenschiff, or *Ship of Fools*. This amusing, provocative volume of poetry consisted of a prologue and 112 clever satirical stanzas lampooning the hypocritical practices of an apostate church. But the enduring impact of this raucous poetic production came from illustrations credited to artist Albrecht Dürer. His fascinating woodcut engravings captivated the interests of readers throughout Europe. Brant's entertaining satire gained momentum in the emerging currents of a more serious critique of the church by Martin Luther, an assistant professor of Hebrew Scripture at an obscure university in Wittenberg, Germany. But the iconic *Ship of*

Fools remained a popular image symbolizing all things unsavory about the church. Brandt's central figure was a court fool named Saint Grobian, patron saint of the vulgar and offensive aspects of blemished Christian behavior.

In 1931, an American journalist boarded a ship leaving Veracruz, Mexico, en route to Bremerhaven, Germany. She was traveling under the auspices of a Guggenheim Fellowship and wisely kept a copious diary of her experiences. In Germany she encountered Sebastian Brant's satirical poem and reflected upon its implications for the horrendous voyage she had just experienced en route to a Europe soon to be consumed by Nazi barbarism. For nearly thirty years she cultivated her one and only novel, *Ship of Fools*. Passengers described in her 1931 diary resemble the despicable characters of her novel. Germans aboard this satirical ship are ardent anti-Semites and contemptuous of all but their own Arian race. Porter's allegorical novel, as with the fifteenth-century poem that inspired her work, showed the ship as a microcosm of the real world's amalgamation of races and divergent cultures. Gypsies, Mexicans, Cubans, Swiss, and Spanish are forced to interact within a caustic atmosphere of intolerance and cultural exclusionism. Racism is cruelly expressed aboard this ship of fools. Herr Rieber, a publisher of anti-Semitic propaganda, addresses Lizzi, his admiring and bigoted apostle, with this torrent of insensitivity: "As a publisher my aim is to direct the minds of my readers to the vital problems of our society. I have lately got a doctor to begin a series of articles, very learned, very scientific, advocating the extermination of all the unfit, at birth or as soon as they prove themselves unfit in any way."[8]

The failure of the church to be an effective extension of the incarnation can be documented in each era of its protracted history. When the Apostle Paul articulated his analogy of the church as the body of Christ in a Letter to the Corinthians, he was keenly aware of the undisciplined behavior of its Hellenistic members, who were taking food offerings to pagan temples on their way to gatherings in the homes of Jewish converts. Sebastian Brant ridiculed the avarice and corruption within the church in Basel on the eve of the Reformation. The European Holocaust was witnessed by a silent, intimidated church whose cowardice and tacit approval contaminated the credibility of the Christian witness and the progression toward spiritual intimacy with Jews for many centuries to come. The church's defense of slavery and bigotry within the Southern church and its resistance to change during the march towards civil rights are indictments against the church's integrity as an extension of the incarnation.

But amidst each of these shameful historical circumstances, the Holy Spirit has sustained a remnant of those whose paradoxical lives reflected the image of Jesus. Instead of abandoning the ship as a viable symbol of the church, I propose that this symbol be reinterpreted in accordance with the church's authentic mission as a vessel of hope that sails to destinations of distress and human need: the impoverished neighborhood down the river, an austere Haitian village in the midst of unfathomable poverty, or a Bolivian settlement devoid of medical treatment. When we see ourselves

---

8. Porter, *Ship of Fools*, 420.

Part III: Paradox and the Holy Spirit as an Extension of the Incarnation

as a pious people gathered in a nave for worship with our eyes focused upon some heavenly hideaway from the pain of this world, we are not the vessel of Christ. The church that sails in destination toward harbors of pain and enters the hurt of a suffering humanity becomes a vessel of hope and good news. The satirical image of a ship of foolish travelers in enmity with one another and seeking escape from a hurting world is transformed into a ship of mercy. This vessel of redemption appears as a ship of fools in a callous world, but the authentic church is a community of people willing to be fools for Christ's sake. Travelers on this ship insist that service to others is the ultimate form of power. This ship of fools does not stay adrift at sea, nor does it dock only at safe harbors. It is a rescue vessel, saving people not only to bear them toward a heavenly destination, but also for a buoyant existence within a renewed earth.

N. T. Wright, in a revolutionary volume that challenges disciples of Jesus to "rethink heaven, the resurrection, and the mission of the church" crystallizes the message of the Apostle Paul and asserts with clarity, "So when Paul says, 'We are citizens of heaven,' he doesn't at all mean that when we're done with this life we'll be going off to live in heaven. What he means is that the savior, the Lord, Jesus the King . . . will come from heaven to earth, to change the present situation and state of his people . . . God intends in the end to fill all creation with his own presence and love."[9]

Thus, any bona fide symbol of the church must point to evidence of extensions of the incarnation within the redemptive activity of actual congregations. Thus, the image of the ship of fools, a dicey community willing to risk all for the glory of God, is a viable contemporary symbol.

I was the senior pastor of Providence United Methodist Church, a congregation that has enthusiastically sustained for over thirty years a medical mission in several remote villages outside Cap-Haïtien, Haiti. The intriguing story of this extraordinary mission has been told with eloquence by another former pastor of the congregation, Rev. Harley Dickson, in his gripping account, *The Real Miracle*. The story begins with a boat owned by Bill and Alice White, a couple within the congregation. This boat was named for the members of their family, *The Pieces of Eight*. They had enjoyed many cherished memories sailing as a family, but due to the scattering of their adult children, Bill surprised the family at a 1979 Christmas Eve gathering by announcing that he was going to donate the boat to the church's mission. Bill's engineering firm had an ambitious agenda, and he had little time for marlin fishing anymore. The United Methodist Committee on Relief (UMCOR) accepted the gracious gift, but the organization's executive director, Harry Haines, insisted that the boat would have to be delivered to a church in Port-au-Prince.

Thus, Bill White, who had no substantive knowledge of Haiti, agreed to depart from Lynnhaven Inlet near Virginia Beach to the capital city of a nation he had never visited. The whole family pitched in to prepare the boat for its new purpose. Bill accepted the responsibility of delivering the vessel, with its primitive navigation system,

---

9. Wright, *Surprised by Hope*, 100–101.

during the Caribbean hurricane season. His precarious voyage in 1980 was indeed the launching of a ship of fools. Four months later, Bill returned to Port-au-Prince with Alice. Their ensuing experiences among the children of the region changed their lives forever. Alice was so overwhelmed by the poor health and living conditions that she returned to Charlotte and enrolled in nursing classes at Central Piedmont Community College and subsequently passed the state's licensing board requirements as a registered nurse.

The boat the couple had donated for the purpose of providing a resource for fishing expeditions among impoverished villagers was a dismal failure due to the scarcity of marlin in coastal waters. But the boat had brought these rejuvenated disciples of Jesus to Haiti. The Holy Spirit now provided a broader vision and furnished spiritual power to pursue its realization. That vision resulted in the creation of medical clinics in the mountain villages of Dondon, La Tannerie, and Tovar. Through the years, teams of medical doctors, nurses, and legions of non-professional assistants joined Bill and Alice. An average of six annual mission teams have participated in these adventures during the past three decades. I had the privilege of accompanying Bill and Alice on a construction project in which volunteers from Providence UMC expanded the facilities at the three medical clinics. Ken and Pam Carter, a clergy couple appointed to this church when I became superintendent of the United Methodist churches of Charlotte, helped proliferate services within the three villages' elementary schools and organized economic cooperatives by initiating a ministry of micro-economics to help women of these parishes become financially self-sufficient through low-interest loans. A cottage industry of useful crafts has now emerged. Sustainable gardens have literally been planted with the seed money provided by Providence UMC.

Christ has modeled for us the paradoxical life by which the world is transformed. Jesus docked his boat along the seashore of Galilee's subjugated poor. He became Israel's Messiah-servant by his healing ministry of compassion among these oppressed masses. He did not pull rank on any of them. He entered proud, imperial Jerusalem looking like a foolish clown riding a peaceful donkey through the East Gate on his way toward a mock coronation as King upon a cross. Truly to follow this paradoxical figure requires a passport on a ship of fools. This ship is neither a vessel of hypocrisy nor of deceitful intentions shown in Sebastian Brant's satire of or the macabre allegory chronicled by Katherine Porter. Nor is the immediate destination of this ship of fools some heavenly port. Its penultimate anchorage is in the harbors of human suffering. Its reliable crew in this redemptive voyage is a small number of disciplined and focused servant leaders trained by a parish theologian. But the ship's Captain is a joyous host who brings all passengers safely home.

22

Less Is More

ECONOMICS IS A CRUCIAL biblical concern. The pivotal event in Hebrew Scripture is the liberation of impoverished masses of slaves from their incessant labors in Egypt. After generations of subjugation, the people who followed the leadership of Moses and Aaron into the wilderness of the Sinai and Negev longed for a home in which the basic resources for life (ample food, shelter, and protection from violence) would be assured. The tabernacle that preserved their greatest treasure—the Ark of the Covenant—honored the laws that defined their unique identity as a theocracy. A spirit of grace permeated these laws, as is evidenced in the fourth commandment of the Decalogue: "Remember the Sabbath day, and keep it holy. For six days you shall labour and do all your work. But the seventh day is a Sabbath to the Lord your God; you shall not do any work."[1] Former slaves who had survived the shame of subjugation by cruel taskmasters greeted with gladness this merciful mandate.

In Hebrew theology, therefore, life is more than labor. Human existence is also much more than the acquisition of money by virtue of toil. All of life is meant to be the activity of praising and honoring YHWH, the giver of existence and the provider of meaningful labor. Money is good when viewed from this perspective. The love of money and obsession with its possession, not money itself, is the root of all evil. The Hebrew God does not desire poverty to be the fate of those whom he loves. Thus, the land of promise is a place of abundance, flowing with milk (herds of oxen, sheep, and goats) and honey (citrus trees and honeycombs). YHWH wants abundant fields of harvest and plenty of productive livestock for his liberated people. A tithe of all these resources that have been graciously entrusted to God's covenant people will sustain the rituals of worship through the priestly descendants of Levi and care for the indigent, diseased, and poor. But acquisition of more than essential resources is a violation of covenant: "A good name is to be chosen rather than great riches, and favor is better

---

1. Exod 20:8–10a NRSV.

than silver or gold. The rich and the poor have this in common: the Lord is the maker of them all."² God wants a pleasurable, fulfilled existence for all. *Qoheleth* addressed the working class of his fellow Hebrews when he wrote affectionately, "I know that there is nothing better for them [the workers] than to be happy and enjoy themselves as long as they live; moreover, it is God's gift that all should eat and drink and take pleasure in all their toil."³

This was the faith of Jesus. He desired that the new community of his followers experience quality of life. His mission was to impart abundant life. But the Galilean multitudes who responded to his preaching were as enslaved by the Roman occupation of Palestine under Emperor Tiberius as were the Hebrew slaves in Egypt during the oppressive rule of Ramesses II. Thus, Jesus announced that he had come to begin the process of liberating the impoverished multitudes. He came as the new Moses (Matthew's theological emphasis) and the one who would make Jubilee a reality (a Lucan theme). He emphatically told his disciples, "Blessed are you who are poor, for yours is the Kingdom of God. Blessed are you who are hungry now, for you will be filled."⁴ The salvation Jesus intended was both economic and spiritual.

In order to be a vital participant in Jesus' kingdom movement one must travel light. He told seventy chosen emissaries that had attended his school of discipleship in Capernaum, "Go on your way. See, I am sending you out like lambs into the midst of wolves. Carry no purse, no bag, no sandals; and greet no one in the road."⁵ Abundant life is a simple, uncluttered existence, centered upon YHWH and his kingdom made visible through the advent of Jesus of Nazareth. Less is more. Thus, he told a listener in the crowd who wanted the Galilean rabbi's advice about dividing his family's estate, "Take care! Be on your guard against all kinds of greed; for one's life does not consist in the abundance of possessions."⁶ He enhanced this counsel with a parable about a man who had been so blessed with plentiful crops that he had decided to tear down his inadequate barns and build larger ones. But the voice of God arrested the self-confident farmer with this disconcerting declaration: "You fool! This very night your life is being demanded of you. And the things you have prepared, whose will they be?"⁷

Jesus' mission indeed brought good news to the poor, but he did not come for the poor alone. The plight of the deprived remains miserable unless the Holy Spirit transforms those entrusted with great resources from greed to generosity. James H. Charlesworth, Professor of New Testament Language and Literature at Princeton Theological Seminary, testifies, "I cannot find one of his Twelve who was poor. James and John, the sons of Zebedee, were well-to-do if not wealthy. Judas certainly was not

---

2. Prov 22:1–2 NRSV.
3. Eccl 3:12–13 NRSV.
4. Luke 6:20–21 NRSV.
5. Luke 10:3–4 NRSV.
6. Luke 12:15 NRSV.
7. Luke 12:20 NRSV.

Part III: Paradox and the Holy Spirit as an Extension of the Incarnation

one of the poor, if he was in charge of the money of the Twelve, as reported in the Gospel of John. Peter and Matthew were probably moderately wealthy. Jesus came to speak to the needs of all, whether they were poor or wealthy."[8] Jesus knew that without the discipleship of the wealthy, there could be little good news for the poor. Moreover, the joy of discipleship is often manifested in a lifestyle of liberality and benevolence among rich converts.

In all his teachings, Jesus was shaping the character of the beloved community. Thus, it comes as no surprise to the reader of Luke's second volume that the followers of his Way in Jerusalem "were of one heart and soul, and no one claimed private ownership of any possession, but everything they owned was held in common."[9] This description of the economics of the early church occurs immediately after the phenomenal movement of the Holy Spirit at the Hebrew festival of Pentecost—a Babel-in-reverse experience by which nationalities and tongues (past and present) were united in an intelligible language of contagious love and altruism. The result was a solidified and exuberant community of generosity that became an extension of the incarnation in the city of the crucifixion and resurrection. For these, less was more—more community, more love, and more joy.

During eras of history when a lethargic church has been dramatically resuscitated by an infusion of the Holy Spirit, it has simultaneously cultivated new generations of generous disciples that live in simplicity. When a young man named Giovanni Francesco di Bernardone, the rebellious libertine son of a wealthy cloth merchant in Assisi, encountered Christ while serving as a soldier through a vision in 1204, he lost his taste for his extravagant lifestyle. He responded to Christ's command to build his church by giving away his possessions and pursuing a life of simplicity. He became such an imitator of his Lord that his exemplary existence became a magnate of reform and cultivation of a contagious joy that swept Europe in the early thirteenth century. Young men from across the land began to share jubilantly their excessive possessions with the poor. Crowds of young women followed the comparable example of Chiara Offreduccio, one of many who Francis inspired to renounce materialism and embrace a self-emptying, paradoxical lifestyle. For each of these, less became more. The rule that defined the new order Clare initiated just days before her death granted her and a group of sisters "the privilege of most high poverty."[10] These sister disciples harmoniously lived as munificent pilgrims during an era of abject poverty in Europe, casting out darkness and creating an atmosphere of joyous charity.

The Wesleyan revival that swept through the British Isles and into colonial America in the eighteenth century was a movement of generosity and distribution of

---

8. Charlesworth, James H., "Evangelization, Creation, and Christians Origins," (unpublished paper presented at "Evangelization and Creation: The Meaning of Redemption" mission and evangelism consultation, Leesburg, Florida, January 15, 1998).

9. Acts 4:32 NRSV.

10. Englebert, *Saint Francis of Assisi*, 122.

resources among the poor. Beginning with the Oxford Methodists in the early 1730s, John Wesley and his student colleagues spent much of their time providing money and mercy to the desolate, distributing food, founding schools for children in workhouses, providing wool for impoverished women to make cloth, and visiting families in debtor prisons. The throngs who gathered in open fields and at entrances to cold mines to hear the proclamation of Wesley were predominantly the common poor of the kingdom. The General Rules of the United Societies required that participants "desire to flee from the wrath to come, to be saved from their sins" by doing no harm, doing good, and attending to the "ordinances of God."[11] These ordinances included systematic and generous sharing of possessions with the poor as an expression of Christ-motivated commitment to do all the good one can do. One observer noted that Wesley himself was charitable to an extreme. To his knowledge, "Wesley never denied relief to a poor person that asked him."[12] During the Christmas season of 1785, for example, John Wesley recorded his efforts to distribute coals and bread among the poor in London in his journal, documenting that for four days he "walked through the town, and begged the hundred pounds, in order to clothe them that needed it most. But it was hard work, as most of the streets were filled with melting snow, which often lay ankle deep; so that my feet were steeped in snow-water nearly from morning till evening."[13] Note that Wesley was eighty-two years old when he penned these lines. In his influential essay titled "Thoughts Upon Methodism," Wesley encouraged those in the movement to follow a simple economic formula: "If those who 'gain all they can,' and 'save all they can,' will likewise 'give all they can;' then, the more they gain, the more they will grow in grace, and the more treasure they will lay up I heaven."[14] This sagacious advice was written only five years before Wesley's death. He considered the greatest threat to sustaining the spiritual vitality of the church to be a growing comfort with an affluence that failed to pursue these imperatives—gain, save, and give abundantly.

While John Wesley avoided a naive, romanticized perception of the noble poor, he maintained confidence in the poor's innate eagerness to respond to God's grace and the contagious, benevolent spirit of a Christ-centered community of faith. When he visited the sick and destitute among the underground prison cells of London in 1753, he encountered those who were "half starved both with cold and hunger, added to weakness and pain."[15] He recorded in his journal, "But I found not one of them unemployed, who was able to crawl about the room. So wickedly, devilishly false is that common objection, 'They are poor, only because they are idle.' If you saw these

---

11. United Methodist Church, *Book of Discipline of the United Methodist Church*, 72–74.
12. Heitzenrater, *Wesley and the People*, 252.
13. Wesley, *Works of the Reverend*, 4:607.
14. Ibid.,7:317.
15. Ibid., 3:546.

Part III: Paradox and the Holy Spirit as an Extension of the Incarnation

things with your own eyes, could you lay out money in ornaments or superfluities?"[16] In 1773 (three years before the publication of Adam Smith's *Wealth of Nations*), he circulated a tract titled "Thoughts on the Present Scarcity of Provisions," in which he argued against those who blamed the poor for their situation in life.[17] Even though Smith never used the term "capitalism," Smith and other contemporaries encouraged many to rail against the poor, blaming their misery upon lack of initiative and slothful behavior. Wesley countered with a biblical message that posited economics as a highly spiritual enterprise. On the fiftieth anniversary of the Methodist movement for which he wrote his famous assessment above, he began with these oft-quoted lines: "I am not afraid that the people called Methodists should ever cease to exist either in Europe or America. But I am afraid, lest they should only exist as dead sect, having the form of religion without the power."[18] Ted Jennings, Professor of Wesleyan Studies at Duke Divinity School, warns that this statement has wrongly been used to explain that the malaise of modern Methodism is primarily due to a loss of evangelical fervor. But Jennings correctly observes that Wesley's essay, "Thoughts Upon Methodism," clearly rehearses the evangelical passion with which the societies have reached out to those economic classes rejected by the Church of England. In this context, Wesley confesses, "I fear, wherever riches have increased, (exceeding few are the exceptions) the essence of religion, the mind that was in Christ, has decreased in the same proportion."[19] Professor Jennings rightly discerns that "what threatens the 'essence' of Methodism, the 'power' of religion, is not a loss of membership, not a lack of emphasis on personal conversion, but prosperity."[20] He feared an insensitive opulence and an obsession with the acquisition of more. He warned an emerging middle class of Methodists that their excessive consumption and diminishing generosity would result in spiritual demise. More, without a spirit of generosity, is less.

In the United States, we are now experiencing what economist Paul Krugman calls "the great divergence."[21] The political cards in the economic deck are stacked in favor of the rich at the expense of the poor and middle class. Writing at the turn of this century, David G. Myers observed that "since 1967, the richest fifth of households have increased their share from 43.8 to 49.4 percent of all income. The incomes of the richest 5 percent have swelled ever faster—70 percent in real terms since 1967 (compared with 23 percent among the poorest fifth, who actually have gained nothing since 1974)."[22] Myers contends that the US is experiencing a dangerous paradox: While the

---

16. Ibid.
17. Quoted in Bonino, "'The Poor Will Always Be with You,'" 188.
18. Wesley, *Works of the Reverend*, 7:315.
19. Ibid., 317.
20. Jennings, *Good News to the Poor*, 137.
21. Krugman, *Conscience of a Liberal*, 124.
22. Myers, *American Paradox*, 141.

accumulation of material goods is at an all-time high, more and more people feel a spiritual emptiness in their lives.

How does this compare with economic trends in other developed countries? Economist Timothy Smeeding's research reveals that "the United States has the highest overall level of inequality of any rich OECD [Organization for Economic Cooperation and Development] nation at the beginning of the twenty-first century."[23] Furthermore, Smeeding reports that "a low-income American at the tenth percentile in 2000 had an income that is only 39 percent of median income, whereas a high-income American in the ninetieth percentile had an income that is 210 percent of the median."[24]

The great divergence was not appreciatively abated by the impact of the 2007 recession. While the plight of the poor is certainly not ameliorated by diminishing the financial resources of the rich, wealth does not "trickle down" without intentional decisions by magnanimous people of wealth. Captains of business and boards of corporations that care about the plight of employees reduce inequities. Many successful businesses have engaged in revenue sharing with workers, provided adequate healthcare insurance coverage, and have made the welfare of people the primary core value over the acquisition of greater profit. Some of these businesses have considered it far better to downsize the workweek than the work force—better to increase family time than cause unemployment. When increasing profits becomes a business's ultimate concern, the moral fabric of that institution is compromised.

Every faithful congregation seeks to become an extension of the incarnation, attuned to the movement of the Holy Spirit. In order to be an extension of the Being of Christ, the corporate body must be engaged in ministries that bless the poor. I have served as pastor of several churches that strived to maintain that identity through crisis assistance funds, food and clothing pantries, community feeding programs, and impressive participation in multifaceted ecumenical urban ministry programs for the poor. In this chapter, I have chosen to limit our focus to the illustrative story of the South Tryon United Methodist Community Church (STUMCC), with which I became acquainted as a superintendent of congregations in Charlotte.

The membership of this incarnational ministry is composed primarily of homeless people and residents of Charlotte's economically stressed Southside, Brookhill, and Wilmore neighborhoods. STUMCC began in the hearts of several leaders within Myers Park United Methodist Church, an affluent congregation located near one of the most prestigious neighborhoods in the city. In August of 2000, these visionary laypeople presented a proposal to the Administrative Board for purchasing an abandoned church building located in the center of these three struggling neighborhoods. They envisioned the creation of a food cooperative, a center for congregate meals, a department store cooperative with affordable prices, a vital teen ministry, and space for neighborhood gatherings and group Bible study. The vision statement for this

23. Smeeding, "Public Policy, Economic Inequality," 956.
24. Ibid., 959.

Part III: Paradox and the Holy Spirit as an Extension of the Incarnation

mission imagined programs "designed to meet the spiritual needs of the community, improve the social welfare of the neighbors, and provide a community gathering space for all."[25] Some who attended the Administrative Board meeting that evening felt the movement of the Holy Spirit in their midst. Reverend Barbara Barden, Minister of Adult Education, described the event as "one of those really amazing meetings where God is clearly moving, calling for action in a bold and hopeful way."

The bishop appointed Rev. Charles Rivens as the initial pastor. He is an African-American with experience as an entrepreneur and business owner. Affectionately known as "Rev. Charlie," this intensely committed servant gave the full measure of his gifts in preaching, teaching, and administration over the first twelve years of the congregation's history. He taught Scripture and theology in the simplest fashion, but he enthusiastically preached for conversion and conviction, often employing emotionally charged illustrations from the experiences of the worshipping congregation. I periodically attended worship there in a supervisory role. On one occasion, Charlie rendered an invitation for discipleship. In a profusion of emotion, a woman raced to the altar and was immediately met by several participants on the worship team. When Rev. Charlie anointed her forehead with oil, she fainted and fell backward, only to be caught in a moment of tenderness by congregants who apparently anticipated her emotional response. In that spiritually charged atmosphere, Rev. Rivens baptized her on the spot. But her expression of emotions was palpable. She screamed, shouted for joy, and danced in that sacred space. No one left the building without earnestly welcoming her into the fellowship of the redeemed.

The following Monday morning, I phoned Charlie to ask for a debriefing. I wanted to know why this woman's emotions were so dramatically and uncontrollably expressed. Charlie replied, "To begin with, she forfeited her entire source of income yesterday." I was stunned when he furthermore explained, "George, you were perhaps the only one in the sanctuary who did not know her identity as a prostitute in this community."

The Myers Park UMCs of mainline denominations must discover how to do ministry *with* the poor if we are to maintain both the form and power of the incarnational, paradoxical church. Within four years after the initiation of this ministry, both congregations began using the language of "sister congregation" and have been working to live that vision of unity through Christ. This vital ministry remains the top budgetary priority for local missions at Myers Park UMC.

The Charlotte District UMC utilized the staff of Crisis Assistance Ministries—an inter-faith non-profit mission—to teach teams from congregations throughout the district in the formation of "Circles," a strategy for breaking cycles of poverty. Volunteers are trained in the psychology of poverty, its many causes, and ways it may be eliminated. "Circles" consist of trained volunteers plus adult parents in households of poverty, unemployment, or homelessness. These local church teams, or "circles,"

---

25. Myers Park United Methodist Church Administrative Board Minutes, August 31, 2000.

demonstrate hospitality and listen nonjudgmentally to the plight of families chosen by the Crisis Assistance staff. Each of these impoverished families desires self-sufficiency and to break the cycles that perpetuate poverty. The success of "Circles" is due to the work of Christ-centered small groups in providing affirmation and accountability. Congregations within the district that have sustained such support groups and continue to collaborate caringly with neighborhood families in poverty have received blessings beyond measure. Funding and facilitating such life-altering ministries requires sacrifice, compassion, commitment, and patience. Church budgets cannot be about *me and my kind*. At the heart of any spirit-filled church budget there is a generous provision for "the least of these." Less for self, more for Christ. Less in the acquisition of things we do not need. More designated for the eternal. This is incarnational ministry, and these are the holy habits of a paradoxical church.

23

Being Alone Together

IN THIS ERA OF Facebook and omnipresent social media, it seems that we are never really alone. We can read the most intimate developments in the private lives of those we have designated as "friends." Following the recent fiftieth reunion of my high school class, I have reconnected through social media with many "friends" who had disappeared from the radar of my awareness. But this delightful technology has not significantly deepened these relationships. We have merely broadened the scope of our accessibility to one another, not necessarily the depth of our spiritual intimacy. While I celebrate the convenience and novelty of these advancements in communication and appreciate the renewal of old friendships, my wispy adventure into the world of social networking has not produced any real evidence of authentic community.

Perhaps this is because to be human is to be alone. Psychologists have written insightful volumes related to the experience of "birth trauma" when the umbilical cord is cut and the infant is separated from its mother's body. There are even those rare individuals, such as novelist Reynolds Price, that "recover or invent persistent and powerful uterine memories."[1] These memories were prompted by his mother's second pregnancy. The novelist verbalized this memory: "Still the images have stayed strong with me for more than forty years. This instant I can see the slow rose light at its sifts through Mother's flesh, blood and water; I can enact a stillness so dense it seems like unearthly music and a safety so total that again I know why I turned my butt to the outer world and very nearly refused to be born."[2]

But we are born to be alone. No one else can do our living, our deciding, our suffering, our laughing, or our dying. Being alive means having this body that emerges from our mother's womb—a body separated from all other bodies. We are not only aware of our aloneness, but we know that we cannot escape it even though every

---

1. Price, *Clear Pictures*, 43.
2. Ibid.

meaningful relationship in life is an attempt to overcome the existential fact of our being alone.

Grace permeates the entire biblical narrative and is especially evident in the second mythological story of creation, in which the Creator says, "It is not good that the man should be alone; I will make him a helper as a partner."[3] God's gift, however, is not an activity that overcomes human isolation or eliminates the pain of loneliness. To be human is to accept and affirm our uniqueness as separate creatures. Even the covenant of intimacy—marriage—does not cure loneliness. The partner helps ameliorate its inevitable pain. Although partners can effectively empathize with the fact of our isolation, those who burden marriage with the false expectation of curing loneliness create the context for marriage's failure. Even God has chosen not to liberate humans from their state of being alone. This is both the majesty and the burden of human existence.

The grace that is woven into biblical narrative is, therefore, paradoxical. Sacred stories from Abraham and Moses to the Hebrew prophets and the apostles of Jesus reveal that while loneliness expresses the pain of being alone, solitude conveys the glory of our separateness. Biblical theology invites the believer to enter a pilgrimage of faith that takes one from the despair of loneliness to the liberating depths of solitude and onward toward the ecstasy of community and communion with God.

The travesty of the current popularity of social media is that such superficial communication raises users' expectations and seduces with the assumption that their sense of isolation and loneliness will be cured, only to discover that these emotions are exacerbated. We never feel lonelier than when we are surrounded by people or when our "inbox" is flush with shallow communiqués from emotional and spiritual strangers. Such experiences confirm our ultimate isolation. Those seeking spiritual intimacy or a quick panacea for loneliness through social media may become intensely hostile. Their feelings are comparable to one from whom love has been withdrawn. They not only feel rejected, but like a jilted lover, they also grow to enjoy the pain of their rejection. This form of neurotic loneliness often mutates toward either repressed anger or explosive violence.

Paul Tillich reminded us half a century ago that "loneliness can be conquered only by those who can bear solitude."[4] He describes solitude as the bridge between loneliness and community. Thus, an essential role of every pastoral theologian is to serve as an administrator of small groups that can become places of redemption through shared solitude, biblical study, prayer, journaling, Eucharist, costly service, and the observance of other holy habits. Through the Holy Spirit's activity within these groups, a community of the lonely is transformed into the mystical and missional body of Christ.

After several months of intense statistical study, analysis of our church's mission in focus groups, a period of prayerful reflection, and an intense retreat of the Church

---

3. Gen 2:18 NRSV.
4. Tillich, *Eternal Now*, 21.

Part III: Paradox and the Holy Spirit as an Extension of the Incarnation

Council of Providence United Methodist Church, this congregation adopted a simple vision statement: "To be the Body of Christ by glorifying God and serving others."[5] A large banner with these words was boldly hung in the gathering room of the Family Life Center. The leadership of this faith community felt strongly that the Holy Spirit was guiding them in a perpetual journey toward the reality of this vision. All small groups, including the administrative committees of this church, were seeking to become *spiritual communities* pursuing the call toward becoming the Body of Christ and guiding individuals from loneliness to solitude to the experience of communion with God and one another.

This movement into solitude toward the formation of community is best illustrated by the experience of Jesus as told in the narrative of Luke the Evangelist: "Now during those days he went out to the mountain to pray; and he spent the night in prayer to God. And when day came, he called his disciples and chose twelve of them, whom he also named apostles."[6] Only after a night of solitude, prayer, and listening to God through sounds of silence did Jesus begin to assemble his intimate band of the twelve. Only after experiencing the vulnerability of isolation on a wilderness mountain and lonely absorption into a dark night of his soul did Jesus arise and walk down to a level place to be surrounded by a crowd of hopeless, diseased people. Only through the empowerment of solitude could Jesus create community amidst such chaotic diversity. Only through the glory of solitude could Jesus touch the lives of the hopeless with healing power. Only through the miracle of solitude can those who now follow Jesus experience the spiritual intimacy of a new community.

Each of the Synoptic Gospels discloses that Jesus' ministry in Galilee was not officially launched until he was driven by the Holy Spirit into the wilderness to be tempted by the Evil One. In solitude he met the potential of his shadowed side—a vulnerability to temptation, obsessive desire for power or prestige, addiction to materialism, insecurity, and self-centeredness. But the God Jesus called upon in the solitude of that wilderness experience supplied him with the power to overcome the Tempter. Therefore, when we also enter solitude and invoke the name of Jesus, he joins us in the barren places of our souls and provides us with the power to resist these temptations. Here we experience a presence at the core of our emptiness and at the epicenter of our loneliness. The mystical path out of our loneliness into the sunlight of a dawning gladness requires the solitude of worship. Tillich eloquently describes this experience when he writes, "In these moments of solitude something is done to us. The center of our being, the innermost self that is the ground for our aloneness, is elevated to the divine center and taken into it. Therein can we rest without losing ourselves."[7]

A central mission of every vital parish is to provide opportunities and space for experiencing solitude. It is imperative that a safe place, such as a chapel or easily

---

5. *Voice of Providence United Methodist Church Newsletter* 31, December 19, 2001, 1.
6. Luke 6:12–13 NRSV.
7. Tillich, *Eternal Now*, 24.

accessible classroom, be made available within the physical facility of each church. I have found it helpful to provide a perpetually burning candle or muted light to illuminate this space with reverence. Kneelers invite communion with God and a spirit of humility. Devotional tracts, lectionary Bible readings, and other resources should be made available for use at home and church. At least twice a year, spiritual life retreats should be sponsored and led by either the pastor or a lay leader trained in spiritual counseling or mentoring. Only through the poverty of solitude can a church discover the richness of community.

Henri Nouwen, who spent his final years as chaplain to the L'Arche Daybreak community for handicapped adults in Toronto, Canada, cautions us against a romanticized concept of community. He warns, "Community is not some sentimental ideal place or time where everybody lives together, loves each other, and always gets along. That's never going to happen. Rather, in living together we come to realize that community doesn't require or offer total emotional harmony. It offers us the context where we try to love one another and receive the love and care of others."[8]

Every pastoral theologian's mission is to guide a congregation from loneliness into solitude in preparation for the ongoing activity of sanctification through the holy habits of life in a Christ-centered community. The pastor will likely discover no greater model for this pilgrimage than that which was clearly articulated and practiced by the martyred Dietrich Bonhoeffer in his straightforward treatise, *Life Together*.

In April of 1935, Bonhoeffer postponed a long-anticipated trip to India at the personal invitation of Mahatma Gandhi and reported to duty as the imminent head of the first seminary of the Confessing Church in Germany. Martin Niemöller had asked this young academic theologian to provide leadership in defiance to the Reich Church that had capitulated to Adolph Hitler's demand for absolute allegiance to the German state. The initial site for this unauthorized seminary was at Zingst, Germany, on a land bridge to the Pomeranian coast. Here Bonhoeffer envisioned a kind of Protestant monastic community, unlike the purely academic environment of the Nazi-controlled universities. In the previous year he had written a letter to a friend that foreshadowed his vision of an entirely new community context for theological education in which he confessed, "I no longer believe in the university, and never really have believed in it—to your irritation. The entire education of the younger generation of theologians belongs today in church cloister-like schools, in which pure doctrine, the Sermon on the Mount and worship are taken seriously—as they never are (and in present circumstances couldn't be) at the university."[9]

Twenty-three ordinands from Saxony comprised his first seminary class, including Eberhard Bethge, who later married Dietrich's sister and became the recipient of a vast number of the martyr's letters from prison as his definitive biographer. Bonhoeffer had come to realize that the rubber and the road were strangers within German

8. Nouwen, Christensen, and Laird, *Spiritual Direction*, 114.
9. Metaxas, *Bonhoeffer*, 247.

churches. He firmly contended that faithful pastoral theologians were obligated to model a nurturing lifestyle within a disciplined communal environment if the contemporary church was to be redeemed from its apostasy and irrelevance.

For practical reasons, this renegade seminary was moved from Zingst to nearby Finkenwalde, where an abandoned estate in ill-repair was renovated in order to accommodate the students. Bonhoeffer set the agenda of solitude, rigorous academic reflection, insightful conversation at congregate meals, joyful worship, and recreational play. He gathered the ordinands in silent meditation at early morning and led them in a forty-five minute period of worship prior to breakfast. Bonhoeffer challenged these young men to focus throughout the day upon a single verse of Scripture, often from the Psalter. He daily integrated academic lectures and required research with reflective periods of worship and vigorous sporting activities, including hiking and soccer. The formation of a supportive, caring community was as important to Bonhoeffer as the digestion of a strenuous scholastic syllabus. Music was integral to the faith formation of this community of students, and Dietrich was a master at the piano, introducing hymns, anthems, and black spirituals that he had learned at the Abyssinian Baptist Church in Harlem. He advocated a method of sharing intimate personal confession that was an alien experience for these young Protestants.

In 1939, the third year of the seminary's brief existence, Bonhoeffer outlined his theology of community in describing the holy habits of Finkenwalde in a brief book titled *Gemeinsames Leben*, which was posthumously translated into the English *Life Together*. This simple work has since become a Christian classic and should be required reading for all lay leadership in any local church. Its directives could easily comprise the format for all small spiritual growth groups within the life of a parish. In his lectures and writings at Finkenwalde, Bonhoeffer felt the urgency of forming viable expressions of authentic, disciplined Christian communities that imitate the paradoxical teachings Jesus' Sermon on the Mount and are empowered by the Holy Spirit to be confrontational communities shaped by the example of Christ. He taught that such communities are divine gifts, explaining, "It is grace, nothing but grace, that we are all allowed to live in community with Christian brethren . . . Communal life is again being recognized by Christians today as the grace that it is, as the extraordinary, the 'roses and lilies' of the Christian life."[10] This new community's atmosphere is filled with praise, even in the worst of times, for Bonhoeffer insisted that "only he who gives thanks for little things receives the big things."[11] He forbade the analytical paralysis that plagues the church of the twenty-first century, concerned as it with fears of extinction. He reminded disciples struggling to remain faithful in an apostate climate that "Christian community is like the Christians' sanctification. It is a gift of God which we cannot claim . . . Just as the Christians should not be constantly feeling his spiritual pulse, so, too, the Christian community has not been given to us by God

---

10. Bonhoeffer, *Life Together*, 20–21.
11. Ibid., 29.

for us to be constantly taking its temperature."[12] Thus, Bonhoeffer set out to make the seminary a model for the imitation of Christ in the anticipation of our Lord's ultimate victory over the evil forces of Nazi apostasy surrounding the ordinands. Moreover, his theology of community was applicable to the transformation of the institutional church in the era following a war Bonhoeffer knew to be inevitable. In practical language he counseled, "A Christian family fellowship should surely be able to read and listen to a chapter of the Old Testament and at least half of a chapter of the New Testament every morning and evening."[13] He clearly articulated the paradox of communal existence within the parish when he insisted, "Let him who cannot be alone beware of community . . . But the reverse is also true: Let him who is not in community beware of being alone."[14] Refusal to participate in the diversity and messiness of Christian fellowship is a rejection of the call of Jesus. Thus, a solitude that does not lead toward community is incomplete and spiritually harmful. Bonhoeffer's wisdom is applicable to much more than the community at Finkenwalde in saying, "We recognize, then, that only as we are within the fellowship can we be alone, and only he that is alone can live in the fellowship."[15]

Throughout my years of pastoral leadership I have initiated and administered various expressions of small group ministry. Some have been effective and others an exercise in futility, but I have learned from each. The most effective and sustainable small groups are those that are biblically-based, Christ-centered, and mission-driven. These ingredients best express the paradoxical character of the authentic church. Through the years, I have found that the Church of the Saviour in Washington, DC, has effectively initiated small communities of disciples that exemplify these essential qualities; therefore, I am grateful for the ways in which that faith community has served to inspire many of the parishes of my pastoral pilgrimage.

In chapter 13's exploration of servant leadership, we explored the story of Gordon Cosby as an exemplary pastoral servant. Following his perilous experiences as a chaplain in combat, Gordon and his spouse, Mary, were joined in 1948 by seven others to form a radically diverse community with a high-octane quality of risky discipleship. Their call to radical obedience combined two foci of a life-long spiritual pilgrimage—an inward journey of scriptural holiness (with growth in love for God, self, and others) and an outward journey of costly service for the purpose of mending a broken creation, beginning with the Adams Morgan neighborhood where their worship center was located, about two miles from the White House.

Gordon often observed that the churches of his acquaintance were too big to be spiritually intimate and missionally effective, but were seeking to become larger. At his insistence in 1994, the Church of the Saviour and its approximately 110 members

12. Ibid., 30.
13. Ibid., 51.
14. Ibid., 77.
15. Ibid.

Part III: Paradox and the Holy Spirit as an Extension of the Incarnation

divided into a scattered community of eight small mission groups. Each of these is independently incorporated with its own vision of calling and identity. These communities share the same intensity of discipleship commitment as the original congregation and seek to follow the radical mandate of Christ to be the paradoxical body of Christ for the world. Mission group membership maintains exemplary integrity, for all participants are held accountable to standards of costly sacrifice and the paradoxical behavior of new beings in Christ. Covenant commitments are reviewed and renewed annually after periods of intentional discernment. There are currently nine mission communities with unique callings to clearly defined outward journeys. Through the years, these covenantal groups have provided affordable housing, procured wholesome family homes for hundreds of orphans, sustained effective feeding programs for the poor, and pioneered numerous other Christ-inspired ministries within this neighborhood and beyond. Diversity of race, economic class, gender, age, sexual orientation, and political philosophy have been the hallmark of each of these small communities. Consequently, these groups' business has always been messy and conflicted, but dependent upon compromise in order to administer an agenda of consensus. Gordon and Mary were catalysts for the entrenched vision of these diverse communities for six decades, but these small mission groups have cultivated a vanguard of lay leadership that ensures a promising future for these faith communities. This is especially important during this time of aging exodus and the recent death of the founding pastor who had spiritually nourished these young servant leaders with the grace of a Moses-Joshua or Elijah-Elisha mentorship. Through the years, I have participated in retreats at Dayspring—a farm in Maryland purchased by the Church of the Saviour as a center for discipleship training that has helped to transform the lives of thousands.

During my high school years, my hometown church pastor taught a theology of community gleaned from the writings of Elizabeth O'Connor, the articulate interpreter of this model of ministry in the nation's capitol. While I was a seminary student, Elton Trueblood, the Quaker philosopher who mirrored many of Cosby's concepts, visited that same congregation. He coached the church and our pastor in the initiation of "Yokefellow," an ecumenical, multi-faceted small group outreach program among the region's poor whose ministries of compassion continue to this day.

In chapter 16, I referred to my participation in *Dunamis*, an ecumenical group sponsored by the Greensboro Urban Ministry and committed to various vital spiritual disciplines. A prominent lawyer within the group named Robin Britt asked for spiritual discernment when community leaders asked him to run for office in the US House of Representatives from our state's Sixth Congressional District. As a result of his theological understanding that the ultimate expression of power is service to others, Robin came to Washington knowing that his political perspective was countercultural. But he was an effective witness and participated, as time allowed, in the ministries of the Church of the Saviour. Through this experience, Robin received clarity regarding his authentic calling to enhance the lives of children in poverty.

Being Alone Together

In my last two appointments before retirement, both congregations gave enthusiastic endorsement to the Stephen Ministry concept, effectively linking well-trained lay caregivers with care-receivers and periodically sending new waves of laity and clergy to the national training for "Equippers." It was at one of those events that I was introduced to ChristCare—an intensely interrelated web for small group formation. All certified ChristCare groups must be Christ-centered, biblically-based, and mission-driven. Lutheran in origin, this program provides a practical methodology for the proliferation of vibrant small groups within the life of a congregation. These groups begin with a period of discernment, seeking the guidance of the Holy Spirit in finding a corporate mission. They are each held accountable for keeping a balance in their pursuit of both inward and outward journeys. While these communities are encouraged to grow in spiritual intimacy, they are also urged to be evangelical, inviting new participants who are drawn to their chosen mission. When a group grows beyond twelve members, it is compelled to divide and grow once again. A ChristCare group of men in Charlotte, for example, developed a meaningful relationship with members of a struggling Hmong UMC nearby, resulting in an enhanced appreciation for these profoundly spiritual neighbors from Southeast Asia. Even though Stephen Ministries no longer provides training for small group leadership or supervision for ChristCare groups, their staff still supplies excellent written resources for initiating effective small groups with the mature threefold purpose of conducting biblical studies, sustaining a Christ-centered spirit, and providing missional service.

The most important small group in the life of a vivacious congregation is the confirmation class. Perhaps the main reason that young adults turn away from our churches is that we expect too little and reflect cheap grace in programs of entertainment that are devoid of substance. When youth participate in difficult mission team assignments and are linked with mentors who imitate the paradoxical life of Christ, their lives are transformed. They gravitate toward sacrifice eagerly. If the church requests and expects little of them, many will seek fulfillment through the Peace Corps, military service, or nonprofit agencies committed to costly service among the destitute. When the church settles for mediocrity in discipleship, youth follow the sanctuary's exit sign. When I encounter inspiring adult leaders who were nurtured within the youth programs of the churches over my four decades of pastoral experience, I recall their inquisitive presence in confirmation class or the sweat on their foreheads during mission trips to Bolivia or Haiti. Through the nurturing environment of small groups in mission, many of these young adults formed lifelong friendships that empowered them to make positive differences in their communities. Through confirmation and subsequent youth small groups, these young people developed holy habits that enabled them to cope with adversity and celebrate community in defiance of their loneliness.

In chapter 16 we elevated the paradoxical, biblical figure of Jesus the pacifist. Since the fourth century and the revolution wrought by Emperor Constantine, many pastors have ignored the contradiction of blessing righteous wars while ignoring Jesus' posture of peace in the Sermon on the Mount. Mainline congregations are not pacifistic in tradition or practice. Those among us who deem this facet of Christ's mission to be of strategic significance often feel lonely and isolated in the just war environment of the standard church. But in nearly all congregations, there are those who are graced with the spiritual gift of peacemaking. Pastors called to this ministry are wise to assemble these fellow peacemakers into spiritual groups of encouragement and accountability. Through the years, I have elicited the beautiful spirits of those called to this aggressive and controversial ministry. The emotional juices stirring within nearly all peace activists dry up unless these peacemakers are brought to engage in an inward journey of spiritual discovery with a supportive small group. I found focus and encouragement in resolute groups in Greensboro and Boone that courageously denounced cruel military oppression in Latin America. I marveled at the creativity and courage of a peace group at First UMC in Waynesville that initiated a sister-city relationship with Mtskheta in the Republic of Georgia at a time of repressive control by the USSR. This peace group hosted a delegation of grateful citizen leaders from Mtskheta, located approximately twenty kilometers north of Tbilisi, shortly after the April 9, 1989, tragedy known as the Tbilisi Massacre. Tbilisi was the capital city of the Georgian Soviet Socialist Republic. On that date, an anti-Soviet demonstration was dispersed by the Soviet Army, resulting in twenty deaths and hundreds of injuries. Our guests from the nearby town of Mtskheta received a full measure of Christian compassion, support, and media publicity during a period of horror and national tragedy that became a prelude to the disintegration of the USSR. That small peace group faithfully fostered hospitality, compassion, and the intimacy of Christian community with newly discovered friends from the Republic of Georgia, truly participating in the Holy Spirit's movement of peacemaking during a crucial time of nonviolent revolution in European history.

But to where is the Holy Spirit leading the church in the twenty-first century? If the church is an extension of the incarnation, and if its size and influence in the Western world is diminishing, what new horizons of hope is God opening for the church? That will be the subject of the next chapter.

24

The Paradox of Church History

I WAS LYING ON a comfortable gurney with a needle in the receptive vein of my left arm, donating a few pints of blood at a neighboring church through the auspices of the Red Cross just days following the brutal massacre of twenty elementary school children in Newtown, Connecticut. The attending nurse broke the awkward silence during the slow drip of platelets, saying, "These are scary times. Even schoolchildren are no longer safe. The end must be near." I ventured no response, for indeed these are times that try the souls of us all. We live in a treacherous world. But is the current era of violence so terrifying as to suggest an imminent apocalyptic day of doom and the sudden end of human history? On the occasion of my birthday a few weeks earlier, I had conducted some speculative research into the events surrounding the date of my birth in 1943. I discovered that on that week, a futile revolt had erupted in a Warsaw ghetto. It was led by a few courageous young Jewish resisters but was brutally extinguished by Gestapo thugs. During each hour of that day, thousands of elementary-aged children with tiny numbers branded upon their gaunt arms had been forced into crowded gas chambers throughout Europe. Their screams of horror seemed to echo in my ear's memory as the nurse spoke of the Newtown carnage and the crazed young man who had stalked into the Sandy Hook Elementary School, pulling the trigger on a semi-automatic rifle in a suburban community that seemed to symbolize the fulfillment of the American dream.

Is the history of humanity progressive or regressive? Are we driven by a divine providence toward a fulfilled future, or are we victims of inevitable self-destruction? What indeed is the direction of our collective history?

There are days when I read the morning news or catch the afternoon broadcast of NPR's *All Thing Considered* only to feel the shock of a regressive, increasingly vulnerable world. On many occasions I have been convinced that I inhabit *Mr. Sammler's Planet*—a depressing environment described in Saul Bellow's novel of the same name.

Part III: Paradox and the Holy Spirit as an Extension of the Incarnation

Aging Artur Sammler had somehow survived the war and merciless captivity in a concentration camp in Nazi-occupied Poland. Now in his seventies, he resides in a fortified, impersonal Manhattan apartment building. The character's environment seems nearly as inhospitable as the banal evil he had endured two decades earlier. Over the course of a single day Sammler is verbally denounced by a radical Columbia University student who erupts with vulgar threats during a lecture he reluctantly delivers at the bequest of a professor friend. On his lonely ride back to his apartment refuge that afternoon, Sammler is shadowed by a belligerent pickpocket he had witnessed stealing another old man's billfold on the subway. This assailant successfully intimidates Sammler into petrified silence as he anxiously enters the lobby. His heart races as he rides the elevator. Upon collapsing on his bed, he spies a sea-green notebook in which his perpetually positive daughter had made ridiculous notes concerning her naive obsession with human colonization of the moon. When Sammler reads her first sentence, "How long will this earth remain the only house of Man?" this brooding father thinks to himself, "How long? Oh, Lord, you bet! Wasn't it the time—the very hour to go? For every purpose under heaven. A time to gather stones together, a time to cast away stones. Considering the earth itself not as a stone cast but as something to cast one's self from—to be divested of. To blow this great blue, white, green planet or to be blown from it."[1]

Artur Sammler's sullen reflections are as ancient as the Hebrew *Qoheleth* he paraphrases. Many of us have our Mr. Sammler moments as we consider our unique interval in the enigmatic progression of time. But just as our pessimism is a rejection of the gospel's redemptive message, so is our retreat into naive optimism. Christian hope is rooted in hardheaded realism and accepts the paradoxical nature of history's movement. From the perspective of biblical theology, the human story is both progressive and retrogressive. We always stand one generation away from either chaotic barbarism or the advent of the kingdom of *shalom* through history's healing and the consummation of biblical hope, for at the center of history is the Christ event that has the power to redeem us and the historical process that carries us. People of faith constantly feel the paradoxical pull of history—the tension between annihilation and fulfillment. Yet we maintain faith that this dilemma will ultimately be resolved by the inexorable movement of Christ's spirit, which cannot be extricated from the historical process. As long as remnants of faithful servants inhabit the parishes of the global church and emulate the self-giving love of Christ, history will be carried toward God's intended destination.

A couple of generations ago, the theologian Oscar Cullmann invited the post-war church to return to the essential faith of the primitive first century Christian community. He suggested a simple, succinct analogy comparing Jesus' death and resurrection to history's D-Day. He warned that there will be many battles yet to fight, but Victory-Day has already been assured. Cullmann further elucidated his point in saying,

---

1. Bellow, *Mr. Sammler's Planet*, 50.

> The entire New Testament, including the Synoptic Gospels, holds the view that the mid-point of time no longer lies in the future but in the past or in the present for Jesus and the apostles . . . The center has been reached but the end is still to come . . . The decisive battle in a war may already have occurred in a relatively early stage of the war, and yet the war still continues. Although the decisive effect of that battle is perhaps not recognized by all, it nevertheless always means victory. But the war must still be carried on for an undefined time, until 'Victory Day.'"[2]

In chapter 16 we have argued that the church's involvement in this struggle is nonviolent. The Kingdom of *shalom* will never be achieved by conquest, military crusade, or violence. Thus, the paradox of human history—its vacillation between manifestations of massive destruction and aspiring hope—is resolved in the context of the church's *meta-narrative*, defined as "an overarching story that gives focus, cohesion, commonality, and meaning to life."[3] The aberrant actions and courageous habits of remnant communities are practically invisible to secular historians. But the church must preserve the narrative of faithful activity in the acts of the apostles and disciples of Jesus. This is the meta-narrative of remarkable congregations, sacrificial saints, and even martyrs who have authentically witnessed to their Christ-inspired faith. These stories are part of the unwritten verbal traditions of many Christian families and a vast number of long-suffering congregations. The meta-narrative of the church carries the human saga towards the Victory Day that was guaranteed by the events in Galilee and Jerusalem nearly twenty-one centuries ago.

Biblical narrative is *meta-history*—the pilgrimage of faith written or remembered by descendants of Abraham and Sarah from the perspective of those who were in persistent dialogue with the eternal Being. Since the discovery of the Rosetta Stone, Egyptologists have searched ancient hieroglyphics in vain to discover an account of an episodic exodus of Hebrew slaves, the horrific deaths of Egyptian children, the capitulation of Ramesses II, and the freeing of multitudes of Hebrew slaves. The Jewish conquest of Canaan was likely a lengthy process and certainly less grandiose than the chronicles of the book attributed to Joshua. Even the impressive account of Israel's apex as a nation-state—under the legendary leadership of David, the conqueror of infidels, and wise King Solomon—pale in comparison to objective data concerning the mighty dominions of Assyria, Babylon, Phoenicia, Egypt, Greece, and China. Yet these sacred texts, in documenting the warp and weft of Hebrew history, have endured the test of time while other ancient civilizations have declined into insignificance. Moreover, holy writ has articulated the most lucid and unambiguous view of human hope and visionary aspiration.

But how reliable and accurate is meta-narrative—the ancient texts of the Hebrew people or the enduring episodes of the Spirit-led church? A careful literary analysis

2. Cullmann, *Christ and Time*, 83–84.
3. Dawn, *Royal "Waste" of Time*, 45.

Part III: Paradox and the Holy Spirit as an Extension of the Incarnation

of the biblical texts can easily identify a myriad of fascinating forms that carry the canonical story: myths, folklore, parables, allegories, poetic imagery, musical psalms, God-centered stories, evangelical proclamation, letters, and apocalyptic writings. But the sacred Scripture of the Hebrews and early Christians is held together by a narrative that attempts to make sense of the movement of time and the human saga. All these forms constitute the meta-narrative of paradox. These stories are linear rather than cyclical. They acknowledge that the human story is repetitive and unique, predictable (dependent upon analogy) but also surprising. Meta-narrative is punctuated by divine intervention. The meta-narrative of the faith community is not a futile cycle of replicated events. God slices into history by surprise and is sewn into the fabric of the human tapestry. We humans are both controlled by circumstance and freed by God's grace to defy determinism and accomplish revolutionary feats. Thus, in his farewell address to the pilgrims of Sinai, Moses articulated the vocabulary of grace through choice: "See, I have set before you today life and prosperity, death and adversity . . . Choose life so that you and your descendants may live."[4]

Thus, the Scriptures hold in paradoxical tension historical accounts that are repetitive and unique, ordinary and revelatory, irrational and purposeful, retrogressive and progressive, and predetermined occurrences as well as events contingent upon ethical choice. The meta-narrative of the Bible contains both meticulously objective records of factual events and internal exaggerations of faith-inspired interpretations. But at the center of biblical story is the belief that God is within time's movement, guiding its destination. Jesus' life defied the notion that humanity is confined in some prison of inevitability. Perhaps George Buttrick, Pastor of Madison Avenue Presbyterian Church in New York, said it best a generation ago when he asserted, "History is Dialogue between God and man-in-pilgrimage in the language of Event; and Christ is the Conversation's middle term, the key to the translation, the light in which the whole pilgrimage can be seen and understood, and the love in which history's brokenness is healed."[5] Jesus' mission was to subvert cycles of misery, violence, and suffering. His seditious teachings challenged the common acceptance of these destructive and repetitive patterns of history. The community formed around those teachings and, infused with his spirit, has prevailed in each era as a threat to principalities and powers committed to the proliferation of violence and economic systems of injustice. Even today, small groups within congregations, remnant voices within mainline denominations, and church bodies committed to pacifism have prophetically insisted that the events of September 11, 2001, did not necessitate a military invasion of Iraq, the intensification of violence in Afghanistan, the domino impact of the Arab Spring, or the increased vulnerability of the US and its allies. The story of incarnational love defies the inevitability of history's cyclical madness.

---

4. Deut 30:15–19b NRSV.
5. Buttrick, *Christ and History*, 44.

Unlike the biblical narrative, secular history is characteristically written from the perspective of victors. This is why the story of Western civilization eclipses the ethnic heritage of the colonial cultures of Africa, the Middle East, India, much of Latin America, China, and the Pacific Basin. But all of that is rapidly changing. The West is discovering records of an Arab Renaissance and intellectual sophistication that predates the European Enlightenment. As the globe becomes more interconnected, we are learning more about an imperial China that was culturally superior to Medieval Europe. When Cortés conquered what is now Mexico and claimed it as a Spanish possession, the first thing he did was to destroy all the libraries that had preserved the history of the Incas, Mayans, and other tribal civilizations. The oral histories of slaves, since the family narrative of Alex Haley in the 1970s, have produced an illuminating narrative of humiliation, suffering, and injustice that humbles the arrogance of American triumphalism. Native Americans are now piecing together cultural records that predate Christopher Columbus. We now know about the tragedy of the Trail of Tears during the presidency of Andrew Jackson, General Custer's Last Stand, and the calamity of Wounded Knee in a more comprehensive historical context. Revisionist historians have a forbidable task indeed! What can we learn from those who have been victims of time's great sword of injustice? What lessons can we glean from the losers of history—the candidates and causes that lost the elections or the civilian women and children that fell victim to warfare?

Paradoxically, the bulk of biblical meta-narrative is the preservation of a history from the perspective of losers that sustained the vision of an ultimate triumph of God's mercy. Hebrew Scripture hangs out to dry all the dirty family stories that reveal the foibles of patriarchs, matriarchs, prophets, and legendary kings. These sacred pages document long periods of exile, ethical decline, military defeat, and national humiliation. In like manner, the gospel writers placed ink to parchment to give prominence to the account of the death of a loving Messiah. Luke's description of the initial church blatantly discloses the persecution of Paul as well as reports of imprisonments and martyrdom. Each of the Letters—the Catholic Epistles, James, and correspondence attributed to Paul—describe the ethos of the church as a subversive community under the heavy heel of Roman oppression. But the corpus of sacred canon has remained largely untarnished by the air-brushing of historical revisionists. The Bible's meta-narrative makes no attempt to provide impeccable factual accuracy. From the point of view of a myriad of authors of holy writ, other cultures played bit roles in the great drama of redemptive history. The pharaohs of Egypt were evil foils in the plot. The Assyrians appear to have been comparable to modern Nazis. The Babylonians were a brief hiccup in history. The Hellenists were misguided by arrogant philosophies, chiseled statues of pint-sized gods, and the tyrannical conduct of pompous monarchs. Roman emperors, with their faces minted on coins, were nothing compared to the Messiah-king on a Roman cross whom God raised from death. The menagerie of authors who collected centuries of oral traditions to contribute to this

Part III: Paradox and the Holy Spirit as an Extension of the Incarnation

diverse assortment of texts were inspired by the Holy Spirit and supported by faithful communities of losers—the authentic ecclesia, the covenant people of promise, and pilgrims of hope. The meta-narrative of these remnant communities of faith is the purest form of historical interpretation. Without the meta-narrative of faith, the human story would move inexorably toward barbarism and eventual self-destruction.

Even though nothing needs to be added to Scripture's account of salvation history, Luke implied that he would only contribute the initial chapter to the saga of the Acts of the Apostles. Luke's Story, therefore, continues through the meta-narrative of God's activity within incarnational communities during each ensuing era. Thus, an essential mission of every congregation is to continue the meta-narrative so that *our stories* receive empowerment and interpretation as they relate daily to the Story.

My pastoral experience has been limited to service within the American South where, in the words of William Faulkner, "The past is never dead. It's not even past."[6] Revisionist historians of the "new South" have done a prolific job of chronicling the lives of the Hugh McColls[7] of Southern culture and the emergence of a financial renaissance. Hagiographic biographies of skillful politicians of the new South, like Terry Sanford[8] of North Carolina, have dramatically documented the qualitative elevation of private and public education. A region of petrified racism, ignorance, and unfair class privilege has begun to change. But we have lived out our decades in the South rooted in the rich red earth of rural communities, small towns, and cosmopolitan cities that have been slowly and painfully transformed by the courageous actions of a few faithful laity and clergy within receptive congregations.

For a considerable period of my ministry I have been an admirer of the Koinonia Farm in Americus, Georgia. Clarence Leonard Jordan was born and reared in southern Georgia. His large family of nine siblings attended the local Baptist church, where Clarence remembered singing as a child, "Red and yellow, black and white, they are precious in his sight." While attending the Georgia State College of Agriculture at the University of Georgia in Athens and participating in Reserve Officers' Training Corps summer camp, Clarence began to feel uneasy with the incompatibilities between military service and the teachings of the Sermon on the Mount. In response to what he considered as God's claim upon his life, he left home in 1938 to attend the Southern Baptist Theological Seminary in Louisville, Kentucky. His studies in the Greek New Testament and his role as an adjunct professor at a nearby seminary for black students drew him to a more radical concept of Christian community reflected in Luke's description of a communal congregation.[9] Later, Clarence wrote, "Never did

---

6. Faulkner, *Requiem for a Nun*, 80.

7. Hugh McColl is the former Chair and CEO of Bank of America, headquartered in Charlotte, North Carolina.

8. Terry Sanford was North Carolina's sixty-fifth governor from 1961 to 1965, President of Duke University from 1969 to 1985, and a US Senator from 1986 to 1993.

9. See Acts 2:44–45; Acts 4:32–33 NRSV.

Paul or Peter or Stephen point to an empty tomb as evidence of the resurrection . . . The evidence was the spirit-filled fellowship."[10] This realization was the seed for a new vision, for as he exclaimed, "If that closeness of sharing in a common life exhibited the spirit of Jesus alive in these men, why not now . . ."[11]

"Now" was the summer of 1942—the time of the experiment. Over five hundred friends received a mailed announcement and invitation to participate in Koinonia Farm, Inc. The new community would be an interracial, nonviolent, Christ-centered populace where all material possessions would be shared in common. The farm was located in the heart of Sumter County, along Route 49, about eight miles southwest of Americus, Georgia.

The global circumstances during this "now" were as perilous during that summer as at any historic crossroads. Hitler's doctrine of Aryan supremacy was catching on in Europe. Allied invasion was a distant dream. Imperial Japan had subdued the masses of China and controlled most of the Pacific. And racism ruled in Georgia's Sumter County. Koinonia was almost bankrupt due to a merchant boycott of the farm. A delegation of the most prominent citizens of the region paid a visit to the farm and tried to talk some sense into Clarence Jordan. After all, violence had erupted when a merchant in Macon, Georgia, agreed to sell flour and seed to Koinonia. An explosion ripped through the front of the bold establishment that had defied the boycott, shattering glass and tearing holes in adjacent buildings. The group insisted that Jordan and members of the interracial commune leave the region in order to restore peace. Clarence explained to this distinguished group of church people that their ancestors had fled Europe in pursuit of a land of freedom of religious expression, for "their practices did offend the people over there and they wanted a measure of freedom where they would be free to worship as they saw fit."[12] Then Clarence clearly articulated the purpose of Koinonia as he asserted, "Now to us our way of life is a very, very important part of worship. Obedience to Christ comes first to us, even before prayer. It is difficult for us to convey to you the fact that what we actually have here is a church which is seeking to be true to Christ."[13]

It is important to note that Koinonia Farm is mentioned only once in the magnificent three-volume, 2,852-page history of the civil rights movement by Taylor Branch[14] (Branch also notes that Mrs. Coretta Scott King escaped there for safety during the November 1962 Cuban Missile Crisis[15]). But the story of Clarence Jordan's extraordinary experiment in Christian community is meta-narrative that has as much

10. Lee, *Cotton Patch Evidence*, 25.
11. Ibid.
12. Ibid., 149.
13. Ibid.
14. See Branch, *America in the King Years*, 3 vols.
15. Branch, *Parting the Waters*, 673.

Part III: Paradox and the Holy Spirit as an Extension of the Incarnation

to do with altering the destiny of the South as did the highly publicized marches and valiant activities initiated by popular civil rights figures.

Many obscure congregations—especially African-American churches—treasure the folklore stories of amazing counter-cultural activity led by their ancestors. When I was the administrative supervisor of several predominantly black congregations in Charlotte, I heard from black laity many tales of courageous social witness. Most are never recorded, but are passed down instead as oral tradition. Many of these folk histories have been lost as generations that participated in acts of daring defiance have departed the land of the living. Why are these stories still so important, especially if they are enhanced with exaggeration or compromised by inaccuracies? The meta-narrative of the church is important because it is infused with the spirit of a God who meets us from the future. The church's meta-history is the vibrant account of those unique revelatory experiences that are a prolepsis of God's coming kingdom. They are true stories because their memory is intertwined with the Story of redemptive history. Accounts of costly fidelity in word and action within ordinary red-clay communities of believers inspire us in the present and remind us of the church's vision of the future.

Jürgen Moltmann contends that Ernst Troeltsch's restricted methodology for historical research—based entirely upon "the almighty power of analogy," cause and effect, and principles of probability—limits the historian's perception of reality.[16] Nothing new under the sun can really happen because the multi-dimensions of the past are denied. In Troeltsch's methodology for studying history, the past is merely an uncoordinated series of dead facts. It has no real vitality or relevance for the present. But the tragedies of recent history have surely taught us, as Faulkner suggested, that the past lives vibrantly in the present. The people and events of our own experience live on at the core of our being. Moreover, the "facts of history" also contain the hopes and aspirations of all the people who have previously occupied this *terra firma*. The facts of the past, consequently, constitute only one dimension of history. They also point toward our corporate future. According to both Hebraic and Christian theology, the past contains the promises of God to the community of the faithful. These glorious past promises constitute present aspirations, goals, and vision for the church. Thus, any thorough study of the past must also probe into promises, expectations, and visions of those who have carried unfulfilled hopes. A conscientious member of a Christian community in the South knows that Faulkner's insight into our history is only partially accurate. The past is not really past, but the present moment contains the future as well! If Faulkner had been a bit more familiar with the Clarence Jordans of the South, he might have articulated the importance of "the history of the future" in the shaping of the new South. Within each parish of my experience, a remnant core of the faithful continue to contend that God is guiding the church and the culture surrounding people of faith toward a more perfect future. These people of hope are carried by the belief that the values articulated in Christ's Beatitudes will ultimately

---

16. Moltmann, *Way of Jesus Christ*, 229.

become a historical reality and his mission statement articulated in the synagogue of Nazareth will be fulfilled. When worship is completed in little country chapels, worshippers often take a detour through the soft green sod of the adjacent cemetery. The stories of these deceased have not ended. Their "facts" are connected with our present longing anticipation of future fulfillment. The history of their future is relevant to present worshippers. The history of planet earth's future is likewise relevant to the faithful. Our hymns of worship point toward that future. Even the administration of the congregation's mission is contingent upon the corporate, biblically-based vision of God's bold future. Worship within these unpretentious buildings is grounded in resurrection faith. Moltmann explains how this faith provides the church with a wholly different methodology for interpreting history. He writes, "If we apply the fundamental metahistorical concepts of experience, we see that 'the resurrection of the dead Christ' talks about the future of this past, and that the hope which it establishes for the raising of all the dead also ascribes a corresponding future to those who have gone. This is a totally unique interlocking of future and past."[17] Thus, when we sing the hymns of resurrection and assert their inherent messages of hope, we proclaim "a future for those who belong to the past, and in so doing, it reverses time's direction."[18]

I shall illustrate this through my memory of an intensely significant personal experience that occurred during a period of high expectation and anxiety in my life—four weeks before my graduation from seminary and eight weeks prior to my first Sunday in that initial parish assignment. I had been among a small colloquy of students that met with visiting Professor Jürgen Moltmann in order to analyze and critique his newly translated *Theology of Hope*. In early April, the seminary hosted a seminar on this topic to be attended by a cadre of American theologians. Various students were assigned practical tasks. I had the duty of providing transportation and hospitality to the moderator of the event—Paul Lehmann, Professor of Christian Ethics at Union Seminary in New York.

On the opening night of the seminar, in a crowded auditorium of professional theologians and students, we all were duly engaged in absorbing critiques and questions by leading scholars. Toward the end of the evening, Professor Harvey Cox from Harvard was handed a note just before his concluding remarks. With a quivering voice, he made this riveting announcement, "I have just received official word: Martin Luther King Jr. was assassinated in Memphis, Tennessee." The seminar immediately dissolved. Within the hour, thousands of students filled the campus chapel or flooded the grassy commons. Violence exploded in hundreds of cities across the nation.

Within a couple of days, a worship service in Duke Chapel was prepared and the chancel filled quickly. The ritual and music were emotionally charged, despite Dean Robert Cushman's efforts to bring a comforting theological word in his eulogy. Excerpts from King's "I Have a Dream" address were recited, and the recessional hymn

17. Ibid., 239.
18. Ibid., 238.

evoked collective guilt and consolation as we sang with somber resolve, "We shall overcome." The majestic sound of the organ echoed down that gothic nave as the doors were opened and worshippers stepped into a sea of voices all singing together: "We'll walk hand in hand . . . we shall all be free . . . we shall live in peace . . . the Lord will see us through . . . some day."

Within weeks I began my four decades of pilgrimage in pastoral ministry in Union County, one of the most racially volatile areas in the state still reeling from a violent race riot just two years prior to my appointment. But the memory of that worship service at the epicenter of a Southern university fortified me to enter my appointment with a resilient sense of resurrection hope.

Fast-forward thirty-five years from this indelible memory. I had just been appointed by my bishop to serve on his cabinet with connectional responsibilities for churches in the metropolitan region of Charlotte. I had only one Sunday's brief hiatus between my last sermon as a pastor and my first service in the old, established First Church in the heart of the city. My wife and I decided to make a surprise return visit to the church of our first appointment in the Union County campus village of Wingate. It was the thirty-fifth anniversary of my initial sermon as a full-time pastor. We arrived unannounced and squeezed into the last pew of a packed congregation in all its racial and cultural diversity. Our joy was uncontrollable as we felt that glorious celebration of gospel reality and were greeted after the benediction by the church's beloved pastor—an articulate and effective young, African-American, female parish theologian.

25

The Urgency of Patience

FROM THE PERSPECTIVE OF the church, historical progress moves like molasses in winter. Nonetheless, we who are followers of Jesus stubbornly hold onto an uncomfortable tradition established at the beginning of Luke's second volume. The Third Evangelist reports that the risen Christ appeared to an assortment of his disciples and insisted that they all remain in Jerusalem to await the arrival of divine power. These befuddled Galileans beseeched he whom God had raised from death to give them some clue as to how long they would need to wait for the consummation of his promised kingdom, anxiously asking, "Lord, is this the time when you will restore the kingdom to Israel?"[1] Jesus' reply has left the church groping through the ages in an eschatological fog: "It is not for you to know the times or periods that the Father has set by his own authority. But you will receive power when the Holy Spirit has come upon you; and you will be my witnesses in Jerusalem, in all Judea and Samaria, and to the ends of the earth."[2] Luke then reports that the risen Messiah ascended into the clouds and out of sight. The Evangelist further complicated matters by reporting that two men in white robes stood among the witnesses to this phenomenon and observed in a tone of authority, "Men of Galilee, why do you stand looking up towards heaven? This Jesus, who has been taken up from you into heaven, will come in the same way as you saw him go into heaven."[3] Jesus was no longer with them physically, but they persisted arduously in labors of love, knowing that they truly had a friend in high places. Thus, none of their efforts, no matter how costly or fruitless, was in vain, for as a result of the ascension, they were convinced that they remained on the winning side of history's inexorable movement toward mercy and reconciliation.

1. Acts 1:6b NRSV.
2. Acts 1:7–8 NRSV.
3. Acts 1:11 NRSV.

Part III: Paradox and the Holy Spirit as an Extension of the Incarnation

What Luke's meta-narrative lacks in clarity it makes up for with the alluring mystery of expectation his enigmatic account creates. Subsequent to the arrival of a compelling spirit of unifying power during the Hebrew festival of Pentecost, those who had witnessed the ascension of the risen Christ initiated an aggressive form of evangelism that began a transformation of the Western world. But as we enter the twenty-first century since Christ commissioned his followers to be witnesses *from Jerusalem to the ends of the earth*, Christ's communal Kingdom of Jubilee ideals and the triumph of his mercy has not yet become a universal reality. The human agenda tolerates escalating violence and seems to be moving rapidly toward self-destruction. Through the centuries, Luke's account of the ascension of the risen Lord has lingered as an embarrassing symbol for the church. Luke's theological message makes it abundantly clear that Christ has left us in charge for the interim, and apparently we have made a mess of things. Consequently, the biblical symbol of the ascension is both the source of quixotic anticipation and eschatological discomfort for the church. The Third Evangelist documents an amazing surge of spiritual energy and the miracle of comprehension among diverse cultures and languages on the birthday of the church. Many of these transformed followers of the Way obeyed Jesus' command to take the good news of a coming kingdom to the corners of the known world. Others remained in Jerusalem in case the departed Messiah might soon descend from the clouds of the Judean sky. So it is that the early church assumed a timetable of "sooner" rather than "later."

James, the brother (or kinsman) of Jesus, became their principle spiritual leader in Jerusalem until his death near the time of the Temple's demolition and the Diaspora of its Jewish population. According to Josephus, James was martyred before A.D. 62. A disciple of this revered kinsman of the Messiah wrote an epistle in which he admonished the faithful to remain patient "until the coming of the Lord."[4] He might as well have suggested that the believer maintain an endurance of faith "until the twelfth of never." This mysterious letter was penned around the end of the first century by a disciple of the martyred Saint James during a time of great impatience for those who had expected the imminent return of the victorious Christ. This pragmatic writer had witnessed the moral restlessness of new Christians who had responded naturally to this prolonged delay in the arrival of a promised *parousia*. Following the destruction of Jerusalem's Temple and the waves of persecution that pursued the scattered Jews, these sons and daughters of Abraham entered the hostile environment of the Greco-Roman world. Leaders of the synagogues in Mediterranean towns and cities turned their hostility toward those within their faith culture who had become followers of the Way. These novice devotees became discouraged in such an alien, antagonistic environment of both Jewish and Gentile hostility. The apostolic fathers had taught them that the ascended Christ would return in power as he had promised, but a full generation had elapsed without any significant sign of the arrival of his visionary Kingdom.

4. Jas 5:7 NRSV.

The Roman government, moreover, had resumed the practice of political oppression after a brief interlude of tranquility. Conflict between Jewish Christians and leaders of the synagogues had reached a feverish pitch. Gentile converts to the Way argued that they need not observe the ethical constraints of Hebrew religious rituals. Devout Jewish converts chastised undisciplined conduct and moral lethargy within the community of those who purported to be followers of a Jewish Jesus. Many of these fragile first-century converts claimed to be bona fide disciples of Paul, maintaining that they had been justified by the sacrifice of Jesus upon the cross and so did not need to be held accountable for performing works of righteousness.

Ironically, the book of James is an impatient response to these appalling attitudes, which reflected a tone of moral lethargy within the church. The author wrote in the style of Hebrew wisdom literature, thereby elevating the importance of obedience to the Torah and its moral mandates. Wisdom literature contains subtle messages of theological paradox, as in the couplets of many Proverbs (discussed in chapter 5) or the astonishing narrative of Job (examined in chapter 3). The writer of James insisted that the faithful believer be urgent regarding spiritual preparation for the coming kingdom. He insisted that the *parousia* would arrive in the fullness of time. Nonetheless, James urged these fretful Christians to wait patiently for the triumphant Christ at some undisclosed tomorrow by conscientiously and urgently performing works of Christ-like mercy each day. The writer of this epistle urged disciples to wait for Christ's return by diligently waiting upon their neighbors. He admonished the pious believer to labor in urgency because of the overwhelming presence of evil, but at the same time, to await the arrival of the full power of God's righteousness and Christ's indestructible Kingdom that cannot be achieved by the good works of Christ's followers.

The book of James is practically devoid of overt references to Christ. Some have even assumed that it was originally a Hebrew document to which a Christian disciple later added this opening phrase: "James, a servant of God and of the Lord Jesus Christ."[5] But this whole epistle implies knowledge of Jesus, the Galilean teacher of righteousness who exemplified the wisdom heritage of Judaism. James echoed the historical Jesus when he wrote, "If any of you is lacking in wisdom, ask God, who gives to all generously and ungrudgingly, and it will be given you."[6] Jesus, sitting upon a Galilean hillside, had explicitly counseled his disciples, "Ask, and it will be given to you; search, and you will find; knock, and the door will be opened for you."[7] When James boldly asserted, "There is one lawgiver and judge who is able to save and to destroy. So who, then, are you to judge your neighbor?"[8] He was paraphrasing Matthew's account of Jesus upon the mountain, "Do not judge, so that you may not be judged."[9]

5. Jas 1:1 NRSV.
6. Jas 1:5 NRSV.
7. Matt 7:7 NRSV.
8. Jas 4:12 NRSV.
9. Matt 7:1 NRSV.

Part III: Paradox and the Holy Spirit as an Extension of the Incarnation

When the book of James was placed in the canon of orthodox Christian witness, the church chose to hold in paradoxical tension the dynamics of law and grace. The disciple who patiently and passively awaits the coming salvation of Christ is also called to work urgently and aggressively in deeds of righteousness as a sign of the authenticity of personal faith. Thus James assertively wrote to his lethargic friends within the congregation, "My brothers, what use is it for a man to say he has faith when he does nothing to show it?"[10] In the style of Hebrew wisdom writings, James compared the patient Christian to a farmer who anticipates a glorious harvest. There is a time in which even the most proactive farmer can do nothing. He cannot produce the rain. He cannot work the soil, for the seeds are already sown. Like this farmer, James reasoned, "You also must be patient. Strengthen your hearts, for the coming of the Lord is near."[11]

The late Peter Gomes, explaining the subtle theology of James' Epistle during Advent to a congregation of students and faculty with fast-paced lifestyles at Harvard's Memorial Chapel, spoke affectionately about his father, a patient cranberry farmer: "This [theology] is not merely a 'waiting around for something interesting to happen,'" he clarified, "but, as with the farmer, a working for that for which we wait. That is what, for Christians, the art of impatient living is all about: working well for that for which we wait. Waiting alone will not do. Working for the sake of keeping out of mischief and keeping busy will not do. Working well for that for which we wait, that is the essence of our peculiar Advent hope."[12]

But what are realistic expectations for a post-Enlightenment Christian? Are we to take literally Luke's symbolic language of a descending Christ who will arrive to establish a paradise on earth? If the time of his Advent is drawing near, what are the signs of his imminent arrival? The diverse New Testament witnesses do not provide systematic answers to these practical concerns. But they each imply that this Jubilee reality will ultimately be established on earth in accordance with the prayer that Jesus taught his followers to pray, "on earth as it is in heaven." Wisely, the writer of the epistle from James' congregation did not predict or specify the time for the consummation of the Jubilee. He merely pointed to the ancient prophets of Israel who had been faithful to the eternal promises even though they would not experience their fruition. He pointed to that paramount figure in Hebrew wisdom literature, Job, citing that this man of unjustified suffering "stood firm" and received the pity and compassion of the Lord. Yet we all know how impatient Job actually was. This Hebrew everyman argued vehemently with his three friends against God allowing such unfairness as the death of his children and devastation of his fortune. Only the voice from the whirlwind quieted his impatient protests. Nonetheless, the story of this impatient man

---

10. Jas 2:4 NEB.
11. Jas 5:8 NRSV.
12. Gomes, *Sermons*, 8.

of righteousness endures because of his forbearance amidst the mystery of unjustified suffering.

Judaism required the discipline of righteous works to achieve salvation. In Christ, according to James, we have received the *perfect law*: "the law that makes us free."[13] Paradoxically liberated Christians are commissioned by Christ to dig into history with a commitment to personal and social holiness that will challenge the evil and brokenness of this world in the certain hope that the fullness of Christ's Jubilee restoration will ultimately become reality. The authentic disciple participates in this revolution of righteousness as if the anticipated future were dependent upon Christian good works. But this same disciple knows that the final transformation of this fallen, corrupt culture of injustice is God's doing. Without such works of righteousness, however, we give evidence to the world that our faith in the victory of Christ is fraudulent.

At the transitional time just before the new millennium, several fundamentalist sects propagated the notion that the time of the end was imminent. With sensitivity to the awkward position of mainline congregations purporting biblical authority while avoiding conversations about eschatology, novelist Gail Godwin published *Evensong* in 1999. This sequel to *Father Melancholy's Daughter* resumed the story of Margaret Bonner Gower, who now pursued her father's vocation as the priest of All Saints in the fictitious Smoky Mountain town of High Balsam, North Carolina. She is married to Adrian Gower, an admirer of Margaret's now-deceased father. Adrian is also an ordained priest serving as chaplain and acting headmaster of a boarding school for troubled children. Because of Adrian's struggle with depression, their marriage is contentious. They struggle to remain passionately focused on their ministry in an environment of monotonous ecclesiastical routine and fundamentalist activity in the community related to the millennium's ending. Adrian reflectively says to his sensitive wife, "Life is a series of transformations, isn't it?"[14] Impatient with her husband's passivity, Margaret cynically replies, "So you just wait, is that it?" Adrian earnestly counters, "Wait and be useful. I wish I were a little more adept at the usefulness part. I know I'm not being of much use to you now, Margaret. Either at home, or in this conversation. But that's what I'm trying to do down here, in my limited way, just give myself fully to a few people in a small place."[15]

Adrian Gower's line echoes countless pastors serving in inconspicuous places with uncommon valor and unappreciated sacrifice, faithfully holding patience and urgency in paradoxical tension. They are being truly loyal to the synoptic tradition that depicts Jesus as a man in a hurry but confident in the reliable promises of YHWH. The word "immediately" depicts nearly all of Jesus' movement throughout the Synoptics. The synoptic writers each project a motif of urgency in the personality of Jesus. These three narratives disclose that the Messiah does not waste any time. He is confident that

---

13. Jas 1:25 NEB.
14. Godwin, *Evensong*, 203.
15. Ibid.

Part III: Paradox and the Holy Spirit as an Extension of the Incarnation

the prolepsis of a kingdom of righteousness is breaking into transitory time through the advent of his ministry. The unique appeal of the film *The Gospel of Saint Matthew*, directed by the Italian cinematographer Pier Paolo Pasolini, similarly insists that Jesus does not walk, but runs.

John Wesley, that patron saint of all workaholics, is rarely associated with the concept of patience. He wagged his gaunt finger in the faces of his preachers, admonishing them, "Never while away time; neither spend any more time at any place than is strictly necessary."[16] Methodists have rightly been impatient with social evils of all descriptions: slavery, child abuse, alcoholism, militarism, and economic oppression. The paradox of biblical patience is that faith in Christ demands impatience with *things as they are* because of a trust in the inevitable and eventual arrival of *things as God shall have them become*. Biblical patience, in fact, is an expression of dissatisfaction and impatience with sin, suffering, and evil. Godly patience, therefore, takes the human form of forbearance and perseverance.

William Wilberforce, a product of the Wesleyan spiritual revolution, spent the decades of his political career fighting in Parliament for the abolishment of slavery in the British Empire. He was well into his seventies and had exhausted his family fortune investing in the abolitionist movement, forcing him to liquidate his home at Highwood, when he confessed to a friend, "I am like a clock that is almost run down."[17] But on the historic Friday evening of July 26, 1833, an aging Wilberforce received word that fulfilled his entire prophetic pilgrimage: Parliament had just passed the bill abolishing slave trade in the British Empire. Throughout the course of his confrontational political struggles, he had practiced an urgency that was rooted in the firm contention that God's righteousness would ultimately prevail.

The Apostle Paul especially understood this paradox when he encouraged congregations throughout the Roman Empire to maintain faith during the present period of suffering "knowing that suffering produces endurance, and endurance produces character, and character produces hope, and hope does not disappoint us, because God's love has been poured into our hearts through the Holy Spirit that has been given to us."[18]

A young pastor who had been callously thrown in jail in Birmingham, Alabama, also advocated this paradoxical expression of urgent patience. Martin Luther King Jr. had been admonished by a group of leading white Southern clergy to be more patient with the insidious Jim Crow laws. Dr. King responded with this battle cry: "Justice too long delayed is justice denied."[19] King cited a litany of injustices with which he could no longer coexist: mobs lynching his kindred, hate-filled policemen cursing and killing black people of faith, children smothered in poverty amidst an affluent society,

---

16. Wesley, *Works of the Reverend*, 5:219.
17. Metaxas, *Amazing Grace*, 274.
18. Rom 5:45 NRSV.
19. King, *Why We Can't Wait*, 81.

and his six-year-old child barred from Birmingham's public amusement park. Black Americans, he explained, had already waited 340 years for their God-given rights to be manifested. "There comes a time when the cup of endurance runs over, and men are no longer willing to be plunged into the abyss of despair,"[20] wrote this urgently patient young prophet from behind the bars of lonely incarceration.

This sort of holy impatience is grounded in the hope of the mathematical equation of God's eternal paradox: "with the Lord one day is like a thousand years, and a thousand years are like one day. The Lord is not slow about his promise, as some think of slowness, but is patient with you, not wanting any to perish, but all to come to repentance."[21] Thus, all disciples of Jesus are called to be God's impatient warriors for justice. When we are internally and spiritually at peace with the God who will ultimately bring the triumph of justice and the reality of God's reconciling Kingdom, we become aggressively impatient with the temporary powers of this world.

As we enter the second decade of the twenty-first century, we of the church are appalled by the widening gulf of economic disparity in the US. We have become passively tolerant of matters that should erode our patience. From 1992 to 2007, the top four hundred wealthiest citizens of this nation saw their incomes increase 392 percent and their average tax rate reduced by 37 percent.[22] This would be a laudatory trend if this repository of unprecedented wealth had simultaneously resulted in an equitable trickling down of good fortune for the poor. According to the research of Tim Smeeding, "We have all but eliminated 'welfare' for single parents in America and in so doing have turned the welfare poor into the working poor. Poverty rates did not go down along with welfare rolls; instead, we have the hardest-working low-income single parents, who also have the highest poverty rates in the rich world."[23]

We have passively accepted such blatant injustices, but have also become increasingly impatient with matters that do not really matter, racing through our days with relentless acceleration. Our personal computers measure time in nanoseconds. Jeremy Rifkin has proposed that all of our timesaving devises have had a dilatory effect on this impatient culture. We prefer to communicate with quick computers rather than slow people. We have even interrupted the natural rhythms of our bodies. Rifkin warns that "the accelerated time frame of the modern age is beginning to drive a permanent wedge between the rhythms of culture and the rhythms of nature, threatening a complete break in temporal bonds between the two worlds."[24] A paradigmatic caricature of our impatient lifestyle was illustrated in the June 23, 1956 *New Yorker* cartoon by Barney Tobey in which a couple races up the steps of the Louvre in Paris. The husband

---

20. Ibid.
21. 2 Peter 3:8b–9 NRSV.
22. See "Only Little People Pay Taxes," in Gilson and Perot, "It's the Inequality Stupid," 25–27.
23. Smeeding, "Public Policy, Economic Inequality," 969.
24. Rifkin, *Time Wars*, 58.

Part III: Paradox and the Holy Spirit as an Extension of the Incarnation

hurriedly turns to the concierge and inquires, "Which way to the Mona Lisa? We're double-parked."

Disciplined saints and courageous martyrs have best comprehended the paradoxical nature of an authentic Jesus follower's urgent patience. When Christmas was approaching war-torn Germany, Dietrich Bonhoeffer languished in prison. He consoled his friends in a letter, telling them that the Advent season, with its spirit of anticipation, connected him with the great communion of saints, "a fellowship transcending the bonds of time and space and reducing the months of confinement here to insignificance."[25]

Terry Waite, with his ironic name and imposing physical height, was a hostage to terrorists in Lebanon for 1,763 days. He struggled daily to maintenance of his sanity. Patience took on an entirely different meaning while he was tortured, intimidated, and confined to a small cell with a ceiling much lower than his physical frame. Time, for Terry Waite, was eradicated. This devout Anglican kept repeating a line from the book of Hebrews: "It is a fearful thing to fall into the hands of the living God."[26] He thought of himself as a captive of God and not of these evil men. When he realized that his captors intended to break his sanity and crush his willpower, he began to resist. He thought, "My active life is over for a while, perhaps forever. Maybe I will never leave this place. My life, such as it is, is in the hands of the living God. I don't feel that God is near. I don't feel comfort from my prayers. All I feel is a searching introspection, as though a light were shining into the deepest parts of my being. Everything will be called to face that light."[27]

The liberating message of the entire Bible is that at the end of all our waiting and longing, there is the light of God's patient love. When we follow that light, we discover that God is there waiting too. When we come close to God's light and love, we grow impatient with the darkness that surrounds us. When we draw near to God's promise of freedom, we hurry to free ourselves from the shackles that bind us. We burn with an impatient urgency fueled by the patience of God, whose love makes our life of impatient works and patient faith worth the wait.

---

25. Bonhoeffer, *Papers from Prison*, 36.
26. Heb 10:31 NRSV.
27. Waite, *Taken on Trust*, 27.

26

Winning by Losing

WINNING IS AN ELUSIVE enterprise. Military strategists are often oblivious to the reality that one can win battles but still lose a war, as was evidenced during the agonizing years of American military presence in Vietnam. Political figures, heedless to the judgments of history, inappropriately celebrate expedient victories without considering the long-range consequences of reckless conquest.

Athletics provide poignant metaphors to interpret the human condition and expose the precariousness of our fixation with winning. A culture that ritualistically rewards the winning of the Vince Lombardi Trophy on that high and holy Super Bowl Sunday is particularly vulnerable. When the defining aphorism of the American people becomes the philosophy of a revered football coach for whom "winning is the only thing," that culture is indeed answerable to the righteous judgments of a paradoxical God who teaches the faithful how to win by losing.

Until a few months before he succumbed to cancer at the age of eighty-six, Joe Paterno was a venerated saint in the Parthenon of American athletics. His Nittany Lions football team had won 409 games and gone undefeated for five seasons, winning bowl games twenty-four times. An impressive 80 to 90 percent of Paterno's players had graduated from the university. Yet winning had become not only the coach's obsession, but also the ultimate concern of many Penn State alumni. When it was revealed that winning had become more important than the safety of young children, many graduates of academic institutions across the nation began to question the values of these schools and our culture's obsession with winning. Jerry Sandusky's young victims will remember the legendary winning coach at Penn State for reasons other than his statistics on the field. According to biographer Joe Posnanski, these children "would see Joe Paterno as the man who should have saved them."[1] Are our most prestigious centers of higher education actually hubs for the amusement

1. Posnaski, *Peterno*, 354.

Part III: Paradox and the Holy Spirit as an Extension of the Incarnation

of superficial students to be treated as mere trade schools for landing lucrative jobs rather than authentic scholastic enterprises that honor the pursuit of wisdom through an atmosphere of academic integrity? Nearly all those in authority at major lending and investment institutions during the economic tsunami that erupted in 2007 were graduates of prestigious schools of business, economics, and law. For most of them, the financial crisis amounted to their first report card failure. The egregious ethical choices of these habitual winners nonetheless caused disastrous deprivation and pervasive suffering among millions of citizens who lost out around the globe.

For over a decade, Lance Armstrong was an athletic Horatio Alger hero for a new generation. He appeared to be the paragon of our most treasured national virtues: reward for hard work, patriotism in international competition, self-reliance, and egalitarian service through lucrative financial gifts. He was already a recognized champion on the global scene when, in 1996, he was diagnosed with advanced testicular cancer that had spread to his brain and lungs. After surgery and chemotherapy, his chances of survival were slim. But Armstrong was determined to continue his career as a disciplined athlete with unprecedented determination and grit. His heroic stature was magnified when he persevered to become the first American cyclist to win the Tour de France. Choking back tears as he recalled his victory lap along the Champs-Elysées, Armstrong told the press, "I would just like to say one thing. If you ever get a second chance in life for something, you've got to go all the way."[2]

That day of seemingly spotless triumph merely fueled Armstrong's greed for more. When Armstrong and his team went on to claim six more victories at the world's most prestigious cycling race, rumors began to spread about his use of performance-enhancing drugs. In hearings before the World Anti-Doping Agency, Armstrong vehemently denied the charges until, in June of 2012, irrefutable evidence that he had used illegal substances with regularity came to light.

In a highly publicized interview with Oprah Winfrey in January of 2013, Armstrong openly confessed his doping, his cover-up attempts, and his arrogant acts of intimidation. When Oprah asked him, "What's the moral to the story?" Armstrong replied, "I don't have a great answer there. I can look at what I did, cheating to win bike races, lying about it, bullying people." Armstrong added, "There's another moral to the story . . . about losing myself . . . And then the ultimate crime is the betrayal of these people who support me and believed in me and they got lied to."[3] The world's most celebrated athletic champion is now a global icon for hubris, for he has lost nearly everything that once mattered to him.

Jesus taught and embodied the paradoxical good news that is the source of salvation for Lance Armstrong and all participants in a culture of winning-at-any-cost. His teachings were recorded, with only slight modification, by each of the Synoptics,

---

2. Armstrong and Jenkins, *It's Not About the Bike*, 262.

3. Lance Armstrong, interview by Oprah Winfrey, "Worldwide Exclusive, Part 2," January 18, 2013.

beginning with Mark the Evangelist, who testified, "He called the crowd with his disciples, and said to them, 'If any want to become my followers, let them deny themselves and take up their cross and follow me. For those who want to save their life will lose it, and those who lose their life for my sake, and for the sake of the gospel, will save it. For what will it profit them to gain the whole world and forfeit their life?'"[4]

These words addressed all those in the crowd—the apostles as well as the curious and uncommitted. Jesus articulated a three-fold expectation for discipleship: self-denial, cross-carrying, and adherence to his precept and example. In order truly to win, one must first deny one's self. But the second facet of discipleship is a metaphorical reference. In the synoptic witness, Jesus does not carry his own cross to the place of the Skull unassisted, as depicted in the account of John 19:17. The Synoptics tell that Simon of Cyrene was compelled by the Roman soldiers to carry Jesus' cross. In a sense, these three gospel accounts "Christianize" this man from Cyrene and make him a prototype for an obedient disciple, in stark contrast with Jesus' closest disciples, who were entirely absent from the crucifixion scene.

All four New Testament Evangelists, transformed by the experience of Christ's resurrection, regarded each follower of Jesus to be an ultimate winner. But in order to be an authentic winner, one must *disregard* or *deny* one's self. The Greek verb *arnasastho*, meaning "to deny, renounce, refuse, or decline," here "connotes a radical renunciation of self, not merely of one's sinful conduct or sins."[5] Thus, taking up one's cross implies not only a readiness for martyrdom but more specifically, a willingness to suffer the opposition of hostility in everyday life.

How is this paradoxical teaching applicable to our contemporary setting that resists paradox in general and the notion of self-denial in particular?

Jesus was acutely aware of the fact that self-preservation is a healthy human instinct. His paradoxical path to winning was an acknowledgement of this reality. He certainly would have preferred that the crowds in Galilee endorse his teachings, that the throngs in Judea recognize and support his nonviolent agenda as he entered Jerusalem on a lowly donkey, and that Herod Antipas would be brought to contrition and conversion through the prophetic preaching of his kinsman John of the Wilderness. But these potential responses to his teaching and ministry were rebuffed. The cross became the only way to accomplish his ultimate victory. The egalitarian society that he envisioned could only be birthed through a new community formed by those who responded to the Holy Spirit's urgings. These people would collectively become an aberrant community. After witnessing his resurrection and receiving his promised Holy Spirit, they began to deny selfish desires and intensify their compassion for others. This peculiar community, consequently, became the real winners in the advancement of the human story. The paradoxical teaching of Jesus and his route to the cross did not create a macabre culture of ailing masochists or gloomy self-haters. It produced

4. Mark 8:34–36 NRSV.
5. Fitzmyer, *Gospel According to Luke*, 787.

Part III: Paradox and the Holy Spirit as an Extension of the Incarnation

a joyous, winning community that followed a reliable path to self-fulfillment and triumphant living.

In conjunction with a Habitat for Humanity building blitz to construct a community of homes in the city of Greensboro, Millard Fuller, founder of this international mission, spoke from the pulpit Christ UMC, where I was the senior pastor. He related his personal story of Pyrrhic victory and empty economic success as a prominent lawyer. He had achieved all his financial aspirations and become affluent and socially influential. But in the process, his marriage was in shambles. Fuller told us how he became a stranger to his own children. Even though he had become a self-made millionaire by age twenty-nine, in 1968 he and his wife gave up their wealth to refocus their lives on Christian service. They moved with their children to Georgia's Koinonia Farm. They lived there for five years until moving to Zaire as missionaries in 1973. Through a sharing of insights, candid conversations with Clarence Jordan, and much time of spiritual searching, Millard Fuller crafted the mission for what would ultimately become the global Habitat for Humanity. By God's grace, Millard Fuller's work will continue to bless millions of recipients of his Christ-centered ministry. His personal spiritual pilgrimage remains a testimony to the fact that by losing one's life, one truly wins.

Some proponents of "Christian realism" place Jesus' paradoxical teachings into their historical context and dismiss their relevance for contemporary living. They remind us that each New Testament Evangelist wrote during an era of encroaching martyrdom, arguing that Christ's teachings have no practical application to the contemporary church, especially in Europe and North America. They contend that Jesus' paradoxical words about self-denial should not to be taken as a mandate for the church's mission today, insisting that to take his words literally is comparable to the mindless attitude of radical Muslim fanatics who commit suicide to inherit the rewards of an eternal Paradise.

Consistently within the chapters of this book, I have made a case for the paradoxical nature of God as manifested in the teachings and being of Jesus Christ, insisting that living paradoxically is indeed God's mandate of the contemporary church. I am certainly not suggesting that a self-denying disciple of Jesus endures a life of misery with the goal of a martyr's ending and the reward of spiritual happiness on the other side of death. Such a demented eschatology is foreign to the Christian message! The first priority of an authentic, sacrificial disciple of Jesus is not a final personal reward beyond earthly reality. To the contrary, existence within a community of self-giving love, with attitudes and actions of authentic altruism, is joyous and fulfilling. The rewards of self-denial are within this present earthly life. Moreover, the perpetual and persistent existence of such a paradoxical community is the driving force of the human saga! These atypical communities of costly witness are transforming the world from the destructive course of greedy self-aggrandizement, the usurpation of nature, the destruction of the environment, and the culture of retaliatory violence.

Many well-meaning theologians and ecclesiastical leaders contend that Jesus' paradoxical words related to self-denial refer only to those rare situations in life that require heroic action. Thus, they have little relevance to one's day-to-day circumstances. But I am firmly convinced that the holy habits of self-denial are daily expressions of the vibrant, transformative life of a joyous disciple. My self-denying hall of heroes includes one Bascom Frazier, a teacher of the Men's Bible Class at Hinshaw Memorial UMC in Greensboro for well over forty years. He began his methodical preparations each Sunday evening, continuing after each day's labor until he was prepared to embody that week's lesson before an appreciative class of men who adored this self-emptying servant messenger. Through the accumulation of my years of ministry among clergy colleagues, I have observed the likenesses of Gail Godwin's *Father Melancholy* who live "by the grace of daily obligation"[6] in people like Bascom Frazier. It is only by the discipline of such grace that heroic response in moments of crisis become natural.

Mrs. Jeannette Allred was a devout member of Providence UMC in Charlotte. This feisty octogenarian widow read her Bible devoutly, attended a circle group for women, prayed earnestly, attended corporate worship enthusiastically, and served without recognition. One horrible night a young man broke into her home seeking to steal anything that might bring him money at a pawnshop. When Jeannette was roused from sleep and came upon the intruder, he began beating her. With a firmness of voice she responded to this humiliation by insisting, "Don't you know that God loves you? You are a child of God." As the intruder began tying her arms with a rope, she continued, "Jesus loves you, and so do I. Why are you doing this to me? I forgive you for what you are doing." The young man proceeded to stuff her into a closet and threatened her with death if she alerted the police. She remained there until morning.

In a motel room along his escape route, this troubled man kept hearing the voice of the old woman he had just beaten. Within a few days, he turned himself in to one of the city's police stations, reported the whole episode, and asked for mercy. Months later, I received a letter from him written from a prison cell in Marion, North Carolina. He said that through the auspices of a prison ministry program, he was learning about this Jesus. He just wanted me to know about the woman in my church who had transformed his life.

Yes, Mrs. Jeanette Allred was a self-denying winner. When she died, her family requested that memorials be sent to the Disciple Bible in Prison Ministry. Many of the people in the parishes I have been privileged to pastor share her qualities. Such individuals are the antithesis of masochism. Church communities that cultivate attitudes of self-giving love are vivacious and happy communities, reflecting sound mental health. Those who live the paradoxical life of compassion and sacrifice are far healthier than those in our culture who are always looking out for Number One. What is missing among these people whose primary objective is self-preservation and self-aggrandizement is the ability to see the whole Number One. A photographer seeking

---

6. Godwin, *Father Melancholy's Daughter*, 209.

to capture the most flattering results rarely poses their subject looking into a mirror. The most revealing photos capture a personality when the subject's mind is diverted to something or someone outside of themselves.

Hellenistic philosophy asserted that the first law of learning is the mandate, "Know thyself." But superior wisdom is found in the paradoxical teaching of Jesus: "deny thyself." He anchored this central theme of discipleship upon the first and great commandment of Judaism, that "you shall love the Lord your God with all your heart, and with all your soul and with all your mind,"[7] adding, "a second is like it, 'You shall love your neighbor as yourself.'"[8] Jesus taught that these dual commandments are the real source of mental and spiritual wellbeing. They are the beginning of a wisdom that transcends knowledge (see theme of chapter 2), for "on these two commandments hang all the law and prophets."[9] By losing sight of self, we discover a fuller, more complete self. We break the vicious, unhealthy cycles of introversion, self-pity, envy, retaliation, and rage. Jesus' paradoxical teachings point the way to a self-knowledge more profound than what we find in the superficial exercise of introspective meditation or the psychological analysis of things that make us tick. A person can discover volumes of information about their id, ego, and super-ego, yet still not uncover their true essence.

One of the most dramatic transformations of intense grief that I witnessed in a life of a parishioner occurred in the Wingate UMC congregation. Lillian Lilly was a widow who had literally pulled the blinds of her existence, blocking the outside world. She had chosen a life of self-pity, intense grief, and bitterness. That began to change when she met Mrs. Alice Nash, another widow and member of the church who lived in the simplicity of a trailer park. This older woman, who had sacrificed her possessions to care for a dying husband and a paralyzed mother, inspired Lillian to join her in a ministry of the congregation at a nearby nursing home. When the energy of her grief was transmuted into the power of empathy and compassion, Mrs. Lilly's final years became a testimony to resurrection empowerment and joyous existence within a supportive community of like-minded sacrificial servants.

When I was a college student working to coordinate Abernethy Memorial Methodist Church of Asheville's summer youth ministry, I was inspired by the exemplary passion of my supervisors, who touched the lives of local youth from broken homes with profound empathy. This young couple's home was constantly filled with runaway youth, some of whom had become addicted to alcohol or drugs. These temporary residents needed a few days of amnesty and hospitality in order to sort out their lives, regain their sobriety, and muster enough courage to contact their parents or a rehab center. When I asked this compassionate mother to explain why she was drawn to such a strenuous, unrelenting ministry, she replied, "When I was their age, I spent

---

7. Matt 22:37; Deut 6:5 NRSV.
8. Matt 22:39; Lev 19:18 NRSV.
9. Matt 22:40 NRSV.

many nights on the streets of this city searching for my inebriated father. I guess I'm still trying to rescue him from the demons of his destruction." Yes—we find our lives and comprehend our greater selves by losing self in costly acts of giving to others.

My wife and I have been blessed by forty-eight years of marriage. When a relationship is based upon the implicit attitude, "I love myself and desire you," it is doomed to failure. The paradoxical goal of the Christian marital covenant is to bring the fullness of joy to another at the expense of self. The fabric of a self-giving covenant is woven into a tapestry of Christ-centered love, as with this admonition from Bonhoeffer's wedding sermon written from prison just months before his execution: "It is not your love which sustains the marriage, but from now on the marriage that sustains your love."[10] The mathematics of grace applies especially to marital love, for paradoxically, the more love we give away, the more we receive in return. We can never exhaust or deplete the infinite abundance of love and grace that increases exponentially as it is given away.

All those who practice the paradoxical ethics of Christ are winners. We need not die as martyrs, but even martyrs experience their rewards in this life as well as in the life to come. Few have stated this proposition of faith more succinctly than Ralph Sockman when he wrote for a previous generation, "The Christian victory does not begin at death, but it requires eternity to complete it."[11]

One memorable Christmas Day morning, I received a phone call from a nurse at Carolina's Medical Center in Charlotte. Doris Beaver, an elderly member of Providence UMC and patient in the intensive care unit, was dying and had requested the presence of her pastor. When I arrived, her devoted husband, their adoring adult children, and members of her extended family surrounded her bedside. She had endured years of labored breathing due to the uncompromising advancement of chronic obstructive pulmonary disease. Knowing that her physical existence was ebbing towards its imminent end, Doris wanted to leave her family and faith community with a final blessing. With the aid of an oxygen tube, she sucked in enough air to speak in staccato phrases. She gave thanks for a life of unconditional love, a husband of valor who had provided her with happiness, and the blessing of two adopted children who had given additional purpose to her existence. She affirmed her faith in a risen Lord and stated that she would soon pass into a spiritual realm free of suffering. Most of all, she articulated gratitude for a faith and community that had blessed her entire family. She requested that we not grieve in despair, but instead celebrate her fulfilled existence. Later in that symbolic day of our savior's birth, this gracious sacrificial servant passed from this blessed life into an existence of eternal victory.

Near the beginning of this chapter we reviewed the choices of an American hero, Lance Armstrong. We shall conclude with a contrasting story concerning Rev. Susan Norman Vickers, my colleague appointed to Christ UMC in Greensboro. We both

---

10. Bonhoeffer, *Papers from Prison*, 150.
11. Sockman, *Paradoxes of Jesus*, 249.

Part III: Paradox and the Holy Spirit as an Extension of the Incarnation

began our ministry there on the same day in June of 1993. She labored vigorously among the youth and families of that extraordinary congregation and continues in that role even as this book goes to press. Susan is a superb pastoral theologian. Her sermons speak the vernacular of youth and touch the emotions of all ages. She has developed instincts for practical applied theology. She brings depth to youth Bible studies, candor to conversations, and discipline to a program tempted by popular gimmicks and vacuous entertainments. Her youth groups engage in annual mission trips to impoverished regions nearby and on foreign soil. Susan rarely compromises the stringent requirements for participation, but the youth fellowship consistently grows in both numbers and quality. Susan is a competitive athlete and accomplished tennis player. Her husband has been a serious cyclist. Both enjoy a variety of sports and know the thrill of victory.

In recent years, Susan has been competing with the advancement of the cancer cells that have spread to several of her vital organs. Between chemotherapy treatments, she still comes to work. She still agonizes with conflicted youth. She still listens for hours to families with relational problems. She still engages in long-range planning for mission trips. She still sees her life as a pilgrimage of uncommon blessing and incalculable joy. A few weeks prior to my writing this chapter, Susan received an updated medical prognosis—Stage Four cancer. The day of her death is likely drawing near. On the week she received this devastating news, she was scheduled to preach at four morning services. She insisted upon delivering a very personal word from the depths of her spiritual struggle. In preparation for the sacred event of corporate worship and her sermon's delivery, Susan wrote this for the week's newsletter:

> You may know, but in case you don't, the breast cancer I battled in 2010–2012 has returned and spread. It is now in my bones (including my right leg) . . . The cancer is also in other bones, as well as a few lymph nodes (above my chest) and in my liver. I am technically in what is called Stage Four Cancer. If you look this up on the Internet, you see that the average life expectancy of a Stage Four Cancer patient is two to three years . . . There is no cure . . . but it can be treated for an indefinite period of time. Now I am back at work. I am your pastor. I will continue to be your pastor until I cannot—which I hope is many, many years from now, but I have not traveled this path before, and I do not have any idea of what lies ahead . . . Remember, no one is promised a "next breath." I hope to have years and years of them, but whatever time I have, I plan to serve Christ Church and Jesus Christ. Thanks for caring.[12]

Who are the authentic winners among us? Only those who have learned that the path to victory is through the crucible of self-giving love.

---

12. Susan Norman Vickers, *The Messenger* 56, February 3, 2013, 6.

27

Good for Nothing

EACH OF THE CHAPTERS in the third section of this volume explore various facets of the work of the Holy Spirit in the life and worship of the church that manifest the paradoxical nature of God's incarnational love through Jesus Christ. When the body of Christ is truly broken on behalf of a fractured world, the Holy Spirit is at work, and the mystical presence of a suffering, redemptive God is made known. It is only through the power of the Holy Spirit that those called out for discipleship receive the courage and persistence to act paradoxically and redemptively. It is only through the movement of the Holy Spirit that a counter-cultural community of defeated winners, acting with foolish, patient urgency, is formed. It is by the creativity of the Holy Spirit that lonely pilgrims discover a community of purpose in their sojourn aboard a ship of fools, moving toward a Kingdom destination. It is only by the vision of the Holy Spirit that the meta-narrative of God's Story is written through the lives and worship activities of a bold people in each new era.

But is the Holy Spirit experienced through the life and worship of the church? If the Holy Spirit is an extension of the incarnation, does Christ manifest himself only through the narrative of the church and the righteous activities of those set aside for discipleship in his name? Does the Holy Spirit operate beyond the pale of the ecclesia? Is there salvation outside this community of paradoxical persuasion? Is the meta-narrative of congregations and ecclesiastical bodies the only footprint of the Holy Spirit? Are the only real winners limited to those self-giving losers who patiently abide in accordance with the mandate of the King upon a cross who filled the earth with divine love by emptying himself to his last drop of life?

Since the third-century writings of Saint Cyprian, the Roman Church has taught *extra Ecclesiam nulla salus*, meaning, "outside the church there is no salvation." The contemporary Catechism of the Catholic Church interprets this ancient dogma to

Part III: Paradox and the Holy Spirit as an Extension of the Incarnation

mean that "all salvation comes from Christ the Head through which is his Body."[1] The redemptive action of the Holy Spirit, according to this teaching, is through the institutional church alone. Thus, the church has the sacred right and obligation to evangelize all people. In acknowledgement of the Apostle Paul's insistence that God our Savior "desires everyone to be saved and come to the knowledge of the truth,"[2] the church's mission is to bring all people into the saving fellowship of the church by the encouragement of the Holy Spirit. The Second Vatican Council expanded the tent of God's redemptive activity with language that seeks to overcome restrictive barriers from centuries of church doctrine that had limited the scope of God's saving grace:

> The ecumenical movement is striving to overcome these obstacles. But even in spite of them it remains true that all who have been justified by faith in Baptism are members of Christ's body, and have a right to be called Christian, and so are correctly accepted as brothers by the children of the Catholic Church. Moreover, some and even very many of the significant elements and endowments which together go to build up and give life to the Church itself, can exist outside the visible boundaries of the Catholic Church: the written word of God; the life of grace; faith, hope and charity, with the other interior gifts of the Holy Spirit, and visible elements too. All of these, which come from Christ and lead back to Christ, belong by right to the one Church of Christ.[3]

This was indeed a word of generous hospitality for Protestants, Christian charismatics, and other sects that practice the rite of baptism, but this tent of ecumenism did not provide shelter for Jews, Muslims, Hindus, Buddhists, or other religious communities. Nonetheless, this decree opened ecumenical dialogue during the 1960s and modified centuries of exclusion from Protestant and other Christian communities outside the Catholic family.

Protestant tradition also lays claim to its version of *extra Ecclesiam nulla salus*. The reformer Martin Luther sternly warned in a sermon, "Now the Church is not wood and stone, but the company of believing people; one must hold to them, and see how they believe, live and teach; they surely have Christ in their midst. For outside the Christian church there is no truth, no Christ, no salvation."[4]

The Trinitarian unity of this book insists upon the harmony of the three manifestations of God's being. We have, therefore, consistently avoided the Marcion heresy by which the Hebrew Scriptures are considered inconsistent with or inferior to the New Testament gospel message and irrelevant to the disclosure of God's being. There are few biblical images of God's activity more arresting than the opening stanza of

---

1. Catholic Church, *Catechism*, 244.
2. 1 Tim 2:4 NRSV.
3. Second Vatican Council, *Decree on Ecumenism: Unitatis Redintegratio*, ch. 1, pt. 3, "Catholic Principles on Ecumenism," http://www.vatican.va/archive/hist_councils/ii_vatican_council/documents/vat-ii_decree_19641121_unitatis-redintegratio_en.html.
4. Luther, "Early Christmas Service," 39–40.

holy writ: "In the beginning God created the heavens and the earth. Now the earth was formless and empty, darkness was over the surface of the deep, and the Spirit of God was hovering over the waters."[5] The second great myth of creation attributes the formation of humanity to the activity of the Holy Spirit by recording, "Then the Lord God formed man from the dust of the ground, and breathed into his nostrils the breath of life; and the man became a living being."[6] This was the Scripture of Jesus of Nazareth, who taught his followers that "if you then, who are evil, know how to give good gifts to your children, how much more will the heavenly Father give the Holy Spirit to those who ask him!"[7] Jesus knew that the same Spirit had called forth Abraham to leave the security of his homeland in Ur of the Chaldeans, had led the Hebrew slaves out of bondage in Egypt, and had prompted the Hebrew prophets to renew Israel's covenant with the God who had chosen a special people.

Hebrew Scripture clearly taught that the Holy Spirit anointed those outside the ecclesia. God's Spirit inhabited even pagans in order to bend history's arc toward justice. The most flagrant example of this reality is Scripture's meta-narrative interpretation of the role of King Cyrus II, a Persian emperor and founder of the Achaemenid dynasty. This pagan monarch is mentioned twenty-two times in Hebrew Scripture and is consistently remembered with reverence and gratitude. His military victories eventually put him in political control of the largest empire the world had yet then seen. With the conquest of Babylon in 539 B.C., Cyrus II initiated a policy of tolerance and compassion, authorizing the rebuilding of the Jerusalem Temple and encouraging the Diaspora to return to the land of their ancestry. As a result, the Hebrew prophets saw him as a virtuous instrument of God's Holy Spirit. The poetry of Second Isaiah, therefore, celebrates the initiation of God's Spirit in the life of this infidel:

> Thus says the Lord to his anointed, to Cyrus, whose right hand I have grasped to subdue nations before him and strip Kings of their robes, to open doors before him—and the gates shall not be closed: I will go before you and level the mountains, I will break in pieces the doors of bronze and cut through the bars of iron, I will give you the treasures of darkness and riches hidden in secret places, so that you may know that it is I, the Lord, the God of Israel, who calls you by name.[8]

The origin of the book of Job was likely an ancient Canaanite or Edomite legend. After all, Job dwelt not in Israel, but in the land of Uz—generally associated with Edom in the Syrian desert east of Palestine. He is, therefore, to be viewed as a universal person. As we discovered in chapter 3 of this book, the drama of Job moves toward a climactic epiphany when the voice of God speaks out of a whirlwind to this man of

---

5. Gen 1:1–2 NIV.
6. Gen 2:7 NRSV.
7. Luke 11:13 NRSV.
8. Isa 45:1–3 NRSV.

Part III: Paradox and the Holy Spirit as an Extension of the Incarnation

unjustified suffering. God's Spirit brings Job to a new understanding of his relationship with the divine Being. By the revelation of God's power and presence, Job's eyes and ears are opened to a deeper comprehension of God's mercy amidst life's unfairness. His previous contact with God had been impersonal, indirect, and secondhand; now it is direct and unmediated. Thus, Job's response to this revelation through the Holy Spirit's whirlwind, recorded in Job 43:6, is best translated as "I repudiate and abandon [change my mind about] dust and ashes." The poetic portion of the drama thus concludes with the righteous man who had suffered severely from life's unfairness suddenly rejecting an attitude of self-pity and lamentation. The God who came to him out of the whirlwind as the spiritual presence of ultimate Being disclosed to him that his attitude of grief and despair was unjustified. This translation of the Hebrew verb *naham* "to change one's mind," indicates that the Holy Spirit saved Job from a meaningless existence of despair and dejection.[9]

The drama had begun in the heavenly court with YHWH observing the righteousness of Job. One of the angels (a messenger in Hebrew theology) was called Satan—literally meaning "the Accuser." This heavenly messenger saw that the only reason Job was righteous was that he expected rewards for his goodness. After all, before his experience of tragedy, he was wealthy with a family of seven children and an adoring wife. If God should take away his blessings, the Accuser argued, Job would curse God, saying, "Skin for skin."[10] Satan, therefore, challenged God with a wager. He bet on the side of Job's unfaithfulness, his weakness, and the selfish motivation of his spurious goodness. The Accuser wagered that if YHWH were to remove Job's blessings by allowing a series of calamities, Job would rebel. God accepted the Accuser's wager and bet on Job's integrity. He wagered that Job would remain righteous because he loved God, not because he believed that his goodness would automatically merit reward, *quid pro quo*. YHWH wagered that Job (as a prototype of humanity) would be good, for nothing.

When the tsunami of calamities hit Job, he was utterly devastated and theologically confused. He concluded that God was not fair. Yet he continued to submit himself to God's sovereignty as a deity who allows tragedy to happen. He remained befuddled and driven to despair until the Holy Spirit spoke to him out of the whirlwind. The God who had bet on Job was not disappointed in this man of intense sorrow. This merciful God never ceased to believe in Job, and the Accuser lost the wager. Job not only refused to curse God, but he continued to obey this deity he could not comprehend. God had now arrived in the form of a mysterious Spirit, speaking through the epiphany of a mighty wind. Job demonstrated the same quality of faith as had Abraham, who had shown himself willing to sacrifice his own son. Job remained devoted to a God who seemed unfair. But this "Gospel according to Job" is not primarily a story of a man's faith in God; rather it is the astonishing drama of God's tenacious belief in Job.

---

9. See Gutiérrez, *On Job*, 86–87.
10. Job 2:4a NRSV.

This mysterious God believed that, despite life's unfairness and the absence of reward for doing good, people of the covenant will continue to trust in YHWH's providential love and sanctifying grace. Only the power of the God who spoke out of the whirlwind as Holy Spirit could transform the man of Uz into a good-for-nothing disciple. Job's only "reward" in the original poetic narrative was a renewed relationship with the most high God who is truly in charge of the process of history and whose ultimate destination for the human story has not yet been fully disclosed. The Spirit of God in the whirlwind did not convince Job that this deity is fair, yet this voice from the funnel of chaos convinced him that YHWH offers something more precious than fairness. God imparted to Job a mercy beyond measure and a trustworthiness that is imperishable. In short, YHWH came to Job empathetically in the form of suffering love.

The Holy Spirit even more clearly defined this suffering love by staking out a cross on a hill outside Jerusalem. In so doing, God consistently bet upon the people to whom he would send his Holy Spirit. Suffering love always knows that the ultimate victory is with God. This is why a Job-like man from Nazareth quoted wisdom literature of trust in his anguishing final moments upon that cruel Roman cross: "My God, my God, why have you forsaken me?"[11] He knew that this Hebrew poem concluded as a psalm of praise for the God who had inexplicably abandoned him. Thus, the dying man nailed to a tree of torture had been good-for-nothing. In an act of passionate trust, like a child separated from his parent in the moment of imminent death, he recited the prayer Mary had taught him to repeat at bedtime: "Father, into your hands I commend my spirit."[12] Yes, Jesus was the victim of this world's ultimate unfairness. But God had bet on him. Jesus embodied suffering love. Thus, it was he whom God raised from the dead in order that all the Jobs of this world might know that their suffering and faithfulness is never in vain.

The compassionate visit of the Holy Spirit to the suffering man of Uz is an indication that this same Spirit envelopes the many who do not overtly articulate faith in the name of Jesus Christ. This Holy Spirit that visited Job through an authoritative voice amidst a foreboding cyclone was the same Spirit that led Jesus in Gethsemane's agony to choose the way of Golgotha's hill of execution. This same Spirit did not neglect the children of Auschwitz, Belzec, Buchenwald, Treblinka, and Dachau as they entered the gas chambers reciting the *Shema*. These precious ones and their loving parents had never affirmed the name of Jesus as Lord. But the gift of the Holy Spirit and the grace of a compassionate God were present at the epicenter of their agony.

This gracious activity was what Jesus had in mind when he told a parable clarifying to his church the nature of the Kingdom his disciples were called to proclaim. The ironic thing about the so-called "parable of the Last Judgment" is that Jesus rarely talked about heaven or a continued existence after death. When he did, he employed the most earthly language. His tongue was not embellished with images of angels with

11. Mark 15:34b; Matt 27:46b; Ps 22:1 NRSV.
12. Luke 23:46; Ps 31:5 NRSV.

Part III: Paradox and the Holy Spirit as an Extension of the Incarnation

harps, streets of gold, or haloed saints gliding around on clouds of ease like celestial couch potatoes. He displayed no interest in the furniture of heaven. Moreover, Jesus said nothing about a millennium or "rapture"—a word that does not appear in sacred writ. His parable regarding God's judgment describes a sort of cosmic ranch roundup or global O.K. Corral. A huge mass of people from all nations and religious persuasions are gathered like an enormous flock of sheep and goats. Jews and Gentiles are herded into a capacious judicial space. Thus, the content of Jesus' story about heaven was far more political than pious, for he utilized the vernacular of practical economics rather than language of angels. According to this parable in Matthew's Gospel, the Son of Man will someday return in order to execute justice. In his first coming, the Messiah called into being the community of his followers and empowered them with his spiritual presence to be his broken body in the world. In his second advent, he will come like an enthroned monarch with expectations of accountability. The mass assemblage will include his disciples (the ecclesia) as well as nonbelievers and those who have never heard the message of God's saving grace. Frederick Bruner compares this setting to "a kind of cosmic Woodstock or Tiananmen Square, the most significant mass meeting of all time."[13] The central theme of this parable in Matthew's Gospel is grace, and this message permeates all five sections of Jesus' corpus of teachings in the catechismal narrative of Matthew's Gospel. Yet, here is a parable of judgment placed in a tale of grace as a prelude to the Passion Narrative. Where is the message of mercy within this sobering description of eschatological judgment? Note that blessing and salvation are offered to those sheep-like people who quietly perform righteous deeds: feeding the hungry, giving drink to the thirsty, welcoming the stranger, clothing the naked, and visiting the sick or imprisoned. Nowhere in this story is there a formula for salvation that requires profession of faith in the lordship of Jesus. It mandates no obligatory theological creed or litmus test. It seems that recipients of heaven's citizenship are those who unwittingly perform acts of mercy and compassion. But the most revealing aspect of the parable is the realization that those who performed good works were surprised by the words of the judicious King, "Come, you that are blessed by my Father, inherit the Kingdom prepared for you from the foundation of the world."[14] Each of those so blessed was astonished at the King's benevolence, exclaiming, "Lord, when was it that we saw you hungry and gave you food, or thirsty and gave you something to drink?"[15] This humble response was indicative of authentic meekness. The old entitlement, according to the Genesis narrative, was the promise of real estate in Palestine exclusively for the seed of Abraham. But through this parable, a new inheritance is offered to Jews and Gentiles as well as believers and nonbelievers who have been faithful in acts of sacrificial love, not in the expectation of reward or recognition. These blessed ones had been good-for-nothing. As with the Beatitudes of

---

13. Bruner, *Matthew*, 915.
14. Matt 25:34b NRSV.
15. Matt 25:37b NRSV.

Jesus, these meek ones will inherit the real estate of God's Kingdom, a blessing that no earthly power can give or take away. It is an inheritance by grace. It is a gift. It is not an earned reward. It is an inheritance from a merciful God offered both to those who are devoutly compassionate disciples and to the nonreligious within this crowded judicial gathering. These are people who have performed acts of altruism naturally, without expectation of compensation. They have been good, for nothing. Their compassion has not emerged from self-interest. They are not Congressional Medal of Honor-types. They have not necessarily done the dramatic, like pulling a traumatized body from the flames of a burning building. They have not miraculously cured the sick; they have simply visited them. They are ordinary people performing ordinary acts of kindness with an extraordinary quality of self-giving love.

This Matthean parable is the story of an *incognito Christ* served by both devout disciples as well as *incognito Christians*. Even these nonreligious disciples will be rewarded with a place in God's gracious, eternal Kingdom. Even non-sacred citizens of earth can perform sacramental acts akin to heavenly citizenship.

An evangelistic task of the church is, consequently, to recognize the many *incognito Christians* within each community. Some may be Muslim. Some may be our Jewish brothers and sisters. Some may profess no religious creed at all. Each of these needs to be affirmed, befriended, and assisted by disciples of Christ. The same Spirit of grace that enfolds the church of Jesus Christ—the ecclesia—also embraces these that serve the *incognito Christ* as they inadvertently live sacramental lives broken for others.

The aging Malcolm Muggeridge, in his valedictory volume titled *Confessions of a Twentieth Century Pilgrim*, stated that his conversion to Christianity came partly from his encounter with Mother Teresa of Calcutta. He had been commissioned to do a casual television interview for the BBC. She regarded Muggeridge as something of a Nicodemus, coming to her under the cover of night. Muggeridge, an intellectual critic of the church and all things religious, was mesmerized by the authenticity of this little nun's life among the desperate and dying peasants of Calcutta. In his account of a life-transforming interview with this unpretentious woman, *Something Beautiful for God*, Muggeridge included a prayer composed by Mother Teresa to be prayed daily by the Sisters of Mercy who labored among the dying children of the city's inhospitable streets. The petition begins, "Dearest Lord, may I see you today and every day in the person of your sick, and whilst nursing them, minister unto you. Though you hide yourself behind the unattractive disguise of the irritable, the exacting, the unreasonable, may I still recognize you and say, 'Jesus, my patient, how sweet it is to serve you.'"[16]

The paradoxical activity of the Holy Spirit touches with grace the covenant community engaged in vibrant worship and costly service. But that same Spirit speaks a word of grace to those who enter the covenant community *incognito* through the back door. They too are the church's kindred within the covenant of God's love. The

---

16. Muggeridge, *Something Beautiful for God*, 56.

inclusive grace so eloquently expressed within the narrative of Luke's Gospel includes the story of the Apostle John complaining to his Lord about an unidentified person casting out demons in Jesus' name. Since he was not a recognized follower, the apostles wanted to muzzle him. Jesus rebuked John, saying, "Do not stop him; for whoever is not against you is for you."[17]

When the young lawyer Mahatma Gandhi approached church officials in South Africa about his being baptized and brought into membership of the church, he was summarily rebuked and dismissed because of the color of his skin. But was there anyone in the last century more attuned to the Spirit of God and connected to the divine vision of Christ's nonviolent Kingdom of *shalom* and reconciliation than this man who remained a Hindu mystic?

In this chapter I have conveyed the paradoxical view that while the Holy Spirit is an extension of the incarnation of Christ, this Spirit is not the limited possession of the church. Yes, the Holy Spirit is abundantly present within the corporate life of all congregations engaged in vital worship and self-emptying ministries. But the being of God cannot be limited. Just as the Holy Spirit has evoked the compassionate gifts of the Cyruses of history, so too does the incarnational Spirit of Christ speak through persons, groups, and movements that do not overtly recognize or acknowledge his lordship. These have become *incognito* followers of the more perfect Way.

Immediately following the tragic events of 9/11, the leadership of Providence UMC initiated dialogue with key Islamic leaders in the city of Charlotte. Seven of our members began to meet with a diverse assemblage of seven adherents of the Islamic faith. Men and women of various ages came together amidst an atmosphere of hostility, mistrust, and condemnation. We were candid about our differences in theology and scriptural heritages. On some occasions these disparities provoked emotional arguments. But ballooned myths were quickly punctured, and God's spirit was felt among those who participated in this challenging experience.

This congregation, which had previously financed and built several Habitat for Humanity houses, had recently responded to the urgent needs of a Muslim family that had suffered in the violence during the Bosnian Civil War. According to Pulitzer Prize-winning reporter David Rohde, between 150,000 and 200,000 people are believed to have died in the war in Bosnia. Tens of thousands of Muslim prisoners were placed in concentration camps in the face of ethnic cleansing in places like Srebrenica, where approximately 38 percent of the war's missing had once lived.[18] This had been the most devastating military conflict in Europe since World War II, and the Providence UMC congregation felt Christ's call to act mercifully. A mission taskforce arranged to sponsor a refugee family—the Rizanowics, a family of two adult parents and their son and daughter. At first the mission group furnished a rented space and solicited donations of furniture, food, and basic necessities. An auto-mechanic job

17. Luke 9:50b NRSV.
18. Rohde, *Endgame*, 349–50.

was found for the father, cleaning service employment was secured for the mother, the son was given work as a waiter, and the daughter was placed in a nearby high school. The Rizanowic family soon qualified as recipients of a Habitat for Humanity project. When I first met with the family, I explained the intended mission of Providence UMC by saying that we considered it a privilege to sponsor their residence, but then I added, "We do not enter this partnership for the purpose of converting you to the Christian faith. We affirm you and the peace-making traditions within your Muslim heritage. We offer you our friendship and the love of Jesus Christ with the hope that this relationship will give you an entirely different and positive view of what it truly means to be a Christian." The Rizanowics continued to experience enormous challenges, including depression due to their separation from all things familiar, but their presence as a refugee family escaping from the trauma of genocide would have been intolerable without the camaraderie of a spirit-filled, Christ-motivated community of faith. The many volunteers who eagerly provided supplies, tutoring, friendship, legal advocacy, and their time did a great deal of good. They expected nothing in return—not even a faith conversion. The emotional scars from the savagery of Christian Serbs were painfully raw for this Bosnian family. Our tireless team of servants continued to do much good, for nothing. What was the "reward" within the paradoxical activity of this faithful congregation?

We surprisingly received the joy of discovering, in the words of Frederick Buechner, that "when the Kingdom really comes, it's as if the thing you lost and thought you'd never find again is you."[19]

---

19. Buechner, *Wishful Thinking*, 50.

28

A Royal Waste of Time

DURING THE EPOCH OF the illustrious prophet Elijah, a great famine struck the land. According to the Hebrew chronicler, this depravation was due to the idolatry of the nation under King Ahab's apostate rule. The drought ended with an epic contest on Mount Carmel between the prophets of Baal and the God of Elijah, who vindicated his servant with fire from heaven. After contriving this act of civil disobedience and regal humiliation, Elijah fled the vengeful wrath of Queen Jezebel by racing into the wilderness of Sinai toward the sacred mountain of Horeb. In a state of acute hunger, this beleaguered prophet yearned for an encounter with God's Holy Spirit. Standing in a cleft upon the desolate surface of Horeb, he felt a forceful wind that initiated a terrifying rockslide. But God's spirit was not in the wind. The earth beneath him trembled and fire came forth like the eruption of a great volcano, but still the prophet was devoid of divine epiphany. Then, through "a sound of sheer silence,"[1] Elijah experienced the mysterious movement of God's affirming presence. He wrapped his face in reverence and awe. At the mouth of a mysterious cave, he heard a commanding voice telling him to anoint a new king (Jehu) to rule Israel. Even though this divine epiphany occurred in the isolated terrain of Horeb's wilderness, the spirit assured this receptive prophet that he was now encompassed by a congregation of "seven thousand in Israel, all the knees that have not bowed to Baal, and every mouth that has not kissed him."[2]

The power of the Holy Spirit is experienced through acts of individual and corporate worship. This spirit comes as a gift to those who are intensely receptive and humbly expectant during occasions of divine worship. The Anglo Saxon origin of our English "worship" is *worthscipe* (from *woerth*, meaning "worthy," plus the suffix *scipe*, for "state or quality of being").[3] Any object worthy of worship must exclusively

---

1. 1 Kgs 19:12b NRSV.
2. 1 Kgs 19:18 NRSV.
3. *Webster's New Twentieth Century Dictionary of the English Language: Unabridged*, 2nd ed., s.v.

possess supreme value. Elijah and all the revered Hebrew prophets risked their lives by denouncing idols or symbols that demanded obeisance to values unworthy of ultimate ascription and honor. The words of only a few tenacious prophets and poets were preserved as the sacred literature of Israel. These were those courageous ones who maintained the notion that only the God of the Abrahamic and Mosaic covenant is worthy of worship. Thus, the judgments of history have vindicated only the righteous biblical prophets who preserved the heritage of authentic worship. Only this God uniquely required observance of Sabbath in order to transform an undisciplined, enslaved population into a grace-filled and grateful people of promise, expectation, and hope. The transforming power of worship in the lives of a remnant of Israel's faithful became the conduit for divine activity that carried God's covenant people into new eras of hope. Through worship, the sons and daughters of Abraham and Sarah received a compass for their pilgrimage toward a promised kingdom of *shalom*.

It is intriguing that Luke the Evangelist, whose two-volume narrative is rightly known as "the Gospel of the Holy Spirit," begins and concludes his first volume in the Jerusalem Temple. Zechariah the priest had been chosen by lot to enter the Holy of Holies—the most sacred space within the revered Temple. He did so while the whole massive assembly of worshippers filled the nave ("Holy Space"), the Priest's Court, the Women's Court, and the space surrounding the altar. As Zechariah wove through the crowd of worshippers and approached the altar of incense before privately entering the Holy of Holies, he was startled by the appearance of an angelic messenger who announced, "Do not be afraid, Zechariah, for your prayer has been heard. Your wife Elizabeth will bear you a son, and you will name him John."[4] The narrative of redemption for Israel and the story of salvation for the Gentiles, therefore, begins with a scene of worshipers crowded into the most sacred space in Judaism. This story is the necessary preface to the birth of the Messiah, for it announces the imminent fulfillment of the hopes of worshipping Jews through centuries of expectation, including the era of tabernacle worship with Moses in the Negev and Sinai, the periods of majestic worship in the two previous temples built upon Mount Zion in Jerusalem, and the generations of exiled worshippers in synagogues throughout the Diaspora of Babylon and beyond. Luke identifies Jesus as the Messiah who was nurtured spiritually by ritualistic pilgrimages to Jerusalem's Temple and Sabbath worship within his hometown village synagogue. The suffering and broken body of the Messiah would become the new Temple and the magnetic spiritual force drawing worshippers to the joy of fulfilled expectation in a Kingdom of Christ's risen glory. Thus, Luke concluded the first volume of his "Gospel of the Holy Spirit" with the risen Christ offering these words of assurance: "I am sending upon you what my Father promised; so stay here in the city until you have been clothed with power from on high."[5] Then, at the apex

---

"worship."

4. Luke 1:13 NRSV.

5. Luke 24:48–49 NRSV.

Part III: Paradox and the Holy Spirit as an Extension of the Incarnation

of a hill in Bethany, a village of extreme poverty, Jesus "was carried into heaven."[6] The disciples remained transfixed in worship at that spot but soon returned with great joy to nearby Jerusalem, where "they were continually in the temple blessing God."[7] Luke's Gospel begins and ends in Israel's place of worship—the Jerusalem Temple. The narrative of the Acts of the Apostles, likewise, begins with an account of expectant worshippers gathered in an upper room during the Jewish spring harvest festival of Pentecost.

The paradoxical title chosen for this chapter recognizes the influence of the writings of Marva J. Dawn, whose monumental reflections upon the significance of worship is a prophetic gift to the church of Jesus Christ in this postmodern era of cultural seduction and apostasy.[8] She reminds the church of something that is elementary and self-evident: namely, that the purpose of Christian worship is to render praise and highest esteem to the God of the Abrahamic covenant whose promises are fulfilled by the risen and regnant Christ. Worship has no utilitarian purpose other than praise *for* and communion *with* the living God. Worship's primary purpose is not evangelism. The role of every Christian who experiences corporate worship is to enter the marketplace and the social arenas of business, school, community, or political discourse with a witness to Christ and the present reality of the seeds of God's Kingdom in our midst through the worship and mission of the church. The whole educational enterprise of the church is, therefore, the activity of teaching the biblical narrative of salvation and modeling scriptural holiness through costly disciplines of prayer and the mission of self-giving generosity. "Seekers" who participate in the catechumenal small groups for biblical and theological studies learn the language of Christian worship, the hymns of this historical faith, and the doctrines of orthodoxy. "Seekers" are then invited to join their Christian neighbors at urban ministry centers among the poor and to travel to places of poverty and pain in beleaguered lands near and far to bring medical care, food supplies, and instructions in agricultural and health technology. This is evangelism that prepares the seeker and the evangelist for full participation in the royal act of worship.

When the central purpose of worship is to convert the unconverted through emotional manipulation, to increase the attendance, to raise the budget, to promote programs, to shine a light on a celebrity pastor, to entertain the congregation, to give prominence to a flourishing church, to establish a religious community with political power, or to tingle the ears of those who crave a musical style suited to individual taste, worship becomes idolatrous. Sören Kierkegaard was prone to observe that God is always to be the audience in the drama of worship. All worshipers gather to do the work of the people—the liturgy. Worshipers sing the music that best interprets the biblical heritage, read the Scripture with reverence and passion, actively listen to sermons that are preached with integrity, pray the prayers of an expectant people, and

---

6. Luke 24:50 NRSV.
7. Luke 24:53 NRSV.
8. The title is taken from Marva J. Dawn's classic discussion in *A Royal "Waste" of Time*.

A Royal Waste of Time

learn the orthodox doctrines with focus on the teachings of theologians who have authentically walked the path of Jesus.

In a utilitarian culture, this God-centered form of worship appears to be a waste of time. In a utilitarian culture, it is always a waste of time for a pastoral theologian to spend an hour in biblical and theological study for each minute at the pulpit. In a utilitarian culture, it is more cost-effective to watch professional musicians entertain through a video production of worship while a smiling evangelist proclaims a soothing message of pop psychology fed by a teleprompter, assuring the listener that God wants each of us to be prosperous and successful. After all, utilitarian worship is all about us—our need to avoid engagement with a suffering world, our need to escape into entertainment, our need to be fed a theological diet of civil religion's tasty desserts, our search for a preacher who agrees with our brand of political philosophy, our need for absolution without confession, discipleship without discipline, epiphany without prayer, and Christ without a cross.

Marva Dawn reminds us that authentic worship through the centuries has been a "waste" of time in the royal presence of God. But because we have encountered in biblically-based, Christ-centered worship a God whose wisdom is foolishness to the world, whose tears appear as weakness, whose suffering servant role appears to be a losing proposition, whose aggressive peacemaking is no match for military intimidation, and whose wounds are the source of human healing; the worshipping church is a gathering of a peculiar people. "Seekers" will find us to be strange indeed! Flannery O'Connor, that irascible mystic from Milledgeville, Georgia, had it right in what she is reputed to have said about following Jesus: "You shall know the truth and the truth shall make you odd." The most important thing that we do in the life and ministry of the church is a royal "waste" of time. As we discovered in chapter 20, when we approach the event of worship with intense receptivity and humble expectation, we enter an *eternal now*. We experience a *kairotic* dimension of time. Our receptive eyes begin to see the end where God resides and toward whose Kingdom we are moving. During the royal, priceless time of worship, we discover who we are and whose we are. We speak the language of theology, not psychology. We are grasped by the Holy Spirit in such a way that we cease to fear the future or any human threat, for we are embraced by the risen Christ who defines and shapes our future.

One Sunday at Hinshaw Memorial UMC, I was disturbed by the sight of a teen in the corner of the narthex as I greeted worshipers after the benediction. He was weeping profusely. Assuming that something during worship had prompted anguish or pain, I approached him to offer a word of consolation. He quickly clarified his emotions by explaining, "You don't understand. These are tears of joy. My life is a mess, but today in worship I felt as though I were swimming in a sea of hope."

Marva Dawn warns those responsible for worship planning against using the terms "traditional" or "contemporary." Worship delineation should be defined by the time of its occurrence. All authentic worship is contemporary. Revered hymns,

Part III: Paradox and the Holy Spirit as an Extension of the Incarnation

ancient prayers, and noble liturgies that touched the hearts of the faithful through the centuries are timeless. Why is it "contemporary" to abandon the repetition of the Lord's Prayer when our Lord instructed his disciples to use this as a model of faithfulness in every generation? The ancient creeds were written with the blood of martyrs. Only a narcissistic, consumer-centered church eliminates the recitation of these time-honored affirmations. Hymns, anthems, and songs of praise as ancient as a Gregorian chant or as recent as an Amy Grant single can resonate with the exalted purpose of honoring the God of the biblical covenant. But worship is not a matter of taste. Robert Bellah's research nearly three decades ago disclosed that the American culture had so gravitated toward the liberal ideals of individual self-interest that postmodern people considered religious truth to be a matter of personal preference. His prototype for this trend emerged from an interview with a woman named Sheila, who described her tailor-made religion as "Sheilaism."[9] When individuals and families church-shop until they find a church that reflects their personal taste in musical form or lifestyle choices, they adopt the idolatry of a consumer-driven religion that has abandoned the centrality of biblically-based, Christ-centered worship. Narcissistic self-interest becomes the primary focus of many peripatetic worshipers in this synthetic shopping mall of Americanized Christianity.

Lest the reader consider this argument to be a defense of musical elitism or rigid, lifeless liturgical tradition, I am quick to insist that worshipers who have certain specific preferences in style need to learn songs or hymns that might not match their taste for the sake of the unity of the body of Christ. Television cable sources provide channels that play music tailored for a variety of exclusive tastes: hard or soft rock, reggae, blues, baroque, late classical, jazz, country and western, easy listening, and a plethora of other modes. Worship planners may draw upon a variety of these styles as long as the theological content is faithful to the biblical message.

Several years ago the worship planners at a newly planted congregation, Good Shepherd UMC in Charlotte, carefully analyzed their music ministry and reached the conclusion that the popular praise band utilized choruses with such mindless repetition that the biblical context was compromised and trivialized. The planners proceeded to introduce musical compositions with a more cutting-edge, prophetic message. The praise band was replaced with musicians that probed deeper into challenging biblical themes. The pastor's blog regularly critiques popular rock artists who communicate prophetic messages with Christian sensitivity, analyzing the impact of songs by Bono (U2), the Eagles, Bruce Springsteen, Gilbert O'Sullivan, Eric Clapton, and Paul McCartney. When the lyrics of well-known popular musicians contain poignant references to the conduct of a Christ-motivated life or provide prophetic insights into ethically sensitive issues, congregational worship at Good Shepherd UMC utilizes these messages appropriately in worship, not because of their entertainment value but because the music addresses relevant biblical texts. When I attended services

---

9. Bellah et al., *Habits of the Heart*, 221.

there as the district superintendent, the worship planners did not come close to meeting my taste in congregational music, for frankly, I have not yet fully recovered from the death of Mozart in 1791. Baroque and early classical styles best suit my personal taste and spiritual needs. Nonetheless, I delight in seeing the reflective participation of twenty- and thirty-year-olds in south Charlotte as they confront the challenges of costly discipleship through engaging explorations into Scripture through relevant musical lyrics. This congregation of young adult families faithfully elevates the triune God and the narrative of the Bible as the epicenter of their worship experience.

When the fifty-voice youth choir of Providence UMC sang at the Annual Conference at Lake Junaluska, North Carolina, the director chose a lively piece that delegates considered to be "contemporary spiritual." In the same service, he inserted a portion of Vivaldi's "Gloria" that equally reflected the morning worship's biblical theme. The youth were comfortable with both styles, for many of them had been nurtured for a full decade by the stair-step choral ministry of their home church. From kindergarten to young adulthood, these young people had opportunities to learn the diversified and rich heritage of sacred music. A wise worship planning team will give credence to Jaroslav Pelikan's distinction between *traditionalism* as "the dead faith of the living" and *tradition* as the "living faith of the dead."[10] All authentic worship is an expression of a living faith. Only that which points toward the ineffable mystery of God's incarnational love will withstand the test of time to become part of a congregation's living tradition. Shallow worship resources will not reveal the truth about God. They will only produce a superficial, trivial congregation that will likely be ineffective or unfaithful in the execution of its mission.

Preaching can be a lonely exercise of wasted time. But it becomes royal proclamation when consistently connected with biblical tradition and the lives of people within the congregation. Preaching and conducting corporate worship is indeed the most important task of the pastor.

When I was appointed to Boone UMC, in the heart of the campus community of Appalachian State University, I received an early visit from a colleague who had been granted an early disability status by our bishop. Sometimes toxic, dysfunctional congregations are cruel to fragile pastors. He was emotionally battered and bruised from taunting critiques by callous parishioners in several of his appointments. After a severe nervous breakdown, his psychiatrist insisted that he relinquish his role as a pastor, apply for disability insurance, and stay away from corporate gatherings—including worship. In the privacy of my office, he shared his tragic story but concluded with this surprising declaration: "George, my ministry shall continue in the form of intercessory prayer. I've come to you in the first month of your ministry at this parish in order to pledge to God and you that upon the opening moments of every Sunday service of worship, I shall be on my knees at home in prayer that your sermon will have power and purpose, that the acts of worship will have integrity, and that the

---

10. Pelikan, *Melody of Theology*, 252.

Part III: Paradox and the Holy Spirit as an Extension of the Incarnation

members will exemplify the mercy and compassion of Jesus throughout the years of your ministry here." There was not a single Sunday during those years that I was not acutely aware of this man's devout act of intercession. He truly elevated his pastor and this congregation to the throne of grace at the majestic moment of royal worship.

Preaching's purpose is to provide opportunity for the congregation to encounter God. I often prayerfully asked myself in moments before the choral procession, "Am I merely leading others in worship, or am I truly worshipping, especially during the presentation of the sermon?"

Topical sermons were the steady diet of Protestant congregations throughout the US in the decades of significant growth from the Great Depression into the 1960s. Harry Emerson Fosdick of Riverside Church in New York City greatly influenced a generation of aspiring mainline denomination preachers through his national radio audience. He consistently insisted that the art of preaching be counseling en masse. One of his listeners on a significant Sunday was young Dietrich Bonhoeffer, who found nothing of valuable theological import in his words, leading this visiting seminarian from Berlin to gravitate towards the dynamic Abyssinian Baptist Church in the heart of Harlem. Here he was exposed for the first time to an emotionally vibrant array of African-American spirituals and socially relevant sermons rooted in the biblical-narrative preaching of the intrepid Adam Clayton Powell, Sr. These intense worship experiences considerably altered his understanding of the Holy Spirit's work in and through the fabric of church life and ultimately contributed to his decision to return home to join the Confessing Church's bold movement of civil disobedience in his apostate homeland. Bonhoeffer had been grabbed by a spiritual power in worship that redefined the nature of the church as a defiant, God-empowered community ready to sacrifice all security in singular allegiance to Christ's Kingdom of inclusive love. Through the inspiration of biblically-based preaching and vibrant worship, Bonhoeffer returned to Germany to confront the sinister madness of unprecedented Nazi cruelty.

Bonhoeffer found that faith communities shaped by a psychology of self-help, positive thinking, or motivational pulpit oratory to be vacuous. Far too many contemporary pulpits have returned to such shallow theological content in preaching. Philip Rieff, in his analytical study, *The Triumph of the Therapeutic*, provides an oft-referenced aphorism: "Religious man was born to be saved, [modern] psychological man is born to be pleased."[11] Topical preaching, grounded in biblical theology and social relevance, can indeed be both faithful and effective. But the congregation's desire to be pleased or counseled may easily seduce the preacher into the passive apathy of entertainment without prophetic engagement amidst the community's pain, poverty, and economic injustice. Topical preaching that avoids collective grappling with the great spectrum of biblical literature and the theological complexities of difficult texts

---

11. Rieff, *Triumph of the Therapeutic*, 25.

produces a shallow congregation that is unable and unwilling to face life's ambiguities and paradoxes.

One of the remarkable residual gifts of my retirement to a faith community where I pastored twenty-five years ago is the opportunity to renew longstanding friendships. On one rare occasion, a member asked me to find in my files the manuscript of a sermon he remembered from his early youth. When he dredged up the memory of the theological theme, I easily identified the text that had challenged him. My sermon emerged from the book of Exodus in which the Lord said to Moses, "I will make all my goodness pass before you, and will proclaim before you the name, the Lord [YHWH], and I will be gracious to whom I will be gracious, and I will show mercy on whom I will show mercy. But . . . you cannot see my face; for no one shall see me and live."[12] I had preached several hundred sermons from this pulpit, but this man recalled from his childhood a difficult text that helped him explore the nature of God's mysterious revelation. He, like most of us, had entered the holy space of worship because he was perpetually asking, "Is there any word from God today?"

During the eight years of my superintendencey, I listened to sermons preached by nearly every appointed pastor. This was generally a royal treat. The problematic sermons, however, were those that erred on the extremes of this continuum: (a) messages so relevant and entertaining that they paid no attention to biblical theology and the authority of a text, or (b) sermons that were boringly biblical, absorbed into exposition and historical context but lacking any semblance of relevance or practical application. Both extremes are equally unfaithful. They prevent encounters with God from happening. A sermon that begins in biblical narrative and never departs is unbiblical.

When a seminary classmate of mine was ordained in his local church, Ed Steimle, a preacher for National Public Radio's "Protestant Hour" and Brown Professor of Homiletics at Union Theological Seminary, gave the ordination sermon. During a church-wide luncheon after worship, the presiding bishop asked the distinguished guest to name those who he considered to be the great contemporary preachers, to which Dr. Steimle replied, "I don't know their names and neither do you. They are all anonymous but faithful men and women preaching each Sunday with fervor and faithfulness in obscure little churches across the land."

The liturgy of worship is literally *the work of the people*, drawn from the innate gifts of the congregation. On a memorable Christmas Eve at Christ UMC in Greensboro, Elizabeth Grove, a gifted high school student, brought her harp along with several other young musicians to provide an ensemble of reflective, heavenly music during the Eucharistic candlelit service. As a district superintendent, I gave administrative guidance for the planting of new congregations. I received special blessings from the exuberant spirit of marvelously gifted volunteer musicians each time I attended the newly planted and predominantly African-American congregations of New Horizon and Sanctuary UMC. Their vitality of praise, emotional energy, and rapturous

---

12. Exod 33:19–20 NRSV.

Part III: Paradox and the Holy Spirit as an Extension of the Incarnation

rhythms truly presented to God's ear the gifts of a grateful people. I especially learned to appreciate the colorful diversity of style and content within the district's ethnic congregations. Cambodian, Latino, Hmong, Liberian, Korean, and Ghanaian churches enriched and broadened my understanding of the diverse dimensions of Christ's body. The most glorious segment of worship within the Ghanaian congregation, for example, was the enchanting offertory celebration in which members dance down the nave dressed in colorful ethnic clothing, creatively tossing sacrificial monetary offerings into a large bowl.

Worship is authentic celebration when it praises God for what the Holy Spirit is doing through the mission of the congregation. It was especially thrilling, therefore, to commission an eager group of adults and teens, including our daughter, as they departed from Christ UMC on mission to Cochabamba, Bolivia, and to celebrate in worship their return.

During the earthquake that struck Haiti on January 12, 2010, Rev. Pam Carter, the spouse of Providence UMC's pastor, had just finished breakfast at Port-au-Prince's Montana Hotel with Rev. Sam Dixon, Executive Director of the United Methodist Committee on Relief, and members of his staff. They were there to discuss Providence UMC's medical work in a rural region near Cap-Haïtien. When the tremors came that morning, Sam was killed in the falling rubble. Pam's life was spared as she stood in the security of a shaking doorframe. Her plight and the horrendous suffering of the Haitian people became the immediate focus of intercessory prayers at Providence UMC's corporate worship. With a history of nearly forty years of medical mission to that beleaguered land, Providence UMC rapidly expanded the scope of its mission, gaining considerable momentum in these efforts through the movement of God's spirit of compassion in worship during the aftermath of so great a tragedy.

Worship is the acknowledgement that all of life is a pilgrimage of hope toward the fulfillment of God's glorious Kingdom. Each stage of our sacred journeys evokes unique opportunities for worship. Every newborn child is surrounded by an abundance of God's prevenient grace; thus, the sacramental moment of bringing the child before the congregation's baptismal font is a majestic, royal moment. Of course, the sacrament is an exercise in fraudulence or cheap grace unless it is coupled with a conscientious program of Christian education at the heart of the congregation's mission, coupled with the commitment of parents who will nurture the child at home in scriptural holiness. Thus, Father's Day in 2000 is a delightful memory, for on that occasion, Dave and Meredith Ritchie presented their newborn triplets for baptism at Providence UMC. During their early years Meg, Will, and Ben became acquainted with a church team that assisted their parents in feeding, changing diapers, and providing protective oversight. The children's extended church family continued to maintain contact through the years by providing musical training, Sunday school classes, Vacation Church School, scouting, and other child-focused ministries. As I compose this chapter, they have just completed intensive membership training through confirmation classes and are now fervent participants in that church's multifaceted small group youth ministry.

In retirement I now encounter in congregational life middle-aged couples whose weddings I conducted approximately a quarter of a century ago. As Steve McClure, the accomplished organist at First UMC, begins the worship prelude, my memory floats back to when he stood before me next to his bride, Karen. She had completed an elective course in the theology of worship at Greensboro College when we designed their wedding. She helped write meaningful additions to the liturgy of the covenant. Their wedding was truly an expression of adoration to the Author of covenant love. That covenant continues to sustain and bless their marriage and children. Occasionally their two daughters play a violin duet while their father accompanies them at piano and their younger brother plays with a hand bell ensemble. Worship is the guiding compass for this family of servant leaders and practitioners of musical creativity.

Authentic worship prepares the lives of the faithful for times of abrupt tragedy. On the morning of September 11, 2001, a steady stream of traffic poured into Providence Road, exiting from the midtown banking epicenter and Charlotte's major skyscrapers. Rapidly the church's chapel filled with terrified worshippers. Impromptu prayers, readings from the Psalter, and silent meditation continued throughout the afternoon. Planning for Sunday worship ensued, but the church's worship team avoided any content that would suggest national idolatry, advocacy for militant retaliation, or a crusade against Muslims. That Sunday, the congregation prayed in union this prayer:

> God of all the ages, in your sight nations rise and fall and pass through times of peril. Now when our land is troubled, be near to judge and save. May our leaders be led by your wisdom; may they search your will and see it clearly. If we have turned from your way, reverse our ways and help us to repent. Give us your light and your truth; let them guide us, through Jesus Christ, who is Lord of the world, and our Savior. Amen.[13]

The choral anthem for that morning was Schubert's "The Omnipotence," which began with the affirmation, "Great is Jehovah, the Lord, for heaven and earth testify to his great power!" The congregation earnestly sang Fred Kaan's consoling hymn:

> For the healing of the nations, Lord,
> we pray with one accord;
> for a just and equal sharing,
> of the things that earth affords;
> to a life of love in action
> help us rise and pledge our word.[14]

---

13. Presbyterian Church, "During a National Crisis," 818.
14. Kaan, "For the Healing of the Nations," 428.

Part III: Paradox and the Holy Spirit as an Extension of the Incarnation

The sermon was based upon the hardheaded hope of the prophet Jeremiah during the worst of times for Israel as the exile in Babylon began. I assured the congregation in those anxious times that "God is the God of creativity. All things are moving toward the completion of God's masterpiece—the Kingdom of God. In all things God is working to accomplish that righteous goal 'for those who love God, who are called according to his purpose.'"[15]

The events within the great span of a pilgrim's existence are most accurately viewed in the context of worship's homage to a merciful God. When we enter the eternal now of a royal "waste" of time, we are "lost in wonder, love, and praise."[16] We are transfixed by Scripture's eternal hope, especially as we enter the valley of the shadow of death. Memorial services are, therefore, corporate expressions of paradoxical joy amidst death's shadow. Due to the privilege of pastoral leadership at funerals, I have recited the liturgy and Scripture of hope upon the death of fragile little children, the tragic ending of a teenager's vibrant existence, the sudden and mysterious disappearance of a young adult due to criminal gang activity, the suicide of a church treasurer, the slow and agonizing disintegration of a life due to ALS, and a vast multiplicity of additional circumstances leading to death. Funerals are perhaps the most royal of all our "wasted" moments in worship.

I arrived early at the Providence UMC sanctuary for the memorial service held for Katherine Ussery. The seating capacity of that sacred space was approximately eight hundred, but it was practically filled as I took a seat near the back. In the memorial tribute, Rev. Ken Carter reminded the grieving congregation that this senior citizen had never held a single office in the church's administration. She had taught no class nor sought any recognition. But each week she had made a special effort to know the names of all the children, greet each guest, and converse with anyone she knew to be experiencing a personal crisis. Throughout any ordinary week she phoned those with birthdays or anniversaries. She contacted many of those whose absence from worship was unexplained. She prayed earnestly and was a guardian angel for many forgotten or marginalized members. In her last decade, Katherine used an oxygen tank to sustain her damaged lungs without having to sacrifice her considerable involvement in the worship and mission of the congregation. Was her entire existence a waste of time? Was this massive display of love and veneration at her funeral a waste of time? Reverend Carter inserted into the eulogy a revealing vignette about a time when members of the congregation offered to take Katherine to the finest restaurant in the city. She could have chosen anywhere, but she insisted that the group gather at Burger King. She never displayed a moment of pretense or postured for recognition and privilege. This is why some of us spoke of her as Queen Katherine of Ussery. A wasted life? Yes, a royal "wasted" life that will never die.

---

15. Rom 8:28b NRSV.
16. Wesley, "Love Divine, All Loves Excelling," 12.

29

Common Nobility

THE SPIRIT OF GOD is counterintuitive and unpredictable. It provokes extraordinary potential from unsuspecting people stuck in a state of inertia. It rouses dormant, latent lives from the obscurity of wasted potential and catapults the most unlikely people into positions of spiritual leadership.

The Holy Spirit recruited leadership for an apostate Israel using the most unprofessional methods. According to the Hebrew chronicler, YHWH became dissatisfied with King Saul's lack of obedience, so the Lord commissioned Samuel, his reliable priest, to seek a more worthy leader. But he directed this resourceful servant's path to the unpretentious village of Bethlehem and the home of Jesse, son of a Moabite mother and a Jewish father. Jesse's mixed-race family was not a likely source for the new monarch for the Hebrew people. Nonetheless, the revered priest invited Jesse and his sons to join him in a sacrificial ritual in the hopes that the spirit of God would reveal the identity of one worthy of regal authority. The saintly eyes of Samuel at first focused with delight upon the seven eligible sons paraded before him, but none satisfied the scrutiny of inspirational selection. When Samuel impulsively thought to anoint the impressive Eliab to replace the inadequate King Saul, the Spirit of the Lord cautioned the prophet, "Do not look on his appearance or on the height of his stature, because I have rejected him; for the Lord does not see as mortals see; they look on the outward appearance, but the Lord looks on the heart."[1] Consequently, in the presence of these astonished siblings and their flabbergasted father, the cautious priest lifted a goat's horn filled with oil and poured it over the humbly bent head of the ruddy, soiled face of the shepherd boy who would become Israel's greatest king. The chronicler recorded that "the spirit of the Lord came mightily upon David from that day forward."[2] The Bible, in point of fact, is the prolific account of common nobility and the surprising

---

1. 1 Sam 16:7 NRSV.
2. 1 Sam 16:13b NRSV.

Part III: Paradox and the Holy Spirit as an Extension of the Incarnation

habits of the Holy Spirit in conducting the movement of history through inspirational leaders arising from very ordinary origins.

Recent attempts by prosperity gospel evangelists to paint Jesus as the prototype for a modern, successful CEO[3] are oblivious to Matthew's simple, straightforward account. This gospel's description of Jesus' non-professional, shoddy business practices is an insight into the trusting relationship Jesus had with the inner urges of God's surprising spirit in his life of radical obedience. Along the placid shore of the Sea of Galilee, Jesus randomly saw two brothers who were entrepreneurs in the fishing enterprise. They were busy casting nets and literally minding their own business—an inherited trade that they knew well. They had not studied Scripture under Gamaliel down in sophisticated Jerusalem. They spoke with a crude northern Aramaic accent and had no formal training in Hebrew theology. The words of Jesus, however, possessed the power of God's spirit, for he merely said, "Follow me." Only by impulse of the Holy Spirit could anything meaningful come from such a simple imperative. But, in one of the most amazing phrases in biblical literature, this miracle occurred in accordance with Matthew's graphic description: "Immediately they left their nets and followed him."[4] Jesus then briskly went about procuring a motley crew from among the most common and unqualified people of the land, beginning with the brothers Peter and Andrew, plus another set of brothers, James and John.

The incarnational activity of the Holy Spirit continues in each era, largely through the witness of ordinary people doing extraordinary things through the indwelling of Jesus in their lives. In the modern era, the extension of the Being of Christ occurs awkwardly and imperfectly in tiny towns and sprawling cities throughout the land. God's spirit moves in and through the lives of common people who live noble, Christ-centered lives. Their stories are rarely told outside these communities. These unheralded followers of Christ go quietly to their graves and are often inadvertently forgotten by disciples who park their cars near the cemetery and walk unawares around rows of marble monuments to church. Contemporary Christians are usually unacquainted with the lives represented by modest tombstone markers with two dates engraved beneath the chiseled letters of obscure names. Yet nearly every congregation that strives to imitate the paradoxical ways of Jesus is carried by the unpretentious witness of individuals, families, or small groups that practiced aberrant lifestyles modeled after Jesus in past eras. Their stories constitute the meta-narrative of the local church. These are the forgotten souls who carry the weight of salvation history toward a future in which human hopes and dreams can be realized. This future is guaranteed by the liberating work of Christ, whom God raised from the dead. When these stories are repressed, lost, or forgotten, the church has inadvertently squandered its most valuable evangelical resource. When congregations fail to preserve their faith stories, they unwittingly practice irresponsible stewardship of the sacred gift of memory, significantly

---

3. See Jones, *Jesus CEO*.
4. Matt 4:20 NRSV.

diminishing the church's evangelical narrative. Recovery of the illustrious stories of the people of common nobility is a primary missional mandate for every local parish seeking to be faithful to its unique role.

In this chapter, I shall provide a brief introduction to the life of a singular representative from each of the seven congregations I served over a period of more than four decades.[5] None of these seven individuals or married couples is the sort to invite voluminous biographies. None has been a dominant figure in the socio-political matrix of their local community. But each has played a unique role in changing attitudes and actions within those communities. Each represents a unique, essential contribution to the meta-narrative of their local church. They are a continuation of Luke's second volume, the Acts of the Apostles. They all play an essential role in God's Story of salvation history.

I shall begin this series of seven meta-narrative accounts by describing the context of that very first appointment. As I describe in chapter 24, I was seated in a crowded Duke University auditorium attending a seminar on Moltmann's *Theology of Hope* during my senior year of seminary, when Harvey Cox interrupted to announce that Martin Luther King Jr. had just been assassinated. Within the next two months, I experienced a major campus protest with thousands of students calling for an increase in wages for nonacademic employees, a historic Duke University graduation ceremony of uncanny seriousness, the formation of a new denomination (the United Methodist Church), the first Annual Conference as a new denomination, and the announcement of my first pastoral appointment. I had to consult a map to find the location of the campus town of Wingate in Union County, North Carolina. This county was the ancestral home of Jesse Helms, who at the time owned and managed a network affiliate television station in Raleigh that derisively ran a Western movie during the network's broadcast of King's funeral. The county seat in Monroe had been a place of dubious hospitality for freedom riders in 1961, thanks to the controversial leadership of the local NAACP president, Robert F. Williams. A minor riot had occurred in that town, resulting in a bogus charge of kidnapping against Williams and his wife. They escaped by traveling to Cuba, drawing international attention. It was obvious from that first week in Wingate that the faith community was tense over matters of race relations and the enormous social changes needed to confront a culture of entrenched racism. Members were anxious about their new pastoral leadership in this intimidating, volatile climate.

---

5. This is entirely a matter of illustrative choice, for many other people within these parishes listed here have appropriately modeled the holy habits of maturing disciples of the paradoxical Christ. The narrative of this chapter will flow less encumbered by the details of dates, but it may be helpful for the reader to know the sequence of parishes I served and the periods during which I shared significant ministry experiences with those honored here as examples of common nobility: Wingate UMC (1968–1972), Shady Grove UMC (1972–1977), Hinshaw Memorial (1977–1983), Boone UMC (1983–1987), First UMC, Waynesville (1987–1992), Christ UMC, Greensboro (1992–1998), Providence UMC, Charlotte (1998–2003), Charlotte District Superintendent (2003–2011).

Part III: Paradox and the Holy Spirit as an Extension of the Incarnation

Very early on, I sought the wisdom and guidance of our congregation's lay leader, Tom M. Walters. As a native of nearby Anson County, he understood the cultural context of racial bigotry. He had been reared on a farm and knew and loved the people of the region, even though his religious convictions prevented his acceptance of the prevailing racial sentiments. After working his way through college, Tom tried teaching in a public school, but the county ran out of money and eliminated his position. He soon landed a job with Seaboard Air Line Railroad and worked as a flagman and freight conductor. By 1958, he had been promoted to the position of Regional Vice President for the southeastern states of the conductor's union, the Order of Railway Conductors and Brakemen (the ORCB). During the Kennedy administration, Tom served in Washington as that organization's representative on national legislation. But two heart attacks prevented his anticipated advancement to the presidency of this powerful national labor union.

After four years of retirement in Wingate due to his physical disability, Tom asked himself, "What can I now do to serve others in the spirit of Christ?" So it was that in July of 1967 he was elected mayor of the town of Wingate, and during the following summer, he was eager to partner with his new pastor in developing effective ways to address the significant racial divide within this community of approximately 1,300 citizens.

When I proposed that the Wingate UMC start by reaching out to Nicey Grove and Piney Grove Baptist Churches, two local African-American congregations, Tom offered his enthusiastic support. He had enjoyed an impressive career of successful negotiations in labor-management disputes. Tom was so filled with the spirit of Christ and a sense of mission to build an inclusive community that he called meetings between leading laypeople from each of the churches, leaders within the college, business owners, and his several golf buddies. He convinced many that an inclusive racial community was the call of Christ and our most urgent agenda in the town of Wingate. Thus, he helped in the formation of "Yokefellow," an inter-racial, ecumenical fellowship based upon the small group concepts of the Quaker theologian Elton Trueblood. We met for prayer and worship, sharing community concerns, fellowship meals, and Bible study. We attempted to reflect the inclusive spirit of the New Testament church and the comprehensive vision of Martin Luther King Jr. None of this came about without controversy and considerable resistance. But Tom Walters was a calm voice of reason and brought an ever-present force of Christ-like influence that affirmed the dignity of every citizen. One of Tom's cardinal rules was the Pauline admonition, "Do not let the sun go down on your anger."[6] On one occasion he said to me with a smile, "We cardiac survivors have to remind the rest of you that anger destroys. Love builds."

Tom Walters died in 1994 at the age of eighty-four, surviving long enough to care for his precious spouse of sixty-one years and to witness the fruition of many of his dreams for both the church and town. His life of integrity, courageous confrontation,

---

6. Eph 4:26b NRSV.

and captivating love for people helped change the course of history in the tiny campus village where he had been placed as God's messenger of visionary hope.

Shady Grove UMC, my second parish responsibility, was the parish in which I was perhaps least effective, but also grew the most. Through this faith community, I discovered that trustful relationships of depth are essential for engaging in the work of the Kingdom. This was not a congregation eager to launch new, panoramic agendas of ministry or to be absorbed into extensive explorations in the meaning of biblical texts. But the members wanted to know that when life was threatened by its deepest crises, a loving, listening pastor would be at their side.

I learned the discipline of nurturing relationships through my association with Gerald and Marian Clodfelter. Both had lived nearly all their lives among the people of this congregation. Gerald had been away from this rural region during the war years, when he was drafted for duty in the European campaign as a teen. Even though he did not talk with much specificity about his grueling experiences, he told me with much emotion about the surprise that had awaited his unit, which was the first military corps to enter the death camp at Dachau. His life was forever changed when he saw, in his words, "the prisoners stacked like cordwood in the box cars and left to die as the Germans retreated."

As a result of this experience, Gerald was the first to respond when his pastor challenged the attitudes of racial exclusion and prejudice that were pervasive in the culture of 1972. When I was his pastor, Gerald was forced to abandon his job driving a laundry delivery truck due to the advancement of his emphysema from years of smoking. After all, this was the land of tobacco farming. Henry Nouwen had just published his classic, *The Wounded Healer*, when Gerald asked to accompany me each week in making hospital visits and special calls to homebound members. Watching the man clutch his oxygen tank and gasp for breath as we entered a hospital ward or sickroom was a poignant experience. Gerald developed immediate rapport with the infirm of the congregation. His presence at my side became an endorsement of my feeble attempts at pastoral ministry. I began to refer to him as Shady Grove's "wounded healer."

Gerald's wife Marian served as a secretary to a High Point business. But her real vocation was teaching youth and leading small groups at the church. She was easily among the most progressive thinker in the congregation, so I fed her some of the most current and insightful volumes in theology. Although she did not possess a full college education, her analytical skills were superb and her teaching was zealous. Thus, I learned through the Clodfelters that the role of the pastor is not to win arguments related to social ethics or political ideology. A pastor is called to live incarnationally— to love people with whom you disagree, to model courageously racial inclusiveness, to forgive those who may reject you and your alien ideas, and to celebrate the joy of Christian community amidst a diversity of conflicting ideologies.

In the years shortly after my departure to a parish in nearby Greensboro, I learned that Gerald's health was in serious decline. Their house was beginning to crumble

Part III: Paradox and the Holy Spirit as an Extension of the Incarnation

with age, deteriorating faster than it could be fixed. Gerald and Marian were vulnerable to winter's cold and the tenacity of summer's heat. Long after their deaths, one of their sons sent me a log that Marian had kept to record miraculous things that had transpired. A considerable number of young adult members of Shady Grove UMC whom Marian had taught in Sunday school class asked for permission to build a new house for them. With the Clodfelter's consent, the church began raising money for this purpose. A young electrician donated the wiring. A team of volunteers installed sheet rock and nailed down floors. Grateful men and women laid cement foundation, sanded walls, painted, constructed cabinets, put up shelves, laid linoleum and carpet, and even fashioned a Chippendale banister. On an exciting June 4, a host of young adults I had known as children of the church moved the Clodfelter's furniture from their old, dilapidated house on the verge of collapse into the comfort of their beautiful brand-new home. Marian shared this excerpt from her daily journal for publication in the church's newsletter, *Leaves from Shady Grove*: "A house built of love—and that's the way we feel—loved. We feel it in every nail, every board, every wire, and every pipe . . . We sincerely appreciate the enthusiasm, comments, visits, and genuine support of the Shady Grove UMC and community as a whole . . . and pray God's blessings on each and every one of you."

I am not surprised that, as I write, Shady Grove UMC is one of the fastest-growing and progressively engaged missional churches in the region.

The geographical distance between rural Shady Grove UMC and Hinshaw Memorial UMC in Greensboro is slight, but in 1977, the corporate personalities and missional agendas of the two churches stood in bold contrast. On the sultry summer's day we moved into the parsonage of Hinshaw Memorial UMC in Greensboro, we met Tom Wilson, who was carrying a sizeable watermelon as a sign of personal and communal hospitality. In subsequent years, we came to know this man whose most palpable spiritual gift was indeed generosity. As we sliced the watermelon in those first moments of conversation, we began a treasured friendship with a man who embodied the didactic formula for Christian stewardship crystallized by John Wesley: "earn all you can," and "save all you can," in order to "give all you can."[7]

Through the years of our growing relationship, I learned more about the spiritual roots of his generosity. Tom was born at the beginning of the Great Depression in 1931. He was only four years old when his parents separated and divorced, making a bad economic situation much worse. His mother retained custody but had no resources to support her son, so Tom lived for a while with an aunt and uncle in an intimidating environment of intense farm labor and strict punishment. When his maternal great-aunt and -uncle, an older couple, became his new guardians, young Tom's life was forever changed. These kind, gentle people surrounded him with love, security, and faith. From age twelve to eighteen, Tom lived in a household of scriptural holiness, a community of joyful worship at Palmyra Methodist Church, and a

---

7. Wesley, *Works of the Reverend*, 1:442–446.

stimulating environment of new friendships through the Methodist Youth Fellowship. Through the Methodist Youth Fellowship, Tom met Ruth at the age of fifteen, a girl one year younger who later became his wife and the mother of their four children.

By the time Tom and Ruth Wilson had become members of Hinshaw Memorial Methodist Church in Greensboro in 1957, he had begun college courses in business, completed nearly two years of military service in Germany, returned to complete his certification as an accountant, and worked as a credit manager in the offices of several major business firms in the city. By the mid-1970s Tom had left his job in the business office of Moses Cone Hospital to become a self-employed rental property investor. When I became his new pastor, he had not yet become successful in this risky venture.

Through all these years, Tom had disciplined his life to model the mandate of Micah the Hebrew prophet: "He has told you, O mortal, what is good; and what does the Lord require of you but to do justice, and to love kindness, and to walk humbly with your God?"[8] As his pastor, I had the privilege of witnessing his considerable spiritual growth through small group Bible studies, ongoing retreat experiences with the Walk to Emmaus program, and innumerable mission building teams. Tom and his entire family learned the art of carpentry, plumbing, and some electrical skills by doing maintenance on his rental properties. Tom was a valuable component of the Hinshaw Memorial building teams that traveled to construct churches at several sites in Mexico, Puerto Rico, and islands of the Caribbean. He attended spiritual life retreats for the laity at Lake Junaluska; the World Methodist Council's global conferences in Rio de Janeiro, Brazil, and Brighton, England; and numerous United Methodist Men's rallies. The enrichment of his spiritual life occurred during a period of exponential growth for his business, resulting in a lifestyle of accelerated generosity. He financed many mission teams by purchasing building supplies. He invested in educational and nutrition programs for children abroad while staying attuned to economic needs of the poor at home through the outreach of Greensboro Urban Ministries. For over thirty years he was an energized, compassionate leader in Civitan International, serving on the Board of Directors for that organization's Boys Home.

Tom Wilson never forgot the lessons of generosity he learned from the relatives who were his compassionate guardians during his youth. He nurtured the embers of a personal faith that had been lit at an early age at Palmyra Methodist Church near Winston-Salem. He always remembered the intensity of care and financial assistance these modest members had provided an economically deprived community during the years of his childhood and adolescence. The Holy Spirit filled him with the gift of generosity through which he blessed his entire family, the congregations of his membership, children around the globe, and pastors with whom he shared watermelon and the joy of his gracious and generous heart.

Because of my personal affinity with campus communities and our favorable experiences at our initial appointment within the collegiate environment of Wingate,

---

8. Mic 6:8 NRSV.

Part III: Paradox and the Holy Spirit as an Extension of the Incarnation

my wife and I were excited to serve in yet another campus setting upon our departure from Greensboro. Anyone that enters the vibrant campus town of Boone, North Carolina, during the spring, summer, and early fall seasons is likely to think that they have arrived in a paradise of floral color. Those of us who are acquainted with the community's cultural heritage know that this is primarily the result of a theology of stewardship in the lives of a devout couple whose fifty-three years of marriage have been a testimony of gratitude. Lee and Vivian Reynolds taught theology by praxis: Their daily lives were a testimony to the living, creative God. They were quick to observe that the biblical canon begins in a garden and concludes in another garden. The first paradise was lost as a result of hubris and disobedience. Humanity broke covenant with God and failed to maintain diligence of stewardship over the natural resources entrusted to human care. Restoration has come through the incarnational God manifested in the witness of Jesus Christ, who came to bring about a new heaven and a new earth and to save this fallen, cracked creation from its destructive fixation on war, its foolish usurpation of nature, and its maddening march toward potential annihilation.

Lee and Vivian Reynolds often cited as their motto this mandate of the Pulitzer Prize-winning author Edward Bok, "Make you the world a bit more beautiful and better because you have been in it."[9] These two disciples of Christ pursued this mission literally. Vivian's love for flowers began on her father's Indiana farm with the loving influence of an aunt who taught her young niece about hundreds of plants and their botanical names. When Dr. Reynolds accepted a position on the faculty of Appalachian State Teachers College in 1949, Vivian divided her time between substitute teaching home economics and leading restoration projects for the local garden club. Lee always assisted Vivian in her beautification ventures, but upon his retirement from the Department of Education in 1973, the two became a dynamic team of astounding energy and productivity in this mountain town. They were forever planting breathtaking beds of flowers, shrubs, rhododendrons, and roses. Without any financial remuneration, they planted bulbs each spring, tended them throughout the summer, and preserved them in hothouses or storage in late fall. City officials estimated that these two citizens planted over twenty-five thousand bulbs, annuals, and roses. At the time of Lee's death in early 1990, they were tending over forty major flowerbeds around the city. All of their labor was donated. When asked by a CBS affiliate WBTV newsman why they worked so arduously, Lee answered that this was a way of showing God his gratitude for the privilege of being a tenant on this earth.

When Dr. Reynolds was a participant in a Disciple Bible group at Boone UMC, he shared with the class his reflections upon Psalm 8 by writing, "When I meditate I become confused as to the vastness of the universe. It boggles my imagination to know that some of the nearest stars are trillions of miles away. But it consoles me to remember that Jesus promised, 'If I go to the Father, I'll prepare a place for you.'" Lee demonstrated with his life that, because of the grace of an incarnational God, this

---

9. Bok, *Americanization of Edward Bok*, xxi.

world is being saved and the natural order is being restored. He believed that both human history and natural history are moving, not toward chaos, but to a new reality—a new paradise. But the present world, through God's love and the restorative activity of God's people, can reflect the beauty and grace of the world that is to be—that future home, that future paradise envisioned by John of Patmos.

After her husband's death at age eighty-one, Vivian Reynolds continued in her unrelenting efforts to make Boone a paradise of colorful flowers and delightful trees. Her leadership by example inspired an army of volunteers to take up her work when she was unable to contribute physical labor. Before her death at the age of one hundred, a 1.5-mile walking trail along the South Fork bank of the New River was named the Lee and Vivian Reynolds Greenway.

It is said that Martin Luther was once asked, "If the day of God's final judgment were tomorrow, what would you do?" He is reputed to have responded, "Today I would plant a tree." On a beautiful day in mountainous Boone, Lee Reynolds meticulously planted seventy-five glorious new roses at Watauga County Hospital. Within a few days, he was rushed back to breathe his last breath.

Yes, the Reynolds truly hold a place of cherished memory in the hearts of all the members of Boone UMC. Moreover, the legacy of floral beauty and community service that they inspired is preserved in a campus town that was truly made a better, more Christ-like place, reflecting the paradise of a coming Kingdom, because of the witness of Lee and Vivian Reynolds.

When we visited our next parish assignment, First UMC in Waynesville, we expected to encounter a number of senior citizens, including at least a hundred retired clergy in the congregation. But to our surprise, we soon discovered that this retirement haven was also the home of a dynamic ministry of Christian education for children. This concentrated mission among the children of Waynesville owes much to the vision and loving legacy of Mary Hale, who served as the congregation's Director of Christian Education from 1976 to 1993.

Mary had always possessed a profound love for children and so she chose to major in early childhood education at North Texas State University. In 1963, she married Joe R. Hale, a recent graduate of Asbury Theological Seminary. In the early years of their marriage they lived in Nashville, Tennessee, where Joe worked with the Board of Discipleship at the national center of Methodism's ministry of evangelism. There they adopted their only child, Jeffrey. Mary learned about the denomination's literature for children in an environment of curriculum authors and strategists. When her husband accepted the position of General Secretary of the World Methodist Council, centered at Lake Junaluska, Mary was asked by First UMC in nearby Waynesville to give guidance to the congregation's ministry with children. She immediately brought to her new job the full measure of her love for children, her grasp of effective teaching techniques, and her comprehensive knowledge of educational resources. Her creative pursuit of excellence in this endeavor established a pattern that persists into the present as subsequent directors have emulated her thoroughness and proficiency in planning and implementation.

During my years as senior pastor at First UMC, I saw that Mary knew the names of all the children and followed their maturation into adulthood. She worked closely with the director and staff of the Christian Development Center, a weekday preschool ministry, and introduced a nurturing, Christ-centered curriculum to the church's comprehensive educational ministry. She developed a task force that intricately planned over half a year in advance the specific activities related to the summer's annual Vacation Bible School. Over 250 adult volunteers were required. Biblical and theological themes varied to allow children and families to experience a Galilean village during the time of Jesus, the Hebrew tribes preparing for exodus from Egypt in the era of Moses, the house churches of Corinth during the missionary journeys of the Apostle Paul, or small group "societies" as the children dressed in eighteenth century costumes as during the Wesleyan revival of England. Dramatists, craftsmen, writers, musicians, and teachers were recruited and trained by this passionate educator who wanted all the children to be saturated in scriptural holiness. One of my favorite memories is the image of Mary Hale blowing a large *shophar* that her husband brought home from one of his many visits to Jerusalem. A bevy of children gathered at her feet as Mary introduced the theme of the morning's biblical drama.

A debilitating, sudden stroke in April of 1993 terminated Mary's continuation of her didactic ministry. She and her devoted husband are now retired and disabled residents at nearby Silver Bluff Village, where they receive medical and nutritional care. Their ministry of intercessory prayer continues to be extensive. When I visit them, Mary always requests updates on the many young adults who had been her beloved students and whose names are indelibly engraved in the memory of her heart.

Episcopal appointments sometimes reflect the movement of God's Holy Spirit and the matching of pastoral gifts with a congregation's needs. That was certainly true when we transitioned from Waynesville to Christ UMC in Greensboro. Occasionally a pastor's faith pilgrimage is amazingly commensurate with the gradational spiritual growth in the corporate life of a congregation. Soon after our arrival at Christ UMC, we discovered that the tributaries of our lifelong pilgrimages converged with this fortuitous appointment.

This realization became evident in our encounters with a leading layman of that congregation. We first met George "Jace" Ralls back in 1970, when he was a guest in our Wingate parsonage and captain of a "lay witness" team from a relatively new church in the growing west side of Greensboro. In 1968, this new congregation had been one of the first of this denomination to experience a lay witness weekend during which a team of keenly focused laity gave verbal witness to their personal faith and explained how their commitments to Christ influenced their sense of vocation and mission within the community. The team that visited Christ UMC that year included Ruth Carter, a sister of the former President. This emotionally charged and intensely relevant experience had so mobilized the membership of Christ UMC that the laity in Wingate specifically requested that laypeople from Christ UMC lead a similar experience in their congregation.

This fortuitous visit introduced me to the faith and authenticity of Jace Ralls—a man who epitomizes the spiritual quality and motivational theology of Christ UMC. A friendship that began in 1970 was exponentially enhanced by my appointment to this remarkable church in 1992. As a result of his participation in several lay witness missions, Jace guided the formation of small groups within Christ Church that regularly meet for Bible study, reading devotional and theological classics, and fellowship meals. Jace has continued to be part of these groups for three generations, actively engaging from 1968 to the present.

Jace was baptized as a child and confirmed as a youth. But he had not personally taken his parent's faith to heart until a near-death experience during his college years. One night he was speeding down Friendly Avenue in Greensboro when his car suddenly skidded out of control, barely missing a telephone pole. Jace reflectively decided that this rescue from a senseless death was a clear sign that God had something important for him to do. During a subsequent Billy Graham Crusade, he solidified his personal commitment to the Christ who had spared his life and initiated his pilgrimage of sanctifying growth.

Naturally he was drawn to the adventure begun in 1956 by West Market Street Methodist Church in launching a new congregation in the Hamilton Lakes region of the sprawling city of Greensboro. Jace worked closely with various laypeople, including Bill Henderson, in making sure that this new congregation would include small group accountability for costly discipleship. Bill was the genius behind the development of Baldhead Island in costal North Carolina and shared Jace's vision for a mature discipleship through small groups and spiritual retreats. In 1975, Jace experienced at nearby Trinity Episcopal Church a life-altering presentation by Gordon Cosby, pastor of the Church of the Saviour. He came to realize that if small groups within the church are to be sustained in faithfulness, they must maintain a balance between the inward and outward journeys. Thus, Jace began the discipline of leading regular trips to the Church of the Saviour's Dayspring Retreat Center near Damascus, Maryland—a place of Pauline proportions in the experience of many Christ UMC members. Three times each year, Jace has guided groups from his congregation to the Dayspring Retreat Center, where seekers participate in silent retreats, discussion themes, and reflective walks in a forested paradise several miles outside our nation's capitol.

When I became Jace's pastor in 1992, the church already had the ecclesiastical structure in place for members to practice the paradoxical character of an authentic Christian community. We expanded options for participation by initiating additional small groups using the methodology of ChristCare, a Stephen Ministries program. Each new group became Christ-centered, biblically-based, and mission-driven in order to sustain a balance between inward and outward spiritual journeys.

Part III: Paradox and the Holy Spirit as an Extension of the Incarnation

Jace accepted a new role as director of the church's "every member in ministry" emphasis. He conducted "spiritual gifts inventories" for members, seeking to match personal passions with community agencies of compassionate outreach. He interviewed each new member, insisting that as a prerequisite for membership, each designate at least one expression of ministry as a personal missional activity. Jace then began a program of "discipleship journeys" by organizing annual trips abroad that were linked to months of biblical or theological study and preparation. Groups of twenty to thirty participants traveled to Israel and the major cites of the Bible, Greece and the lands of Paul's journeys, England and the places touched by the Wesleyan revival, and Germany's major Protestant shrines. Six decades ago, an aimless college student was spared from a senseless ending by grace. This ordinary disciple of Jesus discovered a truly noble purpose for his life and has undertaken extraordinary tasks with a regal spirit.

When guests enter the atrium of Providence UMC in Charlotte and approach the prominent reception desk, they do not have to read any missional brochures or chat with the receptionist to know the core values of this exceptional congregation. Mounted at the right side of this carpeted hospitality area is an unpretentious but revealing sculpture showing the Johannine scene of Jesus washing the feet of Peter, a poignant moment in the narrative of the Fourth Gospel in which our Lord instructed the apostles in their principle paradoxical role—serving others through humble acts of self-giving. The eyes of every visitor who comes through these double doors are drawn to this depiction of Christ-the-servant, who vividly demonstrated that the ultimate form of power is sacrificial love through costly service.

To the left of the receptionist station is a complimentary sculpture of Jesus with a child upon his knee. Those guests who are directed toward the weekday preschool program or the children's Sunday school are likely to pass this artistic reminder of each of the synoptic Evangelists' assurances that our Lord blesses all the children and challenges his resistant disciples to adopt their trusting faith, saying, "for it is to such as these that the kingdom of God belongs."[10] Some venerable members of the congregation who are acquainted with the history of this reflective statue will pause and examine the face of this child to remember the baptized child who was so caringly memorialized in the months after her unfortunate death.

The sensitive artist who so thoroughly comprehends the theology of paradox in the worship and life of this vibrant congregation is Wilton Luther Parr, an active member of Providence UMC for the last four decades. He has captured the heritage and vision of a people who seek to remain receptive to the coming of the Holy Spirit in the midst of their worship, service, and biblical instruction. Wilton models a paradoxical, Christ-centered life, but he rarely holds any official position of authority in the ecclesiastical structure, choosing instead to work behind the scenes. He never seeks power or prominence, yet his mere presence commands such moral authority

10. Mark 10:14 NRSV. See also Matt 19:13–15 and Luke 18:15–17 NRSV.

and respect that he is revered throughout the community. He is best known by many close friends through his oil and watercolor paintings, sculpture, and poetry. Through his introspective and spiritual artistry, Wilton illustrates his pilgrimage as a growing disciple of Christ.

Wilton was born in historic Richmond, Virginia, and spent his childhood and adolescence in Danville, Virginia. He attended Virginia Tech and graduated in 1951 with a degree in mechanical engineering. After serving his country in the Korean War, he returned home to marry Mary Denny Wilson, his wife for these fifty-nine years. For thirty-three years, he labored for the Piedmont Natural Gas Company in Charlotte and retired as that agency's Vice President of Marketing.

Wilton's true vocation, however, is as a disciple of Jesus. At Providence UMC he has participated in over twenty major mission building teams to disaster areas in the US and abroad. He has brought his engineering skills to the congregation's medical clinics in Haiti. He has responded to natural tragedy in his role on disaster relief teams in Saint Croix, the Mississippi coast following Hurricane Katrina, and the flood relief efforts in western North Carolina and the Outer Banks. Wilton is the father of two sons, five grandchildren, and two great-grandchildren, making him a natural youth mentor. He has frequently accompanied the church's youth fellowship mission teams to provide expert counsel in their efforts to repair the homes of the poor and elderly. For the past twelve years, he served as a tutor for youth working on their GED or certification through the local community college. He was the principle force in the church's resettlement of the Rizvanowic family and helped in building their lovely Habitat home. Wilton is an essential component in the congregation's bus ministry, bringing the homeless to the church's facilities for shelter, food, and inspirational hospitality through the "Room in the Inn" ministry. He often provides essential transportation for the elderly and disabled. This skilled artist also has donated many of his remarkable sculptures and paintings to auctions that benefit the church's mission.

Elizabeth O'Connor, that grand interpreter of the diverse ministries of the Church of the Saviour, has written that "we do not experience ourselves as gift until we are engaged in the act of creating... We cannot use our gifts without having unknown chords in us played upon in a whole range of effects that bring us alive."[11] In generously sharing his considerable creative gifts, Wilton Luther Parr has evoked a symphony of harmonious sound that resonates with joy in a vibrant congregation that rejoices in his generosity of spirit.

People of common nobility, much like these seven representatives, provide substance and vitality to every authentic community of faith filled with the generous spirit of the living Christ. It is imperative that their inspirational stories be told.

---

11. O'Connor, *Eighth Day of Creation*, 27–28.

30

One God in Three Persons, Blessed Trinity

WE HAVE ARRIVED IN the belly of a paradox at the final chapter of our theological journey. The roadmap to this destination has taken us on a triangular route. We have encountered biblical stories, parables, and treasured scriptural images pointing to the paradoxical nature of a Creator God whose mercy does not balance the scales of justice. We have been mystified by the wisdom of God's foolishness and the unsystematic manner in which the Almighty discloses power and transcendence. We have gained new perspectives in our discernment of God's purposes as the divine Being who communicates in the language of both good and bad events. We have learned from Scripture and personal experience how to fear a loving God and how to love a fearful God. In acts of worship and compassion through the church's ministry, we have drawn near to the healing power of a suffering God whose tears are our restoration and comfort. We have discovered that our path to purity and sanctification requires the toughness of God's judgment and that divine rejection often leads to a special state of chosenness. We have learned that, while empirical science and harmonious mathematical formulas disclose the logical genius of God's universe, they also point us toward the paradoxical and mysterious fabric of cosmic reality. Only the language of paradox, especially as it is spoken in the prayers and sacraments of worship, remains faithful to the core biblical traditions of the church.

We can only speak of the deity of Christ if we profess that the Man of Nazareth embodied these paradoxical attributes of divine Being. In the fullness of time, amidst a perfect storm of conflicting ideologies and Hebrew messianic expectations, Jesus was born in Bethlehem. Caesar Augustus, an autocratic military dictator, presided over a kingdom whose political power was greater than any the world had yet seen. But mighty Augustus plays only a bit part in Luke's drama of salvation history. Tyrannical Herod the Great, whose self-aggrandizing monuments of stone cluttered the landscape of Judah, is an insignificant foil in the story of the King of kings. However, the regal power of Jesus is manifested upon a cross of humiliation. His route to triumph required an obligatory detour upon a cruciform path of pain and ignominious death. Only this agonizing humiliation opened the horizon of hope and ultimate triumph of the man who rode a humble donkey into Jerusalem surrounded by children holding palm-branches. Only this King with a crown of thorns on a cross of humiliation possessed the power to conquer nations without swords of violence. He emptied himself to the last drop of blood in order that his disciples could be filled with the abundant life of sacrificial love. This paradoxical Being, whose story parallels the narrative of God's paradoxical self-disclosure to the exiled people of Abraham's covenant, is more than an idea or theological concept. The Jesus of history is the Christ of faith whose resurrection validates the paradoxical form of God's indwelling love and its transformational redemption of human history.

The third stage of our triangular theological journey is therefore essential, for unless our pilgrimage toward redemption and the fulfillment of Jesus' mission is sustained within communities that embody the paradoxical attributes of a living God, this theological construct crumbles. Unless the extension of the incarnation is sustained through the paradoxical community that he initiated, the future of humanity will be awarded to the principalities that control the world by Machiavellian power and the politics of military violence. But our theological reflections on the scriptural evidence of the Holy Spirit adamantly assert that history is carried by the movement of Christ's spirit in the lives of individuals and faith communities that embody the characteristics of the paradoxical God revealed in the historical life, death, and resurrection of Jesus the Nazarene. We have especially articulated the importance of telling these metanarratives in the stories of the faithful, but not because these individuals or their faith communities have succeeded in perfect imitation of the life of the paradoxical Christ. Exemplary people of common nobility (as detailed in chapter 29 and in readers' own acquaintance) are imperfect manifestations of Christ's ideal existence. Yet each recognizes that the power to transform human history and rescue natural history from annihilation is clearly the work of the Holy Spirit. These faithful followers of Christ are indeed conduits of that spirit and power. When individuals and communities are molded to the mind of Christ by holy habits, they receive the power to transform the little slice of history to which they have been entrusted. Their submission to the authority of the Holy Spirit is imperfect, and their moral courage is sometimes compromised, but the impact of their imperfect witness is fortified and sustained through recurring, consistent experiences of vibrant worship. Through encounters with the Holy Spirit in worship, these people of common nobility become a force of considerable effectiveness, vision, and change. These Christ-centered disciples of common nobility empty themselves only to be filled with the Holy Spirit and empowered by the vision of Christ's promised future.

Our theological journey has now arrived at its final stanza in our ten-chapter focus upon the Holy Spirit, brazenly affirming the reality of one God in three persons.

Part III: Paradox and the Holy Spirit as an Extension of the Incarnation

We are here asserting that the doctrine of the Trinity is indispensable in our understanding the paradoxical structure of God's self-disclosure. But why is a Trinitarian understanding of God essential to the life and worship of the parish? After all, the term never occurs in Scripture. No schematic triune conception of God is found in the sacred literature of the Hebrews. The Mosaic covenant is firmly rooted in the monotheistic assertion, "You shall have no other gods before me."[1] Jesus affirmed the answer of the young lawyer who asked him what he must do to inherit eternal life. This expert on the meaning of Torah had quoted the *Shema*. Jesus concurred that loving the one God with the totality of one's being and loving one's neighbor as one's self is the essence of authentic faith.[2] The Christian doctrine of the Trinity must consequently be grounded in a monotheistic supposition rather than any suggestion that it is a reference to three gods.

A triadic formula is indispensable language for worship and evangelism if we remain faithful to the context of scriptural witness. The nativity narrative of Luke focuses upon the words of an angelic messenger appearing to Mary, saying, "The Holy Spirit will come upon you, and the power of the Most High will overshadow you; therefore the child to be born will be holy; he will be called Son of God."[3] Pauline doxologies preceded the Council of Nicaea's Trinitarian formula by nearly three centuries. The missionary apostle's Trinitarian Beatitude became a natural expression of his abiding faith, as with the consoling conclusion of his Epistle to the Corinthians: "The grace of the Lord Jesus Christ, the love of God, and the communion of the Holy Spirit be with all of you."[4]

As we move more deeply into the twenty-first century amidst an increasingly pluralistic global environment, the church will likely engage in opportunities for constructive dialogue with Judaism and Islam. It is essential, therefore, that we speak with clarity about our Trinitarian beliefs as Christians. The chief question is not how the three persons of the Trinity refer to the One God, for all inter-faith discussion must begin with the monotheistic framework of each of the three faiths that trace their origins to the Abrahamic covenant. A generation ago, Hans Küng, a renegade Catholic theologian teaching at the University of Tübingen in Germany, was bold enough to articulate the central theological task related to an inter-faith discussion of the Trinity when he asserted, "The monotheistic faith taken over from Israel and held in common with Islam must never be abandoned in any doctrine of the Trinity. There is no God, but God."[5] If the contemporary church is to be an aggressive agent for the building of global peace, we must clearly articulate our identity within the heritage of our Abrahamic faith, grounded in a sacred covenant of obedience to the one God.

1. Exod 20:3 NRSV.
2. See Luke 10:25–28 NRSV.
3. Luke 1:35 NRSV.
4. 2 Cor 13:13 NRSV.
5. Küng, *On Being a Christian*, 476.

One God in Three Persons, Blessed Trinity

The rapidly expanding church of the fourth century and the Council of Nicaea in A.D. 325 had little concern about the divinity of Jesus Christ. That was a universally accepted doctrine within a very diverse Christendom. The more relevant issue was the manner in which the church understood the Son of God to be human. At Nicaea, the assembled theologians wanted to clarify just how Christ was indeed like us. Moreover, these leading Christian theologians wanted to arrive at a consensus regarding the relationship between the persons (*prosoponae*) of the Trinity. Is the triangular symbol of God's being hierarchical, with God the Father taking precedence in time and significance? How should the church hold onto the notion of the one (*homo*) transcendent Being (*ousía*) with three individual realities (*hypostasia*)? How can one being have three personalities? Of course, it is legendary to speak of the Nicene wars that erupted over one letter in the Greek alphabet—a single iota. The African theologian Athanasius was the dominant voice that insisted that Christ was the *same* being (*homoousios*) with the Father. Followers of the rival theologian Arius were condemned as heretics because of their insistence that Christ was not the same being but of *like* being as Christ (*homoiousios*). To modern Christians this controversy may seem like a tempest in a teapot, but church leaders at Nicaea considered it a paramount issue. Thus, the Nicene Trinitarian formula affirms, "We believe in one Lord, Jesus Christ, the only Son of God, eternally begotten of the Father, God from God, Light from Light, true God from true God, begotten, not made, of one Being (*homoousios*) with the Father; through him all things were made."[6] This language had an evangelical purpose. After all, the gospel was being preached primarily in a Greek-speaking culture familiar with the philosophic categories of Plato and Aristotle. This language helped maintain the primacy of allegiance to one God, one common source of being, but with three personalities (*prosoponae*).

This language made perfect sense to Christians steeped in Hellenistic philosophy, but how did the Holy Spirit fit into the orthodox doctrine of the emerging, Western-dominated Roman, Latin-language church? Does the third person (personality of God) have less importance than Father and Son? What is the relationship of the Holy Spirit to the Father and Son? How is God present within the ongoing life and mission of the church if the Holy Spirit has less status and significance in divine revelation?

In the eighth century, the Roman church inserted into the Nicean formula the phrase, "and from the Son" so that the Trinitarian affirmation reads, "We believe in the Holy Spirit, the Lord, the giver of life, *who proceeds from the Father and from the Son*, who with the Father and the Son is worshiped and glorified, who has spoken through the prophets."[7] While this so-called *filioque* phrase (Latin for "from the son") was intended to clarify, it alienated factions within the church, especially Greek-speaking Christians centered in Constantinople. Thus, this theological matter became a divisive, volatile political issue. Christian leaders, primarily from the eastern regions of

---

6. Nicene Creed, 325 A.D., emphasis mine.
7. Ibid.

Part III: Paradox and the Holy Spirit as an Extension of the Incarnation

the Roman Empire, preferred the phrase "from the Father through the Son." But it was the opinion in the eastern regions of the church that whatever the form, the *filioque* phrase created a monarchical concept within the Trinity, giving the Holy Spirit a subordinate role in the reality of God's self-disclosure. I firmly contend that if this phrase were eliminated from the Nicene Creed altogether, the affirmation would sustain the oneness of divine Being without abrogating the importance of the Holy Spirit. Lucan theology, after all, asserts that Christ was conceived of the Holy Spirit. Does it make sense, in this biblical context, to say that the Holy Spirit "proceeds from the Father and the Son"? Jesus was baptized with the Holy Spirit and thereby received empowerment to begin his ministry. The Synoptic Gospels teach that Christ came from God through the Spirit. Hebrew Scripture (that is, the Bible of Jesus) discloses that the Spirit was present at original creation through the breath of God. The Spirit guides Israel through the wilderness toward the Promised Land. As stated in chapters 24 and 29, the Spirit presides over the movement of God's people through epochs of history, as recorded in the meta-narrative of faithfulness within communities of faith. The elimination of the *filioque* in the church's doctrine and teachings would, consequently, restore the essential purpose and prominence of the Holy Spirit in the Trinitarian formula.

In chapter 6, we discussed the healing power of God's wounds. Here we were introduced to the Hebraic concept of *shekinah* and the *indwelling of God*. The insight we gained is that the Hebrews believed that the all-powerful God chose to *indwell* with his covenant people in the era of the exile. God suffered with the people he loved. From the astonishing poetry of Second Isaiah onward, biblical faith dispenses with the notion of a remote, detached deity. Israel's God is not elevated from the passions of humanity. The Hebrew theology that was central to the faith of Jesus was prone to exclaim, "To hell with such an apathetic god!" The God of the Mosaic covenant, the God of the exile in Babylon, and the God of the Maccabees tented with suffering Israel. God's *shekinah* means that divine Being becomes homeless with the fleeing slaves who followed Moses out of Egypt. God pitches tent in the Sinai with his refugee people, bringing manna for daily sustenance. God's *shekinah* was experienced by the impoverished multitudes who listened to the voice of their long-awaited Messiah in Galilee. God dwelled within the persecuted church through the presence and power of God's suffering Holy Spirit. The biblical God, whom we know best through his manifestation in Jesus of Nazareth, continues to indwell with the plight of his people, who gather for worship and scatter to serve in his name.

Even as God's *shekinah* is the hallmark of salvation history and the meta-narrative of the church, this is the *reality* (*hypostasis*, the Greek word employed at Nicaea) of God's authentic *being* (*ousía*). The three vibrant components of God's personality (*prosopon*)—Father, Son, and Holy Spirit—indwell with one another. The Trinity is that paradoxical nature of God's Being by which there is a reciprocal indwelling of the interrelated, unified nature of the divine personhood. The three persons are one Being. Through this reciprocal indwelling, the Christian faith cannot be seen as an aggregation of three separate deities. Moreover, the Holy Spirit is not a subordinate personality of God. Each person of the Trinity indwells with the other in fruitful reciprocity and unity of purpose. No one persona takes precedent over the other. The early church theologians had a term for this mutual indwelling, *perichorosis*. This Greek reference means "a mutual indwelling" out of which a unity-in-the-difference and a difference-in-the-unity is achieved. Thus, a masterful phrase within a Pauline letter provides far more clarity than the Nicean *filoque* as this great missionary apostle and Evangelist simply writes to his friends in Corinth, "in Christ, God was reconciling the world to himself, not counting their trespasses against them, and entrusting the message of reconciliation to us."[8] Paul's simple phrase makes it apparent that God's Holy Spirit is Christ's gift to the church for doing the work of reconciliation. As the church is one body, the deity is likewise one Being with one mission and one goal. Thus, God's Spirit dwells within the church as the gift of Christ. At the heart of Johannine theology, therefore, is the passionate prayer of Jesus for the church on the night before his crucifixion, when he prayed, "Abide in me as I abide in you."[9] In his first canonical Epistle, the beloved apostle cautioned his congregation not to follow just any spirit, but only the Christ-initiated spirit of covenant love (*agape*). The true Spirit of God emanates from Christ; therefore, "Beloved, let us love one another, because love is from God; everyone who loves is born of God and knows God. Whoever does not love does not know God, for God is love."[10]

When we understand the Trinity from the perspective of these biblical references to a *reciprocal indwelling* held together by the costly love of God, the Trinity is no longer a hierarchical community. Jürgen Moltmann insists that "we can speak of the Father's 'monarchy,' if at all, only on the level of the Trinity's constitution, but not in its *perichoretic* [indwelling] life. In the Trinity it is not the monarchy of the Father but the *perichoresis* which is 'the seal of its unity.'"[11]

Why is this intricate, complicated discussion of the Trinity so important to the purpose of this book? What is the relevance of this complex, historical doctrine to the present life of the church and the conduct of its mission?

As the church in the Western world became increasingly enthralled with empirical science, new methodologies for assessing history, and Enlightenment philosophy, it lost interest in such matters as the doctrine of the Trinity to focus on higher criticism's analysis of biblical texts. By the time of Friedrich Schleiermacher (1768–1834), most Protestant theologians considered the doctrine to be irrelevant. Karl Barth (1886–1968) reinvigorated the discussion, but its prominence has never been adequately reestablished in the church bodies of developed Western countries. It is no

---

8. 2 Cor 5:19 NRSV.
9. John 15:4a NRSV.
10. 1 John 4:7–8 NRSV.
11. Moltmann, *Sun of Righteousness*, 154.

Part III: Paradox and the Holy Spirit as an Extension of the Incarnation

accident, however, that this has occurred during the dramatic numerical decline of these ecclesiastical bodies.

During the last few decades of the twentieth century, however, an unprecedented sociological and religious shift has occurred almost unnoticed. This tsunami-like trend was not recognized by the secular press and even by most reputable church historians. In the developing nations of Latin America, the African continent, the Pacific Basin, much of Southeast Asia, and especially China and Russia, there has been a phenomenal outbreak of conversions to a charismatic expression of Christianity. All this is happening during an era in which mainline denominations in the West continue in numerical free-fall. Even though this astonishing growth among charismatic churches has been quietly building for a decade like some gigantic wave, the news media have finally awoken from their passive indifference to the seismic political and economic implications of this spiritual movement. In her April 15, 2013, cover article, "The Latino Reformation," *Time* magazine's Elizabeth Dias revealed while only 17 percent of the current US population is Latino, that figure will likely jump to 29 percent by 2050. As this trend continues, many of those starting their new lives in this country will become Pentecostal or bring a charismatic style to the mainline churches they join. Even those remaining in the Roman Catholic tradition will likely bring a Pentecostal style to traditional worship by uplifted hands, emotional eruptions of spiritual energy, and passionate indigenous music. Dias concluded her analysis of this trend with this observation: "The US—and the entire Latino world—is changing. The rock on which God is building his Latino church all over America is a blacktop parking lot in suburban Maryland and a low-income high school in Illinois. Right now, they may be hard to find. But as Jesus teaches in Matthew, 'May they who have eyes see.'"[12]

With eager eyes I watched several hundred Latinos enter the worship space at Matthews UMC near Charlotte on the first day of their enlistment into the membership roles of that well-established congregation. These Hispanic immigrants launched an additional Spanish-language worship service led by Rev. Diana Wingeier-Rayo, a vivacious Latino elder who preaches in a charismatic style. That service is now integral to this congregation's flourishing ministry of hospitality and evangelism.

When I traveled to China with a group of pastors in 1987 led by Dr. Creighton Lacey of Duke Divinity School, son of the Methodist Bishop in Shanghai, the pastor of a cathedral in that city requested that all members come to auxiliary worship services in order to make room for the avalanche of non-member guests on Sunday morning. When our group of pastors crowded into a large warehouse before sunrise on a Wednesday in Xi'an, it was standing-room only. When the charismatic pastor called for prayers, a cacophony of effusive, emotional voices arose. Tears streaked down the faces of many as we knelt in contrition upon a cement floor. Many of these had suffered horrendously during the recent Cultural Revolution. These sacred moments prior to a full day of arduous labor concluded with shouts of praise and expressions of spiritual joy.

12. Dias, "Latino Reformation," 28.

One God in Three Persons, Blessed Trinity

In a mountainous village outside Cochabamba, Bolivia, a considerable assemblage of Bolivian Methodists gathered in an open field on an occasion designated as Thanksgiving Day. Many of these peasants had walked many miles early that morning over rough terrain carrying sacks of potatoes. Upon reaching their designation, they unloaded gifts of precious vegetables coaxed from rocky, resistant soil. The steep pile of potatoes was deposited in celebration of the harvest for distribution among their brothers and sisters from Greensboro, who had labored in that village to provide dental care and emotional support for families with children. As we worshiped together in that open field, we became a confluence of cultures, with wealth peppered into a population of deprivation. But we North American guests discovered on that day the meaning of poverty of spirit, for on that elevated plateau in Bolivia, we experienced the genuine, emotionally-charged movement of God's Holy Spirit that made us a festive, unified community in Christ.

The Trinity is truly a paradoxical mystery. But as the church restores the efficacy of the Holy Spirit in its expressions of worship and experiences of mission, a new era of exciting vitality will truly emerge.

On April 20, 2008, I faced open-heart surgery and a bypass procedure to correct severe blockages in five major arteries. On the day before the surgery, Rev. David Carl, my colleague in ministry and Executive Director of Spiritual Care and Education at Carolinas Medical Center, guided me in a spiritual exercise. He suggested that I concentrate upon one personally poignant scriptural passage. I happened to choose the intriguing paradoxical language of the early church's first affirmation of faith contained in the second chapter of Paul's Letter to the Philippians. As we discussed in chapter 14, this hymn of affirmation articulates a *kenosis* of the Spirit by which followers of the Way empty self and enter the mind of Christ. The poetry of this affirmation accompanied me to the waiting room as my last thought before sinking into the deep peace of the anesthesiologist's injection.

This experience has made me dramatically aware that each moment I live upon this wondrous earth is a generous gift that comes from the loving spirit of God. Every day and every hour is pure grace and an opportunity to render glory to God. I am supremely grateful, therefore, to the merciful triune deity who allowed me to live and compose this volume of theological testimony and pages of abundant praise. Thus, we shall conclude our theological journey with this remarkable prayer:

> O Christ of contrasts; infinite paradox,
> Yet life's explainer, solvent harmony,
> Frail strength, pure passion, meek austerity,
> And the white splendor of these darkened years—
> I lean my wondering, wayward heart on thine![13]

---

13. Knowles, "To Jesus the Nazarene," 186.

Bibliography

Agosto, Efrain. *Servant Leadership: Jesus and Paul.* Saint Louis: Chalice, 2005.
Anderson, Bernhard W. *Out of the Depths: Studies into the Meaning of the Book of Psalms.* New York: Joint Commission on Education and Cultivation, Board of Missions, United Methodist Church, 1970.
Anderson, Hugh. *The Gospel of Mark.* New Century Bible Commentary. Grand Rapids: Eerdmans, 1976.
Aristotle. *Nicomachean Ethics.* In *Masterworks of Philosophy: Digests of 11 Great Classics*, edited by S. E. Frost Jr., 123–68. Garden City, NY: Doubleday, 1946.
Armstrong, Lance. "Oprah and Lance Armstrong: The Worldwide Exclusive, Part 2." By Oprah Winfrey. *Oprah's Next Chapter*, January 18, 2013, http://www.oprah.com/own_tv/onc/lance-armstrong-one.html.
Armstrong, Lance, and Sally Jenkins. *It's Not About the Bike: My Journey Back to Life.* New York: Putnam, 2000.
Athanasius, Saint. *On the Incarnation.* Translated and edited by a religious of C.S.M.V. with introduction by C. S. Lewis. Crestwood, NY: Saint Vladimir's Seminary, 1996.
Augustine, Saint. *The City of God.* Translated by John Healey. Ancient and Modern Library of Theological Literature 2. Edinburgh: John Grant, 1909.
———. *Confessions.* Edited and translated by Albert C. Outler. Philadelphia: Westminster, 1955.
Baillie, Donald M. *God Was in Christ: An Essay on Incarnation and Atonement.* New York: Scribner, 1948.
Barbour, Julian. *The End of Time: The Next Revolution in Physics.* Oxford: Oxford University Press, 1999.
Bellah, Robert N., et al. *Habits of the Heart: Individualism and Commitment in American Life.* New York: Harper & Row, 1985.
Bellow, Saul. *Mr. Sammler's Planet.* Greenwich, CT: Fawcett, 1969.
Bethge, Eberhard. *Dietrich Bonhoeffer: Man of Vision, Man of Courage.* Translated by Eric Mosbacher et al. New York: Harper & Row, 1970.
Bok, Edward. *The Americanization of Edward Bok: The Autobiography of a Dutch Boy Fifty Years After.* New York: Scribner's, 1920.
Bonhoeffer, Dietrich. *The Cost of Discipleship.* Translated by Reginald H. Fuller. New York: Macmillan, 1963.
———. *Letters and Papers from Prison.* Translated by Reginald H. Fuller. London: SCM, 1953.
———. *Life Together.* Translated by John W. Doberstein. New York: Harper & Row, 1954.

Bibliography

———. *A Testament to Freedom: The Essential Writings of Dietrich Bonhoeffer.* Edited by Geffrey B. Kelly and F. Burton Nelson. San Francisco: HarperSanFrancisco, 1990.

Bonino, José Míguez. "'The Poor Will Always Be with You': Can Wesley Help Us Discover How Best to Serve 'Our Poor' Today?" In *The Poor and the People Called Methodists, 1729–1999*, edited by Richard P. Heitzenrater, 181–94. Nashville: Kingswood, 2002.

Bosley, Harold A. *He Spoke to Them in Parables.* New York: Harper & Row, 1963.

Branch, Taylor. *At Canaan's Edge: America in the King Years, 1965–1968.* Vol. 3. New York: Simon & Schuster, 2006.

———. *Parting the Waters: America in the King Years, 1954–1963.* Vol. 1. New York: Simon & Schuster, 1988.

———. *Pillar of Fire: America in the King Years, 1963–65.* Vol. 2. New York: Simon & Schuster, 1998.

Brooks, David. "Obama, Gospel and Verse." *New York Times.* April 26, 2007. http://www.nytimes.com/2007/04/26/opinion/26brooks.html?_r=1&

Brown, Raymond Edward. *The Death of the Messiah: From Gethsemane to the Grave; A Commentary on the Passion Narratives in the Four Gospels.* Vol. 1, Anchor Bible Reference Library. New York: Doubleday, 1994.

———. *An Introduction to the New Testament.* Anchor Bible Reference Library. New York: Doubleday, 1997.

Brown, Robert McAfee. "Easter: The Demand and the Promise." *Christianity and Crisis* 46 (1986) 75–76.

Bruner, Frederick Dale. *Matthew: A Commentary.* Vol. 2, *The Churchbook, Matthew 13–28.* Dallas: Word, 1990.

Buber, Martin. *Tales of Angels, Spirits and Demons.* Translated by David Antin and Jerome Rothenberg. New York: Hawk's Well, 1958.

Buechner, Frederick. *The Magnificent Defeat.* New York: Seabury, 1966.

———. *Wishful Thinking.* New York: Harper & Row, 1973.

Bultmann, Rudolf. *Theology of the New Testament.* Vol. 1. Translated by Kendrick Grobel. New York: Scribner's, 1951.

Buttrick, George A. *Christ and History.* New York: Abingdon, 1963.

———. *The Parables of Jesus.* Grand Rapids: Baker, 1973.

Carney, Thomas F. *The Shape of the Past: Models and Antiquity.* Lawrence, KS: Coronado, 1975.

Catholic Church. *Catechism of the Catholic Church.* New York: Doubleday, 1995.

Cavanaugh, William T. *Torture and Eucharist: Theology, Politics, and the Body of Christ.* Oxford: Blackwell, 1989.

Charlesworth, J. H. *Jesus within Judaism: New Light from Exciting Archaeological Discoveries.* Garden City, NY: Doubleday, 1988.

Cicero, Marcus Tullius. *De Officiis.* Translated by Walter Miller. New York: Heinemann, 1928.

Cohan, William D. *House of Cards: A Tale of Hubris and Wretched Excess on Wall Street.* New York: Doubleday, 2009.

Commins, Gary. "Woody Allen's Theological Imagination." *Theology Today* 44 (1987) 235–49.

Cosby, Gordon N. *Handbook for Mission Groups.* Washington, DC: Church of the Saviour, 1987.

Coxe, Cleveland A. "O Where Are Kings and Empires Now." In *The Methodist Hymnal: Official Hymnal of the Methodist Church*, 308. Nashville: United Methodist Publishing, 1966.

Crossan, John Dominic. *The Historical Jesus: The Life of a Mediterranean Jewish Peasant*. San Francisco: HarperSanFrancisco, 1991.

Cullmann, Oscar. *Christ and Time: The Primitive Christian Conception of Time and History*. Translated by Floyd Vivian Filson. Philadelphia: Westminster, 1964.

Cusa, Nicholas of. *On Learned Ignorance*. Edited by Paul Wilpert and Hans G. Senger. Minneapolis: Banning, 1981.

Davis, Philip J., and Reuben Hersh. *The Mathematical Experience*. Boston: Houghton Mifflin, 1981.

Dawn, Marva J. *Keeping the Sabbath Wholly: Ceasing, Resting, Embracing, Feasting*. Grand Rapids: Eerdmans, 1989.

———. *A Royal "Waste" of Time: The Splendor of Worshipping God and Being Church for the World*. Grand Rapids: Eerdmans, 1999.

———. *The Sense of the Call: A Sabbath Way of Life for Those Who Serve God, the Church, and the World*. Grand Rapids: Eerdmans, 2006.

———. *Unfettered Hope: A Call to Faithful Living in an Affluent Society*. Louisville: Westminster John Knox, 2003.

de Caussade, Père Jean-Pierre. *The Sacrament of the Present Moment*. Translated by Kitty Muggeridge, with an introduction by Richard J. Foster. San Francisco: Harper & Row, 1982.

DeVries, Peter. *The Blood of the Lamb*. Middlesex, UK: Penguin, 1961.

Dias, Elizabeth. "The Latino Reformation." *Time* 181, April 15, 2013, http://content.time.com/time/subscriber/article/0,33009,2140207-1,00.html.

Dickinson, Emily. "Because I Could Not Stop for Death." In *The Complete Works of Emily Dickinson*, edited by Thomas H. Johnson, 350. Boston: Little, Brown, 1960.

Dickson, Harley. *The Real Miracle*. Franklin, TN: Providence House, 2000.

Dostoevsky, Fyodor. "The Dream of a Ridiculous Man." In *Great Russian Stories*, edited by Isai Kamen, 135–55. New York: Random House, 1959.

Ellis, Joseph J. *American Sphinx: The Character of Thomas Jefferson*. New York: Vintage, 1996.

Elmore, Carl Hopkins. *The Inexhaustible Christ*. New York: Harper, 1935.

Englebert, Omer. *Saint Francis of Assisi: A Biography*. 2nd ed. Translated by Eve Marie Cooper. Ann Arbor, MI: Servant, 1979.

Faulkner, William. *Requiem for a Nun*. New York: Random House, 1975.

———. *The Sound and the Fury*. New York: Random House, 1946.

Faust, Drew Gilpin. *This Republic of Suffering: Death and the American Civil War*. New York: Knopf, 2008.

Fitzmyer, Joseph A. *The Gospel According to Luke, Chapters 1–9*. Anchor Bible 28. Garden City, NY: Doubleday, 1981.

———. *The Gospel According to Luke, Chapters 10–24*. Anchor Bible 28A. Garden City, NY: Doubleday, 1985.

Ford, Michael. *Wounded Prophet: A Portrait of Henri J. M. Nouwen*. New York: Doubleday, 1999.

Fox, Robin Lane. *Pagans and Christians*. New York: Knopf, 1989.

Gerstenberger, Erhard S., and Wolfgang Schrage. *Suffering*. Translated by John E. Steely. Nashville: Abingdon, 1980.

Bibliography

Gilson, Dave, and Carolyn Perot. "It's the Inequality, Stupid." *Mother Jones*, March/April, 2011, http://www.motherjones.com/politics/2011/02/income-inequality-in-america-chart-graph.

Godwin, Gail. *Evensong*. New York: Ballantine, 1999.

———. *Father Melancholy's Daughter*. New York: Avon, 1991.

Goetz, Phillip W., et al, editors. "Heraclitus." In vol. 5 of *The New Encyclopedia Britannica*, 860. 15th ed. Chicago: Encyclopaedia Britannica, 1988.

———. "The History of Mathematics." In vol. 23 of *The New Encyclopedia Britannica Macropaedia: Knowledge in Depth*, 603–633. 15th ed. Chicago: Encyclopaedia Britannica, 1988.

Goldstein, Rebecca. *Incompleteness: The Proof and Paradox of Kurt Gödel*. New York: Norton, 2005.

Gomes, Peter J. *Sermons: Biblical Wisdom for Daily Living*. New York: William Morrow, 1998.

Grant, Michael. *Constantine the Great: The Man and His Times*. New York: Scribner, 1993.

Gray, Thomas. "Elegy Written in a Country Churchyard." In *From Beowulf to Modern British Writers*, edited by John Ball, 543–44. New York: Odyssey, 1956.

Greenburg, Moshe, et al., editors. *The Writings: Kethubim; A New Translation of the Holy Scriptures According to the Masoretic Text*. Philadelphia: Jewish Publication Society, 1982.

Greenleaf, Robert K. *The Servant as Leader*. Westfield, IN: Robert K. Greenleaf Center for Servant Leadership, 2008.

Griffin, Miriam T. *Nero: The End of a Dynasty*. New Haven: Yale University Press, 1984.

Gutiérrez, Gustavo. *On Job: God-Talk and the Suffering of the Innocent*. Translated by Matthew J. O'Connell. Maryknoll, NY: Orbis, 1988.

Hall, Douglas John. "But Where Shall Wisdom Be Found?" Presentation given at the Reclaiming the Text Conference, Montreat, North Carolina, June 1, 2000.

———. *God and Human Suffering: An Exercise in the Theology of the Cross*. Minneapolis: Augsburg, 1986.

Hans, Daniel T. "Absence and Presence: A Good Friday Meditation," *Pulpit Digest* 74 (1994) 43–44.

Hatfield, Mark. *Between a Rock and a Hard Place*. Waco, TX: Word, 1976.

Hauerwas, Stanley. *Matthew*. Brazos Theological Commentary on the Bible 3. Grand Rapids: Brazos, 2006.

———. *Naming the Silence: God, Medicine, and the Problem of Suffering*. Grand Rapids: Eerdmans, 1990.

———. *The Peaceable Kingdom: A Primer in Christians Ethics*. Notre Dame: University of Notre Dame Press, 1983.

———. *War and the American Difference: Theological Reflections on Violence and National Identity*. Grand Rapids: Baker, 2011.

"Hearing before the Subcommittee on Africa of the Committee on Foreign Affairs, House of Representatives, 98th Congress." Transcript of 2nd session, December 4, 1984. Washington, DC: US Government Printing Office, 1985.

Heitzenrater, Richard P. *Wesley and the People Called Methodists*. Nashville: Abingdon, 1995.

Heschel, Abraham J. *The Prophets*. Vol. 2, Perennial Classics. New York: Harper Torchbooks, 1962.

Hilderman, Walter, III. *They Went Into the Fight Cheering: Confederate Conscription in North Carolina*. Boone, NC: Parkway, 2005.

Hochhuth, Rolf. *The Deputy*. New York: Grove, 1964.
Holmes, Robert L. "A Time for War?" *Christianity Today* 67, September 1, 2001, http://www.christianitytoday.com/ct/2001/septemberweb-only/9-17-55.0.html?paging=off.
Howe, Julia Ward. "The Battle Hymn of the Republic." In *The United Methodist Hymnal*, 717. Nashville: United Methodist Publishing, 1989.
Huddleston, Trevor. *Naught for Your Comfort*. Garden City, NY: Doubleday, 1956.
Hunter, Archibald. *Interpreting the Parables*. Philadelphia: Westminster, 1960.
Isaacson, Walter. *Einstein: His Life and Universe*. New York: Simon & Schuster, 2007.
Jacobsen, Jens Peter. *Niels Lyhne*. Translated by Tiina Nunnally. New York: Penguin, 2006.
Jefferson, Thomas. *Notes on the State of Virginia*. Edited by William H. Peden. Chapel Hill: University of North Carolina Press, 1954.
Jenkins, Philip. *The New Faces of Christianity: Believing the Bible in the Global South*. Oxford: Oxford University Press, 2006.
Jennings, Theodore W., Jr. *Good News to the Poor: John Wesley's Evangelical Economics*. Nashville: Abingdon, 1990.
Jones, Laurie Beth. *Jesus CEO: Using Ancient Wisdom for Visionary Leadership*. New York: Hyperion, 1995.
Kaan, "For the Healing of the Nations." In *The United Methodist Hymnal*, 428. Nashville: United Methodist Publishing, 1989.
Kierkegaard, Søren. *Parables of Kierkegaard*. Edited by Thomas C. Oden. Princeton: Princeton University Press, 1978.
King, Martin Luther, Jr. *Strength to Love*. New York: Harper & Row, 1963.
———. *Why We Can't Wait*. New York: Signet, 1963.
Kitamori, Kazōh. *Theology of the Pain of God*. Richmond: John Knox, 1965.
Knowles, Frederick Lawrence. "To Jesus the Nazarene." *Century Magazine* 71, December 1905, 186.
Krugman, Paul. *The Conscience of a Liberal*. New York: Norton, 2007.
Küng, Hans. *On Being a Christian*. Translated by Edward Quinn. Garden City, NY: Doubleday, 1976.
Kushner, Harold S. *When Bad Things Happen to Good People*. New York: Avon, 1983.
Latourette, Kenneth Scott. *A History of Christianity*. Vol. 1, *Beginnings to 1500*. New York: Harper & Row, 1975.
Lawrence, D. H. *Apocalypse*. London: Martin Secker, 1932.
Lee, Dallas. *The Cotton Patch Evidence: The Story of Clarence Jordan and the Koinonia Farm Experiment*. New York: Harper & Row, 1971.
Lincoln, Abraham. "The Gettysburg Address." In *A Documentary History of the United States*, edited by Richard D. Heffner, 151–52. Mentor Book 72. New York: New American Library, 1952.
Long, Thomas G. *Matthew*. Westminster Bible Companion. Louisville: Westminster John Knox, 1997.
Luccock, Halford E. *Unfinished Business: Short Diversions on Religious Themes*. New York: Harper, 1956.
Luther, Martin. "Sermon for the Early Christmas Service; Luke 2:15–20 (1521–1522)." Vol. 52, *Luther's Works: Sermons II*, edited by Helmut T. Lehmann and Hans J. Hillerbrand. Philadelphia: Fortress, 1974.
MacLeish, Archibald. *JB: A Play in Verse*. Boston: Houghton Mifflin, 1956.
Macquarrie, John. *Principles of Christian Theology*. New York: Scribner, 1966.

Bibliography

Mann, Thomas, and Norman Ornstein. *It's Even Worse Than It Looks*. New York: Basic Books, 2012.

Marney, Carlyle. *The Suffering Servant: A Holy Week Exposition of Isaiah 52:13—58:12*. New York: Abingdon, 1965.

McCullough, Stewart W. "Exegesis of Psalms 101–119." In *The Interpreter's Bible*, edited by Nolan B. Harmon, 595. The Book of Psalms and the Book of Proverbs 4. Nashville: Abingdon, 1955.

McNeal, Reggie. *Missional Renaissance: Changing the Scorecard for the Church*. San Francisco: Jossey-Bass, 2009.

Meier, John P. *A Marginal Jew: Rethinking the Historical Jesus*. Vol. 1, *The Roots of the Problem and the Person*. Anchor Bible Reference Library. New York: Doubleday, 1991.

Menotti, Gian Carlo, et al. *Amahl and the Night Visitors: Opera in One Act*, orchestral score. New York: G. Schirmer, 1997.

Merton, Thomas. *The Sign of Jonas*. New York: Harcourt, Brace, 1953.

Metaxas, Eric. *Amazing Grace: William Wilberforce and the Heroic Campaign to End Slavery*. New York: HarperSanFrancisco, 2007.

———. *Bonhoeffer: Pastor, Martyr, Prophet, Spy: A Righteous Gentile Versus the Third Reich*. Nashville: Thomas Nelson, 2010.

Michalson, Carl. *Faith for Personal Crises*. New York: Scribner's, 1958.

Miller, Arthur. *Death of a Salesman*. New York: Viking, 1949.

Moise, Anutza. *A Ransom for Wurmbrand*. Grand Rapids: Zondervan, 1972.

Moltmann, Jürgen. *The Church in the Power of the Spirit: A Contribution to Messianic Ecclesiology*. Translated by Margaret Kohl. New York: Harper & Row, 1975.

———. *The Coming of God: Christian Eschatology*. Translated by Margaret Kohl. Minneapolis: Fortress, 1996.

———. *The Crucified God: The Cross of Christ as the Foundation and Criticism of Christian Theology*. Translated by R. A. Wilson and John Bowden. London: SCM, 1973.

———. *The Future of Creation: Collected Essays*. Translated by Margaret Kohl. Philadelphia: Fortress, 1979.

———. *God in Creation: A New Theology of Creation and the Spirit of God*. Translated by Margaret Kohl. Gifford Lectures, 1984–85. San Francisco: Harper & Row, 1985.

———. *Jesus Christ for Today's World*. Translated by Margaret Kohl. Minneapolis: Fortress, 1994.

———. *Sun of Righteousness, Arise! God's Future for Humanity and the Earth*. Translated by Margaret Kohl. Minneapolis: Fortress, 2010.

———. *The Way of Jesus Christ: Christology in Messianic Dimensions*. Translated by Margaret Kohl. San Francisco: HarperSanFrancisco, 1990.

Morrison, James Dalton, editor. *Masterpieces of Religious Verse*. New York: Harper & Row, 1948.

Muggeridge, Malcolm. *Chronicles of Wasted Time*. 2 vols. New York: William Morrow, 1973–74.

———. *Confessions of a Twentieth-Century Pilgrim*. Vol. 3. San Francisco: Harper & Row, 1988.

———. *Something Beautiful for God: Mother Teresa of Calcutta*. New York: Ballantine, 1971.

Myers, David G. *The American Paradox: Spiritual Hunger in an Age of Plenty*. New Haven: Yale University Press, 2000.

Niebuhr, H. Richard. *Resurrection and Historical Reason: A Study of Theological Method*. New York: Scribner, 1957.

Niebuhr, Reinhold. *The Nature and Destiny of Man: A Christian Interpretation*. Vol. 1, *Human Nature*. Gifford Lectures, 1939. New York: Scribner, 1941.

Nouwen, Henri J. M. *The Wounded Healer: Ministry in Contemporary Society*. Garden City, NY: Doubleday, 1972.

Nouwen, Henri J. M., Michael J. Christensen, and Rebecca J. Laird. *Spiritual Direction: Wisdom for the Long Walk of Faith*. San Francisco: HarperSanFrancisco, 2006.

Oates, Wayne R. *When Religion Gets Sick*. Philadelphia: Westminster, 1970.

O'Connor, Elizabeth. *Call to Commitment: The Story of the Church of the Saviour, Washington, DC*. New York: Harper & Row, 1963.

———. *Eighth Day of Creation: Gifts and Creativity*. Waco, TX: Word, 1971.

Palmer, Parker. *The Active Life: A Spirituality of Work, Creativity, and Caring*. San Francisco: Harper & Row, 1990.

———. *The Promise of Paradox: A Celebration of Contradictions in the Christian Life*. 3rd ed. San Francisco: Jossey-Bass, 2008.

Pascal, Blaise. "Pensées No. 553." In *Pascal*, edited by Robert Maynard Hutchins et al., translated by W. F. Trotter, 268. Great Books of the Western World 33. Chicago: Encyclopaedia Britannica, 1952.

Peck, M. Scott. *The Road Less Traveled: A New Psychology of Love, Traditional Values, and Spiritual Growth*. New York: Touchstone, 1978.

Pelikan, Jaroslav Jan. *The Melody of Theology: A Philosophical Dictionary*. Cambridge, Harvard University Press, 1988.

———. *Vindication of Tradition*. Jefferson Lecture in the Humanities, 1983. New Haven: Yale University Press, 1986.

Peterson, Eugene H. *The Message: The Bible in Contemporary Language*. Colorado Springs, Colorado: NavPress, 2002.

Popper, Karl R. *Unended Quest: An Intellectual Autobiography*. LaSalle, IL: Open Court, 1990.

Porter, Katherine Ann. *Ship of Fools*. Boston: Little, Brown, 1962.

Posnanski, Joe. *Paterno*. New York: Simon & Schuster, 2012.

Presbyterian Church. "Prayer 734: During a National Crisis." In *Book of Common Worship*, 818. Louisville: Westminster John Knox, 1993.

Price, Reynolds. *Clear Pictures: First Loves, First Guides*. New York: Atheneum, 1989.

Richardson, Alan, and John Bowden, editors. *The Westminster Dictionary of Christian Theology*. Philadelphia: Westminster, 1983.

Rieff, Philip. *The Triumph of the Therapeutic: Uses of Faith after Freud*. London: Chatto & Windus, 1966.

Rifkin, Jeremy. *Time Wars: The Primary Conflict in Human History*. New York: Simon & Schuster, 1989.

Robson, Michael J. P. *Saint Francis of Assisi: The Legend and the Life*. London: Geoffrey Chapman, 1997.

Rohde, David. *Endgame: The Betrayal and Fall of Srebrenica, Europe's Worst Massacre Since World War II*. New York: Farrar, Straus, & Giroux, 1997.

Schiller, Bradley R. *The Economy Today*. 9th ed. Boston: McGraw-Hill, 2003.

Schlesinger, Arthur M., Jr. *The Imperial Presidency*. Boston: Houghton Mifflin, 1973.

Bibliography

Shakespeare, William. *The Complete Works*. With an introduction by William Allan Neilson and a "Life of Shakespeare" by James Orchard Halliwell-Phillipps. New York: Collier, 1925.

Sheldon, Charles M. *In His Steps: What Would Jesus Do?* Library of American Civilization 14976. New York: Smithmark, 1992.

Shelley, Percy Bysshe. "Ozymandias." In *From Beowulf to Modern British Writers*, edited by John Ball, 802. New York: Odyssey, 1956.

Sims, Bennett J. *Servanthood: Leadership for the Third Millennium*. Cambridge, MA: Cowley, 1997.

Smeeding, Timothy M. "Public Policy, Economic Inequality, and Poverty: The United States in Comparative Perspective." *Social Science Quarterly* 86 (2005) 955–83.

Sockman, Ralph W. *The Paradoxes of Jesus*. Nashville: Abingdon, 1936.

Söelle, Dorothee. *Suffering*. Philadelphia: Fortress, 1975.

Solomon, Scott. "Four Children Killed in Fire West of Troy." *Greensboro Daily News*, March 1, 1994, A-1.

Stengel, Richard. "A *Time* Gala and an Exclusive." *Time* 179, May 7, 2012, http://content.time.com/time/magazine/article/0,9171,2113158,00.html.

Storey, Peter John. *With God in the Crucible: Preaching Costly Discipleship*. Nashville: Abingdon, 2002.

Studdert-Kennedy, G. A. "My Peace I Give Unto You." In *Masterpieces of Religious Verse*, edited by James Dalton Morrison, 441. New York: Harper & Row, Publishers, 1948.

Tennyson, Alfred. "In Memoriam A. H. H." In *The Works of Alfred Lord Tennyson*, edited with memoir by Hallam Tennyson, 242. New York: Macmillan, 1920.

Tillich, Paul. *The Eternal Now*. New York: Scribner, 1963.

Trueblood, Elton. *The Company of the Committed*. New York: Harper & Row, 1961.

United Methodist Church. *The Book of Discipline of the United Methodist Church, 2012*. Nashville: United Methodist Publishing, 2012.

Waite, Terry. *Taken on Trust*. London: Harcourt, Brace, 1993.

Weatherhead, A. Kingsley. *Leslie Weatherhead: A Personal Portrait*. Nashville: Abingdon, 1975.

Weigel, George. *The Truth of Catholicism: Inside the Essential Teachings and Controversies of the Church Today*. New York: HarperCollins, 2002.

Weiser, Artur. *The Psalms: A Commentary*. Philadelphia: Westminster, 1962.

Wells, Samuel. *Improvisation: The Drama of Christian Ethics*. Grand Rapids: Brazos, 2004.

Wesley, Charles. "Love Divine, All Loves Excelling." In *Hymns for Those That Seek and Those That Have Redemption in the Blood of Jesus Christ*, edited by William Strahan, 12. London: Strahan, 1747.

Wesley, John. *The Works of the Reverend John Wesley, A. M.* Edited by John Emory. 7 vols. New York: J. Emory & B. Waugh, 1831.

West, Morris L. *The Summer of the Red Wolf*. New York: Simon & Schuster, 1972.

Wiesel, Elie. *Night*. Translated by Stella Rodway. New York: Hill & Wang, 1961.

———. *Zalmen, or the Madness of God*. Translated by Nathan Edelman. New York: Simon & Schuster, 1974.

Wigger, John H. *American Saint: Francis Asbury and the Methodists*. Oxford: Oxford University Press, 2009.

Williams, Rowan. *Writing in the Dust: After September 11*. Grand Rapids: Eerdmans, 2002.

Wolfe, Tom. *The Bonfire of the Vanities*. New York: Farrar, Straus, & Giroux, 1987.

Wordsworth, William. "Ode: Intimations of Immortality from Recollections of Early Childhood." In *From Beowulf to Modern British Writers*, edited by John Ball, 704. New York: Odyssey, 1956.

Wright, N. T. *After You Believe: Why Christian Character Matters*. New York: HarperOne, 2010.

———. *Jesus and the Victory of God*. Minneapolis: Fortress, 1996.

———. *Justification: God's Plan and Paul's Vision*. Downers Grove, IL: InterVarsity, 2009.

———. *The New Testament and the People of God*. Minneapolis: Fortress, 1992.

———. *The Resurrection of the Son of God*. Minneapolis: Fortress, 2003.

———. *Surprised by Hope: Rethinking Heaven, the Resurrection, and the Mission of the Church*. New York: HarperOne, 2008.

Yoder, John Howard. *Nevertheless: The Varieties and Shortcomings of Religious Pacifism*. Scottdale, PA: Herald, 1992.

Subject Index

a priori reasoning, 78
Abdullah bin Abdulaziz (King of Saudi Arabia), 144
Abdullah II (King of Jordan), 145
Abernethy Memorial Methodist, Asheville, North Carolina, 236
Abraham, 18, 57
Abyssinian Baptist Church, Harlem, New York, 53, 208, 254
Achaemenid dynasty, 241
The Acts of Pilate (Coptic Church), 149
Acts of the Apostles, 218, 250, 261
Adam (from Book of Genesis), 3, 113
adulteress woman being stoned, 34
Afghanistan war, 14
Africa, Christian population in, xiii, 90, 278
agape, xi
Agosto, Efrain, 108
Ahab (King of Israel), 248
AIDS Action organization, 19
aioniou, 177
Akiba (Rabbi), 88
All Rivers Run to the Sea (Wiesel), 24
All Saints Day services, 163
All Thing Considered (radio show), 213
Allen, Woody, 60, 70
Allred, Jeannette, 235
aloneness, 204–212
Amahl and the Night Visitors (Menotti), 154
Ambrose, Charles, 111
Amnesty International, 93
Amos (prophet), 176–177
Anabaptists, 138
anakrisis, 150
anawim, 88, 89
Anchor Bible Commentary (Ford), 62
And the Sea Is Never Full (Wiesel), 24
Anderson, Bernhard, 37
Anderson, Hugh, 170
angel, parable on alleviating suffering, 101–102
angel of death, 49
anger, 262

Annas (father-in-law of Caiaphas), 147
Antigone (Sophocles), 77
Antioch community, 8–87
Antipas. *See* Herod Antipas
apartheid, 58, 64–65
apatheia, 46
Apocalypse, 60–63, 113
apostate church, 191–193
apostles
 choosing of, 47, 259–260
 wealth of, 197–198
 See also specific apostles by name
Appalachian State University, 110n15
Appian Way, 61, 145
Arab Spring (2011), 144, 216
Archelaus, 149, 157–158
Aristotle, 134, 134n3
Arius, 116, 136, 275
Ark of the covenant, 196
Armstrong, Lance, 232
arnasastho, 233
Arnett, Adam, 118
Asbury, Francis, 117, 172
Ascending Ladder of Wisdom, 14
Ash Wednesday services, 162
Asia, Christian population in, xiii, 278
al-Assad, Bashar, 144
Athanasius (Bishop of Alexandria), 53, 86, 116, 275
Augustine (Bishop of Hippo), 137, 173
Augustus (Roman Emperor), 150, 157, 272
Auschwitz (concentration camp), 24–25, 55
ayt, 175

Babylonian Empire, 31, 44–45, 74, 190
bad news
 biblical narratives, 28–31
 Bivens' story, 33–34
 Jelly's story, 32
 Thompson's story, 29–30
 Weatherhead's story, 32–33
 Williams' story, 34–35

Subject Index

Baille, D. M., 146
Baillie, Donald M., xi
Bar Kokhba, 88
Barabbas, 148
Barbour, Julian, 183
Barman Declaration, 152
Barth, Karl, 139, 277
Beatitudes, 85–103, 178, 197, 244–245
Beaver, Doris, 237
Bellah, Robert, 252
Bellow, Saul, 213–214
Benjamin (son of Rachel), 71
Bergoglio, Jorge Mario, 117
Best, Payne, 171
Bethge, Eberhard, 171, 207
Between a Rock and a Hard Place (Hatfield), 108
biblical paradox, 16, 28–31
birth trauma, 204
Bivens, Ben, 33–34
Bivens, Beth, 33–34
Bivens, Eva, 33–34
The Blood of the Lamb (DeVries), 120
Bohr, Niels, x
Bok, Edward, 266
The Bonfire of the Vanities (Wolfe), 101
Bonhoeffer, Dietrich
    cheap grace and, 39
    on earthly possessions, 93
    Life Together treatise, 207–209
    on Nazi despotism, 89
    in New York City, 53–54, 254
    wedding sermon, 237
    while in prison, 46, 230
Bonhoeffer, Karl, 53
"The Book of His Glory" (Gospel of John), 105
"The Book of Signs" (Dodd), 105
Boone United Methodist Church, Boone, North Carolina, 253, 261n5, 266–267
Borg, Marcus, 167, 183, 183n31
Bosley, Harold, 11
Bosnian Civil War, 246–247
Botha, P. W., 107
Branch, Taylor, 18, 219
Brant, Sebastian, 192–193
Bread for the World (peace-advocacy agency), 93
Brethren in Christ (faith community), 138
British monarchy, 144
Britt, Robin, 210
Broadway Danny Rose (movie), 70
Brooks, David, 139
Brooks, Mel, 144
Brown, Raymond, 113, 150
Brown, Robert McAfee, 171
Bruner, Frederick, 244

Buber, Martin, 101
Buechner, Frederick, 247
Bultmann, Rudolf, 166–167, 183
Bush Administration (George H. W.), 152
Buttrick, George, 8, 216

Caiaphas, Joseph, 15, 147
Caligula (Roman Emperor), 150
Call to Commitment (O'Connor), 109
Calvin, John, 93, 124–125
canticles, 113–114
Cap-Haitien, Haiti (mission), 4–5, 194–195
capitalism, 200
Carl, David, 279
Carney, Thomas, 6
Carroll, Sean, 183
Carter, Ken, 195, 258
Carter, Pam, 195, 256
Carter, Ruth, 268
Cavanaugh, William, 128–129
celestial constellations, 74
Chacour, Elias, 153
Chaplin, Charlie, 70
Charlesworth, James H., 89n5, 197
cheap grace, 39
Chi Rho, 136, 137
children, Jesus' treatment of, 98–99
China
    Christian population in, xiii, 90, 278
    Christian witness story, 18
Christ and Culture (Niebuhr), 167
Christ House (medical clinic for the homeless), 110
Christ United Methodist Church, Greensboro, North Carolina, 4, 19, 181, 234, 237, 255–256, 261n5, 268–270
ChristCare groups, 211
Christian affirmation, 12–19
Christian churches, Nouwen's thesis and, 47–48
Christianity, worldwide population, xiii
Christmas, date set for, 137
Christology, overview, x–xi
Chronicles of Wasted Time (Muggeridge), 9
chronos, 179
church
    in apostate state, 191–193
    authentic mission of, 193–194
    as extension of incarnation, 188–195
    history of, 213–222
    mainstream churches, xiv
    meaning of, 189, 193, 194
    Nouwen's thesis on, 47–48
    ship as symbol of, 192–193
    wounded healers and, 48
    See also specific churches by name

Church of Ecce Homo, Jerusalem, 147
Church of the Savior, Washington, DC., 109–110, 139, 209–210
Church World Service, 110
Chuza (Herod's steward), 98
Cicero, 134, 134n4
The City of God (Augustine), 137–138
City Temple, London, England, 32
Civil War
  Bosnia, 246–247
  U.S., 159–161
Clinton, Hillary, 105
Clodfelter, Gerald, 263–264
Clodfelter, Marian, 263–264
Cochabamba, Bolivia (mission), 4–5
Cohan, William D., 107
Columbia Road Health Services, 110
Columbus, Christopher, 217
Common Cause, 92–93
communal congregations, 218–220
communal life, 208–209
community, 207–212
Cone, James, 39
Confessions (Augustine), 173
Confessions of a Twentieth Century Pilgrim (Muggeridge), 245
confirmation class, 211
conscientious objectors, 135
Constantine (Emperor), 136–137
Convent of the Sisters of Zion, 147
Coptic Church, 149
Cosby, Gordon, 109–110, 209–210, 269
Cosby, Mary, 209–210
Council of Bishops, 142
Council of Nicaea (A.D. 325), 52, 136, 274–276
Council of Providence United Methodist Church, 206
covenant
  context of, 4, 77–78
  fulfillment of, 56
  love, xi, 55
  worship and, 77–78
Covenant United Methodist Church, Charlotte, North Carolina, 94
Cox, Harvey, 261
Coxe, Cleveland, 154
creatio ex nihilo, 167
Crossan, John Dominic, 15
The Crucified God (Moltmann), 63
crucifixion, as ultimate paradoxical event, 100
  See also Passion Narrative
Cullmann, Oscar, 214–215
Cushman, Robert, 221
Cyrus (King of Persia), 31
Cyrus II (King of Persia), 241

Dachau (concentration camp), 243, 263
Dante, 10
Das Narrenschiff (Brant), 192
Dawn, Marva J., 250–253
Day, Dorothy, 141
Dayspring Retreat Center, Damascus, Maryland, 269
de Caussade, Pere Jean-Pierre, 127
de Klerk, F. W., 58
death, 49, 121–122, 155–162
Death of a Salesman (Miller), 95
Decalogue of Moses, 21, 37, 196
The Deputy (play), 55
Deuteronomic theology, 21
DeVries, Peter, 120
di Bernardone, Giovanni Francesco, 198
Diana (Princess of Wales), 104
Dias, Elizabeth, 278
Dickinson, Emily, 162
Dickson, Harley, 194
Didache, 124
Dinah, Leah's son, 71
Disciple Bible program, 92, 180, 235, 266
discipleship, 102
Divine presence, 20–27, 190
Dixon, Sam, 256
Dixon, Simon, 132
Docetic theology, 126
Dodd, C. H., 107
Dostoevsky, Fyodor, 60, 96
The Dream of a Ridiculous Man (Dostoevsky), 96
Dunamis, 210
Dürer, Albrecht, 192

earth, stewardship of, 77
earthquake, Haiti (2010), 256
Eastern Orthodox tradition, 171
economics, 196–203
ecumenism, 240
Edict of King Cyrus, 176
Edict of Milan, 136
The Eighth Day of Creation, (O'Connor), 109
Einstein, Albert, 74, 78, 78–79n14, 80, 182
El Salvador, military regime in, 142
"Elegy Written in a Country Churchyard" (Gray), 26
The Elephant Man (play), 45
Elijah, 122, 190–191, 248
Elizabeth (mother of John the Baptizer), 96
Emmaus, 101, 265
The End of Time (Barbour), 183
Enron, 14, 99
Equippers organization, 211
Erasmus, 17

Subject Index

Espinal, Luís, 65
eternal now, 180, 258
Eucharist, 102, 124, 128–129, 180–181
Europe, Christian population in, xiii, 90, 93, 200, 234
    See also Nazi Holocaust
Eusebius (Bishop), 136
evangelical counsels, 141
Evensong (Godwin), 52, 227
evil, xiii, 4, 31n2, 46, 54
    See also apartheid; Nazi Holocaust
Ezekiel, accountability and, 21

Facebook, 204
failure, resilience and, 95–103
fairness, fallacies of, 3–10
The Fantastics (play), 50–51
Father Melancholy's Daughter (Godwin), 26–27, 52, 227, 235
Faulkner, William, 218
Faust, Drew Gilpin, 160, 161
fear
    and joy, as paradox, 40, 76, 91
    of a loving God, 36–51
    phobias as, 38
Fellowship of Reconciliation, 138
fig tree parables, 158–159, 161
First United Methodist Church, Waynesville, North Carolina, 257, 261n5, 267–268
Ford, J. M., 62
Fortama, Riccardo, 55
Fosdick, Harry Emerson, 254
Fourth Gospel. *See* John, Gospel of
Francis (Pope), 117
Francis, of Assisi, 116–117, 198
Frazier, Bascom, 235
Fretheim, Terence, 68
From Eternity to Here (Carroll), 183
Fuller, Millard, 234
funerals, 258
Funk, Robert, 183

Galerius, 136
"the game of kings," 147
Gandhi, Mahatma, 107, 207, 246
The Gates Ajar (Phelps), 161
Gbowee, Leymah, 92–93
Gemeinsames Leben (Bonhoeffer), 208
General Rules of the United Societies, 199
General Theory of Relativity, 182
George III (King of England), 145
Gerstenberger, Erhard S., 123
Getty, J. Paul, 107
Gifford Lectures, 91n13
globalrichlist.com, 10

God
    as Father/Creator, x
    indwelling of, 125, 276–277
    love of, 25, 36–51
    mercy of, xi
    power of, 59–66
    presence of, 63
    Trinitarian nature of, x, 187, 272–279
    works for good, 30–31, 30–31n1
    wrath of, 39
    See also Holy Spirit; Jesus
God and Human Suffering (Hall), 63
God Was in Christ (Baillie), xi
Gödel, Kurt, 74, 76, 80, 174
Godwin, Gail, 26, 52, 227, 235
Gomes, Peter, 226
Gonxha Bojaxhiu, Agnes (Mother Teresa), 104
Good Shepherd United Methodist Church, Charlotte, North Carolina, 59
goodness without reward, 239–247
Goodrich, Robert E., Jr., 71
The Gospel of Saint Matthew (film), 228
grace
    communal life and, 208
    hesed as, 4
    mathematics of, 237
    paradoxical nature of, 205
    righteousness and, 39
Graner, Gordy, 107
Grant, Amy, 252
Grant, Michael, 137
Gray, Thomas, 26
Grecian thought regarding time, 178
greed, 93, 99, 107–108, 197
Greene, Nathanael, 132
Greenleaf, Robert, 107
Greensboro Urban Ministry, 139, 210
Greenspan, Alan, 14
grief, 171, 173–174, 187, 236
    See also suffering
Grove, Elizabeth, 255
Guilford Courthouse battle (1781), 132
Gutiérrez, Gustavo, 25

Habitat for Humanity, 234, 246–247
Haines, Harry, 194
Haiti
    earthquake (2010), 256
    missionary works, 4–5, 194–195, 271
Hale, Jeffrey, 267
Hale, Joe R., 267–268
Hale, Mary, 267–268
Haley, Alex, 217
Hall, Douglas John, 13, 14, 63
Hans, Daniel, 20

Subject Index

happiness, in biblical narrative, 3
Hardy, William, 132
hasidic parable on alleviating suffering, 101–102
Hatfield, Mark, 108
Hauerwas, Stanley, 44, 90, 91, 139–141, 160–161
healing, 43–51
Heidegger, Martin, 166
Helms, Jesse, 261
Hendricks, Abel, 64
Hendricks, Frieda, 64
Heraclitus, 173
heresies
    of Arius philosophy, 116
    of elimination of the concept of God's wrath, 39
    of Marcion philosophy, 40, 240
Herod Antipas, 15, 87, 96, 145, 148–151, 233
Herod the Great, 15, 149
Heschel, Abraham, 49
hesed, xi, 3–10
Hinshaw Memorial United Methodist Church, Greensboro, North Carolina, 50, 235, 251, 261n5, 264–265
Hitler, Adolph, 53–54, 207
Ho Chi Minh, 93
Hochhuth, Rolf, 55
Holy Communion. *See* Eucharist
Holy Spirit
    facets of, xi–xii
    Jesus' fulfillment of God's salvation, 114–119
    Luke's two-volume narratives and, 249
    redemptive actions of, 239–240
    resurrection and, 101
    transforming hearts, 197, 202
    works of, 259–271
    See also God; Jesus
homoiousios, 275
homoousios, 275
hope, xiii, 171, 175, 221, 226, 261
hospice care, 130–131
House of Cards (Cohan), 107
Howe, Julia Ward, 160
Howe, Samuel, 160
Hughes, Howard, 107
Hume, David, 78
hurricane Sandy (2012), 173
Hussein, Saddam, 152
Hutterites, 138
hymns, 113–114
    See also music in worship services

idolatry of a patriotism, 142
Ignatius (Bishop of Antioch), 86, 124
impatient living, 226–227
"In Defense of Creation" (Council of Bishops), 142
In His Steps (Sheldon), 95
In Praise of Folly (Erasmus), 17
incarnation, mystery of, 145–146, 178–179
incognito Christ, 245
incompleteness theorem, 78–79
indwelling of God, 125, 276–277
Inferno (Dante), 10
information, wisdom and, 13–14
Institute for Servant Leadership, 107
intercessory prayer, 50, 253–254, 256, 268
Irenaeus, 124
Isaac (son of Abraham), 18
Isaacson, Walter, 80
Israel (meaning of), 151
Issachar (Leah's son), 71
It's Even Worse Than It Looks (Mann and Ornstein), 108

Jackson Administration (Andrew), 217
Jacob, marriage to Leah and Rachel, 68–72
Jacobsen, Jens Peter, 7
James (brother or kinsman of Jesus), 224–227
JB: A Play in Verse (MacLeish), 23
Jefferson, Thomas, 3, 41
Jelly, Lillian, 32
Jenkins, Philip, xiii
Jennings, Ted, 200
Jeremiah (prophet), 21, 176
Jesus
    baptism of, 114
    Beatitudes, 85–103
    Divinity of, 113
    future is present, 173–184
    as a pacifist, 132–143
    resilient power of failure, 95–103
    sacramental suffering of, 120–131
    as servant leader, 104–112
    temptation of, 114, 133, 206
    times of solitude, 206
    washing disciples' feet, 106
    witness of adulteress woman, 103
    See also God; Holy Spirit
Jezebel (Queen of Israel), 248
Joanna (wife of Herod's steward Chuza), 98
Job, book of, 21–27, 241–243
Joel (prophet), 176
Johannine Prologue, 113, 123
John, Gospel of
    creation story, 168
    on Jesus as a servant leader, 105
    on Jesus' death, 156
    on Jesus' washing feet, 106

Subject Index

on mystery of incarnation, 145–149
obedient disciple, 233
on Passion Narrative, 148, 151
on resurrection, 165
on suffering, 123, 127–128
John of Patmos (Apocalypse writings), 60–63, 113
John the Baptizer (or John of the Wilderness), 96, 98, 121, 150, 178
Jonah, book of, 135
Jordan, Clarence Leonard, 218–220, 234
Jordan, Michael, 38
Joseph (of Arimathea), 100
Joseph (son of Rachel), 71
Josephus, 147, 157
Josiah (King of Judah), 21–22
Journey Inward (O'Connor), 109
Journey Outward (O'Connor), 109
joy and fear, as paradox, 40, 76, 91
Judah (Leah's son), 70
Judas, the Apostle, 105–106
judgment, 36, 56–57
just war, 137–139, 212
justice, 11, 24, 25
justification, 56–57
Justin Martyr, 124

Kaan, Fred, 257
kairos, 177, 179
kairotic, 91, 91n13, 126–127, 180, 251
Kantian ethics, 140
kenosis. *See* self-emptying
Kethubim, 28
Khalifa (president of United Arab Emirates), 144
khatsotsrah, 76
Khomeini (Ayatollah of Iran), 144
Kierkegaard, Sören, 115–116, 183–184, 250
King, Coretta Scott, 219
King, Martin Luther, Jr., 42, 140, 221, 228–229, 261, 262
King and Kingdom, paradoxical themes of, 147
King of England (George III), 145
King of France (Louis XIV), 144
King of Israel (Ahab), 248
King of Israel (Saul), 259
King of Israel (Solomon), 14
King of Jordan (Abdullah II), 145
King of Judea (Herod the Great), 149
King of Judea (Josiah), 21–22
King of Persia (Cyrus), 31
King of Saudi Arabia (Abdullah bin Abdulaziz), 144
kingship, 144–154
Kitamori, Kazōh, 44, 65

knowledge, wisdom and, 13–14
koinonia, 115
Koinonia Farm, Americus, Georgia, 218–220, 234
Kony, Joseph, 91
Krugman, Paul, 200
Küng, Hans, 274
Kushner, Harold S., 59

Laban (father of Leah and Rachel), 68–72
labarum, 137
laborers
  parable of, 5–8
  prodigal son, 8–9
  Sabbath day and, 196
Lacey, Creighton, 278
laity, role of, xii, xiv
Lake Junaluska Conference, 92–93, 181, 253, 265, 267
L'Arche Daybreak community, 118, 207
Latin America, Christian population in, 90, 278–279
Lawrence, D. H., 53
Lazareth, 99–100
Lazarus, 165
Leah (wife of Jacob), 68–72
Leaves from Shady Grove (newsletter), 264
Lehman Brothers, 99
Lehmann, Paul, 221
Levi (Leah's son), 70–71
Levi, tribe of, 56
Life Magazine, 142
Life of Constantine (Eusebius), 136
Life Together (Bonhoeffer), 207, 208
Lilly, Lillian, 236
Lincoln, Abraham, 160
Lincoln, Mary Todd, 161
Lincoln, Willie, 161
literary forms of biblical writing, x
logical positivism, 78–79
loneliness, 205–207
Long, Thomas G., 90, 92
Louis XIV (King of France), 144
love
  covenant and, xi, 55
  of God, 25
  righteousness and, 39
Love and Death (movie), 60
Luccock, Halford, 171
Luce, Henry, 106
Luke, Gospel of
  as Gospel of the Holy Spirit, 249
  on Jesus' death, 156
  on Jesus' times of solitude, 206
  on Passion Narrative, 122–123, 149–150

on Passover meal, 180
purpose of, 15–16
Luther, Martin, 192, 240, 267

Maccabaeus, Judas, 164–165
Machiavellian view of leadership, 104–105, 107
MacLeish, Archibald, 23
Macquarie, John, 188
Madison Avenue Presbyterian Church, New York, 216
Magnificat, Mary's, 37
Mainline Protestant churches, Nouwen's thesis and, 47–48
mainstream churches, xiv
Malachi (*malakhi*), historical context of, 55–56
Malthace (wife of Herod the Great), 149
Mandela, Nelson, 107, 153, 181
Mann, Thomas, 108
Marcion (Gnostic philosopher), 40, 240
Mark, Gospel of
  date of, 86
  on Jesus' death, 121–122
  on Passion Narrative, 149
  on resurrection, 40, 169–170
  on time for Kingdom of God, 179
  winning by losing, 233
Marney, Carlyle, 50
marriage, 205, 237, 257
Martha (of Bethany), 156
Mary (mother of Jesus), 96–97
Mary (of Bethany), 156
Mary (of Magdala), 172
Mary Queen of Martyrs (German commemorative place of worship), 66
Maryknolls, 141
masochism, 124–126
Mathematical Principles of Natural Philosophy (Newton), 182
mathematics
  monitoring achievement and, 99
  mystery of, 73–81
Matthew, Gospel of
  on Jesus choosing apostles, 260
  on Jesus' death, 156
  on Passion Narrative, 122
  purpose of, 86
  on resurrection, 165
  on second coming of the Lord, 244
Matthew, the Apostle, 87
Maxentius, 136, 137
McClure, Karen, 257
McClure, Steve, 257
McColls, Hugh, 218
McCullough, Stewart, 38

McMannen Methodist Church, Asheville, North Carolina, 32
McNeal, Reggie, 48, 109, 117–118
meek, will inherit the earth, 92, 245
Meier, John P., 87
Mennonites, 138
Menotti, Gian Carlo, 154
The Merchant of Venice (Shakespeare), 10
mercy, xi, 3–10, 92
Merrick, Joseph Carey, 45
Micah (prophet), 265
Michaels, Calvin, 19
Midrash, 168–169
Miller, Arthur, 95
Miriam's House (for women living with HIV/AIDS), 110
misfortune, 85–103
missional renaissance, 48, 109, 118
missionary works
  in Bolivia, 279
  of Church of the Savior, 209–210
  in Haiti, 4–5, 194–195, 256
  L'Arche Daybreak Community, 118
  Room in the Inn ministry, 271
  in South Africa, 64
  Walk to Emmaus program, 265
moed, 175
Moltmann, Jürgen
  on the Beatitudes, 90–91
  The Crucified God, 63
  Gifford Lectures and, 91n13
  on Kingdom of God, 146
  on new creation, 180
  on self-emptying, 114
  on suffering of Christ, 128
  Theology of Hope, 221, 261
  on the Trinity, 277
  on Troeltsch's research, 220–221
  on the understanding of God, 46–47
money, view of, 196
Montagnard refugees, 93–94, 181–182
Montgomery Bus Boycott (1955), 18
Moravians, 138
Morgenstein, Oskar, 74
morphe, 113, 116
Moses, 21, 37, 122
Mother Pollard, 18–19
Mother Teresa of Calcutta, 104, 107, 245
Mr. Sammler's Planet (Bellow), 213–214
Muggeridge, Malcolm, 9, 172, 245
murder, 133
Murdock, Robert, 107
music in worship services, 113–114, 251–253, 255–256
Muslim people, 71, 234, 245–246

Subject Index

mutual indwelling of God, 277
Myers, David G., 200–201
Myers Park United Methodist Church, 201–203
mystery
    of incarnation, 145–146, 178–179
    of mathematics, 73–81
    of time, 173–184

Nag Hammadi texts, 168
naham, 25, 242
Nash, Alice, 236
Nazi Holocaust, 53–55, 65–66, 89, 138, 158–159
Nero (Roman Emperor), 61
neviim, 28
The New Community (O'Connor), 109
New Horizon and Sanctuary United Methodist Church, 255–256
New Yorker (magazine), 229–230
Newton, Isaac, 182
Nicaragua, military regime in, 142
Nicey Grove Baptist Church, 262
Nicholas (of Cusa), 17–18
Niebuhr, H. Richard, 167
Niels Lyhne (Jacobsen), 7
Niemöller, Martin, 207
Nineveh, 136
Noah, 31
North America, population in, xiii, 90, 93, 200, 234
Nouwen, Henri J. M., 47–48, 118, 207, 263

Oates, Wayne, 36
Obama, Barack, 139
O'Connor, Elizabeth, 109, 210, 271
O'Connor, Flannery, 251
Offreduccio, Chiara, 198
olam, 175
Om, Samuel, 41
On Job (Gutiérrez), 25
On Learned Ignorance (Nicholas of Cusa), 17–18
Onassis, Aristotle, 107
Order of Railway Conductors and Brakemen (ORCB), 262
Order of Saint Clare (Poor Clares), 198
Organization for Economic Cooperation and Development (OECD), 201
Ornstein, Norman, 108
Our Many Selves (O'Connor), 109

Pacific Islands, Christian population in, 90, 278
pacifism, 132–143, 211, 216
    See also war
pain, 43–51
    See also suffering

Palmer, Parker J., x, 103
Palmyra Methodist Church, Winston-Salem, North Carolina, 264–265
parables
    on alleviating suffering, 101–102
    of fig tree, 158–159, 161
    of the laborers, 5–8
    of a man blessed with plentiful crops, 197
    prodigal son, 8–9
paradox
    defined, x, 16
    significance of, 85
paradoxa, 16, 164
Parks, Rosa, 153
Parmenides, 174–175, 177, 182
Parr, Wilton Luther, 270–271
Parting the Waters (Branch), 18
Pascal (mystic philosopher), 128
Pasolini, Pier Paolo, 228
Passion Narrative, 100, 121–131, 149–151, 179
pastors, role of, xii
Paterno, Joe, 231
pathetic theology, 46–47
patience, 223–230
Paul, the Apostle
    called to preach in Macedonia, 16–17
    on cosmic reality, 81
    on eternal God, 175
    on Eucharist, 124, 126
    God works for good, 30–31, 30–31n1
    on God's healing, 44
    on meaning of church, 189, 193, 194
    on patience, 228
    on progression of faith, 34
    on resurrection, 164–166
    on salvation for everyone, 240
Pax Romana, 15, 88, 106, 134
peace, 132–143
"Peace without Eschatology?" (Yoder), 139
Peck, Scott, 48–49
Pelikan, Jaroslav, 253
Pentecost, 123–124
Pentecostal sects, 138
perichoresis, 125, 277
persecution
    abolition of, 136
    during Babylonian exile, 55
    in early church, 29, 62, 224–225
    of Paul, 217
    of Peter, 170
Peter, the Apostle, 47, 100, 106, 121, 170
Peterson, Eugene, 16
Pfeiffer University, 110–111, 110n15
Phelps, Elizabeth Stuart, 161
Philip (brother of Herod Antipas), 149

Subject Index

phobias, 38
   See also fear
The Pieces of Eight (ship), 194–195
Pilate, Pontius, 15, 134, 145–154, 157–158
Piney Grove Baptist Church, 262
Pitts, Harold, 110
Plato, 79–80, 174
Plaza Towers Elementary, Moore, Oklahoma, ix
Pliny the Elder, 61
Plötzensee Prison memorial, 66
pneuma, 114
The Politics of Jesus (Yoder), 139
Polycarp, 40
Pomerance, Bernard, 45
Pompey (Roman general), 145
Pontius Pilate, 15
Poor Clares (Order of Saint Clares), 198
poor in spirit, 88–90
Popper, Karl, 182
Porter, Katherine, 193
Posnanski, Joe, 231
post-Stalinist Russia, 12–13
poverty, 88, 229
Powell, Adam Clayton, Sr., 254
power of God, 59–66
Price, Reynolds, 204
Princess of Wales (Diana), 104
Principia Mathematica (Russell), 79
prison ministry, 92, 181, 235, 266
private ownership of possessions, 198
Procula (Pilate's wife), 149
prodigal son parable, 8–9
prolepsis, 89, 89n7
prophets, characteristics of, 49
   See also specific prophets by name
Protestant tradition, 124, 240
Providence United Methodist Church, Charlotte, North Carolina, 4, 180, 194–195, 206, 235, 237, 246, 253, 256, 261n5, 270–271
Psalter, study of, 37–38
Pulpit Digest (Magazine), 20
pure in heart, 92
purifying judgment, 56–57

Qoheleth
   defined, 21
   destination of time, 177
   Job's reflection of, 24
   poetic description of time, 184
   quote from, 214
   restorative justice and, 29
   working class and, 197
Quaker community, 132, 135, 138
Qumran community, 89n5

Rachel (wife of Jacob), 68–72
racism, 193, 218–219, 261–262, 263
Ralls, George "Jace," 268–270
Ramesses II, 197
rapture, 52, 244
Reagan administration, 65
reason, biblical message and, 12
reciprocal indwelling of God, 277
rejection, 67–72
relativity, theory of, 74, 78, 80, 182–183
Renaissance age, 17
repentance, 25, 159, 229
resilience, power and, 95–103
resurrection, 101, 163–172
Resurrection and Historical Reason (Niebuhr), 167
The Resurrection of the Son of God (Wright), 168
retribution, 53–54
Reuben (Leah's son), 70
Revelation
   book of, 52
   context of, 60–63
revenge, 89
revitalization within the church, 116–117
Reynolds, Lee, 266–267
Reynolds, Vivian, 266–267
Richardson, Alan, 91n13
Rieff, Philip, 254
Rifkin, Jeremy, 229
righteous works, 227
righteousness, 39
Ritchie, Ben, 256–257
Ritchie, Dave, 256–257
Ritchie, Meg, 256–257
Ritchie, Meredith, 256–257
Ritchie, Will, 256–257
Riverside Church, New York City, 254
Rizanowics family, 246–247, 271
Rohde, David, 246–247
Roman Catholic Church
   evangelical counsels, 141
      German church commemorative of Nazi holocaust, 66
   Nazi holocaust and, 55
   in oppressive Pinochet government of Chile, 129
   priest scandal, 47–48
   recovery of *kenotic* spirit, 117
   salvation for everyone, 239–240
   on war, 138
Roman military, 88
Room in the Inn ministry, 271
ruach, 114
Russell, Bertrand, 79
Russia

Subject Index

Christian population in, 278
post-Stalinist era, 12–13

The Sacrament of the Present Moment (de Caussade), 127
sacramental suffering of Jesus, 120–131
sanctification, 141
Sandusky, Jerry, 231
Sandy Hook School massacre (2012), Newtown, Connecticut, 213
Sanford, Terry, 218
Sanhedrin, 148
Satan, 54, 242
Saul (King of Israel), 259
Schleiermacher, Friedrich, 277
Schlesinger, Arthur, Jr., 154
Schorr, Daniel, 104
Schrage, Wolfgang, 123
scourging, 149
Search for Silence (O'Connor), 109
second coming of the Lord, 224–226, 244
Second Isaiah, 29, 31, 151, 241
Second Vatican Council, 240
secular history, 217
secularism, 13
self-denial, 233–235
self-emptying, 112–119, 187, 198
self-giving, 235–238, 270
seminary students, xiv, 207–209
September 11, 2001 terrorist attack, 34, 216, 257–258
Sermon on the Mount
  Augustine and, 137
  Chacour and, 153
  Francis of Assisi and, 116–117
  purpose of, 86–103
  on violence, 132
Sermon on the Plain, 98
The Servant as Leader (Greenleaf), 107
servant leader, Jesus as, 104–112
servant songs, 31
Shady Grove United Methodist Church, Winston-Salem, North Carolina, 26, 261n5, 263–264
Shakers, 138
Shakespeare, William, 10
She Danced Only One Summer (movie), 156
Sheilaism, 252
shekinah, 46, 179–180, 276–277
Sheldon, Charles, 95
Shelley, Percy Bysshe, 152
Shema, 88, 274
ship as symbol of church, 192–193
Ship of Fools (Brant), 192–193
Ship of Fools (Porter), 193

shophar, 76, 268
Sicarii, 88, 134
sick theology, 36
Simeon (Leah's son), 70
Simeon (Temple righteous man), 97, 122
Simon (of Cyrene), 233
Simon (the Zealot), 47
Simon Peter. *See* Peter, the Apostle
Sims, Bennett, 107
slavery
  during Babylonian exile, 21–22, 31, 44
  in British Empire, 228
  in Egypt, 28, 70, 193, 196–197, 215, 241
  rebellion in southern Italy, 145
  in U.S., 159–161, 196, 217
Smeeding, Tim, 229
Smith, Adam, 200
Snow Camp, North Carolina, 132
social media, 204
Sockman, Ralph, 237
Söelle, Dorothee, 124–125
solitude, 205–207
Solomon (King of Israel), 14
Sophocles, 77
soul, immortality of, 178–179
South Tryon United Methodist Community Church (STUMCC), 201
Spears, Wright, 92–93
Specific Theory of Relativity, 182
spiritual life retreats, 207, 265
Sprinkle, Kathy, 26
Stalin, Joseph, 138
status, 98–100
Steimle, Ed, 255
Stephen, stoning of, 123
Stephen Ministries, 92, 211, 269
Storey, Peter, 58, 153, 181
Studdert-Kennedy, G. A., 153
success, 96, 101–102
suffering, 43–51, 101–103, 120–131
  See also grief
Summer of the Red Wolfe (West), 101, 101n22
Sunday, origin of name, 137
The Sword of Peace (Hardy), 132

Tbilisi Massacre (1989), 212
temptation, of Jesus, 114, 133, 206, 242
Tennyson, Alfred, 102
"The Latino Reformation" (Dias), 278
theodicy, 23, 157, 157n8
Theology of Hope (Moltmann), 221, 261
This Republic of Suffering (Faust), 160
Thiu Rancho, Cochabama, Bolivia, 110
Thompson, James, 145
Thompson, Nancy, 145

Subject Index

"Thoughts on the Present Scarcity of Provisions" (Wesley), 200
"Thoughts Upon Methodism" (Wesley), 199, 200
Tiberius (Roman Emperor), 97, 150
Tillich, Paul, 91n13, 205, 206
time
   end of, 227
   meaning of, 91n13
   mystery of, 173–184
   solitude and, 206
Time (magazine), 106, 107, 278
tithe, 196
toph, 76
Torah, 28
tornado tragedy (2013), Moore, Oklahoma, ix
Torture and Eucharist (Cavanaugh), 129
Treves, Frederick, 45
trickle down economics, 221, 229
Trinitarian nature of God, x, 187, 272–279
Trinity Episcopal Church, New York, New York, 34
Trito-Isaiah, 178
The Triumph of the Therapeutic (Reiff), 254
Troeltsch, Ernst, 166, 167, 220
Trueblood, Elton, 210, 262
Trump, Donald, 107
trust, xiii, 16, 25, 35, 50, 62, 172
truth, opposite of, 18
Tutu, Desmond, 58, 64–65

unified field theory, 80
United Methodist Church, Charlotte, North Carolina, 41, 141, 143
United Methodist Committee on Relief (UMCOR), 194
United States, Civil War, 159–161
Upham, Samuel, 171
Ussery, Katherine, 258
utilitarian culture, 251

vengeance, 53–54
vicarious suffering, 44
Vickers, Susan Norman, 237–238
Vietnam
   Christian population in, 93–94
   Montagnard refugees, 93–94, 181–182
   war era, 41, 108, 124, 135, 142, 231–238
vineyard, as symbol of God's kingdom, 7
von Harnack, Adolf, 183
von Leibniz, Gottfried Wilhelm, 157n8

Waite, Terry, 230
Walk to Emmaus program, 265
Walters, Tom M., 262

war, 132–143, 211
   See also specific wars by name
wealth, 99–100
Wealth of Nations (Smith), 200
Weatherhead, Leslie, 32–33
Weiser, Artur, 77
Well, Sam, 128
Wesley, John, 117, 171, 199–200, 228, 264–265
Wesleyan revival, 198–199
West, Morris, 101
West Market Street Methodist Church, Greensboro, North Carolina, 269
The Westminster Dictionary of Christian Theology, 91n13
When Bad Things Happen to Good People (Kushner), 59
When Religion Gets Sick (Oates), 36
White, Alice, 194–195
White, Bill, 194–195
Wiesel, Elie, 12–13, 24, 158–159
Wigger, John, 117
Wilberforce, William, 228
The Will of God (Weatherhead), 32
Williams, Robert F., 261
Williams, Rowan, 34
Wilson, Mary Denny, 271
Wilson, Ruth, 265
Wilson, Tom, 264–265
Winfrey, Oprah, 232
Wingate United Methodist Church, Wingate, North Carolina, 33–34, 222, 236, 261n5, 262
winning, 231–238
wisdom
   celestial constellations and, 74
   fear of the Lord and, 37
   information and, 13–14
   Kethubim as, 28
   ladder of, 14
   paradoxical nature of, 12–19
Wittgenstein, Ludwig, 78, 79
Wolfe, Tom, 101
Wordsworth, William, 174
working class, 197
worship, 77–78, 248–258
The Wounded Healer (Nouwen), 47–48, 263
Wright, N. T., 56–57, 165, 169, 194
Writing in the Dust: After September 11 (Williams), 34

Yoder, John Howard, 139–140
Yokefellow fellowship, 262
Yow, Betty, 50
Yow, Pete, 50

Subject Index

Zalmen, or the Madness of God (play and television production), 12–13
Zebulun, Leah's son, 71

Zechariah (father of John the Baptizer), 96, 249
zoe aionious, 177

Scripture Index

Genesis
1:1–2	241
1:27	113
1:31	3
2:7	241
29:17a	69
29:30	70

Exodus
20:3	274
20:8–10a	196
33:19–20	255

Leviticus
19:13	7
19:18	236
23:4	175
25:10–12	97

Deuteronomy
5:29	37
6:4	88
6:5	236
30:15–19b	216
32:35	52

1 Samuel
16:7	259
16:13b	259

1 Kings
19:10–12	190
19:12b	248
19:18	191, 248

2 Kings
15:18	176

2 Chronicles
24:2	176

Job
1:1—2:13	22
1:21	20
2:4a	242
3:25–26	23
41:25	24
42:3b	24
42:6	25
42:7–17	22

Psalms
8:1–2	76
8:4	76
8:5–6	77
10:17–18	38
22	115, 125
22:1	243
27:1b	39
31	172
31:5	243
58:3	53
58:8	54
58:11	53
106:1	184
111:1	37
111:10	37

Proverbs
9:10	37
10:27	37
14:27	37
22:1–2	197

Ecclesiastes
1:2–3	6

Scripture Index

Ecclesiastes (*continued*)

1:4–8a	22
1:7	24
1:8	6
1:9	184
3:2	177
3:8	175
3:12–13	197

Isaiah

4:7–8	31
40:8	156
40:39–40	156
40–60	31
45:1–3	241
52:12–13	31
53:2–4	45
53:5a	46
53:5b	43
53:6b	46
53:7	48
53:7a	46
54:7–8a	175
55:3	176

Jeremiah

29:11	176

Daniel

7:27	164

Joel

1:15	176

Amos

9:11	176

Micah

4:7	175
6:8	265

Malachi

2:17	56
3:3	56

2 Maccabees

12:44	164–65

Matthew

1:15	179
4:3b	114
4:20	260
5:1	87
5:3	88
5:8	92
5:21–22	133
5:29a	36
5:44–46a	133
5:48	141
7:1	225
7:7	225
13:30	179
16:3b	179
19:13–15	270
20:1	3
20:16	3
22:37	236
22:39–40	236
25:34b	244
25:37b	244
25:40	3
26:52–54	152
26:53	122
27:46b	243
27:62–66	165

Mark

1:14	121
1:15	179
8:31	121, 156
8:34	233
9:12	122
10:14	270
10:33	122
10:44	108
14:24–25	126
15:34b	243
16:8	40, 122, 169

Luke

1:13	249
1:14	96
1:35	274
1:37	97
1:50	37
1:52–53	97
2:1	150
2:34–35	97
2:35a	122
4:18–19	97
4:21	178
5:26	16, 164
6:12–13	206
6:20	178

Scripture Index

6:20–21	197
7:25	98
7:28	98
7:32	156
7:34	156
8:3	98
8:58	98
9:23	123
9:24	98
9:48	99
9:50b	246
10:3–4	197
10:4	98
10:25–28	274
10:39–40	156
11:13	241
11:29	135
12:15	197
12:20	197
12:20–21	99
12:48	99
12:49	135
12:51–53	135
13:6–9	158
13:30	99
13:32–33	151
14:10	99
15:29–32	9
16:25	100
18:15–17	270
18:25	11
18:27	11
22:16–18	180
22:26–27	100
23:34	11
23:46	171, 243
24:48–49	249
24:50	250
24:53	250

John

1:1	165
1:14	165
1:14a	123
2:19	156
3:16–17	179
8	34
13:4–5	106
13:8a	106
13:8b	106
13:14–15	106
13–21	105
15:4a	277
16:20–22	128
18:34	148
18:36	134, 145, 148
19:30	123

Acts

1:6b-8	223
1:11	223
2:44–45	218
2:46–47a	124
2:47	124
4:32	198
4:32–33	218

Romans

5:45	228
8:18–19	44
8:24–25	xiii
8:28	30–31n
12:19	52
16:26	175

1 Corinthians

1:18	17
1:20	17
1:25	17
10:16	124
11:24b	126
15:12–14	164
15:33	166
15:58	126

2 Corinthians

5:19	277
13:13	274

Ephesians

4:13	189
4:26b	262

Philippians

2:6–11	113
2:7	112

1 Timothy

2:4	240

Hebrews

10:30	52
10:31	230
11:13b	123

Scripture Index

James

1:1	225
1:5	225
1:25	227
2:4	226
4:12	225
5:7	224
5:8	226

2 Peter

3:8b-9	229

1 John

4:7–8	277
4:8	52

Revelation

1:4	175
1:8a	63
19:9	124
21:1	62
21:3–4	62

www.ingramcontent.com/pod-product-compliance
Lightning Source LLC
Chambersburg PA
CBHW081416230426
43668CB00016B/2254